3 - 08

BATTLE CRIES *and* LULLABIES

BATTLE CRIES

by LINDA GRANT DE PAUW

and LULLABIES

WOMEN IN WAR
FROM PREHISTORY
TO THE PRESENT

UNIVERSITY OF OKLAHOMA PRESS : NORMAN

Also by Linda Grant De Pauw
The Eleventh Pillar: New York State and the Federal Constitution (Ithaca, New York, 1966)
Founding Mothers: Women of America in the Revolutionary Era (Boston, 1975)
"Remember the Ladies": Women in America 1750–1815 (Boston, 1976)
Seafaring Women (Boston, 1982)

Library of Congress Cataloging-in-Publication Data
De Pauw, Linda Grant.
Battle cries and lullabies : women in war from prehistory to the
present / by Linda Grant De Pauw.
p.   cm.
Includes bibliographical references and index.
ISBN 0-8061-3100-4 (cloth : alk. paper)
1. Women and war.   2. Military history.   I. Title.
D25.5.D44   1998   98-21219
355'.0082—dc21   CIP

To Debra E. Morgenstern,
my faithful second in command at The MINERVA Center, Inc.
We've weathered the storm together.

CONTENTS

ILLUSTRATIONS

PREFACE

WOMEN HAVE ALWAYS AND everywhere been inextricably involved in war. This thesis is simple and is supported by an abundance of evidence, but because it has profound, complex, and emotionally charged implications, the roles of women in war are hidden from history. The deep conviction, shared by most people since Neolithic times, that the gendered roles of mother and warrior should be forever distinct, makes it difficult to remember how frequently they have been combined. During wars, women are ubiquitous and highly visible; when wars are over and the war songs are sung, women disappear.

The revival of scholarship in women's history over the past quarter century has scarcely touched the history of women in war.[1] Feminist historians find military history unattractive; women as nurturers and peacemakers, even as victims, are more appealing than women who go to war. For military historians, the absence of women in battle appears self-evident. John Keegan, among the most highly respected military historians of our time, recently wrote, "Warfare is . . . the one human activity from which women, with the most insignificant exceptions, have always and everywhere stood apart. . . . If warfare is as old as history and as universal as mankind, we must now enter the supremely important limitation that it is an entirely masculine activity."[2]

No one has attempted to write a book like this one before, for I wished to place women, in all their diversity, in the context of the history of war.[3] I am well aware of the apparent arrogance of venturing an overview of events that not only contradict common knowledge but also took place over the course of thousands of years across the globe. A thorough study of this subject would require many volumes and the combined efforts of a team of scholars. One historian working alone can do only so much. My ambition for this work is modest; to open a sufficient number of trails, marked in the endnotes with accessible English-language secondary sources, to illustrate the variety of research possibilities and to encourage other writers to follow me. The history of women in war is important and fascinating. To open the field for the explosion of wide-ranging scholarship that is now possible, someone had to go out on point.

The book is structured in a form intended to facilitate correlation with other works that survey military history and are currently used as texts in the United States. Although the history profession is moving away from the long tradition of Eurocentrism and there are useful anthologies that provide a breadth of coverage, including, perhaps, chapters on such diverse topics as war among the Aztecs and war in ancient China, book-length surveys have had only two ways to look at "the rest of the world": either they discuss the spread of Western technology into other parts of the globe, or they discuss wars of imperialism.[4] The first is not helpful for viewing the roles of individual women or men, so I chose the second. Military history texts have not yet managed to create a new model for the narrative form. Indeed, it may require the flexibility of multimedia and hypertext to make such a new model workable. I am not satisfied with this old-fashioned approach to world military history, but I could devise nothing better.

Historians who search these pages for a gendered analysis of war may be surprised by my refusal to provide one. In recent decades women in nontraditional roles have repeatedly told journalists and sociologists that they are not feminists or women's libbers or out to prove anything about women as a group. When Julie Krone won the Belmont Stakes in 1993, becoming the first woman to do so, she used a term familiar to academic feminists in her reply to the reporter who asked her how it felt *as a woman* to win. "I don't think the question should be gendered," she said. Another woman athlete commenting on Krone's remark wrote, "This is what male reporters often don't seem to understand. Women feel like people. We don't think constantly about being women. It's natural for us. We can even forget about it for long stretches of time."[5] Through the centuries one of the most striking characteristics of women in combatant and combat support roles is that they perform them not as women but as human beings. Gender becomes an issue when history omits the detail that some brave warriors were women, and war stories then reinforce prescribed gender roles and expectations. But history books do not alter the truth of what happens on the day of battle.

I wrote this book to provide both information and inspiration. I have controlled the tone of the content primarily through my choices of material to include and to omit. The history of warfare is full of abominations and atrocities perpetrated by both men and women, and the written sources, primary and secondary, are full of misogyny. I could not exclude this unpleasant material entirely without falsifying the narrative, but I made a deliberate choice to keep it to a minimum.

I wrote this book to serve the needs of a diverse readership. Radicals and conservatives and moderates of many varieties will find material here both to support and to challenge their perspectives. Serving a heterogeneous audience, I had to find a way to separate the emotionally charged implications of my subject from the body of the text. I could not ignore or pussyfoot around the controversial topics, first, because like everyone else, I am emotionally affected by them, and second, because writing about these matters with a high level of abstraction would create a book too dull to endure.

During more than twenty years of research on women in war, I have become familiar with the kind of loaded questions that spring immediately to mind for those considering the topic of women in war for the first time. If I were to ignore these questions, they would shout so loudly for attention in the minds of readers as to become a major distraction. But if I wove them into the narrative, they would lurk like minefields to explode as a particular reader's personal beliefs came into conflict with one of mine. So I decided, as far as possible, to tackle all of the loaded questions at once, in the first chapter. My conclusions are based on years of thought and study and conform to no special school of interpretation. The result, as one early reader of the manuscript remarked, is that "there is something here to offend everyone." My purpose was not to offend. Rather, my hope is that by clearing the air up front, even a reader who disagrees with every one of my opinions on every important interpretive issue will be comfortable reading the rest of the book.

Acknowledgments

Women, from Christine de Pizan to Mary R. Beard, who braved ridicule as they called up the memory of valiant women and battled for women's rights.

Writers who over the centuries collected stories about military women to ridicule them or to depict them as curiosities or freaks. They preserved evidence that others may now study with fresh vision.

Historians who pioneered the new field of women's studies and history graduate students who chose to research the subjects of their choice even when these were unfashionable and politically risky.

Academics in disciplines other than my own who marched in where historians feared to tread: my colleagues in and out of academe in sociology, political science, psychology, anthropology, archaeology, theology, and literature.

The army of independent scholars who have worked in isolation without official academic credentials. The accumulated volume of their largely unpublished research is more massive than anyone imagines.

The journalists, novelists, filmmakers, reenactors, lawyers, public policy activists, active duty servicewomen, and military veterans who discovered women's military history and made it a cause.

The hundreds of people who subscribe to publications of the MINERVA Center and buy the books the Center has published, that is, consumers rather than producers of the new scholarship. Their enthusiasm has helped me and many other pioneers in women's military studies keep the faith over the past fifteen years.

Students and friends who have brought me books and photocopies and read preliminary drafts of chapters when I asked for help and listened to me sympathetically when I grew discouraged, including DeAnne Blanton, Lauren Cook Burgess, MaryAgnes Costello, Clare Cronin, Valerie Eads, Chip Harbour, C. Kay Larson, Barbara Maxwell, Regina McNew, Mitch Mitchell, Debra E. Morgenstern, Jennifer Rebecca Peters, P. Joy Sosnowski, and especially Eleanor H. Stoddard, copy editor for the MINERVA Center publications, who, hearing me wistfully longing for a real editor of my own to take charge of my finished work during the long search for a publisher, volunteered her experience. She briskly took the manuscript in hand, tamed my commas and colons, and did many hours of library research to eliminate dozens of errors my own jaded eye would never have caught.

Special thanks to Charles E. Smith, who envisioned *Battle Cries and Lullabies* as a serious scholarly endeavor and encouraged me to transform it from a cheerful unfootnoted romp through history into a thoroughly documented academic work.

And finally, editors and publishers' readers who worked on the manuscript, especially those at the University of Oklahoma Press but also those at other publishing houses that at one time or another have had it in their hands. Many gave considerable time to *Battle Cries and Lullabies* and made valuable suggestions. This book is much better than it would have been without their contributions.

Having expressed my thanks I must now claim responsibility for all the remaining flaws, faults, and omissions in this work.

BATTLE CRIES *and* LULLABIES

INTRODUCTION
Definitions and Presuppositions

T HE HISTORY OF WOMEN in war is buried beneath centuries of sniggering. The tendency to conflate all women's roles into sexual ones
made the presence of women in war zones a natural target for dirty jokes.
Many myths and false assumptions about women and their military roles
still survive. To keep these from confusing the narrative that follows, they are
collected here to be examined systematically at the beginning.

WHAT IS A WOMAN?

AS I CHOOSE TO use the word, a *woman* is any human who self-identifies
as female, whatever her race, class, behavior, or physical appearance. This is
a broader definition than some others have used. In a famous episode in
American women's history, the former slave Sojourner Truth spoke up at a
women's rights convention. Elizabeth D. Gage, the presiding officer, recorded her statement:

*Dat man ober dar say dat womin needs to be helped into carriages, and
lifted ober ditches, and to hab de best place everywhar. Nobody eber helps me
into carriages, or ober mud-puddles or gibs me any best place! And a'n't I a
woman? Look at me! Look at my arm! I have ploughed, and planted, and
gathered into barns, and no man could head me! And a'n't I a woman? I could
work as much and eat as much as a man—when I could get it—and bear de*

lash as well! And a'n't I a woman? I have borne thirteen chilern, and seen 'em mos' all sold off to slavery, and when I cried out with my mother's grief, none but Jesus heard me! And a'n't I a woman?[1]

The response of the gentleman was not recorded, but we can be sure he would have answered in the negative. No, this six-foot-tall, gaunt black figure whom Gage described as "almost Amazon" was not what he meant when he spoke of *woman*. To this day, race and social class as well as behavior and appearance influence perceptions of gender.

Gender is a set of grammatical categories—in English, *he, she*, and *it*—related only indirectly to biological characteristics. For instance, it makes sense to say of a new yacht, "She's a beautiful boat," or of a new baby, "It's a boy!" The separation of grammar from biology is even clearer in some other languages. In French, for instance, both men and women have feminine heads and masculine feet.

Recently, individuals embroiled in the public policy debate over women in combat have often fallen into what the sociologist M. C. Devilbiss calls the "yes, but phenomenon":

I have often been struck by the fact that women's contributions— even when thoroughly documented—have been dismissed by many who listen. Women have participated in war, often in central combatant roles, but these contributions are "explained away," viz., "Yes, but that was not in modern times," or "Yes, but that was a combat support not a direct combat role," or "Yes, but, these were defensive combat roles, not offensive ones," or "Yes, but that was a combat training exercise, not a true combat situation," or "Yes, but, they were Russian (or European or African or Central or South American) women, not U.S. citizens," or—perhaps the best one, said of the involvement of U.S. servicewomen in the 1992 Gulf War—"Yes, but that was not a real *war."*[2]

Less frequently expressed openly, but present in the same public policy debate, is the idea that any female who is a combatant in a *real* war is not a *real* woman. Physically or psychologically, she must be either peculiar or perverted because women by nature require male protection. Women are too weak physically and too gentle psychologically to go to war. So women *can't* have been in war—even if they were.

Binary thinking—the habit of classifying everything as black or white, positive or negative—accepts male and female as categories representing polar opposites. That may make sense as an abstraction, but it clearly does not apply on a physical level. A human female is not the "opposite" of a human male; both are members of the same mammalian species. They have much more in common with each other than either has with a cow or a bull, for example.

Until quite recently, however, even scientists accepted the notion that men and women were "opposite" sexes. A woman who thought like a man or acted like a man was therefore suspected of having some physiological abnormality. Scientists now understand that both physically and psychologically, gender is a continuum. Real human beings, as opposed to symbolic constructs, embody both male and female elements. Some females are taller than some males. Males can be compassionate, and females can be courageous. Furthermore, psychological and physical traits are not directly linked; a small curvaceous female with curly hair and long eyelashes may have an aptitude for car racing while a big, hairy, muscular male may be a sensitive, nurturing parent.

But how about what is under their clothing? In the past it was often assumed that women who cross-dressed and assumed male roles were hermaphrodites. Although that was very rarely the case, humans sometimes do have ambiguous sexual organs. Some females have large clitorises, and some males have small penises. Substantial numbers of babies are born with ambiguous external genitalia. The only way to be sure whether to dress them in pink or in blue is to test their chromosomes, a very recent option. And chromosome testing has problems of its own. Chromosomal abnormalities are twice as common as Down's syndrome, but the individuals affected generally accept a gender role and move in the world as unremarkable males and females.[3] Adult males are not likely to be tested, but female athletes in recent years have been required to prove what they had taken for granted all their lives. And some women with breasts bulging conspicuously under their swimsuits have been told after testing that they were not sufficiently female to compete against others of their sex.

Some female infants have what appears to be complete male plumbing. These children, born with andrenogenital syndrome, have a faulty adrenal gland that secretes large amounts of testosterone, causing embryonic development of a scrotum, penis, and other male accessory reproductive organs. Yet these children carry the XX chromosome and are thus genetically female. Nowadays children with this condition, which occurs in about one in one thousand female births, may have corrective surgery and be raised as girls. In times past, such individuals would have gone through life believing they were male. Historical sources provide no evidence that would identify them, and it would be meaningless to classify them as women even if we now ran tests on exhumed DNA samples.

Biological features have objective reality, but gender identity is a social construct. Children form gender identities very early in life and cling to them even in those cases in which puberty and a new spurt of hormones bring unpleasant surprises. It is extremely rare to find a "mannish" woman who is actually a biological male. As for secondary sexual characteristics and gender markers, having the wrong sort is certainly embarrassing, but humans adapt. A little boy may be teased about his long eyelashes and curly hair, and a little girl may be ashamed of her unusual height or her big feet, but that will not prevent either from developing appropriate gender identity.

Some cultures, notably American Indian cultures, allowed a greater number of gender choices for those who did not easily fit into rigid sex-linked categories. An investigator who did fieldwork on an eastern Navajo reservation originally identified four categories of gender—female/woman, male/man, female/man, and male/woman—but quickly realized that even this was too narrow since the culture recognized at least several dozen subtle gradations between male and female.[4] The dominant cultures of Western nations have, in contrast, been notably intolerant. Difficult as it may have been for some, everyone who could pass as either male or female conformed.

WHORES AND DYKES

"Dyke" is a derogatory term for "lesbian" as "whore" is a derogatory term for "sex worker." Both lesbian and prostitute activists have embraced the epithets as a means of drawing their power to wound. Still, the ugly words are offensive to most women.

A U.S. Army colonel, now retired, tells of reporting to her first military assignment as a young officer and being told by her boss, "All military women are either whores or dykes." Her experience was uncommon only in that the labeling was so promptly and bluntly presented. In the Western world prior to the twentieth century the stigma was simpler: "All women who follow armies are whores." "Whore" and a host of other derogatory terms such as "slut," "trull," "wench," and "harlot," and some even less polite ones were also applied to females in general, those well past menopause as well as those who had not yet reached puberty.

This loose use of language to stigmatize women conflates all roles women play in war into that of sexual object and makes accurate assessment of their true activity difficult. This book defines the words *whore* and *prostitute* narrowly as someone who chooses to provide sexual service for pay— that is, someone who is a "sex worker," to use the term those in the oldest profession apply to themselves today. A prostitute sells her sexual labor as others might sell their muscle as construction workers or brain power as tax consultants. Despite contemporary attitudes that criminalize the activity, commerce in sex has not been universally stigmatized or experienced as degrading. Indeed in many cultures prostitutes and courtesans were highly regarded. Some sex workers still consider themselves healers and therapists, even spiritual mentors to their clients.[5]

The narrow definition of prostitution encompasses all work in what is now called the sex industry, including striptease dancing, sexual massage, and feminine companionship as provided in a chaste form by Japanese *geisha* or ancient Greek *hetaerae*. Military prostitution includes women providing sexual services in a civilian business establishment that caters to soldiers or sailors as well as those in facilities supervised directly by military authorities. It also applies to independent entrepreneurs, including those military wives who might turn tricks to supplement their husbands' pay. And it applies to women for whom the role of prostitute is a cover for covert activities such as espionage or sabotage.

A woman forced to have sexual relations, whether through rape or sexual blackmail, however, is not a whore but a victim. Slaves captured as booty are not whores. Girls kidnapped and forced into military brothels are not whores. If a soldier throws a coin or a pack of gum to a woman he has raped, she does not thereby become a whore. Employers of women in both military and civilian environments may demand sexual service as a condition of employment. The upstairs maid and the regimental laundress often discovered that sleeping with "the gentleman" was the only way to keep the paying job. This is prostitution only if the woman negotiates extra pay for extra service. Otherwise it is simply exploitation. Finally, a sweetheart is not a prostitute. Some women fall in love with soldiers and share sex out of affection and for their own pleasure; not all partners of military men require payment.

Sweethearts often become wives. It has been argued by some that marriage is no more than legalized prostitution, that the marriage contract is simply a lifelong arrangement whereby economic support is traded for sex. Marriage is, however, distinct from prostitution even if the wife marries for money, since the responsibilities of marriage partners include mutual obligations encompassing more than sexual activity, in particular, mutual responsibility for offspring. Marriage need not be a legal agreement. In many cultures, as well as in traditional English law, cohabitation for an extended period created a common-law marriage without any other action by the parties. In many cultures soldiers, in fact, have been forbidden to have legal wives or have had to receive permission from their superiors before they could marry their lovers. Military authorities have treated both husband and wife harshly if they bonded without approval. Ralph Dennison, a navy hospital corpsman in Vietnam, recalled that many soldiers married to Vietnamese women were confined in Long Binh Jail for the offense of wanting to stay with their Vietnamese families when the military wanted to ship them home.[6] Despite the contempt with which they have generally been treated, unapproved military wives are not prostitutes.

A mother is not necessarily a whore simply because there is evidence that she has been sexually active. For some, this may be obvious, but contemporary conservative criticism of women with children serving in the military, while it may focus on child care, carries the suggestion that these women are unwed mothers; that is, they are fornicators or prostitutes. Navy ships carrying pregnant sailors are commonly referred to as "love boats." Bearing children is a natural activity for the females of our species. Pregnancy is not a venereal disease or evidence of bad character. Most human cultures have taken it for granted that in addition to carrying on tasks that may be performed by either sex, women will occasionally have babies as well. Although modern gynecologists would not recommend stressful activities, pregnant women have performed all military roles up to and including engaging in hand-to-hand combat while in advanced stages of pregnancy or while lactating.

Of course, significant numbers of women at all times in history have gone through life without ever bearing a child. Even when pressures to bear children have been strongest, not every female is fertile. Furthermore, even those women who bear the largest numbers of offspring spend substantial portions of their lives—the years prior to puberty and after menopause, if they live to that age—neither pregnant nor lactating. Nevertheless, it is appropriate to focus attention on mothers precisely because it is so tempting to focus on women who do not have children. Motherhood, or the potential for motherhood, is the one irreducible difference between men and women. While it is possible for some women to do everything men can do, even use artificial means to begin a pregnancy, no man can ever be a biological mother.

Despite evidence that pregnancy is not a disability, women who are pregnant or nursing strike a discordant note in contemporary military settings. Both women and men in service today refer to pregnant soldiers and sailors as a "problem." Although there were times in the past when women heavy with child strapped on swords to smite the enemies of their people, embedded cultural archetypes make the symbolic union of mother and warrior repellent to many people. During the Gulf War, the spectacle of mothers leaving their infants behind was far more poignant for most civilians than the spectacle of fathers torn from their offspring. Single military women often spoke disparagingly of those who were married: having family obligations that might interfere with deployment or being visibly pregnant appeared to them to be "unprofessional" and to reflect badly on those women intent on their careers who did not use their reproductive potential while in military service. In contrast, the image of a woman holding a baby in one hand and a sword or rifle in the other may be a powerful symbol of patriotism. Indeed, it is a popular symbol in the guerrilla armies of the Third World, where it serves as an inspiration to both soldiers and civilians.

As applied to military women in recent years, "whore" is an epithet used to describe any woman who does or might have a propensity to sleep with men, and "dyke" is the epithet that covers all the rest. The latter term also stretches to cover any woman who is not stereotypically feminine. Thus some use the term "dyke" to describe any woman who wears combat boots or does not use makeup.

By a narrow definition, *lesbian* would describe a woman who either has sexual relations with another woman or wishes to do so. But perceptions of human sexual activities change dramatically over time and in different cultural contexts. In Western culture prior to the twentieth century, possession of a phallus was believed essential for sexual activities. Consequently, anything women did together was excluded unless one party had an unusually large clitoris. Also, preference for a certain type of sexual activity only recently became part of an individual's self-identification. Male homosexual acts were criminal, but the individuals who committed them were thought to have made a wicked choice rather than to be a special kind of person. An analogy is our current attitude toward food preferences. When a waitress brings a tray to the table and says to one diner, "Are you the rare burger?" and to another "Are you the tofu with sprouts?" neither individual takes the remark personally, even if the tofu eater chooses to feel superior.

Today a woman who has a masculine appearance and behaves in a manner considered masculine may be called a dyke and may self-identify as lesbian, although most transgendered people are heterosexual.[7] The gender category of lesbian, however, did not exist prior to the twentieth century. Neither the word nor the gender construct to which it refers had any meaning. The *Oxford English Dictionary*, which traces word usages back to their first appearances in print, defines *Lesbian* as a native of the island of Lesbos. It refers also to a "Lesbian rule," which was a mason's measuring device made of lead. Even the related word *sapphist,* which derives from the poet Sappho who lived on Lesbos in the seventh century B.C., is a recent invention. It first appeared in a medical dictionary in 1890 and did not come into general use for several decades after that.

To complicate the matter even further, contemporary women who say they are lesbians usually insist that their sexual activity is less central to their identity than their nonsexual emotional, psychological, social, or even spiritual bonding with other women. That is not surprising since women generally value close personal friendship as a context for sex more than men do. Lesbianism for some women may involve nothing more than close nonsexual friendships. Some lesbians prefer sexual activity that is nongenital, the kind of kissing, hugging, holding hands, and sharing a bed once considered totally innocent and celebrated in such books as *Anne of Green Gables,* in which the heroine unselfconsciously seeks out a "bosom buddy."

In this book I limit the use of the term "lesbian" or "dyke" to those who use it to describe themselves. Many lesbians call themselves feminists; most feminists do not identify as lesbians. Some lesbians believe only lesbians can be feminists. Some lesbians believe they are lesbians even though they have husbands whom they love. One lesbian writer uses "lesbian" to mean "a woman who seeks her own self-nurturance,"[8] which would seem to include every woman who is not self-destructive.

This muddle of definitions makes it inappropriate to apply the word *lesbian* to anyone who lived prior to the twentieth century. Readers are free to form their own opinions as to whether certain women of past centuries *would* have called themselves lesbians had they been alive today, but such judgments are anachronistic. Prior to the twentieth century a woman could no more be a lesbian than she could be a Valley Girl.

WHAT IS WAR?

AMONG MILITARY SPECIALISTS, DEFINITIONS of war are considered "notoriously difficult or stupidly arbitrary."[9] An often-quoted example is Pierre Bosquet's comment about the Charge of the Light Brigade during the Crimean War. "It is magnificent," he said, "but it is not war." Similarly, the Prussian general Helmuth von Moltke once remarked that there was nothing worth studying in the American Civil War because it had been fought between armed mobs. Compounding the confusion is the tendency of scholars in different disciplines to adopt different definitions of war. Ethnographers, sociobiologists, and physical anthropologists have favored broad definitions that would encompass the activities of various nonhuman life-forms including insects. Historians, political scientists, and sociologists have formulated narrow definitions for war, distinguishing it from such things as rebellions, riots, massacres, insurrections, police actions, and other activities involving organized applications of lethal violence. *Battle* and *combat* have also been narrowly defined by public policy analysts, particularly after women began to enter Western military organizations in substantial numbers, in an effort to keep women out of combat while letting them do the work of soldiers. The history of these semantic contortions is amusing but not particularly useful.

In this book *war* is defined as a disciplined and socially sanctioned use of deadly force by one group of people against another. The essential part of the definition is the willingness and intention to kill. Only when that is present do other human activities similar to war actually turn martial.

War is a very sophisticated cultural invention and a flexible one. It has taken different forms in different times and places. Although many writers assume the existence of a "universal soldier," the same over millennia, the variety of values and behavior is extreme. Some wars have been fought with a conscious intent to minimize loss of life; others have gloried in maximizing carnage. Some cultures have considered it dishonorable or cowardly to make war on the weak and unarmed; others have sought out helpless victims because they were easier prey. The flexibility of the institution is even more obvious when elements other than killing are considered. War is about killing and dying, but it is also about art, science, religion, poetry, and sport—and male gender identity.

In recent centuries warfare has been rationalized as having economic, dynastic, or political purposes. Soldiers in modern armies consider themselves professionals in applying techniques of destruction to carry out national policy. But war retains elements of ritual and art; indeed these dominate military organizations in peacetime. Marching bands, dress uniforms, flags, and ritualized tributes to the dead hark back to primitive ceremonies that retain their power to inspire.

Practitioners of martial arts, who have adopted as avocation training in techniques used in potentially lethal forms of hand-to-hand combat, frequently find it a spiritual exercise as well as a satisfying form of fitness training. Around the world, reenactors enjoy participating in battles based on campaigns of the past, made as authentic as possible and eliminating only the human corpses and dead horses. Men and women reenactors put on heavy woolen uniforms in the heat of summer, do forced marches, crawl around in the mud, sleep in tents on hard ground, eat bad food, and get bitten by insects. They do this because it is fun. Depending on the outcome and the particular elements of their personal experience, individuals participating in real wars may also find them enjoyable. The danger and the sense of serving a higher cause heighten the intensity of positive aspects of the experience. For many veterans living today, going to war was the high point of their lives.

War as sport has appeal for sedentary folks as well. Strategy games, from chess to Dungeons and Dragons, have been modeled on the intellectual challenges of war. A growing community of war-gamers register for tournaments in which they can command tank battalions or order cavalry charges as they hover over boards set with miniature figures wearing painted uniforms that have been researched for accuracy in every detail.

War can even be enjoyed as a spectator sport. Americans watched the Gulf War on television as they might have watched a football game, adopting the sports fans' chant "We're Number One" and buying commemorative T-shirts. Television coverage of wars around the world shows civilians coming around to have a look at the site of an attack. During the American Civil War, the same spirit of curiosity and desire to be present at a significant event brought civilians from Washington, D.C., with their picnic baskets to the live performance of the first Battle of Bull Run.

Although the horror of modern warfare has made some parents fearful about the effects of war play on children, experts still see positive value in such activity. The new violent computer games or play requiring particular toys to be used to copy story lines presented on television have little to recommend them, but the old-fashioned type of play—"Let's go kill the bad guys! Bang bang, you're dead!"—offers benefits. In their book, *Who's Calling the Shots?* Nancy Carlsson-Paige and Diane E. Levin write,

> *A great many of the parents we've talked with, who grew up to have peaceful values, describe their own war play as children. Often when we talk to a group of adults who are concerned about war play today and ask them how many of them engaged in war play as children, three-quarters of the hands in the audience, those of both men and women, go flying up. And faces usually light up as well, because war play is almost universally remembered by parents of today as a happy part of their childhood experience. These adults realize that children can play at war without necessarily learning to glorify it or wishing to promote it as adults. . . . As a particularly powerful form of pretend play, it offers an arena in which children can feel strong and empowered, and in which they can work on a variety of concepts. In war play, children can work on their understanding of the boundaries between pretend and reality, build basic cognitive concepts, develop a beginning understanding of political and moral ideas, and even learn about cooperation and the needs of others.*[10]

The positive appeal of war is reflected in our language. We use the word *war* loosely and metaphorically to cover almost any kind of assertive or competitive behavior. Both business activity and athletic contests are described in military terms, and many of us wage war on garden weeds, termites, ring around the collar, and flabby thighs. Our language also seizes on the positive connotations of warfare to emphasize dedicated struggle to forward a larger cause. Thus we wage war on drugs, poverty, disease, and crime. Even those practitioners of nonviolence who see militarism itself as the enemy employ rhetoric shot through with martial imagery.[11]

The ultimate war game is the one in which the risks are real and real people are killed. For most of human history, the death and destruction of war were at an acceptable level, at least for the winners. Societies believed it was a price worth paying for the pleasure, stimulation, opportunities for personal growth, and moral or spiritual benefits war provided. As we shall see in later chapters, not until the development of advanced killing technologies in the nineteenth century did peace movements arise to argue that an end to all wars, not just "bad" ones, might be desirable. Even in the nuclear age, ideological pacifism is far from being universally admired.

The intense emotion produced by killing other humans gave war an additional function. As the species developed intellectually, humans became aware of their own mortality, and birth and death became awesome events. Women's bodies, in particular, seemed to contain magical forces. The monthly bleeding that is not an injury is, even today, the subject of superstitious attention, and in primitive cultures men feared they might die if a menstruating woman prepared their food, touched them, or merely looked at them intently. Lactation was equally awe-inspiring, as the mother produced food for an infant out of her own body. But most dramatic were labor and childbirth. Intense pain, blood, and often death itself came as a woman brought new life into the world. Although not all women became mothers, no male could give birth. When binary gender identity became important for the development of individuals, both males and females felt a need for a dramatic ritual by which a boy could become a man as the onset of menstruation made a girl a woman. Since women had already been assigned their roles as givers of Life, men would ritually assume the role of bringers of Death.[12]

In reality, women have always been capable of killing. Even a small woman catching a man unaware or able to add poison when she prepared his food could end his life. Indeed in some cultural and religious rituals that include human sacrifice, including those in which the sacrifice is a captive taken in war, women act as torturers and executioners. But when combat serves as a puberty ritual for boys, girls cannot participate without destroying the meaning. If girls could qualify as both mothers and warriors, there would be no unique identity for boys.

Concern for such rites of passage, which serve to separate the men from the boys, may seem childish to twentieth-century women, who never have to prove their maturity. Even sterile or celibate women are regarded as adults after a certain age. It would be a mistake to underestimate the male need for similar validation. Martin Van Creveld, professor of military history at Hebrew University of Jerusalem, expressed his feelings emphatically and carried his argument to an extreme conclusion:

A way in which . . . war might conceivably be eliminated would be to have women participate in it, not as auxiliaries or surreptitiously, but as full-fledged equal partners. This is not the place to expound on the often imaginary psychological differences between the sexes, nor on the respective importance of biological and social factors in governing those differences. Suffice it to repeat that, with the exception of their disparate roles in the physical acts of procreation, childbearing and nursing, nothing has ever been more characteristic of the relationship between men and women than men's unwillingness to allow women to take part in war and combat. Throughout history men have resented having to perform a woman's role as an insult to their manhood, even to the point where it was sometimes inflicted as a punishment; had they been forced to fight at the side of, and against, women, then either the affair would have turned into mock war—a common amusement in many cultures—or else they would have put down their arms in disgust. However desirable such an outcome may be in the eyes of some, it belongs to the realm of phantasy. One suspects that, should they ever be faced with such a choice, men might very well give up women before they give up war.[13]

Although, as we shall see, men have many times fought "at the side of, and against, women" without abandoning the institution of war, Van Creveld explains very plainly why the *memory* of female involvement in military activity is unendurable.

The use of *warrior* as a male identity corresponding to the female identity of *mother* is clear in many cultures. The African Ashanti, for instance, had almost identical rituals for women who died in childbirth and men who died in battle, and the Aztecs in Mexico believed such women shared with warriors the highest place in paradise because they, too, had fought a battle and died taking another life captive. A related practice is that of the North American Papago, who characterized the scalp of an enemy as a "child" that brought pleasure to the warrior-mother—the man who had killed the scalp's owner. Other tribal cultures found a satisfying balance in the connection between a mother "making life" and the warrior "taking life," sensing that "blood binds the warrior and the child-bearing woman."[14]

Although it is the most powerful, war is not the only cultural invention that can serve to define gender. An example in which, under duress, a primitive society in New Guinea found a substitute is instructive. The Australian colonial government suppressed intertribal warfare in the mid-1960s.

Among the Yomura, war had been the exclusive function of men. The belief that males were uniquely endowed with the ability to protect the village also justified a variety of public and private privileges. Men made political decisions and claimed ownership of family property, although women did most of the work. Women accepted this arrangement because they believed it important to have their husbands free to make war as a condition of the community's survival. The sudden abolition of war created a gender crisis. Very quickly, however, the old forms were back in place. The Yomura found a new threat to combat, a mysterious illness that was attributed to sorcery performed by their traditional wartime enemies. The men created a new healing cult, *assochia,* which was closed to women. As doctors, the men now claimed the same prerogatives they had enjoyed as warriors. This served to maintain gender roles even though the healing was far less dramatic than the earlier killing had been.[15]

Because this book defines war in terms of deadly force, there is no war without lethal intent. No matter how bloodthirsty the threats or the name-calling, trading insults is not war. So-called primitive warfare, in which risk is minimized and the goal is a display of courage and skill rather than carnage, is not war. Games such as football, soccer, and hockey are not war even though they may result in accidental deaths among both players and spectators. If the goal of martial exercise is to develop a level of skill and self-mastery in which the warrior can defend against any enemy without actually killing, the warrior is not engaged in war by my definition even if the warrior "fails" and has to kill someone. Saber rattling is not war; if a society uses threats to achieve political or economic goals, the society is not at war until the threats are carried out—or an attack is launched by a frightened adversary. An individual who kills for personal revenge or to steal is not waging war, nor are groups such as the Mafia or the Japanese *yakuza* which prey on society and advance no moral justification for their activities. But if members of a group consider themselves agents of a higher cause, as, for example, John Brown's small army at Harper's Ferry, they are engaged in war even if the established government brands them criminals and traitors. A group of civilians who organize to use lethal force to resist an attack they believe to be illegitimate are waging war even if they do not wear uniforms and fight without conventional tactics and weapons. Soldiers who unchivalrously use superior weapons against an adversary or attack noncombatants are nonetheless waging war. Armies directed by incompetent or stupid generals or by homicidal maniacs are still waging war if their society sanctions their authority. An individual maniac is not waging war, no matter how high the body count; but a single assassin on a special operation or a terrorist mission serving a larger organization is engaged in war. Finally, a group of killers without a disciplined command structure that is capable of enforcing orders both to kill and to refrain from killing is not an army but a gang of murderers even if they wear uniforms.

War gives soldiers license to kill. Individuals or groups who kill without this license are criminals. In many circumstances, distinguishing the two may be difficult, but all cultures have agreed that there is a difference and that it is an important one.

Broad definitions of war that equate it with any kind of assertive behavior would have us believe humans have always been warlike. When combined with the belief that war has always and everywhere been an exclusively male activity, the conclusion seems to follow that a propensity toward violence and an urge to kill other humans is biologically and genetically based in males. If this were so, our species would be doomed to self-destruct as the technology produced by our brains falls under the domination of raging hormones. This depressing conclusion is complemented by feminist assertions that human females are biologically and genetically programmed to be anti-war and have always resisted or at least not participated in battle. Presumably, locking up all the men and putting power into the hands of women would be the only hope for the future. Unfortunately, if women had an innate propensity to be passive victims, as these writers argue, they would be incapable of exercising power even if the allegedly testosterone-crazed males now in control turned it over to them.[16]

Current scientific knowledge, however, contradicts the belief in biological determinism. In May 1986 scientists specializing in the study of human aggression, distressed by the "misuse of scientific theories and data to justify violence and war," issued a statement presenting the consensus of many scholarly disciplines. The "Seville Statement on Violence," drawn up by twenty psychologists, ethnologists, neurophysiologists, anthropologists, geneticists, sociologists, psychiatrists, and other experts, has since been endorsed by many organizations, including the American Psychological Association and the American Anthropological Association. The report lists five common assumptions about war and violence that are known to be fallacious:

IT IS SCIENTIFICALLY INCORRECT to say that we have inherited a tendency to make war from our animal ancestors. . . . IT IS SCIENTIFICALLY INCORRECT to say that war or any other violent behavior is genetically programmed into our human nature. . . . IT IS SCIENTIFICALLY INCORRECT to say that in the course of human evolution there has been a selection for aggressive behavior more than for other kinds of behavior. . . . IT IS SCIENTIFICALLY INCORRECT to say that humans have a violent brain. . . . IT IS SCIENTIFICALLY INCORRECT to say that war is caused by instinct or any single motivation.[17]

Males are not born killers. Females are not born nurturers and peacemakers. Like the nineteenth-century "science" that believed in immutable races, some of which were naturally "savage" and others of which were "civilized," the belief in the immutability of gender has had its day in the scientific community.

If our species is to invent peace as it once invented war, we shall have to do it together, and there is no biological reason why we cannot. This book presents evidence showing that war is a cultural artifact, an invention, and what humans have created they can also modify. Even more important, this book shows that women as a group and as individuals have always had roles in war. If there is anything fine and ennobling in war, women share the glory. If war is atrocity, women share the guilt.

FINDING THE WOMEN IN WAR

PART OF WAGING WAR is recording the history, telling the story after it is over. Singing the praises of heroes, telling of courage and self-sacrifice, is as essential to the satisfying conclusion of a war as are the tactics and strategy. Since war is a ritualized event, the storytelling is also ritualized, perhaps more so than any other kind of history. As in the hagiography of saints, there is a proper way to tell war stories. Compare war narratives to traditional love stories, which also have a recognizable formula; a love story must end with the two lovers united, if only in death. A story that develops with two protagonists finding each other attractive, then meeting others they prefer, losing interest in each other sexually, and then builds to a climax in which they decide to pool their capital and become partners in a fast-food franchise may be a narrative that is true to reality, but it will be unsatisfying.

In a traditional war story the male heroes do the fighting and embody the martial virtues. Their reward for suffering hardship and risking their lives is woman's love, including, in addition to sex, all the admiration, compassion, and provision of creature comforts that are associated with the image of wife and mother. Focusing on women in any other role spoils the story. For this reason, not only have women been written out of military history, but all of the military functions unrelated to heroic combat or usually performed by women receive scant attention. The study of logistics, military medicine, and military families, for example, is neglected by students of war.

Finding women in both primary and secondary sources requires a special approach because they do not fit into the traditional formula. Although some women in war appear in conventional combat roles, most do not. The reality of women's experience is distorted by focusing exclusively on exceptional females, but it is also distorted by focusing only on the most typical. To achieve an accurate perspective, the student of women's military history must use a wide-lens camera. That means awareness of greater varieties of military roles than are normally considered and sensitivity to overlapping roles.

In any given war, a military participant may at one time lead troops against an enemy position and at other times peel potatoes, dig latrines, polish boots, or treat a buddy's frostbitten feet. Conventional military history will describe a man who does these things as a "soldier." If a woman does the same things, historical sources, if they notice her at all, will probably refer to her as a "nurse." If the male soldier has a lover or a family, it will make no difference to the historical record, but the woman will be placed in a sexually defined category to the exclusion of any others. These are the literary conventions; no matter how heroic and "manly" a woman may be, narrative conventions will deny her gallantry and emphasize her nurturing qualities and sensitivity. He is stalwart and brave; she is cute when she is angry. This practice may be irritating, even infuriating, to contemporary readers, but it must be understood if we are to break the code and see what is actually there.

Women's military roles can be grouped into four categories. The first consists of victim and instigator, which are the classic roles for women in the drama of war. The second category encompasses combat support roles performed by civilian camp followers doing "women's work." The third category, "virago," involves women performing acts requiring "male" boldness and daring without challenging gender construction. The most visible viragos are women heads of state who are commanders in chief by virtue of thier position and march into battle at the head of their armies. Women who guard the rear, protecting their homes and children, also fit into gender expectations. Even women who go into combat in all-female units—"amazons"—are recognizably women. Finally, there is the single androgynous warrior role in which the woman assuming it becomes "a man among men" whether she changes clothing and other gender markers or not. Tolerance for this role varies by period and by culture. At some times in some cultures women in the ranks were considered monsters or criminals, at others they were praised and admired, and at others they were simply taken for granted and ignored. I do not attempt to track every role in evey chapter in this book. That would be impossible. But I do present examples of each in a variety of historical contexts, leaving it to others to explore further.

CLASSIC WOMEN'S ROLES

Victim

By definition, war must have victims. By risking their lives, warriors offer themselves as potential sacrifice even as they strike the enemy. At the same time, since war has a social purpose—defense of unarmed noncombatants whose dependence gives the warrior special status—there is implicit recognition that civilians, too, are potential victims. Women may suffer rape, forced marriage, torture, mutilation, and death during wars without violating gender norms, with one important condition: they must not have made any attempt to defend themselves. Modern military conventions that promise protection for "noncombatants" explicitly exclude from the protected category women who fight back.

From another perspective, if the enemy warrior is found unable to protect his dependents, he will be humiliated and his morale will be damaged. That suggests the use of rape as a military tactic. Enemy women may be perceived as wicked because of their support for the enemy's military activity, which justifies treating them as whores. Rape and murder of women during war do not spring from lust; neither do they spring from hatred or fear of the defenseless victims. Attacking women and children is an attack on the males to whom they are attached.[18]

Until very recently, with the development of urban guerrilla warfare, deaths of civilians in war were not classified as "casualties" and were not recorded in battle reports. The current euphemism for such deaths is "collateral damage." In earlier times they were a minor by-product of the main action, like the deaths of horses or the destruction of fields. Sometimes armies kept records of the number of slaves they took or made "body counts" after the destruction of a city, but there was no accurate recording of civilian victims of war. These war dead are invisible to history. Monuments and memorials were for those who fell in battle.

Instigator

The active face of the woman as victim is the woman as instigator, the one who calls on men to fight or to continue fighting in her defense or for her pleasure. Many cultures personified the inspiration of warriors, their will to fight, in female form. For instance, the Irish Morrigan dating back to 1000 B.C. were a triad of goddesses who haunted battlefields, collecting the severed heads; they were visible only to those about to die. Germanic warriors fighting the Roman legions kept up their courage through the belief that those fortunate enough to fall on the field of battle would be taken by the Valkyries to Valhalla to spend eternity enjoying its pleasures. Similarly, the Houris waited in Paradise for Islamic warriors who died bravely with weapons in their hands.

Real women performed the same function. The common practice, and virtually universal acceptance, of women cheering men on to death and glory contradicts the notion of women as naturally peace loving. While women might use their influence to keep men at home or encourage them to desert, they were much more likely to admire their valor and gallantry and speed them off to war. Encouraging men to fight has taken many forms. The most dramatic involves women on the battlefield itself, sometimes clutching their children, singing war songs, screaming or cursing to inflame the fighting spirit of their men and terrify the enemy. The voices of women in this role have been as much a part of war as the beat of the drum.

Examples of women shaming men into fighting are Eleanor of Aquitaine handing out distaffs to men reluctant to go on the Second Crusade and English ladies handing white feathers to men out of uniform during World War I. Praying for soldiers, or working magic for them, is a related form of womanly support that helped keep up morale; so is writing letters from home and sending cookies. Certain kinds of sexual activity, such as giving sex to a soldier about to face death, perform a similar function.

CAMP FOLLOWER ROLES

Camp followers are civilians, both male and female, who follow an army to sell goods and services and perform support functions. Before the mid-nineteenth century, when many of their functions were given to military personnel, camp followers did such "woman's work" as cooking, laundry, nursing, and preparing the dead for burial. Such people also performed logistical duties. Until the development of modern transport, in which uniformed personnel have taken over supply, medical, and other support functions, no army could go to war without camp followers. Contemporary military organizations have begun once more to rely heavily on civilian employees, although they no longer call such individuals camp followers but speak instead of "outsourcing" and "privatization" of combat support functions.

Traditionally, camp followers provided food and drink for the soldiers, foraged for firewood and fodder for the horses, and carried spare clothing, cooking pots, blankets, and other supplies needed by a marching army. Although women on average have less upper body strength than men, their greater lower body strength and greater endurance made them useful for carrying things on their heads, strapped to their backs, or in sledges dragged behind them. Such arrangements reduced the soldiers' loads to small packs, leaving their arms free to carry their weapons and use them if necessary. Since baggage trains slowed down the movement of an army, commanders were often impatient with them; but lack of a supply convoy reduced the length of time a force could continue to operate in the field.

Female camp followers were usually wives, widows, or daughters of soldiers. Although most historical sources call them prostitutes, that usually meant that the women slept with their men after the day's work was done. Men without wives might pay for such service when they could not successfully court a sweetheart. Sweethearts as well as wives were valued for more than satisfying a pressing sexual urge. Caring for the soldier's physical needs —preparing his food, keeping him warm, dry, and clean, nursing him in illness—was the usual work of his woman. Another important, though rarely appreciated, contribution of military wives was production of a new generation of soldiers. Particularly in cultures where the military was widely separated from civilians, new recruits were born into the service. The boys enlisted as soldiers, and the girls grew up to marry them.

VIRAGO ROLES

War Leader

Throughout history some women have stood at the top of a power hierarchy, through inheritance or by battling their way to success. Control of military power is prerequisite to retaining authority in all societies, from pre-Columbian American tribes to the empires of Egypt and China. Europe also has had its share of what Antonia Fraser calls "warrior queens."[19] An example is Isabel of Castile, remembered in our time as the patron of Christopher Columbus, who used the Italian form of her name, Isabella. In her own time, however, Isabel was known as a military genius, first in wars to secure her own succession and later in a ten-year campaign to drive the Moors from Spain. Isabel combined martial activity with a series of pregnancies, and the hardships of the field were probably responsible for her many miscarriages.[20]

Although donning male attire was customary for queens leading troops into battle, and even for those who made an appearance only to rally the troops while delegating actual battlefield command to others, such cross-dressing was emphatically *not* a disguise. Recognition as leader was essential to her exercise of command.

In feudal societies, women war leaders were most often found in defensive roles, acting as agents for their husbands by defending castles. Sometimes sorties outside the gates were necessary to break a siege. Other women, however, have raised armies to carry out aggressive action. Elizabeth I of England and Catherine the Great of Russia were both war leaders who prided themselves on having "manly hearts." In more recent times, Margaret Thatcher was such a leader.

Rear Guard

It is always appropriate for a mother to protect her babies. Guarding the wagons in the baggage train when an army is hard-pressed is woman's work. Forming home guard units for defense when males are absent is work expected of mothers and wives. In siege operations, when the men were gone, ordinary women have been on the walls, hitting attackers with whatever may have been the objects of choice—stones, tiles, bricks, burning oil, or artillery shells.

Related to rear guard activity is the widespread tactic, known in early America as "making a show of hats," by which a defending force is made to appear more formidable by dressing the women present in male clothing. The ancient Germanic tribe of Lombards, meaning "long-bearded people," believed that their name derived from the practice of having their women go into battle with their hair tied under their chins. This disguise was intended only to deceive the enemy. Men fighting alongside such crossed-dressed women knew perfectly well who they were and expected them to pitch in to aid military operations when it was necessary.

Covert Operations

Covert operations require deviousness and manipulative skill, characteristics cultivated by women and slaves in patriarchal systems. Since Delilah, women have exploited their presumed helplessness and innocence for espionage, sabotage, smuggling, and assassination. Working in such accepted roles as sex worker or peddler, women could enter military camps without arousing suspicion and be uniquely situated to make observations about the physical condition of the soldiers, discipline, and morale. They were also positioned to put poison in food, steal documents, or plant bombs. Covert operatives have a dubious reputation; they may be patriotic and courageous, but to warriors their activity is neither heroic nor gallant. Nevertheless, the tide of more than one war has turned because of the dedication and daring of these secret soldiers.

Masquerade and disguise are stock-in-trade for covert operatives. Men passing as women and women passing as men feature in the history of both espionage and diplomacy.

Amazons

The word *Amazon* originally referred to a race of warlike women in Libya. The Berbers of North Africa claim descent from these bellicose females and still call themselves "Amazigh." Writers in the ancient world and in modern times have used the word to refer to any group of combatant women regardless of their geographic origins or nationality.

Although the word *amazon* may be applied to any woman who fights, it is here confined to those fighting in segregated units. Women who wage war while organized in all-female units are a recurring phenomenon in military history. Many home guard units formed when men were away at war have been exclusively female, although others have included elderly men and boys as well. In sexually segregated units, there is no need for women to adopt male clothing as women do when serving in integrated units. Amazons may fight in skirts or other clothing that serves as a female gender marker. Although amazons often wear male clothing for convenience, it is not intended to serve as a disguise. Some amazon units have been formed to shame men into more warlike efforts, as a variation on the role of woman as instigator. The implicit suggestion is that if the men cannot protect them, the women will become men. In another specialized role, kings have sometimes used amazons as elite bodyguards. Chandragupta Maurya, founder of the first great state in India in the fourth century B.C., had gigantic Greek women in such a corps. The king of Dahomey's armies of women also began as personal bodyguards.

The original Amazons described by the ancient Greeks were illiterate nomads who left no records of their own to describe their culture. Greek sources say they lived in a society that entirely excluded men. Amazon units may develop by default if war kills all able-bodied males or some other activity, such as prolonged sea voyages, pulls most men away from home. Obviously, if men are not available, women must undertake all roles in society. Most amazon units, however, have been tools of male rulers; often they have had male officers.

ANDROGYNOUS WARRIORS

Women who fight in integrated units are no longer distinguishable as women. This does not mean that they are always "in disguise," or that their fellow soldiers are not aware of their biological sex. As we shall see, a surprising number of women who have served in integrated armies have done so openly. In revolutionary or guerrilla armies, women soldiers have carried weapons while wearing their usual female garments.

More commonly, women serving in integrated armies in the West, particularly in this century, accepted the fact that warrior is a male role as unalterably as mother is a female role and became "honorary men" for the duration. "Feminine" behavior, like giggling, or a female appearance, like having a large bosom, would be considered "unprofessional." A woman who swears and has a lean, boyish build would fit in better.

The degree of disguise a woman in the ranks assumed has been related to the degree of tolerance for women who joined male combatants. It is instructive to compare the situation to challenges faced by members of other groups who adjusted to intolerance in a culture by "passing." Thus, not so long ago, a black woman could find work in a white-collar clerical job only if her appearance allowed her to fit in as a white person. Similarly, a Jew could attend an elite school or become a member of a prestigious men's club only if he was assumed to be gentile. A gay man could serve in the military only if he seemed to be straight. How much effort it cost to keep up appearances well enough to remain in the group depended on the attitudes of other individuals. If the environment proved to be tolerant, others would collaborate through their silence with the individual who was passing, pretending not to notice, for example, when some slip revealed that a co-worker's mother had very dark skin or that a fellow student regularly missed classes on Jewish holy days. An individual who surreptitiously entered a closed institution might even find that so many others were already inside that the secret could be widely shared so long as outsiders were not alerted to the true state of affairs.

Paradoxically, evidence of the presence of a stigmatized group inside a presumably closed institution is greatest when tolerance is lowest. When disgrace, punishment, or death is inflicted on those discovered passing, the result of any discovery is etched into the record. When no one much cares, nothing is said. In the chapters that follow, we will find many women who made no attempt to hide their gender identity and served armies alongside men. As in the American military today, they might look like men when in the field, but they kept their female names and feminine identity when off-duty. When such women fell in battle, enemy soldiers who came to strip the dead would make a "discovery" that might or might not be a surprise, depending on their own experience of women combatants. Such women might simply be buried like the rest, thus leaving no mark in the historical record, or they might gain special mention either as heroines or as victims.

In standard war stories, all soldiers are heroes. Soldiers who do not view themselves and their comrades as heroic will have no will to fight, and soldiers who view their enemies as passive victims cannot perceive of themselves as heroic. Although many innocents have been slaughtered in wars, the glory comes in meeting a worthy foe in battle.

In some cases, soldiers may also be viewed as victims. War stories celebrate soldiers who fall in battle equally with those who survive to drive the enemy from the field and find no conflict in the notion of heroic sacrifice. Even soldiers who are killed by accident or as a result of their own incompetence are deemed worthy of honor. Pacifists, however, take a different view. In their eyes soldiers, particularly those who have been conscripted, kidnapped, or forced into service by economic pressures, are victims of military systems that dupe them into believing a life of brutality and suffering is glorious when it is in fact pitiable.[21]

Because *victim* is a feminine role, women performing as androgynous soldiers may be distinguished from their male comrades if they can be moved into this category. By making them objects of pity, they are denied honor. Thus the appearance of women in an enemy army's ranks may be cited as an example of desperation or inhumanity whereas if they appear among friendly forces they are "heroines"—patriotic, courageous, and braver than ordinary females.

A NOTE ON HISTORY AND PUBLIC POLICY

WOMEN IN THE MILITARY have become a controversial issue in American society since the introduction of the all-volunteer force two decades ago. Public policy makers operate on an advocacy model and use facts, including historical facts, not for illumination but as ammunition. Historians, in contrast, practice a discipline that attempts to discover what is true despite possibly embarrassing or even dangerous implications. Discovering evidence that some people have gotten away with murder is not the same as arguing in defense of homicide. Describing what people have done in the past does not dictate any public policy conclusions for the present.

It must be remembered that contemporary American attitudes toward women in combat have not been shared by every age and culture. Some peoples have not had the luxury of deciding to exclude some members of the population from the hazards of war. Some peoples, particularly those who practiced aggressive warfare as a way of life, saw no incompatibility between military service and pregnancy or motherhood. It is not necessary to agree with such attitudes and practices in order to study them. Just as we understand that cannibalism and slavery were once common in many places without endorsing their reintroduction into our society, we can understand that pregnant and lactating women have been in combat. Much larger numbers of women who were not at the time actively exercising their reproductive potential have been involved in military operations over the centuries. Whether one applauds or deplores their presence and their actions, women have always been part of war. To ignore this fact grossly distorts our understanding of human history.

CHAPTER TWO

PREHISTORY

SOMETIME AROUND 6500 B.C. a young woman died at Jebl Sababa in what is today the Sudan. Archaeologists call her Burial no. 44, Cemetery 117. She is among the casualties in the earliest known act of war. Of those who died with her, twenty were adult males, twenty were adult females, seven were adults whose sex could not be determined, and eleven were children. Burial no. 44 was the most savagely assaulted of the victims: twenty-one chipped stone arrowheads were discovered in her remains. Three of these points, attached to a single arrow shaft, were shot into her mouth.[1] Probably none of those found in Cemetery 117 had weapons to defend themselves, but we may imagine that Burial no. 44 died screaming curses at those who would murder her children.

Archaeologists are not certain exactly what happened at Gebel Sababa. Almost certainly it was not a battle with forces of armed warriors facing each other. It may have been an ambush in which an organized force attacked others able to defend themselves. Or it might have been a ritual execution or blood sacrifice with no military element involved. Some of the victims were killed while lying on the ground with their heads thrown back. Other archaeological remains and some cave paintings indicate that human sacrifice, if not war, appeared in human cultures in many parts of the world during the Mesolithic epoch (12,000 to 4500 B.C.).

✦ ✦ ✦

ONE HUNDRED THOUSAND YEARS OF PEACE

WAR IS AS OLD as recorded history but not very much older. Humanity required millennia to become a warlike species, and learned war long after developing highly sophisticated cultures. For 90 percent of the time our species has lived on this planet, we practiced only the arts of peace. Once wars began, they so thoroughly dominated human history that it is very difficult to believe this earlier peaceful heritage. Archaeologists and anthropologists searched hard and long for evidence to the contrary before concluding that peace was, indeed, the original human condition.[2]

It is difficult to comprehend the scale of time used by students of human prehistory. A useful way is to translate it into familiar units. The limits of "living memory" are about a century. When a woman tells her granddaughter stories she was told by her grandmother, the span of five generations is approximately 100 years. A line of fifty women passing down stories spans 1,000 years. A group this size could easily fit into a classroom. A line of five hundred women—a number that could fit comfortably into a theater or concert hall—spans 10,000 years. For 100,000 years, we will have five thousand women and would need a stadium to seat them all.

Everyone living today is connected in an unbroken line through five thousand great-great-grandmothers to the time when *Homo sapiens* began. Scientists tell us that we were cooperative, family-centered people. Family meant mother with her immature offspring, her grown daughters, her husband or husbands, and her sons-in-law. Sons would leave a mother's home to live with their wives and mothers-in-law. As the population grew, the single family might combine with others, forming a clan, and eventually many clans might band together as a tribe. The mothers remained the defining link, and all known human cultures before the invention of war followed a matrilocal pattern. From the earliest hunter-gatherer bands to the highly advanced urban culture of Crete, human societies centered on and revolved around women.

As a species, humans are creators of both material artifacts and ideas. One hundred thousand years ago humans had already invented many objects to improve their quality of life. These included baskets for carrying infants and pots to carry food. Such objects were necessities for a species whose new offspring could not even walk for many months following birth and who could not forage for food and feed themselves for several years. Humans developed communication skills far beyond those of other animals in order to create emotional bonds and socialize the younger generation, whose unique human brains required nurturing as much as their bodies required food. Because females both birthed babies and created their earliest food within their bodies, the primary association of the mother and child developed naturally. In societies where the women were promiscuous, a new baby was taken to be related to everyone in the family circle, creating an extended biological bond. Other members of the family, men and girls and other women without babies at the breast, protected mother and child while the early dependency of the youngster made the pair vulnerable.

Before the advent of war, protecting nursing mothers and babies was not difficult. Other animals might be stronger and faster, but human intelligence created safe shelters. If a dangerous animal came too close, humans had weapons to kill it. Shock weapons, hand axes and clubs, were known to several now-extinct hominid species one hundred thousand years before *Homo sapiens* evolved. Had they wished to, they could easily have used such weapons on each other, but they did not. To deal with the mysterious unseen forces that ruled the universe and sometimes sent illness and pain, humans developed religious rituals. When one of their number died, they buried the body with appropriate ceremony.

Thirty thousand years passed (1,500 grandmothers leave the stadium), and humans learned to use fire. Another twenty thousand years passed, (another 1,000 leave their seats), and humans invented the first long-range weapon, the fire-hardened, wooden-tipped spear. After another sixty thousand years (and the departure of another 3,000 grandmothers) humans had bows and arrows with stone points. (The 500 remaining grandmothers can move to the theater.) With the equipment now available, humans could have killed each other on a grand scale, leaving the unmistakable evidence that wars burn and bury deep in the earth. But ten thousand years ago weapons were still merely hunters' tools.

More significant than the invention of efficient hunting weapons had been development of technologies that contributed to the quality of life. Humans learned to herd wild animals, to fish, and then to domesticate sheep, cattle, goats, and dogs. Early experiments with vegetation led to systematic harvesting of wild grains and eventually to cultivating domesticated cereals. Humans, before they learned war, learned to construct houses, to make rugs and furniture, to weave and to sew. They developed rudimentary forms of writing, complex religious theories, knowledge of astronomy and medicine, and sophisticated art forms.[3]

Before the invention of war, some human cultures had left hunting behind entirely to live exclusively on domesticated grain and meat. Civilization developed in different ways and at different rates. While some humans took up farming, others were nomadic. Once warfare was invented, such cultural differences were pretexts for violent engagement. Many writers postulate that war began because nomadic people coveted the wealth of the agriculturalists. But nomadic tribes and early agriculturalists coexisted peacefully for hundreds of years before the invention of war. Curiosity and impulses toward cooperation are far older than the impulse to combat.

For many centuries hunter-gatherer cultures outnumbered those based on agriculture. These systems are the most ancient and are characteristic of the so-called living fossils archaeologists study today for insights into our prehistory. The "living fossils" exist in Stone Age societies that have survived into the present or recent past. All of these societies had many features in common, hinting at what life may have been like in our own Neolithic age before the invention of civilized warfare. In combination with archaeological finds, these kinds of anthropological data are the best evidence we can hope for.

In hunter-gatherer societies young adult males were peripheral to routine survival activities. Gathering and preparing food and child rearing were women's work. Since women did not dominate men in these cultures, it is incorrect to call them matriarchies. But neither did the men dominate the women. Nor did anyone have servants or slaves. Neolithic societies had no power hierarchy of any kind. The sexual division of labor generally assigned gathering to women and hunting to men, but it was not rigid; women sometimes hunted, and men sometimes gathered.

In Neolithic communities, hunting produces only a small part of the food supply. Meat comes in irregularly while gathering proceeds continually. Among the surviving Stone Age societies, women's work produces 80 percent of the food, meat is a luxury, and hunting is not a daily activity. For instance, the !Kung! bushmen of Botswana hunt no more than one week in three or four. Sometimes they do not hunt for a month or more, instead spending their time visiting with each other and dancing, and the women's gathering provides all the food.[4]

While men dominate hunting in hunter-gatherer cultures, women are almost never entirely excluded. Although a hunter alone might kill small game like mice or rabbits, groups of hunters are required for larger animals that travel in herds. These groups are organized bands, and all members of hunter-gatherer societies, including the women and children, join in this kind of activity.[5] To hunt big game successfully requires the application of strategy and tactics: prey must be ambushed and surprised or stampeded over a cliff or into a bog. For such complex operations, there must be a hunt leader, but the leader's authority extends only to the direction of the hunt and does not carry over into other family activity. Long before the invention of war, early hunters following a leader could deploy in column and line, movements essential to military operations before the twentieth century. But they did not direct this ability to hunting humans.

Artifacts, cave paintings, and even myths survive from Neolithic history. From these we know a good deal not only about hunting but also about spiritual practices and ritual life. Once war began, about six thousand years ago, weapons and warriors dominated religion and art. Yet in the oldest remains we see no evidence of battle or glorification of weapons. Humans had the means to slaughter each other long before they had the will.

WAR GAMES

Anthropologists disagree about the ferocity of or propensity to violence in surviving hunter-gatherer societies. In such societies people may be killed by accident and individuals may fight and even commit murder in a fit of rage. Women in some cultures may be as pugnacious as men in interpersonal relationships. When contemporary Stone Age people experience territorial pressure, they will fight to defend their space. Such pressures, however, did not exist in ancient times when so few humans roamed the earth.

More recently even the most peaceful hunter-gatherers have fought against encroachment by farmers or to defend their sources of food and their way of life from "civilized" invaders. In all such cases, however, the warlike activity is tied to physiological needs, the sort of reaction that forces any lifeform to fight for survival. It has not led to the development of specialized man-killing weapons, formal training, rituals, or glorification of fighting and bloodshed. This fighting was not institutionalized warfare. In a thorough review of the research, the anthropologist Eleanor Leacock has concluded that "gathering-hunting societies, the type of society that has characterized by far the longest part of human existence, is the most peaceful type of society; not without problems, but they have *social* strategies for dealing with them."⁶

Among these strategies were ritualized war games. Like hunting, these events involved the entire community, though warriors had the central roles as they afforded the opportunity to demonstrate courage and skill. The purpose of a battle was neither to kill nor to destroy, nor was it to acquire wealth or take slaves. According to the historian Gwynne Dyer, the activity is "an important ritual, an exciting and dangerous game, and perhaps even an opportunity for self-expression, but it is not about power in any recognizable modern sense of the word, and it most certainly is not about slaughter."⁷ Since skill rather than slaughter has been the essence of ritualized war games, primitive warriors took care to avoid the most dangerous hunting weapons or modified them in a way that made them less effective. They might, for example, fight with bows but only after removing the feathers from the arrows.⁸

For Neolithic people, a typical "war" brought a dozen or so warriors to an open field. Other tribal members stood around cheering them on or cursing the opposition. The warriors would wrestle, spar with clubs or spears, make rude gestures, shout insults at each other, and perhaps chase each other around to make physical contact with a bare hand. Killing an opponent would be "bad form," even cowardly, since a dead opponent was no longer dangerous. As soon as anyone was hurt, even one of the cheering-cursing spectators, the battle ended. Primitive warfare was a rough game, and a few people were seriously hurt or killed—but only a few.

An Englishman who was a spectator at one such intertribal contest in northeastern Australia late in the nineteenth century left a detailed description. The combatants began by putting on their best clothing, and then they took up their weapons, in this case spears, clubs, boomerangs, and hard wooden swords. Everyone, including the women and children, assembled at the battle site.

There was no regularity in the fight. The duel usually began with spears, then they came nearer to each other and took to their swords. Sometimes the matter was decided at a distance, boomerangs, nolla-nollas [clubs], and spears being thrown against the shields. The natives are exceedingly skilful in parrying, so that they are seldom wounded by the first two kinds of weapons. On

the other hand, the spears easily penetrate the shields, and sometimes injure
the bearer, who is then regarded as disqualified and must declare himself
beaten. . . .

The women gather up the weapons, and when a warrior has to engage in
several duels, his wives continually supply him with weapons. . . .The old
women also take part in the fray. They stand behind the combatants with the
same kinds of sticks as those used for digging up roots. . . .They cry to the
men, egging and urging them on, four or five frequently surrounding one man,
and acting as if perfectly mad. The men become more and more excited, per-
spiration pours from them, and they exert themselves to the utmost.

If one of the men is conquered, the old women gather around him and
protect him with their sticks, parrying the sword blows of his opponent, con-
stantly shouting, "Do not kill him, do not kill him!" . . .

With the greatest attention I watched the interesting duels, which lasted
only about three-quarters of an hour, but which entertained me more than any
performance I ever witnessed.[9]

Casualties resulted from this battle. One man was hit in the arm by a
boomerang and became the object of solicitous concern. Another was
pierced by a barbed spear that could not be removed and died three days
later. Still it is clear that the participants in this activity did not have killing
as their goal. This was not war; this was sport.

Contrast another incident in Australia witnessed and described by a
German observer two decades later.[10] A chieftain of one of the Aranda tribes
invited chiefs of other tribes to join him in an alliance. Those who accepted
the invitation came to his home with their warriors. The men painted themselves and then practiced a sacred ritual that involved opening their circum-
cision wounds with sharp bones and letting the blood flow over the right
shoulder of another warrior to make his arm strong.

They spent the rest of the evening singing songs celebrating the blood
that "flows like water from the long penis" and describing how, the next day,
"the barbed spear" would strike an enemy fatally. Then, in the dead of night,
the warriors crept up to the camp of their enemies. Equipped with magical
talismans including rope made of dead men's hair, they attacked while their
victims were sleeping. "First, crying 'Wai, wai, wai,' they spear[ed] the sleeping men. Then, crying 'Kukukukuku,' they kill[ed] the women with cudgels,
and finally, they deal[t] with the young children, grasping them by the feet

and smashing their heads on stones or on the ground." Then they washed the blood from the spears, and the youngest warriors drank the mixture of blood and water. They took nothing from the camp, left the dead unburied, and went home. Purists may argue that this example should not be called a military operation but a massacre or an atrocity. In the history of warfare, however, massacres and atrocities may have claimed considerably more casualties than did battles in which noble foes clashed face to face. According to Lawrence H. Keeley, small raids or ambushes targeting helpless victims are "the most common form of combat employed in primitive warfare."[12] Wars raging around the globe today are filled with horrific example of savage slaughter in which helpless noncombatants are the targets of choice. This was not sport; this was war.

LEARNING WAR

EVIDENCE OF INSTITUTIONALIZED WARFARE enters the record of the human past suddenly in about 4000 B.C. How can we explain why, after tens of thousands of years, such behavior entered the human repertoire? It is easy to understand why once exposed to lethal combat, people adopt its forms. When one side plays for points and the other side plays for blood, the only way to survive is to learn the new rules. But how did it start? The mass killing at Jebl Sababa in 6500 B.C., 8,500 years ago, that was described at the beginning of this chapter appears to be an isolated incident. Furthermore, there is no way of knowing what was in the minds of those who carried out the slaughter. But literate practitioners of so-called civilized warfare which began two thousand years later, tell us clearly that orders to slaughter other humans came as a divine inspiration.

In the fifth millennium B.C., a totally new kind of social organization emerged almost simultaneously in Egypt and Iraq, claiming legitimacy from an angry deity that demanded human sacrifice. Cities devoted to militarism rapidly grew and prospered. No gradual transition occurred between the peaceful cultures of the ancient agricultural towns and the bloodthirsty urban societies of the Middle East. The contrast between them could not be more extreme. Hierarchical social systems replaced the egalitarianism of older human cultures. Slavery, subordination of women, and the organization of warriors into professional armies appeared simultaneously. Lewis Mumford, in his classic study, *The City in History*, wrote, "To exert power in every form was the essence of civilization; the city found a score of ways of expressing struggle, aggression, domination, conquest—and servitude."[13] And Dyer states, "The roots of human civilization lie in states so absolutist and so awesomely cruel that even the death camps of Nazi Germany would have been regarded as a moral commonplace."[14]

The founders of these militaristic states did not themselves invent war. Rather they refined a practice first introduced into the "cradle of civilization" by nomadic people from the steppe. This vast plain occupies an area from southeastern Europe to Mongolia with no natural boundaries, and it has always seemed vague and mysterious to people at the center of Western civilization. Since the steppe people were illiterate and did not live in permanent settlements, they left nothing by which the early development of their homicidal inspiration might be traced. Several elements in their way of life, however, supported efficient warfare once they decided to take up the practice. For millennia after their first appearance, people from the steppe erupted periodically into the civilized world and thus into history, each fresh wave of Sythians, Goths, Huns, or Mongols bringing the horror of galloping hooves and merciless slaughter with them.

The grasslands of the treeless steppe offer the best place in the world for grazing the horses that were essential to the conduct of war until the invention of motorized transport in our own century. Nomads, who lived with their herds of horses, became pastoralists, domesticating flocks of sheep and goats. These domestic animals were slaughtered for food by mounted herdsmen using techniques far more efficient than those used by hunters pursuing wild animals.[15]

At some point that historians will never be able to identify precisely, someone conceived the idea of using such techniques to kill humans. Because the nomads had no territorial roots, their warriors had great mobility. Because they did not depend on cultivated fields, they could put their whole population on horseback, and all those fit for fighting could be sent into battle.

Warriors fighting from horse-drawn chariots, killing humans as keepers of domesticated flocks slaughtered animals, swept into prehistoric Europe in waves beginning about 4300 B.C. and continuing at intervals for more than two thousand years. If they followed the pattern observed by those writers who described later incursions, children rode in wagons behind the body of the tribe, but all others, including women, rode on horseback. The agricultural communities that had never seen or even imagined such an invasion were helpless before the onslaught.

The first wave of warlike hordes from the steppe was Indo-European. In India, they were called Aryans. In the Middle East, the invaders were called Hittites and Mitanni. In Anatolia, they were Luwians; in Greece, Achaeans and Dorians; in eastern Europe, Kurgens. Later, as we shall see, they came to be known by other names. But wherever they went with their weapons and horses, they spread their ideology and their martial culture among the survivors of their conquests.[16]

As the civilized societies of the Middle East absorbed and elaborated the martial ethic, they replaced the older woman-centered and family-centered social structures. The complementary roles of mother and warrior were replaced by a single dominant male warrior god as obedience to higher authority and killing enemies replaced caring for children as the most highly valued activities. The "parasitic" classes—warriors, priests, and tax collectors—who have dominated civilized societies ever since have consumed a great deal without producing anything of substantive value. They justify their existence by claiming to be intermediaries for superior wisdom and power. Only they can protect the society as a whole from the wrath of a deity or from external human threats. As these classes established themselves at the top of a social hierarchy, those who produce food and nurture infants went to the bottom.[17]

Only a species with powerful intellectual ability could have thought up such an ideology. The patriarchal view of the world has involved a high degree of abstraction. One result of this abstraction has been the rupture of the connection between aggression and empirical reality. Instead of reacting only to real threats, as Neolithic people did, humans now reacted to imagined ones as well. Fighting for abstractions leaves no objective way to limit aggression. One may know that when an attacking tiger is running off, it is time to cool down. But how can one know when a deity's demand for blood is sated? Or when the imagined implacable hostility of another tribe has been extinguished? Or when the enemy's essential evil has been sufficiently punished? As artificial ideologies replaced physiology as motivators, humans lost the ability to respond automatically to submissive gestures, which is the way other animals limit aggression between members of the same species.[18]

With this level of psychological development, warfare emerged full blown and spread with unprecedented speed. The older peaceful societies could not survive unless they also militarized. Under such circumstances women as well as men supported the transition of cultures; the alternative was to be passive victims of attacking armies. War spread more rapidly than any previous human cultural invention. Starting from nothing, the period between 4000 B.C. and 539 B.C. saw constant warfare of almost unimaginable destructiveness.[19] Whole populations were wiped out so completely that not even their languages survived, and cities were totally destroyed. In less than a thousand years an improved weapons technology created instruments designed for the sole purpose of killing humans: the sword, dagger, and mace. Bronze weapons and iron weapons followed, as did large-scale defensive fortifications and war chariots.

By 2700 B.C. Sumer had a fully professionalized army complete with military academies, general staff structures, military training programs, a permanent arms industry, books on tactics, military procurement, distinct combat arms branches, logistic systems, conscription, and military pay.[20] Soon the armies of Persia and Assyria learned to conduct the whole range of tactical applications required of modern armies: cold weather operations, desert warfare, obstacle crossings, movement at night and in rugged terrain, movements to contact, and siege warfare.[21]

OLD TESTAMENT WARS

ALTHOUGH THE WAVE OF invasions that brought the idea of war into the Middle East came primarily from the north and east, another tribe of warlike nomadic pastoralists came from the deserts to the south. The Semitic people known as Hebrews invaded Canaan, later called Palestine, in successive waves of conquest that lasted for several centuries. They fought under the leadership of warrior priests, the Levitic tribe of Moses, Aaron, and Joshua, who spoke in the name of Yahweh, a fierce and jealous god who ordered them to destroy, plunder, and kill. The similarities between the Indo-Europeans and the ancient Hebrews are so striking that some scholars believe that they must have had a common origin or at least some contact leading to cultural diffusion.[22] But the warrior-god model developed independently in other parts of the world, and the Hebrews may also have developed it independently.[23]

The Old Testament, which is the Hebrew Bible, records some of the earliest episodes in military history from the viewpoint of invading nomads. It also provides a sample of women's roles in war.[24] In Numbers 31, we learn how Moses followed Yahweh's directions to attack the Midianites.[25] The troops followed orders. They killed the five kings of Midian, the priest

Balaam, and every man in the city. They carried off all portable wealth and then burned the settlement to the ground. Yet Moses was outraged when he discovered that they had disobeyed in one respect. In addition to the cattle and flocks, the soldiers took all the Midian women and children as booty.

Moses reprimanded the commanders. "Have you let all the women live?" he demanded. "Behold, these caused the people of Israel, by the counsel of Balaam, to act treacherously against the Lord." The Midian women had been giving psychological support to the enemy. Moses ordered his soldiers to make up for their oversight: "Now, therefore, kill every male among the little ones, and kill every woman who has known man by lying with him." Then relenting just a bit, he concluded "All the young girls who have not known man by lying with him, keep alive for yourselves." The Lord ordered Moses to count the virgins with the rest of the booty so they could be distributed. According to the Book of Numbers there were thirty-two thousand of them.[26]

The famous Battle of Jericho began as a siege. Jericho was an ancient Canaanite city, at least seven thousand years old when the Hebrews attacked it. It is called the "earliest town in the world." Originally, it was home to about 2,500 people supported by agriculture. It flourished for one thousand years before going into decline because the soil had been exhausted. An unusual feature of the town was its walls. When the Hebrews besieged it, six thousand years after its prime, the walls were in total disrepair.[27] Joshua followed Yahweh's directions by ordering the Hebrew tribes to march around the town behind the armed men and priests. As with other nomadic armies, women and children were present. At a signal from the priests' trumpets the people gave a loud shout, which brought down the wall.

Joshua had a collaborator inside the town. A woman named Rahab, described as "a harlot" sheltered two young men whom Joshua had sent into the city as spies. Perhaps Rahab was engaged in the sex trade, perhaps not. The Bible sometimes calls all people who worship "false gods" whores and harlots.[28] At any rate Rahab was a woman capable of taking care of herself. She told Joshua's men, "For we have heard what you did to the two kings of the Amorites that were beyond the Jordan, to Sihon and Og, whom you utterly destroyed."[29] These people were dangerous enemies, and they seemed likely to overcome Jericho as they had the other towns. So she offered her support to Joshua in return for a pledge to keep her and her family safe. The men agreed. "Our life for yours! If you do not tell this business of ours, then we will deal kindly and faithfully with you when the LORD gives us the land."[30]

When the king of Jericho came looking for the spies, Rahab helped them escape down a rope through a window of her house, which was built into the city wall, and told them where to hide.[31] After the walls fell Joshua honored the pledge. The Hebrews "utterly destroyed all in the city, both men and women, young and old, oxen, sheep, and asses, with the edge of the sword," but the two spies brought Rahab and her entire family out in safety. The story ends "So the LORD was with Joshua; and his fame was in all the land."[32]

In the Book of Judges, the Song of Deborah praises a woman who was general, judge, and prophet and who led the Israelites in military action during a campaign that took place in the twelfth century B.C.[33] The verses, with an accompanying retelling in prose, describe an operation designed to hold the Valley of Jezreel against a Canaanite army of horse-drawn chariot squadrons. Deborah went into the field of battle with her general, Barak. She made the crucial tactical decision to prepare an ambush in a narrow gorge where the superior force could be picked off piecemeal. Her song of triumph is the lengthiest piece of writing in the Old Testament, the oldest surviving Hebrew verse and among the earliest military songs known.

Besides Deborah, another woman receives special mention in the song: Jael, the wife of Heber the Kenite. When the enemy leader Sisera came to Jael's tent asking for water, she played the hospitable hostess and offered him milk and a bowl of curds. Once she had put him at his ease, "She put her hand to the tent peg and her right hand to the workmen's mallet; she struck Sisera a blow, she crushed his head, she shattered and pierced his temple. He sank, he fell, he lay still at her feet; at her feet he sank, he fell; where he sank, there he fell dead."[34] For driving a tent peg into the man's brain, Jael merits this high praise: "Most blessed of women be Jael, the wife of Heber the Kenite, of tent-dwelling women most blessed."[35]

Judith is another heroine of early Hebrew warfare. A book of the Apocrypha records her history. The story begins with an Assyrian siege of the Hebrew settlement of Bethulia. Judith, a wealthy widow, took a woman servant carrying a basket of figs, wine, and bread, left the city, and marched up to the enemy camp. Holofernes, their leader, found her attractive and took her to his tent. There she flirted with him, filled him with wine, and when he was sufficiently inebriated took his sword, cut off his head, and handed it to her maid who put it in the basket. Then the two women returned to the city. In the morning, the Assyrians saw the head of their commander displayed above the walls of Bethulia. This demoralized them to such an extent that the Hebrews easily defeated them. As a reward for her heroic deed, Judith received part of the battle spoils, including Holofernes's tent. She took these to Jerusalem and put them in the temple as an offering. Yahweh also blessed her with long life; she lived to be 105.[36]

These examples do not exhaust the number of biblical women celebrated for their sanguinary activities. Queen Esther, Delilah, and Salome are other familiar names. In societies dominated by the warrior-god model, women conform to the accepted behavior.

ASSYRIANS

EUROPEAN ARCHAEOLOGISTS, WHOSE FINDINGS have given us so much insight into the prehistoric past, brought their preconceptions with them to the study of ancient artifacts. For example, Hammurabi's code of laws, which governed ancient Babylon in 1830 B.C., gave women legal rights that were still denied to French women at the beginning of the twentieth century. It would be difficult for French archaeologists to entertain the possibility that women were accepted as equals in a group of fighting men. Thus when a series of Assyrian bas-reliefs, most of which are now in the Louvre, were discovered in the nineteenth century, the visual evidence puzzled the scientists.

The Assyrians were remarkable for cultivating long, luxuriant beards. Yet here, depicted in battle scenes and in military camps were "beardless, somewhat full-faced men, revealing a slight tendency to fat."[37] The first interpretation was that they were eunuchs. But there were a great many of them, and it seemed implausible that Assyrians would castrate so many of their males. The French scholars then concluded that the figures were really boys and that depicting them as fully grown adults was an artistic convention. A third alternative may already have suggested itself to the reader. Women's clothing in the early Babylonian period was identical to that worn by men, so costume offers no clue to gender.[38] The beardless soldiers use the same weapons as do those with beards and are not obviously smaller. Indeed, those shown at work in camp, cooking, tending fires, and doing similar chores, look to a nonspecialist who has seen drawings and photographs from other eras depicting female camp followers at work very much like women.

Whatever one makes of the bas-reliefs of beardless soldiers among the rank and file, we have evidence that the Assyrians had a warrior queen in the last years of the ninth century B.C. She was Sammuramat, known to the Greeks and later historians as Semiramis. Sammuramat was among those early rulers whose history was collected and immortalized by the Greek historian Herodotus in the fifth century B.C.[39]

Herodotus, known as "the father of history," was the first to put into writing the record of the past that had earlier been preserved only in oral form. Modern scholarship can confirm very little about Sammuramat.[40] That she did rule the New Assyrian Empire from 811 to 806 B.C. is established by archaeological evidence. But archaeology cannot tell stories. For events that occurred centuries before his birth, Herodotus drew on oral tradition.

Since oral history is limited by the power of memory, narrators customarily weave stock stories, descriptions, and situations into narratives with reiterated themes. For example, a description of an evening meal may be used unchanged in several tales. Herodotus and other classical writers introduced additional imaginative elements themselves. They wished to convey the essential truth of their stories rather than strive for the sort of literal accuracy that modern historical scholarship demands. They had no photographs or tape recordings and very scanty archives. So they made up descriptions of individuals whom they had never seen and wrote speeches for prominent personages whom they had never heard. Their work is what scholars today would describe as "partially fictionalized." The best of them, like Herodotus, nevertheless brought a critical intelligence to their research and strove to record the evidence accurately. It must be emphasized that these limitations apply to all history from the ancient world, not just to histories of women.

According to his sources, Herodotus wrote, Sammuramat was married in her early teens to Menon, a principal courtier of the Assyrian king Ninus. When the king took command of an army during an invasion of Media, she went with him. At first the campaign was an unqualified success, as one city after another fell to the Assyrian hordes. Then they reached the capital city of Bactria, which was defended so fiercely that Ninus decided to pull back. At that point Sammuramat addressed the council of war and proposed that she lead an assault on the citadel. Her success in this operation impressed the king. He asked her husband, Menon, to give her up, offering to trade her for his sister Sosana. When Menon refused, Ninus threw him into prison where he committed suicide. The widow married the king. Then she manipulated Ninus into giving her supreme power for five days. When he consented, she threw him into prison and had him executed.

Next Sammuramat set out to extend the empire she had inherited. She conquered Babylonia where she erected the famous Hanging Gardens, one of the Seven Wonders of the ancient world, which archaeologists are now excavating. When Alexander the Great later made the long march to Babylon, his detractors accused him of trying to imitate Sammuramat, who made the march with an army of 100,000, of whom 20,000 were still able to fight at its conclusion.

Sammuramat's final and most famous expedition was an invasion of India. Except for Alexander, she was the only general in ancient times who carried a war beyond the Indus River in northern Pakistan. The historian Ctesias says that she launched this campaign with 300,000 foot soldiers and 5,000 horses. Because she lacked elephants, which were the special strength of the Indian military, she procured several thousand camels to which she attached the accoutrements of elephants. These substitutes, however, were no match for the genuine article. Although Sammuramat made valiant efforts to rally her troops from the thick of the fighting and was twice wounded herself, a disorderly retreat followed. Officers and soldiers pressed together to cross the bridge back across the Indus. Thousands were trampled, and others were thrown into the river and drowned. When Summuramat and all those who could manage to save themselves crossed over, she ordered the bridge destroyed. The Indian commander, after consulting an oracle, decided not to pursue.

Back home again, Sammuramat, in the fashion typical of her times, erected a monument, which Herodotus describes, celebrating her exploits. A bronze statue of herself armed with a sword surmounted a pillar bearing this inscription:

Nature made me a woman yet I have raised myself to rival the greatest men. I swayed the scepter of Ninos: I extended my dominions to the river Hinamenes Eastward; to the Southward to the land of Frankincense and Myrrh; Northward to Saccae and the Scythians. No Assyrian before me had

*seen an ocean, but I have seen four. I have built dams and fertilized the barren
land with my rivers. I have built impregnable walls and roads to far places and
with iron cut passages through mountains where previously even wild animals
could not pass. Various as were my deeds, I have yet found leisure hours to
indulge myself with friends.*[41]

In the years following Sammuramat's reign, Assyrian power was at its
height. At that time the most formidable military weapon was the war chariot. It took two people to operate. The driver managed the team of horses
and urged them along at high speed, sometimes clashing the chariot against
one of the enemy vehicles, while an archer used the chariot as a platform.
This was certain death to anyone trying to oppose on foot. Women were
capable of serving as drivers. Herodotus observed that among the Zavecians
in North Africa, it was customary to have women drive the war chariots.[42]
But as has happened repeatedly with weapons systems, the chariot was eventually overtaken by an improvement: mounted cavalry.

Once again, the steppe peoples were the military innovators. They had
invented the horse-drawn chariot that had made their earliest attacks on
people to the south and east so terrifying. They also rode on the backs of
horses, certainly by 2000 B.C. and perhaps even before 4000 B.C. But the first
evidence of horses being ridden into battle is in the ninth century B.C.[43] At
the end of the seventh century B.C. Iranian tribes from the steppe, for some
now-unfathomable reason, involved themselves again in the ongoing wars of
Asia Minor, where archaeological and historical records are available.
Cimmerians and then Scythians charged into battle firing arrows while
mounted on the backs of horses. The Scythians allied with the Babylonians,
and in 604 B.C. brought about the fall of the great Assyrian empire, which
could not resist despite having help from Egypt.

EGYPTIANS

THE HISTORY OF EGYPT goes back even farther than that of the
Assyrians. Long before Sammuramat, Egypt had warrior queens. About
3000 B.C., Maryet-Nit reigned and erected for herself a particularly large and
fine monument at Abydos.[44] Queens named Khenkaues, Nefrusobek,
Ahhotep, and Ahmiose Nofretari left their marks on records dating between
the twenty-fifth and sixteenth centuries B.C. Then from 1503 to 1482 B.C.,

Hatshepsut ruled Egypt. She was an exceptionally able leader, who focused on commercial enterprises rather than on the military conquests that had engrossed the attention of her immediate predecessors. But when military action was necessary, she fought at the head of her troops. Hatshepsut adopted the false beard signifying wisdom, which was worn only by pharaohs, and some of her monuments show her wearing other articles of male adornment as well.[45]

LIBYAN AMAZONS

THE STRIKING, WELL-PRESERVED monuments left by the Egyptians are so conspicuous that the histories of other African cultures are eclipsed by them. Egypt was by no means the only part of Africa to have women rulers. Detailed written history for most of Africa is relatively recent. However, one group, the Libyan Amazons, grew so powerful and endured for so long that it left a record in the written sources that is the equal of that of any other illiterate empire in prehistory.

The Greeks called all of North Africa except Egypt Libya, and it was from this region that the first Amazons set out on military campaigns of conquest. Rock drawings in the Sahara studied by the French archaeologist Henri Lhote show a party of women warriors armed with bows, one of the few pieces of hard evidence left behind by the illiterate, nomadic Amazon tribes. But they did not have to depend on their own writing to pass on their history; the classical writers of Greece and Rome did that for them.

It is fashionable today to deny the existence of historic Amazons, to scoff at them as pure fantasy, like unicorns or centaurs, found in ancient texts because of the credulity of the authors. Even feminist scholars shy away from asserting their literal reality for fear of being considered naive.[46] But the classical writers who created the discipline of history and first developed the principles of logical analysis and laid the foundations of scientific method were not fools. Significantly, very few of them questioned the reality of Amazons even centuries after the disappearance of the Amazon empire. One who was skeptical was the first-century geographer Strabo:

> Our accounts of other peoples keep a distinction between the mythical and historical elements; for the things that are ancient and false and monstrous are called myths, but history wishes for the truth, whether ancient or recent,

and contains no monstrous element, or else only rarely. But as regards the Amazons, the same stories are told now as in early times, though they are marvelous and beyond belief. For instance, who could believe that an army of women, or a city, or a tribe, could ever be organized without men, and not only be organized, but even make inroads upon the territory of other people, and not only overpower the people near them to the extent of advancing as far as what is now Ionia, but even send an expedition across the sea as far as Attica? For this is the same as saying that the men of those times were women, and the women were men.[47]

But is there anything self-evidently absurd about a tribe dominated by women? Few other scholars of antiquity shared Strabo's sweeping dismissal of Amazons, particularly since, as we shall see, Amazons continued to appear in battle. Some details of older accounts might be questioned, but as the historian Arrian wrote in the middle of the second century, "I do not think it credible that this race of women, often mentioned by good authorities, never existed at all."[48] The historian Sarah Pomeroy cautiously writes, "Whether the Amazons had a historical existence is unprovable. It appears not to be beyond the realm of possibility that exclusively female societies existed."[49]

What kind of evidence must be produced to prove the existence of historical Amazons? There is far more evidence, both literary and archaeological, than survives for other people such as Hittites or Massagetae, whose existence is unquestioned. Must we establish beyond a reasonable doubt that a Greek named Heracles stole a belt from a woman named Hippolyta to quiet skeptics? Should it not be sufficient to identify one or more nations of belligerent women who repudiated permanent matrimonial ties? It would be instructive to review archaeological literature from the past two centuries, particularly that not published in English, to examine the hypothesis that Amazons were real. If Amazons did not found the dozen cities in the Aegean and Asia Minor that claimed their founder was Amazonian, then who did? If Amazons did not erect the great image of Artemis at Ephesus, then who did? If Amazons did not live in Libya, who did? Absence of evidence proves nothing unless there has been a reasonable search for evidence. If the history of African women in ancient times has been neglected by scholars, that is no proof that there were no African queens.[50] Indeed, as soon as there were European histories of Africa, evidence of powerful women rulers appeared everywhere, suggesting that serious investigation of the early period would be fruitful.

The first-century Greek historian Diodorus of Sicily included the rise and fall of the Amazon empire in his ambitious history of the world. According to Diodorus, the homeland of the Amazons in North Africa supported a hunter-gatherer culture. Like other nomadic empire builders, these people eschewed farming and concentrated on war. Under Queen Myrina, they began by attacking a neighboring tribe known as Gorgons in a battle in which thousands died. But the Amazons grew careless, and while they were celebrating their victory some of the three thousand prisoners they had taken managed to arm themselves and signal to companions who had been routed earlier and were hiding in the hills. They returned during the night and massacred the sleeping women.

Myrina, however, escaped with a few of her followers. She recruited another army of women and headed east. The Egyptian pharaoh allowed her safe passage through his kingdom. Her army continued to Arabia and conquered it. Like other fierce nomadic warriors, the Amazons piled up conquests quickly. They subdued the countryside from Syria to Asia Minor, founding cities as they went. Most of the cities named after Amazon commanders were unquestionably real: Cyrene, Gyneion, Smyrna, Anaea, Thebes, Sinope, Pygela. At the Amazon city of Ephesus, they built a magnificent temple to the goddess Artemis, which came to be regarded as one of the Seven Wonders of the Ancient World. Here the Amazons performed war dances to the music of pipes, rattling their shields and quivers and beating the ground.[51]

Today many writers associate goddess worship with the matriarchal cultures that flourished prior to the invention of war. Unfortunately, once war was set loose, older goddess-worshiping cultures became just as adept at killing as those that took up the newer patriarchal religions. Had they not learned war, they could not have survived. The Amazons waged aggressive wars of conquest. Their devotion to Artemis drove them forward just as devotion to Yahweh inspired the Hebrew nation.

Artemis, the moon goddess, like all moon goddesses, had a changing nature. She was virgin, mother, and crone. As mother of all life, the Amazon image of her at Ephesus depicted her with a torso covered with breasts, showing how bountifully she nurtured all living things. But Artemis was also the crone of the waning moon, the Hunter, or as the Spartans called her, the

Butcher. Originally Artemis was worshiped with human sacrifice. Herodotus described the practice at Taurus where the priestesses killed all men who landed in their territory and nailed their heads to crosses. At Hierapolis artificial trees in Artemis's temple were hung with the corpses of her sacrificial victims. The ritual softened over time, as it did in other cultures over the world that originally practiced human sacrifice. In Attica Artemis was satisfied with a few drops of blood drawn from a man's neck with a sword instead of demanding his head, and eventually the sacrifice of a bull was sufficient.[52]

The stories of the Amazons that are remembered today are those in which Greek heroes are triumphant. Tales of Heracles, Theseus, and others come from a late period in Amazon history when Greek heroes sought out contact with Amazons to test their bravery. Earlier, Amazons were not accustomed to losing and those who were wise did not provoke them. When Jason and the Argonauts went looking for the Golden Fleece, they carefully avoided Amazon territory.

The Libyan Amazons had a naval force as well as an army. Myrina's sister, Mytilene, who had a town named for her on Lesbos, was an Amazon naval commander who extended the women's imperial ambitions into the Aegean. While the Amazons were a match for any army, their navy was as subject to storms and foul weather as any other. Caught in a sudden squall, the Amazon ships barely escaped destruction to land on the island of Samothrace. From this position, Myrina planned an invasion of Thrace in the southeastern part of the Balkan peninsula. Faced with the Amazon invasion, the king of Thrace called for help from Scythian allies in the Black Sea region of the steppe. In the battle that followed, Myrina was killed. Although the Amazons continued to wage a Thracian campaign, they suffered a series of setbacks and withdrew to their strongholds in Asia and North Africa. But some of the Amazon women remained behind.

SCYTHIAN AMAZONS

NO ONE HAS EVER suggested that Scythians were mythical, but like the Amazons their nomadic lifestyle and lack of a written language left their history to be recovered only through excavations by archaeologists and descriptions from outside observers, in this case primarily Herodotus. Russian archaeologists, who in the past few decades have uncovered many remains of the mixture of peoples and tribes who crossed the steppe in the sixth and fifth centuries B.C., call them Early Nomads. Herodotus called some of them Sauromatians and others Scythians. The standard history of them in English, published in 1970 by the Polish scholar Tadeusz Sulimirski, calls them Sarmatians. The historian John Keegan calls the steppe people simply "the horse peoples of the steppe."[53]

To the Greeks, a peculiarity of the Sarmatians was their female warriors. Herodotus explained this phenomenon as a direct transfer from the African Amazons. He says that some of these women who came to Thrace were courted by young Scythian men and finally agreed to mate with them on the condition that they leave their own tribe and accept the freedom for women that the Amazons were accustomed to enjoying. The men accepted and thus became the fathers of the first Sarmatians. For Herodotus, this explained why women north of the Black Sea were found "riding to the hunt on horseback, sometimes with, sometimes without their menfolk, taking part in war, and wearing the same sort of clothes as men."[54] It is not necessary, however, to hypothesize direct cultural transfer to account for women warriors in the steppe. Herodotus's own investigation of steppe societies indicates that strong matriarchal elements were pervasive all the way from Turkey to Central Asia. Thus, among the Illsseonians, "the women [had] equal authority with the men."[55] Similar arrangements prevailed among the Massagetae, whom Herodotus considered strange because, unlike Greeks, they drank milk and while on the move had their children live in wagons drawn by oxen.[56]

Sarmatian history extended over a millennium and covered territory from Siberia and the East China Sea to the British Isles. Huns, Mongols, Cossacks, and many others will reappear in the following chapters, sporadically erupting into the settled communities of Europe and Asia, raiding, killing, taking slaves, and sometimes holding empires. Their women were always a sturdy lot. Among the Cossacks into modern times, so eyewitnesses say, "the womenfolk were as free as the men to change partners, and participated as freely in the Cossack orgies of drink and sex. . . . They also fought alongside their men when necessary."[57]

The Sarmatians were never a unified political entity, and the cultures of the many smaller tribes and groups had distinctive variations. For many centuries all of eastern Europe was called Sarmatia, and that they are today such a shadowy presence among the peoples of antiquity says much about the unkindness of history to those who do not preserve their own heritage. Excavation of Sarmatian burials reveals that up to 20 percent of the female graves from the sixth and fifth centuries B.C. contained weapons and sometimes horse skeletons.[58]

For several centuries after the death of Myrina, Sarmatian Amazons made no further impact on world history, although steppe peoples continued to train both girls and boys for war and probably experienced as much combat as any other people. But eventually a war came which nearly destroyed them. Some troops of mounted women fought their way out. Their leader, Queen Lysippe, took them south to a new homeland and established Themiscrya at the mouth of the Thermodon River in northern Turkey. Whether or not Thermiscyra existed, the Turks certainly produced a race of women who were superb riders. According to Keegan, "legend had it that Turkish women conceived and gave birth on horseback."[59] Under Lysippe's leadership, the Amazons reconquered some of the land first won by Myrina. Lysippe died in battle, and her daughter continued campaigns to expand Amazonia, extending her domain as far as Thrace and Syria. The Amazon empire continued to grow and flourish for many generations.

THE TROJAN WAR

WHILE THE AMAZON HISTORY is known only through the writings of other people, the Greeks, who invented history, preserved vivid, highly individualized stories about themselves and their military exploits. Earlier records left by ancient peoples were repetitious catalogs of atrocities, numbers of casualties, and threats by conquerors of what they would do if anyone challenged them in the future.

The first Greek contact with war came between 1200 B.C. and 1000 B.C. At that time the Greeks were badly mauled by the Indo-European invaders and fell into a Dark Age. For the next four centuries the Greeks were outside the mainstream of military development and had no written language.[60] As a result, when they began to write history, much of the record was well beyond living memory. Once they recovered writing, the oral tradition that was transcribed included the stories of martial women.

The earliest women warriors said to be natives of Greece were Harpalyce and Atalanta. Harpalyce was the daughter of King Lycurgus of Thrace. He trained her in warlike exercises, including riding, racing, throwing darts, and using the bow and arrow. When the king of Thessaly invaded Thrace, defeating King Lycurgus's best troops and taking him prisoner, Harpalyce assembled an army, attacked the enemy, and freed her father. Unfortunately for him, the king then started an anti-alcohol campaign to eliminate drunkenness among his subjects, and his order to uproot all the vines in his domain provoked a rebellion. He fled to the isle of Naxos, where he went mad and killed himself. Harpalyce turned outlaw and lived in the forests of Thrace until some shepherds captured and executed her. Atalanta is famous as the only woman among the Argonauts, whose heroic expedition was said to have taken place in 1263 B.C. Although her fellow voyagers praised her bravery and military skill, her greatest talent was wrestling. She once defeated young Peleus, who later became the father of Achilles, the great hero of the Trojan War.

The oral traditions relating to Persia and Egypt were supported by monuments and other corroborative archaeological evidence. The Greeks, however, far from the Near Eastern centers of civilization, had only their own stories and artifacts to cite as sources. The skepticism of modern scholars eventually put Harpalyce, Atalanta, and the whole pantheon of male heroes who feature in early Greek history in the category of myth. Even King Theseus, the man credited with founding Athens, which certainly did exist, was dismissed as myth because the lists of kings containing his name could not be verified. Indeed, until the archaeologist Heinrich Schliemann's excavations in the twentieth century, the city of Troy itself was dismised as pure fantasy.

The history of the last great undertaking of the Greeks before they succumbed to the Indo-European invaders was preserved in oral form by bards during the Greek Dark Age. When the Greeks learned to write again, they preserved two of these epics as the *Iliad* and the *Odyssey*. The poet Homer is credited with providing the text for the written form.[61]

The *Iliad* is a war story. In part it reflects oral tradition stretching back to the time of the original events, and in part it reflects the desire in the Dark Age to look back to relearn the art of war and to celebrate the glory of heroes. This Greek war poetry introduced a new view of war. The Indo-European invaders and the Hebrews had adopted a positive view of battle and slaughter, explaining the duty to fight as obedience to a god whose orders might or might not make sense in human terms. The Greeks conceptualized war as a spiritual practice in itself, a kind of activity that ennobled the human spirit. Martial virtues—courage, bravery, self-sacrifice, endurance, and military skill—could become manifest only in combat. All of this would be familiar to the people who engaged in nonlethal forms of primitive warfare.

But unlike the older forms of ritualized war, which was undertaken as sport and a demonstration of skill and courage, Homer's heroes did not fight to minimize casualties. Their warfare was lethal, and Homer dwells with loving detail on descriptions of a variety of ghastly wounds. The heroes did resemble earlier practitioners of ritual war, however, in that they fought as individuals. It is not the strategic and tactical skill of generals that the poet celebrated but single combat between particular champions. Indeed, the participants in the war at Troy seemed unable to coordinate even small groups of soldiers to achieve a battlefield objective. While professional armies have required subordination of the individual to coordinated group formations, discouraging flamboyant performances carried out to gain personal fame, the myth of martial glory that the Greeks introduced has had an impact that persists into the present.

The *Iliad*'s purpose is to celebrate male heroes, yet women abound in the story.[62] The Trojan War began because Paris, son of the king of Troy, kidnapped Helen, wife of Menelaus. During the war the fierce quarrel between the two heroes, Achilles and Agamemnon, started because Agamemnon took away "Fair Briseis," Achilles' prize of war. Achilles refused to fight until he got the girl back and received assurances that Agamemnon had not slept with her.

Other women appear in active roles as well. Hecuba, mother of the Trojan hero Hector, encourages the men to fight. "Why child," she asks him, "have you come here and left behind bold battle? Surely it is these accursed sons of the Achaians who wear you out. . . . But stay while I bring you honey-sweet wine. . . . In a tired man wine will bring back his strength to its bigness. . . ."[63] Andromache, Hector's wife, advises him on tactics. "Stay here on the rampart," she counsels at one point, "but draw your people up by the fig tree, there where the city is open to attack, and where the wall may be mounted. Three times their bravest came that way, and fought there to storm it."[64]

Large numbers of women accompanied the invading army as servants, although Homer does not tell us much about the menial support functions they probably fulfilled. We do know that when Hector fell in battle,

Achilleus, one of Achilles' female servants, washed and anointed his corpse. Presumably the bodies of other fallen heroes received similar treatment.[65] The story ends with the fall of Troy and the Greeks returning home with their booty, which included large numbers of Trojan women.

An intriguing element in the history of the Trojan War is the participation of the Amazons. The army of women came to the aid of Troy after the death of Hector. Homer refers to the Amazons twice,[66] but his story ends before the Amazons enter the war. Although some of the earliest manuscripts of the *Iliad* contain a final verse describing the arrival of the Amazons, it is too scanty to be of any value.[67] However, another poet, Arctinus of Miletus, composed *Aethiopis* at the same time Homer was writing his account. He tells the rest of the story, describing how Memmon, king of Ethiopia, and Penthesilea, queen of the Amazons, came to Troy during the final year of the war.

Amazon connections with Troy predated the war. The first great Amazon queen, Myrina, was said to have been buried there after her death in Thrace.[68] Once engaged at Troy, the Greek sources say, Penthesilea killed many Greek heroes, including Achilles, outside the walls. But then, in one of those interferences by deities that cause skeptics to dismiss the entire tale of Troy as myth, the god Zeus brought Achilles back to life so that Penthesilea had to fight him again. On the second try, he defeated her. Some of his friends, not knowing when to stop, mutilated her dying body by gouging out her eyes. In one version, Achilles was so overcome by lust at seeing the bloody remains of the Amazon queen at his feet that he raped her corpse.[69]

In later years, Amazons became a popular subject among both Greek and Roman artists. Schliemann, the same archaeologist who discovered Troy, discovered the earliest-known representation of an Amazon. He found a fragment of a terra-cotta shield at Tiryns dating from the end of the eighth or early seventh century B.C. which shows an Amazon with a Greek hero. Somewhat more recent bronze reliefs, dating from the late seventh and early sixth century, have also been discovered.[70]

It is worth observing that in none of these representations are the Amazons missing a breast. In the third century A.D. a Roman author named Justin asserted that the word *Amazon* derived from the Greek *a* meaning "without" and *mazos* meaning "breast." This odd notion has had enormous staying power and is still commonly cited today.[71] Female breasts are not an obstacle to the use of any weapon, including the bow and arrow, and mastectomy is not an effective way to increase the strength of chest muscles. That some women in some parts of the globe may have practiced ritual mutilation to prevent the development of a breast is possible—humans have done all sorts of odd things in the pursuit of beauty—but the Amazons of the ancient world were not among them. At any rate, Justin was off to a bad start because the word *Amazon* is not of Greek derivation. The *American Heritage Dictionary* gives the origin as the Old Iranian word *ha-moz-an,* meaning simply "warrior." Or, even more likely, as suggested earlier, it derived from *Amazigh,* which was what Libyans called themselves before the Greeks gave them the name Berbers.

THE AMAZONOMACHY

THE GREEKS HAD ONE more major encounter with Amazons after the Trojan War. This time the mounted women invaded Athens itself, and the war the Greeks fought to resist conquest was known as the Amazonomachy. The Greek victory in the conflict was the first time the Greeks succeeded in repelling an invasion of their homeland, and it remained a popular subject in art and literature for hundreds of years.

Greek tradition traced the origins of the Amazonomachy to the goddess Hera, who ordered the hero Heracles to carry out twelve tasks, one of which was to obtain the girdle worn by the Amazon queen Hippolyte. In a style reminiscent of the vision quests and dares characteristic of puberty rituals, Heracles went forth to prove his manhood. What followed was not a war but a ritualized contest between champions. The Greek hero made his way to the Amazon capital city of Thermiscyra and sent an envoy to the queen demanding that she give him her girdle. She refused, and soon battle lines were drawn on the plains of Thermiscrya.

Heracles dressed for the occasion in a lion skin, putting his head through the mouth of the dead animal and wrapping its paws around his neck. Except for that he was naked, and to emphasize his bravery he carried a sword but not a shield. His first opponent in the duel of champions was the Amazon Aella. She also fought without armor, but carried a round shield, a spear, and a sword. The two circled each other as spectators on both sides shouted encouragement for their champion and called out insults at the opponent. The Greek storytellers went into detail about the parries and thrusts, but to make a long story short, Heracles eventually got in a heavy blow to Aella's head and brought her down. Several more women, each a famous Amazon champion, took turns facing off with Heracles, but he won each round. Then he took the girdle, burned the city, and sailed home. One of his companions on his quest was Theseus, known as the founder of Athens. Theseus took a souvenir of his own, the Amazon warrior Antiope.

According to the Greeks, these events left the humiliated Amazons lusting for revenge. They retaliated with a full-scale invasion conducted in conjunction with Scythian allies. The combined force advanced through Thrace into Attica and camped outside Athens. The Amazon warriors were garbed in the Scythian fashion of tight-fitting trousers and adorned their horses as the Scythians did with antler headdresses of gold and bronze. They fought Scythian style, shooting bows from horseback and using lances, swords, and axes in close combat. The Greeks persist in describing their enemies in this first great battle of their history as a distinct group of Amazons.[72] It is possible, however, that the attackers were Scythian women fighting in all-female cavalry units.

Theseus made the first move in the battle, taking his right wing down from the Museum Hill and attacking the Amazon left wing. The women on horseback surged forward, firing arrows as they came and breaking the Greek lines so that the Greeks were forced back as far as the Shrine of Eumenides. But the Athenian left wing held fast as the screaming Amazon cavalry thundered past in pursuit of the routed Greeks. Theseus then advanced again from the Palladium, Mount Ardettus, and the Lyceum, targeting the Amazon right wing. In bitter hand-to-hand combat, axes smashed against shields, and swords and spears broke in the clash. Curiously, Theseus had a new champion at his side—Antiope, who chose loyalty to her new husband over loyalty to her own people. Her reward was an Amazon javelin through her body. Theseus continued to push the attack; the Amazon line broke and they retreated to their camp.

The most complete account of the Amazon siege of Athens is in Plutarch's *Life of Theseus* written about A.D. 100. He relied on the work of a fourth-century B.C. historian named Cleidemus, whose work no longer survives but from which Plutarch must have drawn for his detailed description of the battle.[73]

Archaeological evidence lies tantalizingly just beyond reach. A century after Plutarch, and fourteen hundred years after the Amazon invasion, a Roman writer named Pausanius wrote a travel guide for his second-century contemporaries. He included a walking tour of Athens, describing as a site not to be missed a line of Amazon graves along the side of a road leading from the citadel to the port of Piraeus. He also mentioned monuments that earlier writers had described—the Amazonium, the Temple of the Furies, and the Horcomosium—all related to the famous war.[74] Pausanius's travel guide is now eighteen hundred years old, and anthropologists continue to search for remains of ancient times. It is not beyond the realm of possibility that traces of Amazons, the women warriors from the city of Thermiscrya on the Thermodon River, will one day be found, if not in Athens, then near the River Therme in modern-day Turkey as they have already been found in the ancient Scythian lands in Ukraine.[75]

CHAPTER THREE

CLASSICAL WARFARE

F OR CENTURIES THE SIGN of an educated person was the ability to read Latin and Greek, and most of what there was to read was about wars. Schoolchildren in Europe and America learned about wars between Greeks and Persians and then about wars between the city-states of Athens and Sparta in Greece itself. Next came the rise of Macedon and the heroic career of Alexander the Great, who conquered the world but died young. Next came Rome, with its invincible legions, which also conquered an enormous empire and held on to it for more than one thousand years. Then European barbarians brought down the western part of the empire in A.D. 476 and started the Dark Ages.

Children today no longer read the histories of Herodotus or Tacitus or the memoirs of generals like Xenophon and Caesar. Classical history has become a field for specialists. Our knowledge of this history, however, still depends on the same Greek and Latin texts supplemented by archaeological discoveries.

In the previous chapter, the classical historians cited relied on oral history for narrative accounts of events of the past. But in the fifth century B.C. Greek writers also began to record events they had seen themselves or which were related to them by eyewitnesses. Other literate cultures also left records that provide a variety of perspectives from which to evaluate individual accounts. For this more recent period, there are also more surviving archaeological remains. The difference in the quality and quantity of the evidence creates a vast divide between earlier events, which some may choose to dismiss as entirely fictional, and those of the classical era, which scholars consider proven fact.

To readers who are not classics specialists and are accustomed to the kind of evidence that historians have available when writing about the twentieth century, the line between prehistory and history will appear very uncertain. The same writers who described the rise and fall of the Amazon empire wrote about the rise and fall of Greece and Rome. They used the same rhetorical devices—making up dialogue or guessing at numbers when they did not have precise counts—that modern scholars abhor. And while some wrote from personal knowledge, others produced books centuries after the fact, books that have become essential sources because the older accounts they took their information from did not survive.

Modern military historians discuss classical warfare as if no women were involved, but the same sources they cite in their books include information on women that is as well documented as that about their male contemporaries. The overview of classical warfare that follows is a synthesis based on the literature of antiquity combined with modern secondary accounts in a form that makes most sense to me. Modern scholarly writing is acknowledged in the endnotes in the usual way, and when I included material drawn from the classical canon, I identify the original writer. Readers interested in investigating the evidence for themselves can trace the references in any edition of these ancient books.[1]

THE GREEKS DISCOVER WAR

CLASSICAL HISTORY BEGINS WITH Greece emerging from its Dark Age, a slow process that took several hundred years. Despite the battering they took from various invaders, the Greeks were still ignorant of the military practices of the advanced civilizations of Egypt and the Middle East. Instead they had developed a unique type of fighting based on heavy infantry, the hoplite phalanx. This formation consisted of tightly packed masses of soldiers armed with spears, short swords, and shields. They could not maneuver, and since they could move in just one direction, they could fight only in an open field. The front ranks in the phalanx made the first contact with the enemy while all the rest pressed forward with their shields trying to force the opposing formation to break. No one could keep this up for long, and after fifteen or twenty minutes something had to give. Once a unit broke, the killing stopped. A phalanx could not pursue without breaking its formation, and the Greeks had no cavalry, one reason they had found the Amazons so formidable. Although this form of combat was terrifying, casualties were low. It thus retained many characteristics of war as sport and male bonding ritual, minimizing the blood sacrifice that was the essence of the newer civilized forms of war.

As the Greeks were discovering the larger world, the main military action continued to be in Asia Minor, which had elaborate and deadly military institutions. Greek historians recorded their observations of Asian war making, including the participation of women. Since most of what we know today is filtered through the eyes of the Athenean Greeks, it is important to remember that the military roles of women in their culture were less prominent than they were among the people they observed. Thus, they might be surprised, shocked, or skeptical of what was routine for cultures they describe. For example, Xenophon, who was a general as well as the author of *Anabasis,* one of the major classical histories, described the musicians who led the Lydian army of King Croesus into battle—women playing harps and flutes. Music helped morale and was useful for keeping troops marching in step without breaking rank, which is essential for maneuvering large formations. Besides this corps of musicians, Xenophon wrote, all the armies of Asia brought women to the battlefield. They claimed that having their families with them motivated them and increased their lust for battle. "Perhaps this is so," he observed cynically, "but perhaps they want to satisfy their passion."[2] Here is an example of a male historian conflating all female roles into sexual activity, in this case elevating his preconceptions over the direct testimony of his informants. Although we must be grateful to Xenophon and other classical writers for recording what they saw and heard, we must also be alert to their biases.

THE PERSIAN EMPIRE

CYRUS, THE FOUNDER OF the Persian Empire, began his career in the middle of the sixth century B.C. when he defeated the Medes and merged them into his Persian kingdom. He also conquered the Lydians, sacking Sardis, the capital city of the Lydian Empire, in western Asia Minor and capturing Croesus himself together wih all his female musicians. He subjugated the country of Sacae after defeating a fierce army of men and women, who fought side by side with bows, arrows, daggers, and battle-axes. And in 539 B.C. he conquered Babylon, bringing to an end the great Chaldean empire. At this point his empire extended from the Indus to the Mediterranean, from the Caucuses to the Indian Ocean. Then he cast his eye on the domain of Queen Tomyris, ruler of the Massagetae.

The Massagetae were steppe people of Central Asia, east of the Aral Sea. In the first millennium B.C. the region was well watered although today much of it is either desert or semidesert. Herodotus noted that these nomads "resemble the Scythians in their dress and mode of life." They were ferocious fighters, both on foot and on horseback, with bows, javelins, and battle-axes. Their social organization was matriarchal, and, as Herodotus put it, they "use women promiscuously," which meant that they practiced polyandry, with women taking as many partners as they chose.[3]

In 529 B.C., Cyrus took an army of two hundred thousand[4] men plus a large baggage train to add another conquest to his empire. Rather than openly challenge the Massagetae to battle, he laid a trap. He set up a camp in which he spread out a banquet, including great goblets of wine. Then he left a few hundred of his least skilled soldiers to guard the camp and took the body of the army off to wait at a distance. The Massagetae soldiers took the bait, captured the camp, then ate and drank until they passed out. Then Cyrus returned, gaining an easy victory in which he killed or captured most of the Massagetae, including Tomyris's son Spargapises. Queen Tomyris sent him a message: "Glutton as you are for blood, you have no cause to be proud of this day's work, which has no smack of soldierly courage. Give me back my son and get out of my country with your forces intact, and be content with your triumph over a third part of the Massagetae. If you refuse, I swear by the sun our master to give you more blood than you can drink, for all your gluttony."[5]

Herodotus believed the battle that followed was more violent than any other fought between foreign nations. Tomyris drew the Persians into a narrow pass, where she did not bother to take prisoners but slaughtered them all, including the camp followers. Learning that Spargapises had killed himself while in captivity, she had her soldiers search through the heaped corpses until they found that of Cyrus. She plunged the head of the dead man into a skin filled with human blood. "See now," she cried, "I fulfil my threat; you have your fill of blood."[6]

Cambyses, Cyrus's son, left Tomyris alone, contenting himself with the conquest of Egypt in 525 B.C. The Persian Empire continued to prosper under Cambyses's successor, Darius, and Darius's successor, Xerxes.

THE EARLY GREEK WARS

AS WARS CONTINUED IN Asia Minor, the Greeks fought among themselves. The city-state of Argos claimed to be the rightful ruler of all Greece because it represented the remnant of the preinvasion Greek state that went to war against Troy. This ancient claim did not impress Athens or Sparta or such other city-states as Tegea, Corinth, or Megara. Sparta, in particular, developed a rigid militaristic society that expanded its influence during the seventh and sixth centuries.

Early in the fifth century, when Spartan power was at its height, Sparta's young king, Cleomenes I, invaded Argos in a campaign that ended with a memorable victory for the Argive women. After defeating the Argive army in battle, Cleomenes had pursued the survivors to a sacred grove where they had taken refuge. There the Spartans surrounded them and set fire to the grove, where all of them died in the flames. Next the Spartans marched to the city, which now had no men to defend it. A poet named Telesilla rallied the women, calling on them to protect their homes and children. Armed with ceremonial weapons from temples or with implements found in private dwellings, the women followed Telesilla to the walls and after heavy fighting repelled the enemy.

The women who fell in that battle were buried with ceremony close by the Argive Road. A statue of Telesilla was erected in the Temple of Aphrodite and the poet composed a victory hymn. The women also erected a statue of Ares "as a memorial of their surpassing valor." According to Plutarch the defense of Argos was still commemorated more than five hundred years later. At an annual Festival of Impudence, women dressed "in men's shirts and cloaks, and the men in women's robes and veils" in memory of the manly valor of the Argive women.[7]

This incident was unusual in that women were the sole defenders. It was not unusual, however, for women to help to defend a town when attackers broke through the walls. Heavy infantry could not operate in the narrow, crooked streets with dead-end alleys, and civilians who were familiar with the street plans could easily set ambushes and booby traps. Anyone who could climb to a rooftop could bombard soldiers with heavy stones or tiles. Plutarch in his life Pyrrhus tells how the general died when a roof tile thrown by an Argive woman hit him on the head.[8]

THE PERSIAN WARS

THE PERSIAN WARS OF the fifth century B.C., brought Greece into the mainstream of military history for the first time. The Greeks learned about cavalry, skirmishers, and light infantry from Persia while the Persians learned about heavy infantry from the Greeks. In 498 Athens sent some ships to help in a revolt against Persian rule led by Aristagoras of Miletus, although Sparta refused to get involved. Darius, the Persian ruler, defeated the Athenian fleet and sacked Miletus, which ended the revolt. The Persians then set out to punish the Athenians. Their first attempt was frustrated when the Persian fleet was destroyed while attempting to round the promontory of Mount Atlas in a storm, and their second effort was stopped when the Athenians won a decisive victory in the Battle of Marathon in 490 B.C. Darius returned to Asia.

Four years later Xerxes became ruler of Persia. He made extensive preparations before he launched a second invasion in 480 B.C. Persian forces arrived in Greece with a large train of women and children as part of a joint operation in which Xerxes required participation by all his subject states from Asia Minor, across the Middle East, and on to India. One of his allies was Artemisia, queen of Caria, a land in southwestern Asia Minor on the Aegean Sea. She reported as ordered, but throughout the war she had reservations about the wisdom of the enterprise.

The force Xerxes assembled for the Greek invasion was among the largest ever known in the ancient world. Herodotus, who modern authorities say grossly overestimated, said it consisted of 1,700,000 men, not counting the baggage train. After crossing the Hellespont, this massive army marched around the northern Aegean Sea. At the same time, a huge Persian navy crossed the Mediterranean from the south. Herodotus says there were 1,207 triremes plus 3,000 smaller ships, including light galleys and transport boats. Artemisia's contribution consisted of a fleet 70 ships, including the one she commanded.

At first, the Persian invasion went well. Xerxes broke through Greek resistance at Thermopylae and occupied Athens, where he burned the

Acropolis. Several Greek states began to consider negotiating terms with the invader. But Xerxes wanted total victory and planned to finish off the Greeks by destroying the fleet anchored at Salamis. He told Mardonius, his chief military officer, to ask his naval commanders for their opinions.

All except Artemisia encouraged Xerxes to go ahead with his plan. An aggressive fighter in an earlier naval operation off the coast of Artemisium, Artemisia emphasized to Mardonius that her reasoning was not colored by fear of combat, although Herodotus assumes, in the words he imagined her speaking, that she must have shared his ideas about feminine weakness:

> Tell the king that it is I who say this and clearly I have not been lacking in courage against the Greeks. But I counsel you not to offer their fleet a battle. The Greeks are much stronger at sea than we, just as men are stronger than women. So why endanger yourself at sea? You have possession of Athens, the aim of this campaign. On land, no man stands against you. You could even advance into the Peloponnese and easily gain victory. The Greeks cannot hold a united front and will scatter to their individual cities. I hear the Greeks on Salamis are short of food and if you lead your army into the Peloponnese, then those Greeks will be fully occupied and have no wish to support the Athenians in a sea battle. But to push for a naval confrontation now risks great harm to both your fleet and your land army.[9]

A consideration that Artemisia did not mention was even more telling. The channel between the island of Salamis and the mainland was very narrow, which gave an advantage to the smaller Greek navy. But Xerxes was in command, and it was his decision to go after the Greek fleet. The Battle of Salamis was a disaster for the Persian side. Artemisia was the only senior officer to survive and to save her ship, a feat she managed this way, according to the Roman historian Polyaenus: "Artemisia in the naval battle at Salamis, finding the Persians defeated and herself near falling into the hands of the Greeks, ordered the Persian colors to be taken down and the master of the ship to bear down upon and attack a *Persian* vessel that was passing by her. The Greeks, seeing this, supposed her to be one of the allies, drew off and left her, directing their forces against other parts of the Persian fleet. Artemisia in the meantime sheered off and escaped safe to Caria."[10]

Xerxes soon went home as well, and the Athenians celebrated their triumph by rebuilding their shrines. Relief sculptures of combat adorned the major temple, the Parthenon. The subject, however, was not combat with

Persians. Instead the great sculptor Phidias depicted mounted long-haired Amazons in combat with nude Greeks, a celebration of the historic conflict with the Amazonomachy, which the Greeks would always consider their greatest triumph.

THE PELOPONNESIAN WAR

AFTER THE PERSIANS RETREATED, the Greeks were free to go back to fighting each other. Between 431 and 404 B.C., Athens and Sparta, already enemies of long standing, fought the Peloponnesian War. The war ended with Athens trapped in a land and sea siege. The city capitulated, and for the next thirty years, Sparta was the dominant power in Greece.

Athenians generally saw only the sexual role for women in their armies. Aristophanes, the satiric dramatist, claimed that the great beneficiaries of intra-Greek conflict were the sex workers. When Pericles besieged Samos, the prostitutes accompanying his army made so much money that they erected a temple to Aphrodite known as Aphrodite-in-the-Swamp.[11] If they were not prostitutes, so thought the Athenians, they should not be with armies but at home procreating. In a famous oration, described by Thucydides, Pericles is said to have stated, "Women are . . . to be neither seen, heard, nor spoken of, yet they reproduce the generations of warriors who constitute Athens."[12]

Spartan women were different. Unfortunately, everything we know about Sparta, we know from outsiders. The Spartans deliberately repudiated all cultural pursuits; we are not certain that they could even read and write. But they fascinated their contemporaries, who made up for Spartan reticence in their own writings. Spartan women were famed for their beauty—since the days of Homer they were reputed to be the most beautiful women in Greece[13]—but they were also totally unfeminine. Spartan law prohibited them from wearing jewelry or using cosmetics and perfumes. Women wore plain garments made of undyed fabric, and for her wedding, a Spartan bride had her hair cut short like a man's and put on male clothing.[14]

In Sparta, boys and girls grew up and played together naked, the girls sharing in athletic sports and contests. Lycurgus explained that there was nothing "shameful in the nakedness of the young women; modesty attended them and all wantonness was excluded. It taught them simplicity and a care for good health and gave them some taste for higher feelings, admitted as they were to the field of noble action and glory."[15] Perhaps most important, the Spartans gave girls as much food as boys. In Athens the boys nursed twice as long as girls, and girls had less food throughout childhood.[16]

In time of war Spartan women stood by their men. Plutarch wrote that when Sparta was attacked by Pyrrhus, there was some talk of sending the women and children to safety in Crete. "But the women unanimously refused and Archidamis came into the Senate with a sword in her hand, in the name of them all asking if the men expected the women to survive the ruins of Sparta." The women then tucked up their clothing and went to work digging trenches around the city with the old men while the young men who were to face the enemy were told to rest. The next morning the women brought the soldiers their weapons and put them in charge of the trenches they had dug, giving them a last-minute pep talk explaining it would be "glorious to die in the arms of their mothers and wives, falling as became Spartans." The women did not, however, always leave the fighting to the men; if they were needed, they pitched in there as well. Lactantius told how Spartan women routed an attack by the Messenians. Young wives with their close-cropped hair and male clothing would have been indistinguishable from their husbands and brothers in a fight.[17]

The customs of Sparta were Plato's inspiration when he suggested in book 5 of his *Republic* that women should be part of the political community and have the same occupations as men. Those who had the inclination would even be employed as soldiers. In a later book, the *Laws,* Plato retreated somewhat, saying that women should become fighters only after menopause and then only during emergencies. The Spartans themselves had no such reservations and trained their daughters as well as their sons in the martial arts. From the age of five all children learned the Pyrrhic dance, performed in the nude, which trained them in the movements required for spear and shield warfare. Xenophon gave the most detailed description of these martial exercises in his *Anabasis,* noting particularly the dance performed by a girl with a light shield.[18]

Of course, motherhood was a duty for Spartan women as it was for Athenian women. Giving birth to a new generation of warriors was service no male could perform. But Spartan motherhood was peculiarly ferocious. These stalwart mothers rejoiced at the news that their sons had died in combat. One mother, whose son survived a battle in which all his comrades died, made things right by killing him herself with a tile. Another reveled in her good fortune as she buried her son, saying, "I bore him that he might die for Sparta, and this is the very thing that has come to pass for me."[19]

+ + +

THE RISE OF MACEDON

THE WARS IN GREECE took a new turn with the rise of a major military power in Macedonia in the fourth century B.C. During the reign of Philip II the Macedonians altered their culture under the influence of non-Greeks, who even though conquered in war, won by marriage. According to Satyrus, Philip's biographer, every time the king made a war he also made a marriage, and he had at least seven wives. Although Philip's last wife, Cleopatra, was a native Macedonian, his other wives came from cultures that taught their daughters to ride and fight. His first wife, the Illyrian princess Audata, was trained as a warrior. Another one of his wives may have been Scythian, although we do not have her name, and another wife, Meda, was a princess of the Getae of Thrace. A royal grave believed to be hers contained weapons as well as items suitable for an upper-class woman.

Audata raised her daughter Cynane in Illyrian fashion, and when she was grown, Cynane went with her father to war. As his oldest child she thought herself entitled to inherit and fought at the head of a mercenary force in the dynastic wars that followed her father's death. Cynane's daughter, Adea, also trained to hunt and fight, took up the cause and challenged Olympias, who claimed to be Philip's first wife. The war that followed was said by Duris of Samos to be the first war waged between women. It ended with Audata's capture and death. Olympias was mother of a son, Alexander, who was reared to be a worthy successor to his father by his mother and his Greek tutor, Aristotle.

Philip II and Alexander were notable for bringing greater mobility to their armies by revolutionizing the logistical system. Traditionally the Greeks had a casual attitude toward logistics. Unlike the Near Eastern armies, they had no organized commissariat but relied on civilian merchants who followed the armies. Before the Peloponnesian War, these merchants set their prices and arranged for supply without any formal connection with military leaders.

Other civilians also followed the armies—musicians, sex workers, and other entertainers, plus the families of soldiers with their servants. The Greeks, for all Xenophon's early suspicion of Near Eastern armies and their lust, now believed that a soldier's love for his children gave him the incentive to fight and that bringing some of the comforts of home into the field motivated men to accept self-sacrifice for the good of the community.[20]

For mercenary troops, it was even more important to encourage family attachments because they lacked Greek patriotism to keep them fighting. Philo of Byzantium recommended promising mercenaries proper funerals and care for dependents: "If any of them die they must be buried with as much ceremony as possible at the expense of the community, and if they leave children or wives behind, these must be looked after scrupulously. This is the best way to instil in them loyalty to the generals and citizens, so that they confront danger bravely."[21]

What this system provided in motivation, it sacrificed in mobility. Philip of Macedon increased the flexibility of his army by reducing the size of the baggage train, even requiring the soldiers themselves to carry most of their equipment and supplies. The Spartan infantry normally took as many as seven servants apiece on a campaign simply to carry the food and weapons.[22] Philip permitted only one servant for every ten soldiers, plus one for every four cavalry. He cut the number of carts to a minimum, though they were still necessary for siege equipment, ambulance service, and such heavy items as tents and firewood. He also ordered the soldiers to leave their families at home.[23] These reforms cut the size of the marching army by almost two-thirds.

Operating with these strict rules, Philip laid the foundations for the original success of the Macedonian armies. His son, Alexander, later relaxed the rules as his own military success grew. The decision to force austerities on the soldiers was tactical, not based on any moral reservations or disapproval of family life or any other sexual activity. On the contrary, as we have seen, the Macedonian kings practiced polygamy and Alexander himself had both wives and mistresses and an intimate male companion as well. Alexander's dearest friend was Hephaiston, and although there is no contemporary evidence, Greeks of that time assumed that close male friendships would have a sexual element. That did not, however, exclude sexual relationships with women. Indeed, Alexander planned one of his marriages so that Hephaiston's children would be his nieces and nephews.

ALEXANDER THE GREAT

ALEXANDER, LIKE HIS FATHER, appreciated the benefits of sexual alliances. He favored alliances with bilingual women. His first connection was with Barsine, the daughter of a Persian governor who traced his lineage back to King Darius. His wife Roxanne was the daughter of an Iranian baron. Alexander and Roxanne married while his mistress Barsine was pregnant. We do not know whether Barsine or her father objected. A few years later Alexander married two more Persian princesses.

When he was very young, Alexander attempted to become the groom in a marriage his father wished to arrange for another son which would connect Macedonia with Caria, the land on the Aegean Sea once ruled by Artemisia. This arrangement fell through, but Alexander later accepted a proposal from Ada, a former Carian queen who wished to adopt him as a son. Ada suffered some unhappy experiences with matrimony. Following a common practice, she first entered into an incestuous marriage with a brother. Then, after his death, she married another brother. A third brother exiled her and shut her up in a fortress. The aging queen had seen enough of marriage and preferred to bring young Alexander into the family as son rather than husband,[24] assuring Alexander's inheritance of the throne. Shortly after Alexander's adoption, Ada proved herself still more valuable to her Macedonian son. She managed to force the surrender of Persians holding the citadel of Myndus, which Alexander himself had been unable to achieve.[25]

Several writers of ancient times, including Diodorus and Plutarch, described a brief affair between Alexander and an Amazon queen named Thalestris. In 330 B.C. Alexander was in Parthia, just south of the Caspian Sea, resting up after a bout of diarrhea. He had many visitors at this time, including a representative from the Scythian king, who offered him the hand of a princess, which Alexander politely refused. Then Thalestris appeared with three hundred women warriors in full armor. According to Diodorus, she was "remarkable for beauty and for bodily strength [and] admired by her country women for bravery."[26] She had made the trip from Thermiscrya, a matter of several hundred miles, because "Alexander had shown himself the greatest of all men in his achievements, and she was superior to all women in strength and courage, so that presumably the offspring of such extraordinary parents could surpass all other mortals in excellence."[27] Alexander found this proposal appealing, especially since she agreed to give him any male offspring that might result. She wanted a girl. They spent thirteen days together, but Thalestris died without giving birth to the hoped-for wonder child.

The soldiers who in 334 B.C. marched from Greece with Alexander ahead of stripped-down baggage trains left wives and families back in Macedonia. In 330, Alexander gave them official permission to marry Asian women and to live with them in camp. Ten thousand of them took advantage of the offer.[28] Then in 324 B.C. Alexander sponsored an opulent mass marriage celebration at Susa where he ordered more than ninety of his officers to take Iranian brides. To set an example, he himself married two. The children of these marriages would share Greek and Persian culture, and, in the next generation, descendants of the old Iranian nobility would again be in positions of power in the court and in the army.[29]

Later, when some of his older or disabled veterans wanted to return home, Alexander assumed responsibility for the families they had established during the campaign. In addition to their full pay and enormous bonuses, he gave the soldiers his promise that "if they had any children by Asian wives, they were to leave these with him so as not to import quarrels into Macedonia between foreign children and the native families and wives whom they had left at home."[30] He would see that they were raised "in the Macedonian fashion," with appropriate military training. When they were grown, they would be sent back to their fathers in Greece. The Asian mothers, it was assumed, would find new husbands.

Before he died in 323 B.C. at the age of thirty-two, Alexander had founded more than twenty-five cities, extending Greek influence throughout the known world. Yet at his death, despite his having fathered two sons, no one could take his place. The next world empire would be that of Rome.

THE ROMAN WAY OF WAR

THE GREEKS INVITED Romans to participate in the Isthmian Games and the Eleusinian Mysteries in 228 B.C. in gratitude for their participation in the First Illyrian War. Illyria, known today as Albania, was ruled by the pirate queen Teuta. Illyria produced many warlike women, including Audata, who was the first wife of Philip II, Alexander's father. For the Illyrians, piracy was simply a way of making a living, as it would be later for the Vikings and the North African state of Tripoli. Their business was capturing ships and raiding Greek coastal towns. Unfortunately, success made them greedy. Rome was provoked when Illyrian pirates began seizing Roman-owned trading vessels and killing Roman citizens or selling them into slavery. Roman ambassadors sent to Illyria to resolve the problem found Teuta engaged in directing a siege of Issa, the only island still holding out against her. She told the ambassadors that although she planned no action against Rome, piracy on the high seas was an Illyrian custom. The ambassadors replied that Rome intended to alter that custom. Teuta resented the threat and murdered the ambassadors.

Rome's response was to send two hundred ships to eliminate the Illyrian menace. In cooperation with the Greeks, they lifted the siege of Issa. Teuta retreated to an inland fortress and opened negotiations with Rome. Still it took a second war against her successor ten years later to end the Illyrian threat.[31]

Meanwhile Rome had begun the second of its three great wars against Carthage. In the First Punic War which began in 264 B.C., Rome mobilized manpower and production to an extent unmatched until the twentieth century. At the height of the Second Punic War, 29 percent of Rome's male citizens were in military service. In the last two decades of war, 10 percent of the entire male population died in battle. The conflict between the two empires ended in 146 B.C. The Romans demolished Carthage, and those who survived were sold into slavery. Nothing whatever remained of Carthaginian culture; even the language disappeared.[32] In this context the Romans perfected the military skills that would conquer and secure their great empire in the following centuries.

In 264 B.C., the year that the First Punic War began, Rome introduced military training programs employing a shield and a short sword known as the gladius. This was the most lethal shock weapon ever developed. The Roman soldier killed with a shield parry followed by an undercut to the chest—very simple and very fast.[33]

When Roman armies adopted the gladius as their basic weapon, the Roman people watched gladiatorial contests held in public arenas for entertainment. Eventually women as well as men trained for these performances and fought in the arenas.[34] Some were slaves who could earn their freedom by serving for three to five years as gladiators. A first-century marble bas-relief in the British Museum commemorates the release from service of two female gladiators from Halicarnassus who performed under the names Amazonia and Achilla.[35] Other gladiators were free women, including well-to-do matrons. Upper-class women, both wives and courtesans, invested in personal weapons and armor. They trained for the contests with regular workouts and practice sessions. Juvenal describes a woman training with weights:

"At night she goes to the baths and sweats amidst the noise and hubbub. When her arms fall to her sides, wearied by the heavy weights, the skilled masseur presses his fingers to her muscles and makes her buttocks resound with a smack."[36]

Some Roman women, obviously, were capable of bearing arms. Did any of them ever fight in the ranks? The question is valid; the silence of sources proves nothing. In later periods of history for which evidence has survived in far greater quantity, the occasional woman among fighting men has sometimes generated considerable paperwork. But not always, and women virtually never appear in official accounts of battles. If the Romans had a few women soldiers, they may not have considered them worth mentioning. However, the classical authors do take note of women who fought against them. It is clear that Roman legions faced large numbers of fighting women in wars across Italy's northern border.

For some reason, Roman historians idealized the ferocity of barbarian women. They also carried on the Greeks' traditional admiration of the Amazons. As in Greece, Amazons were popular images on Roman sarcophagi and other funerary monuments. In the first century A.D., the emperor Nero became intrigued by the idea of fighting as an Amazon. According to the historian Suetonius, Nero prepared to put down an uprising in Gaul by trimming the hair of the concubines he planned to take with him and equipping them with axes and shields of a design thought to be used by the ancient women warriors. Nero's Amazons, however, had only a ceremonial function; he did not use them in combat.

BARBARIAN WARS

Late in the first century B.C., the Cimbri, who were German or Celtic people, invaded modern-day France and Spain and threatened Italy. The Roman sources report that they destroyed two Roman armies. Among the casualties were the camp followers, but the sources do not say whether women in the baggage trains attempted to defend themselves. Cimbri women certainly did. At Aquae Sextiae (Aix en Provence) in 102 B.C., the Romans battled the Celts, broke through their lines, and pursued them to their wagons to complete the slaughter. "Here the women met them," Plutarch wrote, "holding swords and axes in their hands. With hideous shrieks of rage they tried to drive back the hunted and the hunters, the fugitives as deserters, the pursuers as foes. With bare hands the women tore away the shields of the Romans or grasped their swords, enduring mutilating wounds. Their fierce spirit unvanquished to the end."[37] The Roman writers also noted that Cimbri priestesses performed a ritual when their people took prisoners. The women stood on ladders brought onto the battlefield, decapitated the prisoners, and caught their blood in pots. They gave this liquid to their soldiers as a tonic, believing it would double their strength.[38] It took another year for Roman legions to crush the Cimbri. In 101 B.C., at Vercellae (Campi Raudii), south of the Alpine Brenner Pass, the battle ended again with Romans confronting the rear guard: "women in black robes who stood at their wagons and slew the fleeing warriors—their husbands, brothers, or fathers—and then strangled their own children and cast them beneath the wheels of their wagons before cutting their own throats."[39]

Meanwhile historians continued their observations of women among the enemies of Rome. Tacitus described the effectiveness of German women, who provided moral support to husbands and sons: "Close by them, too, are those who are dearest to them, so that they hear the shrieks of women, the cries of infants. They [women] are to every man the most sacred witnesses of his bravery—they are the most generous applauders. The soldier brings his wounds to his mother and wife. . . . Tradition says that armies already wavering or giving way have been rallied by women who, with earnest entreaties and bosoms laid bare, have vividly represented the horrors of captivity." According to Dio Cassius, Roman soldiers found the bodies of women in full armor among fallen Marcomanni and Quadi. Other writers told of Goth prisoners of war who proved to be women and described numerous instances of women wielding weapons at the side of their men.[40] Ammianus Marcellinus, who had faced Gallic women in battle, warned that a whole troop of Roman soldiers would not be a match for a single Gaul if he called his wife to his aid, for "swelling her neck, gnashing her teeth, and brandishing sallow arms of enormous size she delivers blows and kicks like missiles from a catapult."[41]

BOUDICCA

Of all the warlike women encountered by the Romans, the most memorable was the British queen Boudicca who led a revolt against their occupation of Britain in A.D. 61. Now wrapped in myth and usually called Boadicea, she is remembered by few Americans, but she is as famous today in Great Britain as Joan of Arc is in France. Her history rests entirely on three written sources. Tacitus is the author of two of them; two centuries later, Dio Cassius produced the third, but his work survives today only in an edited form set down nine hundred years after that. Archaeological evidence confirms certain elements of the accounts of this memorable revolt by Britons against the mighty Romans, but all the colorful detail comes from the same three texts.

Julius Caesar led a brief expedition into Britain in the first century B.C., but he withdrew without leaving an outpost behind. The Romans chose to invade Britain again in A.D. 43. The reason is not known, although greed is probably an adequate explanation. Prasutagus, the king of the Iceni tribe in southeastern England, certainly believed the Romans to be greedy. When he died in A.D. 60, he left half his fortune to his daughters. He left the other half to the Roman emperor, hoping that would satisfy the invaders. It was not enough for Catus Decianus, the chief procurator. He sent an army of Roman veterans to Icenian territory with orders to confiscate everything that had belonged to Prasutagus—the fields, the animals, and all the treasure they could find. When his widow Boudicca protested, the Romans brutally put her in her place. They beat her with rods and raped her two daughters.

Although historians generally assume that the Iceni must have done something to provoke the Romans, the three sources do not say so. Still, after suffering their abuse, Boudicca naturally wanted revenge on the Romans, as did the other Iceni, the people living on the confiscated land. And they were not the only Britons who had had enough of Roman rule. Dio Cassius imagined Boudicca rallying the angry people to her cause:

> *It is our own fault that the Romans are here, for we should have expelled them as we did with Julius Caesar. But even at this late day, let us do our duty while we still remember what freedom is, that we may leave to our children not only its name but also its reality. Have no fear of the Romans, for they need to protect themselves with armor and earthworks, whereas we can fight from the swamps and mountains, eating only the roughest grass and roots. Let us show them they are hares and foxes trying to rule over dogs and wolves.*[42]

According to Dio, 120,000 volunteers responded to this appeal.

Boudicca led her forces in an attack on the Roman settlement at Camulondunum. The colonial governor, Caius Suetonius Paullinus, had taken the main Roman army to Wales to break the power of the Druids, religious leaders who had their own reasons for resisting Roman domination. To make matters worse for Camulondunum, the defenses of the town were in bad repair. According to Tacitus, the Romans had put more effort into building a temple honoring the deceased Emperor Claudius than they had maintaining the walls. Faced with a sudden massive attack, the Romans withdrew to the partially completed temple and held out for two days. Then Boudicca's force stormed the walls and slaughtered everyone in the town— men, women, and children. Archaeological evidence confirms that they burned Camulondunum to the ground with the same ruthless thoroughness that the Romans had displayed at Carthage.[43]

Meanwhile, Paullinus was far away, off the coast of Wales, on the island of Mona in the Irish Sea, the sanctuary of the Druids. Many Britons opposed to Roman rule had taken refuge there, and Paullinus intended to eliminate them and their Druid protectors. Tacitus described the scene. Standing against the Roman army were "black-robed women with disheveled hair like Furies, brandishing torches" as the Druids stood close by, "raising their hands to heaven and screaming dreadful curses." For a moment, the Romans hesitated, but their famed discipline held; they cut down the screaming multitude in their sacred grove and then burned it.[44]

When he heard about Boudicca's activities in the south, Paullinus sent a legion to put down the rebellion. As the Romans marched through the forest of East Anglia, the Britons followed. They broke the extended line of march into small vulnerable groups and destroyed them. Only the legion commander, Petillus Cerealis, and a few cavalry escaped alive.

At that point Catus Decianus, the procurator who had started the whole business, left the country and went to Gaul. Then Paullinus arrived in London to take command himself. London was smaller than Camulondunum, but it was an important trading center. The wealthiest merchants had already fled with the procurator. The citizens begged Paullinus to protect them, but he could see no practical way to defend the city and recommended they abandon it. When Boudicca arrived, only the very poor and the sick remained.

The Britons stormed into the defenseless town, slaughtered everyone, and destroyed it completely. Modern excavations in London bear mute testimony to their thoroughness, revealing a sixteen-inch-deep "red layer" thirteen feet below the modern streets. Here, writes the archaeologist Peter

Marsden, "the events of A.D. 60 are indelibly scorched on the soil."[45] Then, with scarcely a pause, Boudicca's force ravaged the nearby settlement at St. Albans, killing the romanized Britons there as collaborators. Tacitus said that Boudicca had no interest in taking prisoners and estimated the total number slaughtered in this town and at yet another massacre at Verulamium at seventy thousand. Modern writers who extol "Boadicea" as a national heroine avoid examining the list of atrocities, but the vengeful queen did not give the victims easy deaths. "They could not wait to cut throats, hang, burn, and crucify," Tacitus wrote. Dio's account is more detailed: "They hung up naked the noblest and most distinguished women and then cut off their breasts and sewed them to their mouths, in order to make the victims appear to be eating them; afterwards they impaled the women on sharp skewers run lengthwise through the entire body."[46]

Paullinus chose the ground for the final confrontation with Boudicca's forces. He placed his army where an open plain lay in front of them, with thick woods protecting their flanks and rear. After sacking Verulamium, Boudicca's army was larger than ever. With each success, more of the local tribes joined in the rebellion until, according to Dio, she led a force of 230,000. Even allowing for exaggeration, her army clearly outnumbered the Romans.[47] In Celtic style, they advanced with music and shouting. Women, children, and wagons took up positions at the edge of the battlefield. The warriors carried the traditional Celtic sword but wore no armor and no clothing except, perhaps, a pair of baggy trousers. Although the Celts craft-ed elaborately decorated helmets and shields, these were for the nobility only. The queen and others of high rank rode to battle in light wickerwork chariots, dismounting when the fighting began.[48]

The force Boudicca faced was composed of thorough professionals with years of training and experience. They carried carved wooden shields and wore helmets with neck protection. Body armor extended to the waist, and a broad leather belt with metal-tipped leather thongs hung below. On their feet the soldiers wore studded open boots. Each soldier carried a two-foot gladius, a dagger, and two javelins. The javelins, seven-foot-long spears with iron points three feet long, were easy to throw and almost impossible to remove once embedded.[49]

Tacitus imagined Boudicca speaking to her troops from her chariot, exhorting them before the battle: "This is not the first time the Britons have been led to battle by a woman. But I do not take to arms merely to boast of an ancient lineage or even to regain my kingdom and possessions. I fight, like the humblest warrior among you, to assert my liberty and seek revenge for the physical outrages wrought on myself and my daughters. . . . On this ground we must either conquer or die with glory. There is no alternative. Although a woman, my decision is made. The men, if they wish, may survive in shame and live in bondage."[50]

Fighting began and continued until late in the day as the Romans eventually broke through Boudicca's force. They pursued the Celts to the wagons, fighting with the women there. Then they killed everyone and for good measure slaughtered the cattle as well. Tacitus put the Celtic casualties at eighty thousand.

Boudicca did not die on the battlefield, but Tacitus tells us she died soon after, taking poison rather than fall into Roman hands. Perhaps she poisoned her daughters as well. At any rate, the trio of women passed into legend as the Romans methodically destroyed the land of the Iceni. It remained a barren waste for more than a century.[51]

CLEOPATRA

Britain was merely a minor appendage of the Roman Empire. Indeed, the Romans believed the entire region north of Italy was a land of barbarians who had to be kept down as a matter of self-defense. The real wealth of the empire was in Africa and the Middle East. In these lands, home of the ancient civilizations, local nobility might be useful political and military allies for ambitious Romans.

A century before Boudicca's revolt, Cleopatra VII of Egypt made her mark on history.[52] She was of mixed ancestry, the sort of cosmopolitan ruler Alexander's policies had hoped to encourage. Her language was Greek, but she had Macedonian, Persian, and Syrian ancestors as well. She probably had no Egyptian blood. The Romans had taken control of Egypt some years earlier, and Cleopatra's father ruled at their pleasure. She understood how to play power politics and worked her influence with both Julius Caesar and Mark Antony. Although Antony handed over lands and wealth, his brother-in-law Octavian denounced the Antony-Cleopatra alliance, charging that they planned to found a new dynasty based at Alexandria rather than at Rome. In 32 B.C., Octavian declared war, not on Antony, but on Cleopatra. Antony continued to support the Egyptian queen.

The crucial event in the war pitting Octavian against Antony and Cleopatra was a naval action, the Battle of Actium. Cleopatra, believing that a land battle would mean the loss of her fleet, overruled the advice of her admirals not to risk the sea action. On the day of battle, Cleopatra's galley went out with the fleet. The queen probably intended to give moral support by her presence and did not serve as an operational commander. The details of the battle are uncertain, but at one point, when Cleopatra's galley turned back toward the Egyptian coast, all sixty of the Egyptian ships followed, thus losing the battle by default. Soon after, Antony's army surrendered to Octavian. When Octavian arrived at Alexandria, Cleopatra tried to work out an arrangement with him as she had with his predecessors. When he refused her, she committed suicide rather than face the humiliation of being taken to Rome as a symbol of his victory.

ZENOBIA

The fame of Cleopatra over the following centuries has obscured a long military tradition of pre-Islamic Arab queens. More than sixty years ago, Nabia Abbott published a study identifying more than two dozen of these women, beginning with the queen of Sheba who visited Solomon in the tenth century B.C.[53] Later, several Arab queens besides Cleopatra faced the Roman legions. Roman historians had a very negative opinion of Cleopatra; they depicted her as a scheming siren whose ambition was to ruin Rome. But they were enthusiastic about the queen they called Septimia Zenobia, a Latinized form of the Aramaic name Bat Zabbai. Here is what Trebellius Pollio had to say: "Her face was dark and of a swarthy hue. Her eyes were black and powerful, her spirit divinely great, and her beauty incredible. . . . Her voice was clear and like that of a man. Her sternness, when necessity demanded, was that of a tyrant; her clemency, when her sense of right called for it, that of a good emperor."[54] Perhaps they liked her because she put up a good fight but was also a good loser in the end.

Zenobia became ruler of Palmyra, a city-state in Syria, in the middle of the third century.[55] She repelled a Roman invasion launched by the emperor Claudius, and he did not try again. His successor, Emperor Aurelian, however, was a much abler military leader. He took care of Rome's northern threat, successfully retaking land from the Goths, Gauls, Vandals, and Franks. Then he turned his attention to the erosion of Roman claims in the

East. At the height of her power, Zenobia controlled much of Asia Minor—Arabia, Armenia, and Persia—as well as Egypt and Syria. She put up stiff resistance against Aurelian's attempt to take it back. She sent out an army of seventy thousand. The advancing Romans trapped the queen in Palmyra and began siege operations. Aurelian wrote to a friend, "There are Romans who say that I am waging a war against a mere woman, but there is as great an army before me as though I were fighting a man. I cannot tell you what a great store of arrows, spears, and stones is here, what great preparations they have made. There is no section of the wall that is not held by two or three engines of war. Their machines even hurl fire." [56]

Attempting to negotiate a surrender, Aurelian sent a letter to the queen:

From Aurelian, Emperor of the Roman world and recoverer of the East, to Zenobia and all others who are bound to her by alliance in war. You should have done of your own free will what I now command in my letter. I bid you to surrender, promising that your lives shall be spared with the condition that you, Zenobia, together with your children shall live wherever I, acting in accordance with the wish of the most noble senate, shall appoint a place. Your jewels, gold, silver, silks, horses, and camels shall be handed over to the Roman treasury. As for the people of Palmyra, their rights shall be preserved. [57]

Zenobia resented Aurelian's tone, especially his use of a title for himself without recognizing hers. She replied:

From Zenobia, Queen of the East, to Aurelian Augustus. None save yourself has ever demanded by letter what you now demand. Whatever must be accomplished in matters of war must be done by valor alone. You demand my surrender as though you were not aware that Cleopatra preferred to die a Queen rather than remain alive, however high her rank. At this very moment we are expecting reinforcements from Persia. On our side also are the Arabs and Armenians. The bandits of Syria have defeated your army, Aurelian. What more need be said? When these forces arrive, you will surely lay aside the arrogance with which you demand my surrender. [58]

Actually, Zenobia was not so confident, and taking the advice of her generals, she slipped out of the city on a female camel, "which is the swiftest of that kind of animal, and much more swift than horses." [59] Aurelian learned of her flight, and his Arabian horses chased after the camel and caught the queen just as she was about to cross the Euphrates into Persia. Unlike Cleopatra, Zenobia decided to make the best of the situation. When

Aurelian asked her why she had defied the emperors of Rome, she replied, "You, I accept, are an Emperor because you win victories. But your predecessors I have never regarded as worthy of the Emperorship. I desired to become a partner in the royal power, should there be enough land."[60] She blamed her advisers for the actions that had brought on the war. The advisers were executed; Zenobia was taken to Rome for display in a great triumphal parade.

The Romans loved parades almost as much as they loved gladiatorial contests and war, and Aurelian's procession was spectacular. He rode in front in a chariot drawn by four stags. Then came twenty elephants and two hundred other animals including tigers, giraffes, and elks. After the parade, Aurelian gave the animals to various citizens, who appreciated exotic pets enough to be willing to foot the bill for feeding them.[61] Following the animals were eight hundred pairs of gladiators and ambassadors from as far away as India and China. Next marched assorted prisoners from Arabia, India, Africa, Bactria, and Persia plus captives from the "barbarian" nations: Hibernians, Vandals, Franks, Swabians, and Goths, all identified with appropriate placards. A group of Goth women captured fighting in male clothing were labeled Amazons.

The highlight of the parade, however, was Zenobia herself, who walked in front of her own magnificent chariot, so heavily covered with gold chains and jewels that she could barely stand. The parade continued with Roman dignitaries of various sorts, concluding with the senators. It took a full day for the procession to pass by the Capitol. Aurelian declared the day of his triumph a national holiday and gave the Roman people bread, meat, and gladiatorial games to top it off.

Once this ordeal was over, Zenobia got on with her life. She married a senator and retired to a villa just outside Rome. Two sons who marched with her in Aurelian's Triumph became well known in senatorial circles, and her daughters married into influential families. Even Emperor Aurelian sang her praises, telling the senators "what manner of woman she is, how wise in counsel, how steadfast in plans, how firm toward soldiers, how generous when necessity calls, and how stern when discipline demands."[62]

SOLDIERS' WIVES

Before leaving the history of Roman wars, we must remember another group of women, the Roman soldiers' wives. Ignored or casually dismissed as prostitutes by conventional military history and nearly invisible in the primary sources, the wives were, as always, the most numerous group of women in the military and not without value to the army. Roman military leaders were ambivalent about soldiers' wives. On the one hand, they believed devotion to family could motivate a soldier to fight. Describing qualities desirable in a general, Onsander wrote in the first century A.D., "I would prefer him to have children. . . . If, in effect, it happens that his children are of tender years, these act as powerful philtres conveying courage which can guarantee a general's dedication to his country."[63] On the other hand, families in a baggage train slowed an army, creating problems both for logistics and for defense. But if families were left at home or in garrison, the soldiers were reluctant to march away. While authorities might casually dismiss soldiers' families in foreign lands as "whores and bastards," the men who loved them were nonetheless bound by emotional ties.

Originally, Roman regulations would not permit a soldier below the rank of centurion to contract a legal marriage; the idea was to have a celibate army. But human nature was not so easily restrained. The average Roman recruit was a teenager, and soldiers served for at least twenty-five years. Often they stayed in service for much longer.[64] If legal marriage was forbidden, soldiers would go to courtesans. According to Lucian, a Greek satirist writing in the second century A.D., sophisticated women were wary of proposals from soldiers. "What is there in military love affairs?" Lucian has one of them say. "Beatings and lawsuits. They always try to pass for colonels and captains, but when it comes to payment then 'wait until the war taxes are collected, when I get my pay, I will take care of everything.' The demon take these braggarts; I am wise enough not to let myself in with them any more."[65]

Nevertheless, Roman soldiers always found willing women. Before the spread of Christianity and its association of sex with sin, there was no guilt associated with having an extralegal relationship. Absence of a legal tie might be a financial disadvantage, but that was all. And military concubines felt entitled to make some demands. In 172 B.C., a mission came to Rome speaking for Spanish women whose children (a total of more than four thousand) had been fathered by Roman soldiers forbidden to marry. The women petitioned for a city in which to live.[66]

Many extralegal marriages formed between soldiers and women in the frontier areas, where most troops were stationed, lasted for a lifetime. The partner who predeceased the other would erect a tombstone with an adoring inscription that made no reference to the absence of a legal contract. If both survived until the soldier's retirement, they could then regularize the relationship. The rules changed over time and were different for each branch of the service, but one benefit of a legalized marriage was often the grant of Roman citizenship to both the sons and the daughters. Sons who did not receive citizenship could acquire it by joining the military themselves. That practice was common. In time, a hereditary military caste developed, providing a reliable supply of recruits. The historian G. R. Watson writes, "It is noticeable that though the interests of the fathers were usually considered, and the interests of the children were protected more and more, the mothers appear to have been looked upon merely as an unavoidable necessity."[67] That may have been the attitude of those who wrote the regulations, but the moving inscriptions husbands placed on their wives' tombstones indicate that soldiers had affection for their wives as well as for their offspring.

The authorities rarely appreciated the humble contributions of women to the health and comfort of the fighting force. Instead, they charged that soldiers who had good food, clean clothing, and warm beds were going soft, as if indigestion, lice, and sleeping with horses contributed to combat effectiveness. Those for whom the wars were a spectator sport strove to keep the male bonding features of military organization intact. Here is Severus Caecina addressing the Roman Senate in A.D. 20:

> There is something in the female followers which hurts the peace through luxury, hinders war through fearfulness, and lends the Roman army the aspect of an Asiatic caravan. These women are weak and unable to bear hardship; the women are given freedom to stalk among the soldiers; and these women are cruel, ambitious, domineering, and have even the centurions in hand. Recently while the cohorts were engaged in practice it was suggested that a woman command legions during a drill. The proposal fell through, and all agreed that in war, weapons were to be the only accompaniment.[68]

About A.D. 197, Septimus Severus decreed that it would henceforth be legal for soldiers to live with their wives. This decree legitimized what had been going on for a long time anyway. Soldiers' families lived in settlements that grew up around the fortresses. Often retired veterans and their families continued to live in these settlements after their enlistments ended. The demands of the military force and its dependents attracted merchants and others from the local population to the settlement. Camulondunum in England was such a town. Its Roman inhabitants and their local purveyors were the people slaughtered by Boudicca's force.

Gradually the communities on the Roman frontiers took on distinct identities. They felt more like home to those posted there than did the distant imperial capital. Soldiers resisted transfers, and eventually Rome had to create a separate, more mobile force, known as the field army, that could serve as a strategic reserve. Even then soldiers wanted to take their families with them and the long baggage train hindered operations. Eventually what had once been a series of frontier garrisons became static settlements. As Watson writes,"The desire to make the army self-perpetuating had led first to the connivance of the authorities in the creation of unofficial domestic establishments, and then progressively to the recognition of these establishments as part of the military organization. The ultimate effect was to create an army, largely based on the frontiers, which was too immobile to make large troop movements practicable."[69]

Ultimately even more serious was the assimilation of the frontier force into the local community. Soldiers, especially new recruits, were prone to desertion, to disappearing into the civilian population during a crisis. The trend was apparent as early as the fourth century A.D., and "barbarians" came to make up a growing part of the Roman army.[70] In A.D. 476, the barbarians brought down the Roman Empire as a German chief named Odovacar deposed Emperor Romulus Augustulus. In history books, this event came to mark the end of the Roman Empire in the West. The military activity of the European barbarians makes up the next chapter in the history of war.

CHAPTER FOUR

EUROPEAN WARFARE

$\mathbf{F}$OCUSING THIS CHAPTER ON warfare in Europe during the thirteen hundred years between the fall of Rome and the final decades of the eighteenth century is conventional but arbitrary. By the fifth century A.D., war had long been a universal cultural institution. Asia, in particular, continued to take the practice of mass carnage to spectacular heights. As Geoffrey Parker has pointed out, Asia pioneered in the invention of gunpowder (in the ninth century), in the perfection of metal-barreled gunpowder weapons (in the thirteenth century), and in cannons mounted in ironclad warships (in the sixteenth century).[1] Asia also had women warriors.[2]

In Central and South America, the history of warfare from pre-Columbian times to the modern era shows less technological development, but it, too, includes women in war. Columbus himself was once fired on by a party of women archers. Indeed, wherever there was war, women were part of it, and all instances are worthy of study. The ideal global perspective, however, does not yet inform the work of mainstream military historians. Because this book is designed to supplement currently available surveys, I cover these years from the traditional vantage point. Although the wars of medieval Europe may not have been the most significant events on the globe at the time, they are the wars in the mainstream of Western history.

✦   ✦   ✦

CHRISTIAN EUROPE

DURING THE CENTURIES FOLLOWING the collapse of the Roman Empire, Europeans made relatively modest advances in military science. Nothing comparable in scope to the revolution caused by the introduction of cavalry occurred. Even after Europeans began to use gunpowder weapons, the fundamentals of war changed relatively little. The strategic thinking supporting European sorties, sieges, and set battles would have been understood easily by commanders of the Roman legions.

For most of the period discussed in this chapter, the Europeans fought each other, occasionally breaking off local conflict to respond, with indifferent success, to threats from the north, south, and east. Not until the end of the fifteenth century did Europe begin to expand its influence into other continents and start the drive toward technological development that eventually would make it the center of world military power. Nevertheless we will proceed with the familiar series of "important" wars.

Christianity was perhaps the most significant legacy of Rome's long domination of Europe. In the centuries following the fall of Rome, the influence of Christianity permeates the history of Europe. Wars were commonly fought in the name of Christ, just as the Hebrews earlier fought in the name of Yahweh. Christians were not supposed to make war on each other, although combatants got around that restriction by charging their opponents with perverting the true faith. But fighting under the sign of the cross was simpler when the enemies were pagans—as when, early in the ninth century, England's famed Alfred the Great confronted the Vikings of Scandinavia.

The English themselves had not been Christian very long. After the Romans withdrew from Britain early in the fifth century, seven Anglo-Saxon kingdoms replaced their authority. Christianity had not made much progress under the Romans, and it was not until 597 that Augustine the Monk converted the first of the English kingdoms for the Roman Catholic church. Another three centuries passed, and then the still-pagan Scandinavians began their assaults on Britain. For twenty years, they pressed the attack, until Alfred the Great finally defeated them. In 878 he came to an agreement with the Vikings whereby Guthrun the Dane became a Christian and the two kings divided England between them. Guthrun's share was known as the Danelaw.

Alfred was never reconciled to the loss of the Danelaw. He negotiated various diplomatic and military arrangements designed to increase his strength, with the goal of ultimately recovering the lost territory. His daughter Aethelflaed began her service to England by marrying in her late teens to seal an alliance with another of the Saxon royal families. Her husband, Aethelred, ealdorman of the Mercians, was old and ailing, willing to accept political direction from his young wife. When Alfred died, Aethelflaed and her brother Edward worked together to hold the ground Alfred had won. Aethelflaed bore one child and after that refused further marital relations with her husband, saying, according to the twelfth-century historian William of Malmesbury, that "it was unbecoming the daughter of a king to give way to a delight, which after a time produced such painful consequences."[3] This return to chastity and symbolic virginity was much admired by the Christian English. In 911, Aethelflaed was widowed. What had been a de facto exercise of power earlier now became hers to exercise in her own right as Lady of the Mercians.[4]

William of Malmesbury described Aethelflaed as "a woman who protected men at home and intimidated them abroad."[5] The protection began with a construction program. In 912, she built a fortress at Bremesburh about one hundred fifty miles north of London and within three years completed nine more. Edward also built forts, furthering their joint plan to use strongholds both defensively and offensively. Soon they had a continuous line facing the Danish military centers in northeastern England.

The Danes, however, were not the only threat. Aethelflaed built more forts in the northwest when Irish and Norwegian settlers made inroads and raided English towns. Next, as the Viking threat waned, the Welsh became assertive. Aethelflaed then proved she could do more than build. She sent an army into Wales and captured the wife of a Welsh king and thirty-three members of his court. This campaign so impressed the Welsh that they bowed to her authority.

Aethelflaed's major military activity, coordinated with her brother, began in the summer of 917. As Edward fought in the south, she took the Viking military center at Derby by storming it without so much as a preparatory siege. It was a decisive victory, but not a bloodless one; four of Aethelflaed's captains were cut down within the gates. When Aethelflaed suddenly fell ill and died the next year, her territories passed to her brother. Edward continued to fight the Vikings until his death, and his son Athelstan finally completed the conquest of the Danelaw.

There were, of course, two sides to the Norse wars. Families lived in the

Danelaw, although we know virtually nothing about the women there except that they took their share of casualties. There were other Scandinavian women who took on manly roles. We know a bit more about them even though their histories are overladen with myth. Their chief chronicler, Saxo Grammaticus, wrote in the thirteenth century, "There were once women among the Danes who dressed as men and devoted every waking moment to the pursuit of war. Those who had force of character or were tall and comely were especially apt to enter into such a life."[6] Among these was Wisna, "a woman filled with sternness and a skilled warrior,"[7] who commanded a unit that fought with long swords and small round shields in the Battle of Bravellir, an engagement between Danes and Swedes that Saxo claimed involved two hundred thousand soldiers, five thousand ships, and kings of twelve nations. Another woman at that battle was Heid, who led one hundred regular soldiers plus a company of berserkers, Norse warriors famous for fighting in a violent frenzy. There was also a band of Viking pirates—Saxon, Goth, and Swedish women—led by the princess Alvilda (or Alfhild) of whom Saxo writes, "They offered war, not kisses, and went about the business of arms, not amours. They devoted those hands to the lance, not the loom. They assailed men with spears. They thought of death, not dalliance."[8]

More decorous than the fierce females of the North was the martial lady Matilda, whose life was dominated by her devotion to the Italian papacy. Catholic historians through the ages have extolled her. She was a decidedly Christian ruler, proudly bearing the title "Matilda by the Grace of God." As her soldiers stormed into battle their cry was "For Saint Peter and Matilda!"[9]

In 1052, when Matilda was only six, her father was assassinated. Some said the German ruler Henry III, the Holy Roman Emperor, had been responsible for the murder. Matilda's brother and sister died soon after, leaving her the sole heir to a vast estate that represented the greatest concentration of power in Italy. It included all of Tuscany, parts of Liguria and Umbria, and a dozen cities including Pisa, Florence, Mantua, and Verona. The family's castle at Canossa, set 1,500 feet high in the Apennines, dominated the countryside for miles. Matilda's mother realized that her daughter would have to fight to defend it. Accordingly, in addition to embroidery and other arts suitable to her station, her mother saw to it that Matilda learned to ride with a lance, carry a pike like a foot soldier, and wield the battle-ax and sword.

Matilda first went into combat at her mother's side defending the interests of Pope Alexander II. An account written several centuries later says of the 1061 battle, "Now there appeared in Lombardy at the head of her numerous squadrons the young maid Matilda, armed like a warrior, and with such bravery, that she made known to the world that courage and valor in mankind is not indeed a matter of sex, but of heart and spirit."[10] Five years later, at the battle of Aquino, she is said to have shared command of four hundred archers, an equal number of warriors armed with pikes, and a detachment of cavalry.

In 1073, a charismatic Church reformer named Hildebrand became Pope Gregory VII. Although Matilda was married in a political alliance to a stepbrother known as Godfrey the Hunchback, her real emotional attachment, revealed in her letters, was for Pope Gregory. He addressed her as "my most beloved and loving daughter," and she affirmed her fervent devotion to the Holy Father. After Godfrey died, Matilda had no husband and no heir to challenge her authority or interfere with her activities. She put all of her power and energy into support of the pope.

Holy Roman Emperor Henry IV and Pope Gregory attempted to undermine each other's authority by issuing official edicts. The emperor declared the pope deposed, referring to him as "Hildebrand, now not Pope but false monk," and accusing him of licentiousness and necromancy. The pope responded by excommunicating the emperor. The excommunication gave Henry's subjects an excuse to rebel and elect another king of Germany. To hold his kingdom, Henry and his wife crossed the Alps to ask the pope's forgiveness. Under an armed escort, provided by Matilda, Gregory came to the fortress at Canossa. There Henry was kept waiting in the snow for three days, after which Gregory felt compelled to forgive him.

Three years later, Henry defied Gregory again and directed the election of an antipope, Clement III. Gregory excommunicated Henry a second time, but the move was less effective than it had been earlier. The clergy in northern Italy were unhappy with Gregory, and they rebelled against both the pope and Matilda. In the warfare that followed, forces loyal to the German ruler defeated Matilda's troops, and she retreated to Canossa. As Henry's armies ravaged her lands, Matilda for the first time was unable to send troops to help the pope when Henry entered Rome in 1083. Henry's antipope presided at a coronation for the emperor and his wife in St. Peter's Church. But Henry soon discovered that he had another problem.

Norman warriors, some generations removed from the Vikings who battled Aethelflaed, were now operating in the south. Their reputation for ferocity had not diminished over the years. Two decades earlier, in 1066, they had conquered England, for good this time, and they also controlled territory on the other side of the English Channel that they called Normandy. Henry learned that the Norman commander, Robert Guiscard, had augmented his troops with Saracen mercenaries who had a mean reputation of their own. This combined force was heading for Rome. Guiscard's wife, Sichelgaita, customarily accompanied him on campaigns. A tall, powerful woman with an imposing presence, she routinely put on full armor and went into battle at her husband's side. Henry packed up his antipope and his non-combatant wife and fled. Guiscard's army sacked Rome, and incidentally rescued Pope Gregory, taking him to Salerno in the south of Italy where he died the following year.

Meanwhile Henry's allies in the north continued to attack Matilda's possessions. She had one moment of success in defense of Sorbara, when she launched a surprise attack late at night. As her troops screamed out their war cry, "For St. Peter and Matilda!" she led them to victory, tradition says carrying her father's sword and cutting down the enemy soldiers just awakened from sleep. But political squabbles and military uprisings continued, with Matilda clinging to the papacy and resisting any overtures from Henry or his son. In 1114, when she was close to seventy, in failing health, Matilda was still able to take personal command of an army against rebels in Mantua. She died the following year. Over the centuries, Matilda's reputation for piety and devotion to the Church continued to grow. Five hundred years after her death, her remains were reinterred at St. Peter's in Rome with a marble effigy by Bernini marking the place.

Matilda was not the only noblewoman to command armies in medieval Europe. The historian Oderic Vitalis described a conflict over land in northwestern France late in the eleventh century which he blames on two noblewomen: "Countess Helwise took offence at insults uttered by Isabel of Conches and used all her influence with Count William and his barons to take up arms. Thus through the quarrelling of women, the hearts of brave men were stirred to rage and there was much bloodshed, the burning of farms and villages." According to Oderic, Helwise was "clever and eloquent, but cruel and grasping." Isabel, however, was generous, and "when her vassals took to war, she rode armed as a knight."[11] The quarreling of men was the usual trigger for feudal warfare, and women became involved only as loyal wives.

In the fifteenth century, the woman scholar Christine De Pisan[12] wrote of the upper-class woman's need for education in military matters. She observed in *Treasure of the City of the Ladies* that "if her land is attacked by foreign enemies—as frequently happens after the death of a prince with underage children—it will be necessary for her to make and conduct war." To facilitate study, she produced a tactical manual entitled *Feats of Arms and Chivalry*[13] based on historical sources and interviews with various knights. She described the qualities desirable in commanders and in soldiers, how to choose a campsite, and the supplies that should be assembled before launching a campaign, including an exhaustive list of items required for an assault on a castle.

Christine De Pisan also collected examples of women who had successfully mastered the arts of war. Hers was the model for a genre of biographical literature, still produced in our time, where one may find portraits of dozens of women in small-scale military operations defending castles and leading sorties to lift sieges.[14] The major military operations in medieval Europe were the expeditions to the Near East known as the Crusades.

THE CRUSADES

IN 1095, WHILE MATILDA of Tuscany was still holding her own in the hills of northern Italy, Pope Urban II proclaimed the First Crusade to "defend Christendom" against Moslems. Crusades directed against Islamic forces in the Middle East and Turkey continued until the fifteenth century. Women of all sorts were involved in these campaigns. Christian chroniclers liked to snigger in Latin, *castra non chasta,* meaning there was nothing chaste about the encampments, and later historians continued the tradition of assuming that every woman who followed the cross was actually interested only in selling her body. Wilhelm Haberling, writing in 1943, called them "lewd women, a crowd of run-away nuns, women who deserted their husbands, and other loose persons."[15]

It was in Christian Europe that camp followers first became objects of scorn and disgust. In earlier times commanders might find the baggage train an inconvenience and complain that soldiers cared for in the "Asian manner" grew soft, but Christian armies were the first to identify the baggage train with moral contamination. Military wives and all women associated with military activity, especially those who are pregnant, have faced such slander ever since.

The root of these negative attitudes derives from early Christianity's equation of sex with sin. The pagan religions of Greece and Rome and polytheistic cults generally had deities devoted to sex and considered sexual union a religious act. In the classical world, marriages were celebrated under the auspices of the goddess Aphrodite-Mari from whom the word *marriage* itself is derived. Early Christian writers, by contrast, were opposed to both marriage and family. Saint Paul had grudgingly conceded that it was better to marry than to burn: "If his passions are strong, and it has to be, let him do as he wishes: let them marry—it is no sin," he wrote to the Corinthians. Nevertheless, he said, "he who refrains from marriage will do better."[16] Later, the Christian fathers were less forgiving. Origen declared, "Matrimony is impure and unholy." Saint Ambrose called it a crime against God because it destroyed virginity. Tertullian called marriage *spurcitiae,* meaning *"obscenity"* or *"filth,"* a state "more dreadful than any punishment or any death." Saint Augustine declared flatly that marriage was a sin and the act of childbirth an abomination that produced babies "between feces and urine." Marriage did not become a Christian sacrament until the sixteenth century. Bonding between men and women was a legal transaction with resort to the older pre-Christian traditions when a blessing was wanted.[17]

European interest in "rescuing" Jerusalem dated back to its conquest by the Arabs in 637. Even so, peaceful pilgrimages to the Holy Land by European penitents had gone on for centuries, and were generally tolerated by the Moslems, who recognized that Jerusalem was a shrine for other religious faiths. An average of more than one pilgrimage a year took place during the century before the proclamation of the First Crusade in 1095. But the Arabs conquered much more than the Holy Land. They took over considerable European territory as well, including Spain, Sardinia, and Sicily, and this pressure ultimately encouraged an aggressive European response.

The First Crusade began with mass migrations of inspired people; sometimes whole villages took off for Jerusalem. William of Tyre, mustering his troops before Nice, claimed he had one hundred thousand cavalry in mail armor and helmets and about six hundred thousand civilian Crusaders, many of them children. Some women wore men's clothing and considered themselves soldiers. That they could be identified as women, however, indicates that they were not in disguise. A poem written to celebrate the party led by Godfrey of Bouillon, which took a route through Hungary, describes companies of women, marching in rank and file, armed with clubs and carrying their own flags.

The First Crusade was not a well-coordinated military operation, nor were the Crusaders a disciplined army. Two groups following the inspirational leaders Peter the Hermit and Walter the Penniless were annihilated as soon as they reached Asia Minor. Other leaders, in particular a Norman, Bohemund of Taranto, were more effective. Bohemund managed to reach Antioch in Turkey, which he captured by siege and treachery. Then the Christians faced a siege themselves. Characteristically, the Christians assumed that sex, that is to say, women, were to blame for their difficulties.

According to the chronicler Albertus Aquensis, a priest named Stephanus declared that Christ had appeared to him "full of anger at the lechery of the Crusaders who abandoned themselves with Christian and heathen women." Thus the leaders decreed that sexual activity was to cease: "If caught in the act of lechery, both the man and the woman were stripped naked in the presence of the army; hands bound behind their backs, mercilessly they were flogged by jailers' helpers equipped with rods and forced to exhibit themselves to the entire army, so that the sight of their terrible punishment would deter others from committing such a shameful crime."[18] And to keep temptation at a minimum, the Crusaders went to the fortifications in the area, where several thousand women had taken refuge from the fighting, and drove them all away

Meanwhile the tradition of martial women in the Arab world had not ended with Zenobia. In the fourth century, a Syrian queen named Mawia, at the head of an army, invaded Phoenicia, Palestine, and Egypt and defeated Roman legions. In the seventh century, women were conspicuous in the wars marking the birth of Islam. Hind al-Hunud was one of the Quaraish people who were in power in Mecca when Muhammad arrived. In the battle of Badr in A.D. 624 she engaged directly with Muhammad, and her father, uncle, and brother were killed.

The Hind, as she was called, was a devotee of the Cult of the Lady of Victory, an ancient tradition in which noblewomen motivated men by putting themselves in danger. The Lady of Victory, surrounded by her retinue, would let down her hair, partially expose her body, and sing martial songs accompanied by lute music as the battle raged around them. This practice persisted in some form into the nineteenth century. William Palgrave, who traveled through Arabia in 1862 and 1863, described a "huge girl" who rode a camel into battle with the Bedouin Arabs, encouraging the men to fight and reciting poetry. Her death from an enemy lance was said to be the chief reason for the defeat of the Bedouin army.[19]

For a time, the Hind continued to resist, but she was outnumbered and surrounded, and she ultimately submitted and converted to Islam. Other women fought on the side of Muhammad from the beginning. Salaym Bint Malhan fought in the ranks with swords and daggers strapped around her pregnant belly. Aishah, "the beloved of Muhammad," who was the prophet's last wife, took part in the fighting at the Battle of the Camels. Khawlah Bint al-Azwar al-Kindlyyah, with other female captains, fought at the Battle of Yermonks. She was described as "a tall knight muffled in black and fighting with ferocious courage."[20]

Khawlah was captured at the Battle of Sabhura and rallied the other women prisoners to revolt. She is quoted as saying, "Do you accept these men as your masters? Are you willing for your children to be slaves? Where is your famed courage and skill that has become the talk of the Arab tribes as well as the cities?" Another of the women is said to have replied, "We are as courageous and skillful as you describe. But in such cases a sword is quite useful, and we were taken by surprise, like sheep, unarmed."[21] Khawlah suggested that tent poles could serve as weapons. She formed the women into an old-fashioned phalanx, and they successfully fought their way to freedom.

An Islamic writer, I Mâde ad-Din, recorded his impressions of both Moslem and Christian women who fought in the Crusades: "A great and rich woman also came to the sea, she had 500 horsemen, horses, grooms, equipment and war supplies; she had to pay her people's expenses; this woman rode with us and participated in the attacks. In the enemy army there also were women on horseback, in armor and steel helmets who fought manwise; they hurled themselves into the thick of the battle by the side of the men, and only the ornaments on their feet betrayed the women." But there were some women warriors who could not be distinguished from the men at all. He wrote, "On the day of the battle, we found many strong women in garments similar to those of the horsemen. This was discovered only after they were stripped and plundered." He also noted the presence of "many old women who spurred the fighters on," evidence that not only the young and beautiful could serve in the equivalent of a Lady of Victory role. I Mâde ad-Din concluded with a remark typical of historians reporting on women in war with knowledge derived from limited experience. "Is not this activity of men and women together in such an undertaking something altogether peculiar?" he asked. Actually, as we have seen, it had been, and continued to be altogether common.[22]

Back in Europe, the pope proclaimed the Second Crusade in 1145. King Louis VII of France took the cross, and his wife, Eleanor of Aquitaine, pledged her vassals as well. The papal bull calling for the Crusade expressly forbade concubines to follow the army, but the queen, naturally, did not think such a prohibition applied to her and her noble ladies. She came to take the cross, riding a white horse and dressed in a costume thought to be Amazonian, including gilded buskins on her feet and plumes in her hair. Her ladies accompanied her, also on horseback and appropriately garbed and armed with lances and battle-axes. In addition to volunteering their military service, the ladies went through the crowds handing out distaffs used in spinning to men who seemed reluctant to take the pledge themselves.[23]

By the time of the Third Crusade, forty-three years later, King Henry II of England and his son Richard the Lionhearted for the first time officially recognized the lower-class women charged with doing women's work for the army. The English leaders forbade anyone to bring a woman on the Crusade with the exception of a laundress. This woman was to be prepared to march on foot and must be of good character. At the conclusion of the Crusade, when the army pulled out of Acre, Richard ordered that any women who had joined the army during the campaign be left behind. Only the laundresses were to follow the troops.[24]

Today, the word *laundress* is likely to trigger images of snowy shirtfronts, ironing boards, and starch. For an army to have laundresses seems a frill and meshes with the usual assumption that "laundress" was merely a euphemism for "prostitute." Until military organizations began to include women who were not wives at the beginning of the twentieth century, however, those officially on the rolls as laundresses were expected to do all "women's work," including nursing as well as washing clothing. What they washed was incredibly filthy. By the time even an aristocratic officer's linen went into the laundry, it stank. Linen for the hospital was soaked with sweat, blood, and excrement and was often crawling with lice. Cloth was expensive in the preindustrial age. Bandages were washed and reused. If clothing had to be cut from a wound, it was not discarded but carefully mended.

Technology for cleaning clothing did not advance as rapidly as that for weapons systems. Laundresses beat the bloody fabric with stones or scoured it with sand or ashes if they had a source of running water. When water was scarce, they used and reused whatever was collected in a kettle. When wash water was heated, doing laundry meant shifting cauldrons weighing fifty pounds or more empty over a fire and sweating in the steam when they were full. It was not dainty work.

In medieval Europe, excessive cleanliness was looked on with suspicion. Bathing and the use of sweet-smelling oils and soaps were practices identified with the Moslem enemy. But if washing the body was close to sin, engaging in sexual activity, or even in sexual thoughts, was clearly over the line. God would punish an army that indulged in carnal delights. Women by their nature were a temptation to sin. Those in command believed it their duty to enforce chastity. Holy Roman Emperor Frederick Barbarossa threatened dire punishment: "No one shall have a woman in his quarters, and whoever dares to keep one, will be deprived of his armor and shall be considered excommunicated; but the woman's nose shall be cut off."[25]

King Louis IX, known as St. Louis, dismissed sensualists from his service. John of Joinville, an official in the king's service during his Crusade, reported, "The men in general amused themselves with loose women; thus it came to pass that the King dismissed a large number of men when we returned from captivity. And when I asked why he had done so, he replied that he knew for certain that within a stone's throw from his pavilion, they held their meetings of debauchery and this at a time when the army suffered the greatest hardship." Under the circumstances John took good care to preserve his own reputation. "My bed was so placed in my tent that no one could enter without seeing me in my bed," he wrote, "and I did this to prevent any ill suspicions that I have any dealings with women."[26]

Not every man was willing to make such sacrifices. Members of the nobility commonly took mistresses. Furthermore, the distinction between a woman whose sexual conduct is sanctioned by a legal contract and another woman of the same ethnic background and social class who lacks such a contract is murky at best. Mistresses (or concubines) are not necessarily promiscuous; unmarried men can be just as jealous and possessive as legal husbands. A twelfth-century monk who recorded the presence of twelve hundred concubines in the French army toward the end of the twelfth century added that "public opinion did not relegate them into a class of their own; it appears that great ladies often mistook them for most respectable women." Legal wives, of course, wanted to claim moral superiority. A French queen who was embarrassed to learn that a lady she had greeted as an equal in church was actually unmarried convinced her husband to issue an order forbidding unmarried women from wearing cloaks so that they would not be mistaken for decent wives.[27]

THE MONGOL INVASION

PERHAPS THE MOST IMPORTANT result of the Crusades was the broadened perspective they brought to Europeans, who had lost contact with most of the rest of the world after the fall of Rome. The perspective was broadened further in the thirteenth century, when once again an inspired warrior from the steppe set out to conquer the world.

The steppe peoples, with their shadowy history of women warriors, come in and out of the Western historical record as they came to the attention of literate people, generally those they conquered. In A.D. 450, Atilla, king of the Huns, whose armies included women, invaded the Roman province of Gaul, also known for its ferocious fighting women. In 452, Attila invaded Italy and had to be bribed to leave. Yet by 453 Atilla was dead, and by 469 both of his sons were dead, and the Huns sank below the historical horizon again. As John Keegan reminds us, however, the steppe people "were to remain an ever-present menace to the civilizations of Europe, the Middle East and Asia for the next millennium."[28] That they failed to leave written records is an explanation for their apparently spectral presence, but not an excuse for ignoring them or denying their reality.

Amazons, those mysterious mounted women warriors from the steppe, never really disappeared. They were there when Genghis's horde swept into Hungary and began terrorizing the West. The so-called Mongol armies that he led were largely Turks. Others were Tartars, a people Genghis had subjugated. The exact composition of these people remains an ethnolinguist's nightmare. But if their origins and ethnicity are tangled and murky, the ferocity of their women is clear. Children followed the fighters in wagons, but able-bodied women rode and fought like men.[29]

Genghis Khan and other Mongol leaders left a deeper impression on history than the rank and file that followed him. The dynastic warfare that preceded and followed his reign is sprinkled with reminders of the power of

Mongol women. Genghis's mother, Oelun-eke, like the mother of Alexander the Great, was a formidable woman. And the wife of his son Ogotai, who was Great Khan from 1229 to 1241, was regent of Outer Mongolia from 1241 to 1246.[30]

That there were influential women in his life and fighting women in his armies did not make Genghis Khan a feminist and certainly no lover of peace. "Happiness," he said, "lies in conquering one's enemies, in driving them in front of oneself, in taking their property, in savoring their despair, in outraging their wives and daughters."[31] One source of pleasure was a genocidal war in China in which an estimated forty million people were slaughtered. The Mongols went on to conquer most of Asia, the Near East, and eastern Europe in the same jovial spirit. Iraq, for example, was visited by the Mongols for just two years, but the devastation was so thorough that the population did not return to its preinvasion level for more than seven hundred years. The Mongol armies swept across Russia, Poland, and Hungary and halted before reaching Vienna only because they were distracted by political complications following the death of the Great Khan in 1241.

Before the end of the thirteenth century some Europeans, notably Marco Polo, would be actively seeking contact with Asian rulers, believing they would be splendid allies in the wars against Islam. Pursuit of this goal led to the first voyages of discovery in the fifteenth century and eventually to the development of European imperialism. But that story must wait for a future chapter as we return to the memorable wars of Europe.

THE HUNDRED YEARS WAR

THE FOURTEENTH CENTURY WAS remarkable for two events. The first was the appearance of the Black Death, an epidemic of bubonic plague that began in the camp of a Mongol prince besieging a city in the Crimea and then spread rapidly throughout the Mediterranean on ships, continuing to rage across Europe and much of Asia for several years. It killed as much as one-third of the population in England in 1348 and 1349. The second, less lethal event, was the Hundred Years War, actually a series of wars between France and England, which began a decade before the epidemic struck and continued for 116 years.

The conflicts began in 1337 with the usual feudal squabbles over land. In Brittany the French king favored the Blois family claim to succession to the duchy. The claim was challenged by John of Montfort, who took out an army to enforce it. When he was captured, his wife, the countess of Montfort, looked for an ally and found one in King Edward III of England to whom she suggested a marriage between her son and one of his daughters. Edward promised to send an army, but a storm kept his fleet at sea for forty days.

While waiting for her ally, the countess had to break a siege at Hennebont on the Britanny coast. Wearing a suit of armor with a mail shirt and iron plates, the countess rode a war horse through the streets of the town, rallying the citizens to defend themselves. The women got their usual assignment of gathering rocks and stones from the buildings to throw down on the enemy from the walls. Pots of caustic quicklime supplemented the solid bombardment. Meanwhile, the countess studied the enemy positions from a tower and discovered that most of the Blois army was concentrating for a major assault on the town, leaving their camp exposed. She led three hundred horsemen out from a side gate and charged into the enemy camp, setting the tents on fire. Seeing the flames, the Blois abandoned the assault, and the countess escaped to Brest where she met the English army.[32]

In 1431, exactly one hundred years after coming to the support of the countess of Montfort, the English arranged to burn another Frenchwoman at the stake. The only charge against her that they could make stick was wearing male clothing, but Joan of Arc had done more than offend the English sense of sartorial decency by cross-dressing. She had rallied the failing French cause and by her inspired, and inspiring, military leadership had snatched victory from the English army.

Joan's cross-dressing was not a disguise. Indeed, during her lifetime she was always known as la Pucelle, the Maid, and the surname d'Arc was not used until late in the sixteenth century. She was an uneducated peasant, and remarkably young. If the documentary evidence were not so overwhelming, her history would surely be dismissed as fantastic. Even with hard evidence, the facts of her life and her canonization by the Catholic church, made Joan a woman soldier distinct from her mundane sisters.

Joan's military career began in 1428, when at the age of sixteen she had a vision in which Saints Michael, Margaret, and Catherine told her to go to the aid of the king of France and raise the siege of Orleans. The voices also told her where to go to get the necessary military training and troops. By April 1429, she had the title *chef de guerre*, a suit of armor, a squire, two pages and two heralds, two elaborate banners, a sword mysteriously discovered buried behind the altar of the church of Saint Catherine at Fierbois, and an army of four thousand infantry and archers. She headed for Orleans with a company of priests marching in front of her, singing *Veni Creator Spiritus,* having sent messengers ahead with a warning for the English commanders and their king: "I have been sent by God, the king of Heaven, to drive you, body for body, out of all France. If you do not believe this news sent to you by God and the Maid, we will strike you, wherever we find you, and make such a great attack that France has not seen in a thousand years."[33]

The French knights discovered to their astonishment that this child had somehow acquired all the skills necessary to command an army in the field. "Apart from the matter of war, she was simple and ignorant," wrote Thibaud d'Armagnac, "but in the conduct and disposition of armies, in their drawing up in battle order and the raising of soldier's morale, she behaved as if she had been the shrewdest captain in the world and had all her life been learning the art of war." The duke of Alençon was impressed by her "management of the lance in drawing up the army in battle order and in the preparing of artillery. All marvelled that she could act in so prudent and well-advised a fashion as might a captain of twenty or thirty years experience, especially in the preparation of artillery."[34]

The English were forced to withdraw from Orleans, and in July 1429, Joan stood beside the king at Rheims as his rule was consecrated. A year later, a mob of Burgundian soldiers captured her and turned her over to the English for one hundred thousand francs.

Several elements in Joan's career made her a particularly appealing model for female heroism, memorable even when all other military women are forgotten. First, she was a virgin, a fact established repeatedly by physical examinations. Thus she was different from the ordinary peasant women who marched with the armies. Second, she went into battle and suffered wounds, but she never killed anyone by her own hand. Thus she fits easily into the female role of instigator, encouraging others to kill without drawing blood herself. Third, her career ended at the stake—as a glorious victim, the most feminine of all roles.

MILITARY PROSTITUTION

MILITARY HISTORIANS SPEAK OF the Hundred Years War as a time of transition from medieval to early modern warfare. Gunpowder weapons appeared on the battlefield for the first time, although the longbow was still more important, and semipermanent royal standing armies were established. At this time, too, the large number of women accompanying the armies came under military regulation.

The laundresses who went on crusade with Richard the Lionhearted were told to march with the baggage but were not otherwise supervised or protected. A few years later the French ruler Philip Augustus created a battalion of mercenaries from the mass of lower-class civilians with unsavory reputations who were always around army camps. Despite the Christian belief in the virtue of poverty, real poor people were not expected to be good Christians. In particular, devotion to chastity was not expected of them. The French *ribauds* became an elite corps that was famous for bravery and served as the king's bodyguard. Philip permitted this unit to have as many women —wives, mistresses, or prostitutes—among them as they wished. A noble officer, holding the title Rex Ribaldorum, was in charge. Anyone running a brothel had to pay the Rex Ribaldorum a fee of two sous a week, as did each of the female residents. At the same time, any man who committed adultery with a married woman belonging to the army would have to pay the Rex Ribaldorum five sous.[35]

The Germans soon established a similar system. A chronicler reports that an army entering Strasbourg in 1298 included eight hundred women supervised by an officer to whom they paid one pfennig a week. In 1380, Emperor Frederick II instructed his marshal to collect one groschen from every woman each Saturday. Eventually the English made comparable arrangements.[36]

Clearly, military authorities saw nothing inappropriate in pimping, and more or less open arrangements of this kind continue to the present day. Sometimes prostitutes came to camp under civilian sponsorship. For example, during the Swiss siege of Strasbourg in 1476, patriotic citizens sent a boat full of public prostitutes out to the soldiers. Significantly, however, these were not women regularly attached to the army but what might be called a "special issue." Soldiers in garrison had access to civilian houses of prostitution not connected with the company of women attached to the camp.

Still, some "public women" had official recognition in armies. Only an officer of unusual virtue would exclude them. Of one fifteenth-century commander a source says, "his continence as regards women surely is admirable; for him as for others, speaking generally, there is no greater pernicious enemy to the vigor of the body and soul than woman; it is necessary, by work and assiduous night-watch, by sleeping on the ground, to master the body and tame the momentary ardor for luxury. Thus by his example and advice he admonished soldiers too eager to visit the houses. There were no wretches nor lechers in his camp."[37]

For most commanders, it was sufficient to limit the number of officially designated prostitutes and put them under the supervision of an officer. Thus a military unit marching through Paris in 1465 was described this way: "The superb company of mounted archers passed through the city in good order, well equipped, lacking nothing not even eight daughters of joy on horseback, who with their father confessor followed the company."[38]

By the sixteenth century, German war ordinances were spelling it out specifically. For example, a list of "female persons" necessary for the occupation of a castle includes one seamstress, two kitchen maids, "and two or three other females who shall be everybody's women and regarding whom there must not be any rivalry. The captain shall take these poor women under his protection and care, and no one must think that he can have them alone." All of the "female persons" were to be paid "suitable women's money of two kreutzer." Carefully distinguishing between fornication and adultery, the regulation adds, "Those who have wedded wives must have no share in the common property under the punishment of God."

Another German ordinance issued by Duke Carl III of Lothringen is equally explicit:

> No military man entering the service of this army shall bring with him any special woman, unless she is his legitimate wife having been married or affianced to him; all other women present with this army shall be public women and the common property of all and that in each company there shall be no more than eight women under penalty of flogging [for the excess women] and the man shall be deprived of his effects; and if it is proved that soldiers or officers of our military forces have, or bring into our army such women for their own privacy, they should be driven off and henceforth declared incapable of carrying on the war, and be further chastised at our pleasure."[40]

The duke of Alba went so far as to establish price controls, ordering, "Let there be none among them who from now on refuses a soldier who asks to be admitted to her room for 5 solds the night."[41]

Although public women in the army provided sexual services, this was not their sole function. Wilwolt of Schaumburg describes their work in the fifteenth-century armies of Charles the Bold: "Through the provost, Charles had the common women, of whom there were 4000 here, called together for the work [of carting earth]. The Duke gave them a small flag showing the picture of a woman, and when they went to or from work, the flag, and drum-and-fife preceded them."[42]

Genuine prostitution, however, may have been less prevalent than casual reading of sources suggests. The word *whore* was often employed loosely to mean any woman who was "common" in the sense of being of low social status. For instance, the sixteenth-century "Articles for German Artillery" stipulate that "no soldier may possess a whore unless for serious reasons permission is granted him by his colonel; and that the women are to be formed into platoons in the regiments and shall be assigned to do nursing and cooking."[43] A "whore" who is "possessed" by one soldier is not promiscuous. She is what would later be recognized as a common-law wife.

Prior to the sixteenth century, virtuous commanders strove from religious motives to prevent all fornication. After syphilis appeared in Europe, promiscuity rather than sex became a medical problem for the military. The first cases were recorded in 1494 following a French invasion of Italy. Charles VIII advanced with a mercenary army that included Flemish, Gascons, Swiss, Spaniards, and a few Italians. The usual train of camp followers and beggars accompanied it. After the battle of Fornovo on July 5, 1495, doctors recorded symptoms of syphilis for the first time. As the French mercenaries demobilized, they spread the disease in their respective homelands. By the end of the century, syphilis was everywhere in Europe. Gonorrhea, which was thought originally to be a form of syphilis, spread simultaneously. The two had one important feature in common: they were spread through sexual intercourse and were called venereal diseases, the term carrying connotations of both sex and sin for Europeans.[44] Henceforth, prostitutes would be considered physical as well as moral contaminants.

The earliest reference linking military prostitution and disease is in a pamphlet entitled "Discourse Pertaining to the Present German Army." The author believed he was dealing with a peculiarly German problem:

No other nation causes the field marshal and the paymaster so much trouble as do the Germans with the "military baggage and conveyances." A soldier who is without a wife or whore at the time of his induction in the army, is enjoined from acquiring one afterwards. As far as possible, women must disappear from camp because, due especially to the prostitutes, much sin and mur-

der is committed. Other nations more ardent than the Germans such as Italians, Spaniards, French do not have so large a woman-load. Even the German cavalry had not got a tenth part of what the foot-soldiers have and is better taken care of.[45]

The author knew that women performed essential duties in camp, but he thought there were other ways to cover them. "Each squadron should employ sutlers, cleaners and cooks to take care of the single men," he wrote. "These single lads could, as they do among the Spaniards, form friendships and help each other in case of illness or other needs. In addition, there is to be a field medicus, surgeons, and male nurses; also an efficient apothecary shop. Thus we will have no need for women to keep a soldier alive and the camp will be protected against contagious diseases."[46]

Yet considering how rapidly the disease spread and the severe impact it was to have on all armies, medical supervision of military prostitution developed with surprising slowness. In 1580, for the first time, an edict issued by Albert the Pious of Belgium specified that only women free of disease could be admitted to the army. Instead, commanders limited their efforts to preventing promiscuity by limiting women on the march to legal wives, even if that meant encouraging marriage to prostitutes.

THE THIRTY YEARS WAR

IN THE SIXTEENTH CENTURY, the Protestant Reformation split the religious unity of Christendom and removed whatever inhibitions Christianity imposed on the behavior of Europeans warring against each other. In 1568, Protestants in the Netherlands rebelled against their Catholic ruler, the Spanish Hapsburg king, Philip II. The Dutch Revolt, which lasted for eighty years, became one of the longest wars in European history. England's Protestant queen Elizabeth I, became involved, as did French Protestants who opposed Philip's army, which was diverted from Flanders to aid the Catholic side in the French religious wars. These conflicts, remarkable for their ferocity, were followed by an even more savage conflict known as the Thirty Years War.

The fighting in the years 1618–48 was actually not one war but four. What began as a protest by Protestants in eastern Europe developed into a full-scale conflict between European Protestants and Catholics and finally evolved into a political struggle in which Swedish and French armies invaded Germany. The slaughter, especially the slaughter of civilians, was of a magnitude not seen in Europe since Roman times. Fully 25 percent of the German population of 16 million died in those years as the result of the fighting and associated famine and disease. Two-thirds of the population of Bohemia died. Whole towns and villages disappeared. In 1631, 25,000 of the 30,000 people in Magdeburg were butchered in what has been called the "Hiroshima of the Thirty Years War."[47]

In short, these were dangerous times. Not until the twentieth century would civilian losses again outnumber military casualties and put similar pressures on women to assume military roles. The desperation of civilians explains the long trains of camp followers found with all the armies of these years. At the end of the Thirty Years War, in 1648, a report to Elector Max of Bavaria stated that the combined Imperial and Bavarian armies had 40,000 soldiers drawing rations and 140,000 others who got nothing.[48] Of course the armies plundered.

Johann Jacob Wallhausen, a chronicler of the seventeenth-century wars, describes how soldiers and camp followers alike would descend on a farmhouse, even in supposedly friendly territory, pounce on livestock, break down doors, and pull out trunks and boxes while intimidating the inhabitants. When they had eaten all they could hold, they took the horses and oxen and the farmer's carts and loaded them with objects they had stolen. "Then ten to twelve women and as many soldiers and some six boys sit on top of the heavy packing like caterpillars in heads of cabbage," Wallhausen wrote. "The vehicle is frequently so heavily overburdened that the horses or oxen cannot budge it."[49]

For soldiers, women represented not simply sex but all the creature comforts, and the men vigorously resisted being separated from their female servants. Wallhausen described the situation in the German infantry: "A regiment of three thousand men usually had not less than three hundred vehicles and each wagon was filled to overflowing with women, boys, children, prostitutes and plunder." One regiment of three thousand had two thousand followers and their baggage. The captain thought of a clever scheme by which he hoped to reduce these impedimenta. When the army crossed a river, he told the boatmen to stop ferrying people for a few days after the soldiers had crossed. But when they discovered what was happening, the women began to weep and scream, so that the whole regiment broke ranks and returned to the riverbank. Then, we are told, "The soldiers called out in chorus: 'Ho, what the devil, I must have my whore back; she has my shirts, collars, shoes and stockings.'" The captain had to accede to their wishes, but he hit on another method. He mustered the men with a trumpet call and announced that every soldier without a lawful wife must get rid of his mistress immediately or be flogged. So the soldiers took their women and went off in all directions looking for a church. "In two days 800 prostitutes, including some most miserable creatures, became duly wedded wives."[50]

Lawful wives, no matter how "miserable," considered themselves superior to those without marriage certificates. This could lead to fights. Wallhausen described a typical scene, in which the camp followers rushed for places in the wagons. When a legal wife could no longer find a place, she would shout, "You miserable prostitute, you want to ride, and I am an honorable wife of a soldier who has made many campaigns with him." Then sticks and stones would be thrown until finally the soldier's wife ran to her husband crying, "Look, Hans, there is this or that one's whore; she sits in the wagon, wants to ride and I have to go on foot, I, your honorable wife." The soldier would go to the wagon and try to pull the other woman off so his wife could have the place. Then her soldier would show up, saying, "Leave my girl alone; I am as fond of her as you are of your own wife." Next the two soldiers would go at it, drawing their sabers, and often wounding or even killing each other. "This is no rarity," Walhausen insisted, "for when in transit, hardly a day passes in which three, four or even ten soldiers do not lose life or limb for the sake of their women."[51]

At this time the Germans called the soldier in charge of the baggage train the *Hurenweibel,* or whore sergeant. He was usually an older man, often suffering some disability from wounds. The others treated him with respect because he was guarding both their families and their booty. The whore contingent had its own flag and marched in military order with the sergeant at the head and the most attractive women close to him so that he could keep them from being annoyed by the boys. Despite the large number of wagons, most camp followers had to walk and carry on their backs whatever did not fit into the carts.[52]

In a manuscript dated 1612, an anonymous German officer described their condition with a degree of sympathy unusual among aristocrats, who usually disdained camp followers:

Seldom did the woman carry less than 50 or 60 pounds; whenever the sol-
dier provided himself with victuals or similar portable goods, he piled it with
straw or wood on top, not to mention that the woman already carried one or
two or more children on her back; in addition the woman usually carried on
her person the man's clothing consisting of one pair of pants, one pair of
socks, one pair of shoes; for herself, the same number of shoes and stockings,
one skirt, two shirts, one pan, one pot, one or two bowls, one bedsheet, one
cloak, one tent, three poles. Furthermore, if she could not get wood in their
quarters, she collected it on the way, and piled it up on her back. And as
though that were not enough, she usually leads a small dog on a cord, and if
the weather is bad, she even carries the animal.[53]

Another contemporary confirms the description: "The women or the prostitutes of the common foot-soldier are not unlike the Spanish mule burdened as they are with knapsacks, cloaks, shawls, pots, kettles, pans, brooms, small bags, roosters and all kinds of trash, with their skirts trussed up to their knees, with mud up to the shoetops, many of them barefoot, of course." Nor did they get much gratitude for acting as pack animals, the writer adds. "With all that they are not well treated, and for the slightest reason mercilessly trampled on and beaten as their black eye bears witness."[54]

Like regular soldiers, women with the army were subject to martial law, which prescribed ferocious punishments for misbehavior. For the French, these included flogging and amputation of nose or ears, branding, and dyeing a woman's face black or shaving her head. The English favored a device called the whirligig. For this punishment, the offender was placed in a circular wooden cage that turned on a pivot at high speed. Soon "the delinquent became extremely sick and usually emptied his or her body through every aperture." An entry in an English garrison order book records that one "Mrs. Malone was committed to the whirligig for 2 hours" and that "it gave great pleasure to the spectators."[55]

The custom of military service also gave husbands the right to punish their wives by their own authority. A German source says a husband could, as a matter of right, "turn her over to the stableboys and camp hirelings; the miserable woman would then be set upon by the wild pack of men and camp dogs and chased into the bushes."[56] And, of course, he could beat her himself, as the black eyes referred to above suggest.

Wives carried baggage on the march, but they were not idle in camp either. Camp followers were responsible for cleaning the latrines and sweeping the streets. They were also required to help bind fascines, the bundles of sticks used to construct earthworks. Digging pits, filling ditches, and mounting cannon were also women's work, as was caring for the sick. It was the responsibility of the whore sergeant to see that they carried out these assignments and "that they never refuse either on the field or in garrison, runnng, pouring out, fetching food and drink, knowing how to behave mostly with regard to the needs of others and taking it in turns to do what is necessary according to orders."[57] When her work for the army was over, a wife went to work as an entrepreneur to supplement the miserably poor army pay.

Hans Jokob Christoffel von Grimmelshausen, a musketeer during the war, described some of this economic activity in his novel, *Simplicius Simplicissimus:* "In their misery, a few troopers took on wives (some of these formerly two-bit sluts) who could increase their income by such work as sewing, washing, spinning, or by selling second-hand clothing or other junk, or even by stealing."[58] There was also work for midwives and the always-in-demand laundresses. Grimmelshausen also describes women sutlers who sold pipes and tobacco or brandy. Some of the last, he says, had the reputation "of adulterating it with water distilled by their own bodies—but that didn't change the color of the liquor in the least."[59] He knew others who had gone back to the ancient hunter-gatherer practices out in the fields: "they dug for snails in the winter, collected grass for salads in the spring, and in summer knew where to find thousands of tidbits; some carried wood on their backs like donkeys and offered it for sale." More unusual, Grimmelshausen knew one woman, married to an ensign, who drew her pay as a corporal. This example points to another opportunity the wars opened for women in the seventeenth century—enlisting as paid soldiers.

WOMEN SOLDIERS

WOMEN WHO CHOSE TO put on male clothing and become soldiers or sailors during the Thirty Years War and the wars that followed in early modern Europe were very much like the camp followers in age, class, and background. Joining the military was for them an alternative to becoming military whores. Other than simple economic pressure, their motives included patriotism, a longing for adventure, or a desire to keep an eye on a special man who had become a soldier. Most women soldiers and sailors we know of in these years came from Holland, Germany, and England, where there was an insatiable demand for recruits during the wars and, coincidentally, a fascination with disguise and cross-dressing that assured publicity to women discovered masquerading as men.

In the early years of the Dutch Revolt, women fought alongside men during the siege of Haarlem and other cities. They used the familiar tactics, including pouring boiling tar from the city walls. Two Haarlem sisters, Kenau and Amaron Kenau Hasselaar, put on swords and organized a battalion of three hundred women who fought outside the walls as well. Both of these activities are well within women's traditional wartime roles, and the participants made no attempt to conceal their gender. Later in the wars, the novelty was significant numbers of women concealing their sex in order to take on male gender roles in armies and navies.

Isolated examples of women passing as men appeared prior to the sixteenth century. We cannot assume that women discovered in male clothing on battlefields were necessarily keeping their sex secret from their comrades—Joan of Arc certainly did not—but there were traditions in European folklore that emphasized an element of disguise. In medieval hagiography, a number of female saints preserved their virginity by turning into men. Whatever may have been the case earlier, from the late sixteenth through the eighteenth century, there were hundreds of women soldiers and sailors[60] passing as men, and everybody knew about it.

In 1762, an Englishman joked that so many disguised women were serving in the army that they ought to have their own regiments. Earlier, a Dutch statesman wrote, "I could give you many examples of women on our own ships who did men's service and were exceptionally brave. . . . I could also tell you how I myself have discovered women in soldier's clothing in our armies and made them change their dress. During my days in the army a girl in the cavalry was caught plundering and suffered herself to be hung without making her sex known. This the sergeant on duty told me; he had her undressed after she had died and felt sorry about it."[61]

Popular culture supported young women who might contemplate putting on male dress and following a military career. Songs celebrating female warriors began to appear in print at the end of the sixteenth century and grew in popularity over the next two centuries. The folklorist and musicologist Dianne Dugaw has collected more than one hundred separate Anglo-American female warrior ballads, and her list of variants of these songs runs to more than five hundred pages. "Ballad-makers regularized this heroine as they did few others," Dugaw tells us. "Far from being isolated and idiosyncratic, the Female Warrior and her story assumed the status of an imaginative archetype in popular balladry, a standard motif." The "bold, bonny lass" celebrated in these songs is simultaneously an outstanding warrior and a perfect woman. "Far from being marginalized or monstrous, most of them are attractive, virtuous, and loving sweethearts," Dugaw writes. Significant-ly, those few in the songs who are "discovered" because of pregnancy turn out to be the most viraginous and heroic of them all.[62]

With so much popular admiration for the fictionalized heroines of the songs, it is not surprising to find that substantial numbers of real women who cross-dressed to enter military service published the stories of their adventures. The success of these biographies encouraged imitation, and a good many fictional autobiographies reached the bookstalls as well. Printers issued translations of these books, proving the existence of an international market for writing on this theme. Some women war veterans became local celebrities who took advantage of their fame to go on the stage or open taverns. The romance attached to women in disguise persists, and of all military women of the past, those who fought disguised as men have had the most written about them.

Once stories of women in uniform were circulating, each example encouraged other women to consider a military career. Besides revealing the fact that disguise could be successful, a few books or legal documents included practical hints on delicate matters. One Catharina Lincken had "a leather-covered horn through which she urinated and [which she kept] fastened against her nude body."[63] Christian Davies, an Englishwoman who first enlisted as a man but later fought openly as a woman, described a useful urinary device, a "silver tube," which she said she learned about from another woman soldier.[64] That final comment is revealing. Modern historians, with their shameless twentieth-century curiosity, want to know specifically how women could have maintained a disguise, how they managed urination and menstruation, for example, or how they concealed their breasts when sleeping crammed between male comrades on a troop transport or in a small tent. The sources rarely answer such questions. Maria van Antwerpen, for instance, does say she "sometimes" kept her trousers on at night when sleeping in a bed with other soldiers, but then she merely refers to "a certain precaution about which chastity forbids [her] to tell."[65] Details omitted in the published autobiographies were probably shared privately with other women considering enlistment.

Some individuals made a living recruiting women for the army or navy, and they almost certainly had a wealth of useful information. Anna Spiesen was recruited by another woman who took care of everything, even making sure that a man registered in her place when the articles were signed just in case physical scrutiny was keen. In a few cases, two disguised women enlisted together, cooperating to maintain their joint disguise.[66]

Twentieth-century readers who learn about these female comrades tend to assume the existence of a "lesbian" relationship. We must be careful about reading too much of the present into the past. That women might join forces to go after male lovers reveals a different kind of partnership. Even in the small number of cases in which a woman soldier took a wife, the motive was often to help maintain the disguise and to get the same domestic services other soldiers got from their wives. Surprising as it may seem, the wife might remain innocent of the true sex of the soldier husband for many years. One woman soldier explained her failure to consummate the marriage by claiming to have syphilis.[67] A conveniently located wound would serve as well. It might very well be true that if these couples lived in our time, they would have looked at each other differently. But they lived in their time, not in ours. As the historian of cross-dressing Marjorie Garber reminds us, "the very concept of 'sexual orientation' as a self-definition is itself of relatively recent, and local, vintage."[68]

If the cross-dressing military women of early modern Europe confuse the twentieth-century mind, an even more baffling case is that of the Chevalier d'Eon. Perhaps s/he is a puzzle because s/he was so far ahead of his/her own time that s/he is still ahead of ours. D'Eon was a French nobleman, born in 1728 about one hundred miles east of Paris. He was educated in Paris, held a law degree, published articles in literary journals, and produced a treatise on finance. His close ties to government and court circles led Louis XV to employ him as an espionage agent in Russia. Following his successful completion of that mission, he entered the military, served with distinction during the Seven Years War, and rose to the rank of captain of dragoons. At the conclusion of the war in 1763, he was part of the diplomatic team that negotiated peace with England. That business concluded, he remained in England as a spy.

Meanwhile rumors circulated that d'Eon was actually a biological female. By the mid-1770s, London newspapers ran countless articles discussing the Frenchman's gender. Gentlemen fired up with curiosity placed bets on what might be found underneath his clothing. Eventually even the London Stock Exchange handled wagering on the subject. Since d'Eon was an aristocrat, a diplomat, and an officer in the French dragoons no one could order him to strip and be examined. Although he was offered enormous sums of money to consent to an examination, he flatly refused. Finally, gamblers sued each other in a dispute over payment, and a British court formally ruled that d'Eon was a woman.

D'Eon returned to France and there "confessed his true sex." At this point in the chevalier's history, at the age of forty-nine, *he* became *she*. The gender change was a free choice. But Mademoiselle d'Eon still wore with pride the uniform of a Dragoon captain and the prestigious Cross of Saint Louis, awarded for valor. The foreign minister, Vergennes, summoned her to a meeting at Versailles. D'Eon went happily, hoping for a new diplomatic assignment. Instead she was given a signed order from King Louis XVI ordering her to "lay aside the uniform of a dragoon" and forbidding her "to appear in any part of the kingdom in any other garments than those suitable to females." D'Eon was devastated; she did not understand why being a woman should exclude her from the diplomatic service or require her to wear clothing that she considered uncomfortable and inconvenient. But d'Eon followed the king's orders and lived the rest of her life in women's clothing. When she died at the age of eighty-two, the body was prepared for burial. Anatomically, it was unambiguously male.

How do we label this soldier? D'Eon was not a transvestite but wore women's clothing only under duress. D'Eon was not a transsexual, for s/he did not wish to live as a woman; s/he wanted a military and diplomatic career. S/he was neither homosexual nor heterosexual; despite the intense interest in d'Eon's anatomy, no one ever gossiped about possible sexual activity. In an age of flamboyant sexual behavior by the upper classes in both England and France, d'Eon did not form any close relationships. And he was not an androgyne; there was no ambiguity in his genitalia.

If the word had been invented in his/her time, we might call d'Eon a feminist. S/he owned a large number of books arguing that true virtue was not derived from virility but from a feminine source and elaborated the theme repeatedly in autobiographical manuscripts. For example, a manuscript d'Eon wrote in 1805 reads as follows:

During all ages the French have respected the courage particularly of women. Their ancestors, the Gauls, would not go to war without women, nor ever go to battle without their advice. So, can I become a man without becoming a woman? What foolishness! If man has bodily strength and courage, woman has virtue and prudence. She possesses a special spirit that allows the quick perception of things that are difficult to understand. She sees through the most hidden deception of a common enemy; and through the court intrigue of an ambitious minister. A woman who has made war and peace must be as wise as Thales, Solon, Bias. . . . In addition, she must have the virtue and courage of Judith, and of Deborah, and of Joan of Arc.[69]

D'Eon longed for a society in which biological sex would not predetermine gender identity, a world in which an individual might choose from both "masculine" and "feminine" virtues and then act freely without being confined to either masculine or feminine roles. Such a vision has interesting implications for contemporary women who would like to serve as military professionals without being forced to assume gender characteristics more "feminine" or "masculine" or more "neuter" than those that are comfortable for them as individuals.

CHAPTER FIVE

THE AGE OF REVOLUTION

A T THE END OF the eighteenth century, European warfare witnessed a new type of fighting, most conspicuous at first in the British colonies in North America. The American form of combat consisted of very small scale engagements with civilian combatants. A battle might involve only a handful of people who did not wear uniforms or carry conventional weapons or bother with tactical formations. During the American Revolution, British as well as American military units learned to fight "Indian-style." Before the end of the century, civilians who fought in the Napoleonic Wars had discovered the value of similar irregular tactics. The term coined to describe this kind of fighting in Europe was "guerrilla warfare," but it was practiced earlier by Europeans fighting American Indians.

INDIAN WARS

THE PATTERN OF INDIAN wars that developed in America was a product of the clash between the European form of "civilized" warfare and the "primitive" warfare of the Indians. The Indian way of war was the old-fashioned combination of ritual and sport, which did not last any longer than tempers stayed hot and in which relatively few people were killed. The Europeans, whose warfare was a far more lethal activity with long-range goals, including the appropriation of land, did not understand the cultural assumptions supporting Indian warfare and concluded they had no rules.

Meanwhile, the Indians very quickly learned that for Europeans war was no game, and they abandoned their own traditions in a desperate fight for survival. The consequence was a form of fighting in which neither side practiced restraint.

Ultimately disease and ecological damage rather than war were responsible for the virtual extinction of most of the nations of indigenous peoples in North America. But that process took several centuries, and so long as the Indians remained a significant military force, wars of sporadic attack and reprisal continued. Europeans attempted to make "alliances" with various tribes to use them in their own conflicts, but the Indians understood that they had interests of their own to protect, and peace treaties negotiated on the other side of the Atlantic that ended various European wars did not ensure peace on the American frontiers.

The first contact between Europeans and Indians came about A.D. 1000 when Norse voyagers, sailing far out into the Atlantic Ocean, established settlements in Iceland, Greenland, and North America. Both men and women were in the expeditions. *Eirik the Red's Saga* describes the first battle between Karlsefini and his warriors and people they called Skraelings.[1] The Skraelings arrived in "a great multitude of boats" and attacked the Norse settlement. At this time Europeans had no technological advantage in weapons. Indeed, after the first clash with staves and missiles hurled from slings, the Skraelings were the ones who unleashed a strange and terrifying weapon, a big ball-shaped object, launched from a pole, that made a tremendous noise when it hit the ground. At the sound, the Norse defenders panicked and ran away up the river.

At this point one of the Norse women, Freydis Eiriksdattir, came onto the scene to change the tide of battle. Seeing the men running off, she screamed at them, "Why are you running from wretches like these? . . . If I had a weapon I think I could put up a better fight than any of you!" Freydis was in an advanced state of pregnancy, which slowed her down but did not interfere with her will to fight. Snatching up a sword from beside a dead Viking lying in the path, she went after the men with the Skraelings behind her. As they began to overtake her, she turned and prepared to defend herself. "The Skraelings were now making for her," the saga relates. "She pulled out her breasts from under her shift and slapped the sword on them." This unexpected act was a psychological match for the Skraeling's noisy ball, for "the Skraelings took fright, and ran off to their boats and rowed away."

Recognizing a heroic act when they saw one, "Karlsefini's men came up to her, praising her courage." Soon after, the Norse abandoned their settlement.[2]

For the next five hundred years, the Skraelings were left alone. Then, in the sixteenth century, Europeans returned to North America, and settlers from many nations established colonies. Most of these colonies eventually came under the control of Great Britain. Conflict between the indigenous inhabitants and the newcomers was continuous.[3] Yet the pattern of attacks and counterattacks on individuals or small settlements was only occasionally labeled war. Europeans considered bloodshed in the colonies to be real war only when it fitted into the context of European politics and was conducted between armies fighting in a European style.

British colonists distinguished between routine raiding and the wars fought by the Indians as allies of the French when France and England went to war in Europe. Between 1689 and 1763, American colonists fought a series of wars that they named after the reigning British monarch. The first was King William's War, linked to Europe's War of the League of Augsburg (1688–97). This was followed by Queen Anne's War, the American contribution to the War of the Spanish Succession (1702–13). Then King George's War (1744–48) coincided with the War of the Austrian Succession. The last war with France, also fought during the reign of King George, was called the French and Indian War in America, the Seven Years' War in Europe, and the Great War for Empire in England.

The deadliest war waged by Americans, however, took place twenty years before King William's War when New England colonists fought what they called King Philip's War (1675–76). This conflict had nothing to do with European events, for "Philip" was Metacom, an Indian leader. Metacom succeeded his father, Massasoit, as sachem of the Wampanoags. Incursions into Indian hunting grounds and attempts to Christianize the native inhabitants of Cape Cod motivated the Wampanoags to form a league of tribes that included most of the Indians from Maine to Connecticut. This alliance launched attacks on white frontier settlements. Two of the tribes in Metacom's confederacy had female chiefs. One of them, Awashonks, and her warriors fought for a year and then negotiated a separate peace. Weetamoo was more persistent. Known as the Squaw Sachem, she led a force of three hundred warriors in raids against fifty-two of the ninety English settlements. She annihilated twelve of these. Eventually, she was betrayed, and the English surprised her with twenty-six of her comrades. She drowned in a river while trying to escape. The British retrieved her body, mutilated the corpse, and put her head on a pole to display before her weeping followers.[4]

By European standards the casualties in King Philip's War were trivial, but in seventeenth-century New England, with its tiny population, they were enormous. In per capita terms, King Philip's War was the costliest war in American history. A recent scholar sets the total number of casualties for this conflict at nine thousand, two-thirds of them American Indians. Military records, however, do not include civilian casualties. None of the dead were professional soldiers, so in European terms this was not a war at all. Nevertheless, a total of losses recorded for white men, who made up the civilian militia, showed five hundred captured or killed and, before the fighting ended, more than forty New England towns damaged, half of them so badly that they were abandoned.[6]

The death of King Philip ended his war, but it did not mean peace between Indians and settlers. An event the following year illustrates how women might develop their own military response to a dangerous situation. Leaders of the Sokokis and Canibas tribes devised a plan to burn Boston by seizing English fishing and trading boats and sailing into the harbor, taking the city by surprise. In the early summer of 1677, they captured twenty ships, killing the crews or taking them hostage. Most of these sailors came from Marblehead, Massachusetts. Then on July 15, a group of white men recaptured one vessel and took it into Marblehead with two Indian prisoners aboard. The women of the town saw no sense in keeping them alive. One of the English mariners gave a deposition describing what happened next:

The women surrounded them, drove us by force from them, (we escaping at no little peril), and laid violent hands upon the captives, some stoning us in the meantime, because we would protect them, others seizing them by the hair, got full possession of them, nor was there any way left by which we could rescue them. Then with stones, billets of wood, and what else they might, they made an end of these Indians. We were kept at such a distance that we could not see them till they were dead, and then we found them with their heads off and gone, and their flesh in a manner pulled from their bones. And such was the tumulation these women made, that for my life I could not tell who these women were, or the names of any of them. They cried out and said, if the Indians had been carried to Boston, that would have been the end of it, and

they would have been set at liberty; but said they, if there had been forty of
the best Indians in the country here, they would have killed them all, though
they should be hanged for it. They suffered neither constable nor mandrake,
nor any other person to come near them, until they had finished their bloody
purpose.[7]

The French and Indian Wars that constituted the next phase of warfare
for the American colonies embraced several generations of conflict. Except
for the last one, the series of European wars were sparked by events that had
little or nothing to do with the American colonies. Yet each time a new war
was declared, colonists were expected to fight for their sovereign. Both
France and England tried to maintain alliances with the Indian tribes, who
held the preponderance of military force in North America until after the
American Revolution. Consequently, every time a new war was declared in
Europe, the French governor of Canada mobilized Indian allies to attack
English frontier settlements. In such circumstances, no one was a noncom-
batant.

The most famous heroine of the colonial wars is Hannah Duston. On
March 15, 1697, she became part of the conflict known in Europe as the War
of the League of Augsburg. For people like the Duston family, living in the
remote wilderness of Haverhill, New Hampshire, the Indians were the only
visible enemy. They came on the scene that fatal day in March as Thomas
Duston worked in the field. When he saw a small "Band of Salvages"
approaching, he ran to the farmhouse to try to save his family. He was partially successful. He rounded up seven of his children and got them ready to
abandon their home. But Hannah had just given birth again and was in no
condition to make a mad dash through the woods for safety. So Hannah, her
infant daughter, and a woman who was nursing her were left behind to fend
for themselves.

The Indians captured them and marched them north, toward the French
colony in Canada. According to Cotton Mather, who published the earliest
contemporary account of the affair, the baby was a nuisance for the Indians
and "e'er they had gone many Steps, they dash'd out the Brains of the *Infant*
against a Tree." The party made slow progress north and after a journey of
about one hundred miles, paused at a small island near what is now
Concord, New Hampshire. On the island lived an Indian family of twelve—
two men, three women and seven children—relatives of the man in charge of

the Haverhill raid. Also living there was an English boy who had been taken captive about eighteen months earlier. Hannah Duston chose this place to make her break for freedom and in passing strike a blow for king and country. Sometime before dawn on the night of March 30, Hannah and the boy seized hatchets and attacked the Indians as they slept. The boy killed one; Hannah killed nine. One of the Indian women and one child escaped. The blood-soaked pair then packed up the nurse, appropriated an Indian canoe, and returned to Haverhill. They brought with them the scalps of those they had killed. In appreciation of a job well done, the General Court in Boston awarded a bounty of twenty-five pounds to Hannah Duston and bounties of twelve pounds five shillings each to the boy and the nurse.[8]

Late in the nineteenth century, Hannah Duston was honored with two monuments. She was the first American woman to be recognized by such a memorial. Victorian sensibility apparently was not offended by the representation of a female brandishing a hatchet in one hand while clutching a handful of scalps in the other.[9]

THE AMERICAN REVOLUTION

PERIODIC INTERVALS OF PEACE interrupted the wars in Europe, but the Indians and the white settlers remained in a continuous state of war. The colonists were accustomed to providing for their own defense. British troops participated only in the last of the wars, the Seven Years' War, in which acquisition of French Canada was an aim. A fundamental cause of the American Revolution was the British decision, following the French defeat in 1763, to send an army of regular troops to North America on a permanent basis, ostensibly to protect the colonists from the Indians. The colonists, who had managed for almost two centuries without such help, resented being asked to pay the costs of maintaining professional soldiers. Even more than the cost, they resented having redcoats posted in their cities.

Professional soldiers had an unsavory reputation, which they lived up to whenever they could escape the vigilance of their officers. Although their ostensible mission was on the western frontier, the troops ended up in port cities on the Atlantic coast. Street fighting between civilians and off-duty soldiers provoked riots in New York City, and a similar incident in Boston led to the Boston Massacre in 1770 in which six civilians were killed. Although moving the troops out of the city calmed matters for several years, a new tax on tea enflamed the colonists again. When King George III sent troops and ships to punish Boston for the destruction of private property known as the Boston Tea Party, civilian militia resisted their attempts to seize colonial military stores at Concord. The resulting Battles of Lexington and Concord on April 19, 1775, began the American War of Independence. From that first day women had muskets in their hands.

Although it would be more than a year before the British colonies officially declared their independence from Great Britain, the Continental Congress supported the local militia besieging Boston by appointing a Virginian, George Washington, to take command. Washington's challenge was to form and lead an army that would appear to Europeans as a professional fighting force. Americans had never had standing armies of their own. Indeed they detested the whole notion of standing armies, regarding them as a tool of tyrants. The hastily organized Continental Army could be no match for England's force of seasoned professionals who would battle Napoleon to the ground a few years later. But if the Americans could look good enough, England's enemies in Europe might be persuaded to support them. France and Spain might find aiding the colonists a cheap way to annoy the British and an opportunity to take advantage of England's preoccupation in America to gain advantage elsewhere on the globe.

Most Americans who fought and died during the Revolution did so in actions that were not connected to the famous "battles" waged by George Washington and his generals. As had been the case throughout the eighteenth century, Indian warfare formed the background to all other military activity. In addition, divided loyalties among the colonists introduced elements of civil war. Most Americans did not want to get involved in the fighting between Continentals and redcoats and hoped that King George and the Continental Congress would somehow work things out. But as years passed and troop movements eventually affected every one of the colonies, all Americans were forced into the conflict, whether they liked it or not.

Organizing for self-defense was nothing new for American women. As the men in Massachusetts transformed their militia companies into rapid-response units of minutemen ready to move toward Boston, the women prepared to take up the slack for local defense by organizing home guard companies. The best-documented example is a company of women at Pepperell, Massachusetts. It was known as Prudence Wright's guard, after its elected captain. Sarah Shattuck was the lieutenant, and we know the names of several other members, the youngest of whom was seventeen. These women dressed in men's clothing when they went on patrol, some armed with muskets and others with farm tools, such as pitchforks. New England women were familiar with the rank-and-file drill of the male militia, and groups of them marched in good military order when on a mission.[10]

While the propriety of women taking up arms as regular soldiers might be questioned in later years, their role as defenders of home and families against Indian "savages" never drew anything but praise at this time, although Indian fighting was hand-to-hand combat and particularly gory and gruesome. In European warfare, muskets and bayonets had become the standard weapons; the standard weapon for women who fought Indians was the hatchet. But because these women did not fight as part of a male fighting unit or while wearing male military uniforms, their military role could easily be conflated into that of wife/mother.[11]

Women living on the New York frontier or in the backcountry settlements from Pennsylvania to Georgia did their fighting against Indians or small parties of Loyalists, and, as was customary in such combat, they were not concerned with tactical formations or hierarchy of command. They defended their homes, as they always had, by braining or disemboweling attackers with hatchets, beating them with shovels, or blinding them with pots of boiling lye. One woman, Nancy Johnson, won fame by dispatching a Loyalist with a well-placed kick that knocked him down a flight of stairs. Another, known to the Indians as Mad Ann Bailey because of her ferocity in combat, received pay from the army for work as an Indian "scout and courier," which somehow sounds more feminine than the modern equivalent, special operations. In her later years she was a local celebrity, living in a log cabin she built herself. The writer Ann Newport Royall interviewed Bailey in 1825 when she was eighty-three years old. "She was quite a low woman in height," Royall wrote, "but very strongly made, and had the most pleasant countenance I ever saw, and for her, very affable."[12] Dozens of these case histories were lovingly preserved by descendants in the nineteenth century and later in the archives of the Daughters of the American Revolution.

The romance of border warfare notwithstanding, conventional military histories concentrate on the Continental Army, considering both the Indian warfare and militia actions between Loyalists and Patriots a distraction from the main events. This perspective conveniently edits out most women who fought in the Revolution. But there were women with the "real" armies as well.

As far as possible, Washington imitated British practices. He had help from a Prussian volunteer, Friedrich Wilhelm Ludolf Gerhard Augustin von Steuben, who was not the baron he claimed to be but who did know how to drill troops in the intricate maneuvers required in eighteenth-century European armies. American volunteers were eager to learn, and in addition to receiving Steuben's training, new officers studied maneuvers in books. Some Americans, including some women, had had military experience in the Seven Years' War, for armies in America required the services of camp followers just as did those in Europe.[13]

The commanders of the professional armies, English and Hessian, arranged for the transport of soldiers' wives to the American war by ship. These included the lower-class "trulls" who foraged for horses, stripped the dead in the aftermath of battle, and did the washing. The elegant baroness von Riedesel, wife of the Hessian general, also made the trip. She traveled with her three daughters, all of them under five, and during the war gave birth to a fourth child whom she christened America. For six years, she and the children, together with two women servants, followed the army. The baroness kept a detailed journal during the war, in which her contempt for the filthy habits of the American lower classes occasionally flashes out. But as a good military wife, she was not above getting her own hands dirty. On an occasion when both English and Hessian camp followers took refuge in a farmhouse during a battle that was going badly for their side, "Mrs. General," as she was known, directed its conversion into a makeshift hospital and supervised the operation.[14]

Rank was attached to officers' wives on the American side as well. The wives of the high-ranking American officers who came to camp experienced the war differently from those who marched behind the wagons. Martha Washington was proud to say that she had heard the first and last gun of every campaign of the war, and she spent the hard winter at Valley Forge. Lucy Knox, the wife of Gen. Henry Knox, remained with him both in camp and on the march, thoroughly enjoying military life.

Aristocratic British officers who went to war without their wives saw no objection to taking mistresses. In the eighteenth century adultery was fashionable for kings, dukes, counts, and others of high degree. Those of King George's generals who so wished followed the traditional upper-class practice of taking "camp wives," sometimes more than one. Such uninhibited behavior disgusted bourgeois Americans. The most notorious mistress was Gen. William Howe's "Mrs. Loring," whose husband raised no objection to her spending three years as Sir William's courtesan. Perhaps he was satisfied with his appointment as commissary general of prisoners, a position he was said to have used for his own enrichment while American prisoners died of starvation.[15]

American officers, with their middle-class Puritan attitudes, had none of the sophistication of contemporary Europeans and proudly remained faithful to their lawfully wedded wives. One American officer even hesitated to hire a washerwoman for fear it might compromise his virtuous reputation.[16]

Thousands of German, Irish, and English wives came with the armies of King George, and American girls with Loyalist sympathies joined their ranks. One of these was Jane McCrea, who unintentionally became a contributing factor in the stunning British defeat at Saratoga. Jane lived with her brother, a colonel in the American army, near Fort Edward in upstate New York. But she loved Lt. David Jones, a Loyalist serving in Gen. John Burgoyne's army, which was advancing south in the fall of 1777. As the British force approached Fort Edward, she refused to leave, expecting Lieutenant Jones to arrive so that she could marry him and follow the British flag. Unfortunately, Britain's Indian allies were the advance party for the main forces; they captured, tomahawked, and scalped Jane McCrea.

News of this atrocity spread though New York. New Yorkers who had previously been neutral now took up the Patriot cause in response to the outrage. And Loyalists now questioned the wisdom of supporting a cause that allowed Indian savages to murder even its friends in the civilian population. Burgoyne felt it necessary to reprove his Indian allies, who were already growing restless, with the result that they deserted in droves. As his dwindling army moved south, it was picked to pieces in small engagements with American forces, the kind that were typical of colonial warfare. On October 7, 1777, during the Battle of Bemis Heights, the wails and curses of American camp followers were heard over the gunfire. When the battle ended at sunset, they performed one of the traditional duties of camp followers, crawling over the battlefield and stripping the dead and dying of the clothing their own men could use when winter came. Ten days later the entire British force surrendered to the Americans at Saratoga—approximately eight thousand men, two thousand women, and an undetermined number of children.[17]

As the prisoners were marched into captivity, civilians, who had been spared most of the hardships of war, watched in amazement. A Boston woman wrote,

"I never had the least Idea that the Creation produced such a sordid set of creatures in human Figure—poor, dirty, emaciated men, great numbers of women, who seemed to be the beasts of burden, having a bushel basket on their back, by which they were bent double, the contents deemed to be Pots and Kettles, various sorts of Furniture, children peeping thro' gridirons and other utensils, some very young infants who were born on the road, the women bare feet, cloathed in dirty rags, such effluvia filld the air while they were passing, had they not been smoking all the time, I should have been apprehensive of being contaminated by them."[18]

Americans, of course, had a better opinion of their own army wives and recognized that a soldier's concern for his family was a legitimate concern for the army as well. Washington did not enforce the same strict quota on wives that was customary in European armies since he feared many of his soldiers would desert if their wives were not permitted to work for the army to support themselves and their children. Joseph Reed, governor of Pennsylvania, tried to persuade the executive council of the state to use gifts to the army women as a way to improve morale among the men and assure that they remained at their posts. "A new gown, silk handkerchief, and a pair of shoes, etc.," he wrote, "would be but little expense, and I think as a present from the State would have more effect than ten times the same laid out in articles for the men."[19]

Except for rejecting the quotas, Washington's orders regulating "women of the army" were similar to those of the British. As in Europe, the women were supervised by a sergeant. In an order dated September 1782, Washington directed, "As there are many orders for checking irregularities with which the women, as followers of the army, ought to be acquainted, the ser[g]eants of the companies to which the women belong, are to communicate all orders of that nature to them, and are to be responsible for neglecting to do so."[20] A recurring concern was about the baggage train slowing the march. As the war dragged on, large numbers of women and children became war refugees. Although there were never so many with the American army as with the British and Hessian forces, they became, in Washington's words, "a clog upon every movement."[21] Repeated orders to women not to ride in the wagons show that they continued to ride in them when they could, understandable behavior especially for women advanced in pregnancy or carrying small children.

Distinct from "women of the army," who were valuable to the army even if occasionally inconvenient, were those described as "lewd and disorderly." They did more than create a drag on the baggage train; they were seen as responsible for spreading venereal disease and encouraging alcohol abuse, and were suspected of spying for the enemy.

Surviving medical reports reveal that venereal disease posed a threat to combat readiness for American soldiers. In October 1778, Dr. John Cochran had twenty men sick with venereal disease at Fredericksburg, New York. In the summer of 1779, at West Point Dr. George Draper had twenty-five cases on August 2 and thirty-three on August 10. "General Return of the Sick and Wounded in the Military Hospitals," a report prepared by Dr. William Brown for the month of February 1780, recorded a total of 115 venereal disease patients. These figures are modest compared to those reported in other armies. Apparently American officers were aware of the potential danger but did not react with the flurry of orders and regulations that the British army directed against possibly infected women among those authorized to accompany the troops. Indeed, only one such order survives. On July 1, 1777, the commander of the Delaware regiment ordered, "That the Weomen belonging to the Regt. be paraded tomorrow morning & to undergo an examination from the Surgeon of the Regiment at his tent except those that are married, & the husbands of those to undergo said examination in their stead. All those that do not attend to be immediately drummed out of the Regiment." A few days later the regimental orderly book recorded, "Woman ducked and drumed out of camp for giving men venereal disease."[22]

Although regular army women might spread disease, professional prostitutes were more likely to be suspected of being the source of infection. The commander of a regiment encamped in New York in May 1776 ordered, "No Woman of Ill Fame Shall be permitted to Come into the Barricks on pain of Being well Watred under a pump, and Every Officer or Soldier who Shall Bring in Any Such woman will be tryd and Punished by a Court Martial."[23] But officers could not control the prostitutes who worked outside the camp; soldiers got into trouble when they went into town. An area in New York City known as the Holy Ground because the property was owned by Trinity Church was a notorious center for prostitution. An officer who visited "out of Curiosity" expressed his disgust in his diary:

During the Course of the last Week I several Times visited the Holy Ground, before described. When I visited them at first, I thought nothing could exceed them for impudence and immodesty; but I found the more I was

*acquainted with them the more they excelled in their Brutallity. To mention
the Particulars of their Behaviour would so pollute the Paper I write upon that
I must excuse myself. . . . [It] seems Strange that any man can so divest himself
of Manhood as to desire an intimate Connexion with these worse than brutal
Creatures, yet it is not more strange than true that many of our Officers &
Soldiers have been so imprudent as to follow them, notwithstanding the salu-
tary advice of their Friends, till the Fatal Disorder seized them & convinced
them of their Error.[24]*

He had heard that these "horrid Wretches" had infected forty men from
one regiment.[25] By the end of 1776, however, the city was in British hands,
and if the Holy Ground prostitutes were really as careless about their own
health as their American critics charged, at least they spread infection
among the redcoats for the rest of the war.[26]

Alcohol abuse was a more persistent problem. Camp followers were
expected to provide alcohol for the troops; it was a staple of all European
armies and considered a necessity. A soldier who had been on campaign with
Gen. James Wolfe in 1759 recalled the period prior to the attack on Quebec:
"The swarming flies, short rations, dysentery and scurvy were as plaguing as
the painted Red Indians, prowling around the old posts with tomahawks and
scalping knives. The only relief was in the almost lethal spirits provided by
the women sutlers."[27] But what was useful in moderation was harmful in
excess, so sutlers were subject to army regulations in their sales to soldiers
and could be banned from the camps and otherwise punished if they violat-
ed them.

Women gathering military intelligence and carrying messages are found
on both sides during the Revolution. They did not have to be with the army
to offer this kind of combat support. Sixteen-year-old Sybil Ludington made
a midnight ride in April 1777, passing the word to members of the local militia that the British were raiding Danbury, Connecticut. Pennsylvania Quaker
Lydia Darrah reported on conversations she overheard between the British
general William Howe and his staff when they boarded in her home. Women
selling alcohol and other merchandise in army camps had unmatched cover
for espionage and access to the most valuable information.

A sample of the kind of information sutlers might gather comes from
the British records that preserved intelligence reports. In 1778, one of their
best agents was a woman who sold "thread and other supplies" to

Washington's army. Between sales she wandered around outside the general's quarters, eavesdropping. On one mission from August 11 to August 15 she overheard officers debating the prospects for taking Long Island; she learned that two officers had taken light infantry to positions somewhere near Dobbs Ferry and that the Marquis de Lafayette had marched for Rhode Island with three thousand army troops and two thousand militia. Then she had a look at the artillery units and counted the equipment and had a chat with a friend who told her that a certain Captain James's whole company was ready to desert. Her report also included the information that on Thursday, August 13, the soldiers were given two months pay and as a result the whole army was drunk. She ventured the opinion that had the British attacked at that time, they could have destroyed the entire American army.[28]

Washington had women agents, too. One of these, who worked with a network on Long Island, is known only by the code name 355. When Benedict Arnold changed his allegiance and joined the British, her cover was destroyed. She was arrested and confined on the prison ship *Jersey* where she died five months later after bearing a child.[29]

Since the American War of Independence occurred at the time when women disguised as men were numerous in Europe and England, it is surprising at first glance to see how few disguised women left evidence of regular military service in the Continental Army. On the British side there is evidence of two women discovered while attempting to enlist,[30] and one female career soldier had a service record suggesting she may have fought at Bunker Hill, although that minor incident was not thought worthy of inclusion on her tombstone. Her grave marker in St. Nicholas Churchyard in Brighton, England, reads,

In memore of Phoebe Hessel, born Stepney 1713. Served for many years as a private soldier in the 5th Regiment of Foot in different parts of Europe. In the year 1745 she fought under the Command of the Duke of Cumberland at the Battle of Fontenoy, where she received a bayonet wound in her arm. Her long life, which commenced in the time of Queen Anne extended to the Reign of George IV, by whose munificence she received comfort and support in her latter years. Died at Brighton, where she had long resided, 12 December, 1821. Aged 108 years.[31]

According to a sergeant of the 13th Light Dragoons, Hessel's military service ended when, after committing a misdemeanor, she was " brought to the halberts to be whipped, and, having her neck and shoulders bare, her sex was discovered. Her answer was 'Strike and be damned.'" No additional punishment was ordered for her masquerade; indeed, as her obituary indicates, she received the usual pension for her years of service.[32]

Americans knew about such soldiers at the time of the Revolution even though Phoebe kept her cover until after the war ended. People in Boston, New York, and other cities read occasional accounts in their newspapers of women "discovered" in the ranks or on shipboard during European wars. Biographies of Hannah Snell and other women soldier celebrities were sold in American bookshops, and Americans bought reprints of broadsides and sang the songs about "bold, bonny lasses" that were so popular in London.

Of the tiny number of American women known to have served in the American military, two came to light because they got into trouble. In 1777, a woman in uniform was formally drummed out of the 1st New Jersey Regiment, driven "threw the town with the whores march beating." And financial chicanery rather than sexual misbehavior put an end to the career of the highest-ranking woman known to have served in the American army. "Samuel Gay" made such a good first impression on her officers that she was promoted to corporal immediately after enlisting in a Massachusetts regiment on February 14, 1777. In less than three weeks, however, she deserted and her captain swore out a warrant for her arrest: "Please take into your custody Nancy Bailey who dressed herself in mens Cloths, inlisted as a Soldier in my company in Col. Patterson's Reg. Rec'd fifteen pounds & ten shillings Bounty from this State and then absented herself." In due course she was apprehended and charged with "the Offense of having appeared in Man's Apparel" and with having taken the bounty money from the state. The trial did not take place until August, when Bailey, now identified as Ann rather than Nancy, was found guilty, fined, and sentenced to two months in prison. At this point she was also put out of the army. Her service record in the National Archives states, "Discharged. being a woman, dressed in mens cloths Aug 1777."[33]

The other women known to have worn the uniform served with more distinction. A number of these used their own names on muster lists or petitions for pensions, suggesting that Americans may have been so familiar with women moving into male roles in time of need that the practice was tolerated. After all, a society that praised women for scalping Indians is unlikely to have been overly squeamish about having a few kill English soldiers with bayonets. But some women apparently sustained a disguise. It is impossible to estimate their number. Sally St. Clair, a Creole woman, was found to be female only after her death at the Battle of Savannah. "Two females" recruited for the 2d South Carolina Regiment were never named and left no further record. Women soldiers who survived the war and did not seek government pensions are untraceable.[34]

Still, when all is said and done, the numbers are surprisingly small. There are two possible explanations. One is that despite the high visibility of Washington's army in the history books, most of the fighting during the American Revolution was small scale and local; women who had patriotic motives for military activity did not have to join the Continental Army to take part. The other explanation is that America did not have a social class as impoverished as that which provided soldiers for European armies. In the seventeenth century, after the end of the Thirty Years War, professionalized royal regiments came into existence. Joining these, soldiers lost their individuality. They were no longer free to select their own uniforms, for instance, and they were put under such firm discipline that Keegan describes it as a "military slave system."[35] The attraction for recruits was the security military life offered. Kings and queens were always waging wars, so lifetime employment was guaranteed. The Continental Army, by contrast, was mustered for an emergency; Americans continued to be hostile to standing armies and expected to demobilize when peace came. Thus there was little economic incentive for women to enlist.

Only one American woman deliberately courted celebrity and sought out financial recompense for military service as so many European women soldiers and sailors had done. Deborah Samson[36] enlisted under the name Robert Shurtleff or Shirtliff on May 20, 1782, seven months after Charles Cornwallis surrendered at Yorktown, and was discharged on October 25, 1783. She collaborated with one Horace Mann on a fictionalized autobiography that was published in 1797 under the title *The Female Review: Life of Deborah Sampson [sic] the Female Soldier in the War of the Revolution.* Deborah married a farmer named Banjamin Gannett in 1785, and after that she was officially Deborah Gannett. But with the publication of Mann's book, the extra *p* crept into her maiden name and has remained there in writing about her ever since. *The Female Review* enjoyed only modest success, but a few years later Mann again tried to write a script for her and organize a lecture tour. Beginning in March 1802, she appeared in several

New England towns, including Boston, and in New York City. After delivering Mann's dramatized, apologetic account of her history, she would finish off by performing the manual of arms. She also pursued veterans' benefits vigorously, collecting references from her former officers. She succeeded in winning back pay from the state of Massachusetts and a small pension from the federal government but none of the lavish gifts sometimes presented to fortunate women in European armies. After her death her husband successfully petitioned for benefits for himself and three children on the basis of his wife's military service. Ironically, this one woman soldier who clearly wanted to be known and remembered has to this day had no serious biographer to reveal the real woman behind the media hype created by her pursuit of fame and fortune.[37]

MOLLY PITCHER

We cannot leave the discussion of women in the Revolution without mentioning the one who is the best known of all American military heroines. As England has Boadicea and France has Joan of Arc, the United States has Molly Pitcher. Perhaps it says something about America's scant contact with war that the woman memorialized on posters, postage stamps, and a rest stop on the New Jersey Turnpike was not a real person at all but a mythic figure constructed by artists and writers many years after the war.

Every third grader has heard the story of the woman who courageously took over an artillery position when her husband fell. The story has endless variations, often including a cameo appearance by George Washington who gives her either a gold coin in one version or a whole hatful of gold coins, or a promotion to sergeant or captain. The birth and growth of the Molly Pitcher legend is a fascinating story in itself,[38] as it illustrates the double standard of evidence applied to the mythology of women heroines as opposed to actual history. Should a writer assert the reality of Amazons or of Soviet women fighter pilots in World War II or of women Viet Cong officers, the level of evidence demanded by skeptics soars to the impossible. But if a writer is content to tell a pretty story without insisting that it is as true as war stories told about men, poetic license is easily granted, leaving writers free to exercise their imaginations with total disregard of documentary evidence or even common sense. Anyone with knowledge of the Battle of Monmouth, where Molly Pitcher is said to have had her moment of glory, knows that on that day George Washington had other things on his mind. Indeed, he was in a towering rage, in no mood for polite chitchat with a soldier's wife.[39]

In 1981, in one of my earliest forays into women's military history, I speculated that Molly Pitcher was a generic name used to describe any woman of the army.[40] After more than twenty years of searching, however, I have not been able to find a single contemporary use of the sobriquet. I now believe Molly Pitcher was entirely a postwar invention. The heroine of the Battle of Monmouth first appears as "Captain Molly" in patriotic prints and not until 1848, seventy years after the battle, did Nathaniel Currier produce the first print of a woman identified as "Molly Pitcher." The first written mention of the heroine, in 1851, also called her "Captain Molly," and "Molly Pitcher" was not named in a book until 1859.[41]

Artists would not have to reach far for the image of a woman at a cannon. Ever since the introduction of artillery pieces for the defense of fortifications, women under siege could be found carrying powder, shot, and water and sometimes helping load or fire the weapons. The role fit in with traditional women's activities during sieges when they had thrown tiles or rocks or burning oil to repel attacks. In North America, a famous heroine was Madame de La Tour who served at artillery in New Brunswick's Fort La Tour in the 1640s. Another was Madame Drucour, wife of the governor of Louisbourg, who, during a siege in 1758, several times appeared on the ramparts to fire a cannon. In the United States a number of folk heroines were remembered, if not widely celebrated, following the Amercian Revolution. A soldier's wife was supposed to have fired the last shot in the defense of Fort Clinton, New York, in October 1777, and the Library of Congress has an early-nineteenth-century engraving labeled "A Soldier's wife at Fort Niagara" depicting a woman loading shot in a cannon. But the most famous example of a woman at a cannon was Agostina of Saragossa, whom we will meet later in this chatper. She was celebrated by many artists, and an engraving made from a romanticized painting owned by the British royal family was widely distributed. Showing the heroine of Saragossa in a flowing gown rather than in the military uniform she actually wore, it bears a suspicious resemblance to portraits of Molly Pitcher.

The figure of a Revolutionary War woman at a cannon was not identified with a specific person until 1876 when certain citizens of Carlisle, Pennsylvania, decided to claim her as a local heroine. The spark was an article by one Wesley Miles, a middle-aged gentleman who published his recollections six weeks before the great centennial celebration on July 4. He remembered an Irishwoman, Mrs. Mary Hays McCauley, who worked for his father when he was a child. (McCauley's granddaughter said her grandmother had been German—"Dutch as sauerkraut"—but no matter.)[42] He remembered her funeral, he said. She was buried with military honors by the volunteer companies, but no marker was placed on the grave. Miles concluded his piece with a startling revelation: "Reader, the subject of this reminiscence is a prototype of the 'Maid of Saragossa.' The heroine of Monmouth, Molly Pitcher."[43]

A local fraternal organization, Patriotic Order of the Sons of America, took up the cause and on July 4, 1876, placed a marker on the grave of "Mollie Pitcher," taking it on faith that Mr. Miles had picked out the right one and without taking time for any further research. (The Carlisle centennial coup reminds one of another display of Pennsylvania civic pride, which succeeded in convincing Americans that Pauxatawny Pete is the "real" groundhog of Groundhog's Day.) After the grave marker had been placed, a local historian, John B. Landis, conducted interviews with elderly citizens—who now knew all about the centennial ceremony and had encouragement to remember things they may never have remembered before. Eventually the Patriotic Order published his book about the heroine of Monmouth. Not everyone in Carlisle approved of the new Molly Pitcher cult. Jeremiah Zeamer, a respected genealogist, spent years attacking Landis's flawed and distorted research, but no one wanted to hear his pedantic objections to the legitimacy of the new homegrown heroine.[44]

Although no one called her Molly Pitcher in her lifetime, Mary Hays McCauley, who lived in Carlisle after the Revolution, had probably served in a military role during the war. The evidence for her wartime service is a pension granted to her by the state of Pennsylvania in 1822. McCauley made her application for a pension simply as "widow of a soldier" of the Revolutionary War, and the bill granting the request went through three readings in the Pennsylvania Senate and two readings in the Pennsylvania House without amendment. Then, with no explanation, the phrase "for services rendered" was substituted for "widow of a soldier" before it passed into law.

When McCauley died, the Carlisle newspaper *American Volunteer* published an obituary. The notice mentioned her pension but said nothing about what "service" she had performed to deserve it. The only hint of what that service might have been appears in a New York newspaper article published a few weeks after the approval of her Pennsylvania pension petition. The news story makes no mention of the Battle of Monmouth or of a cannon but presents quite a different picture of the woman who would become Carlisle's local heroine: "Molly Macauly [sic], who received a pension from the State of Pennsylvania for service rendered during the Revolutionary War, was well-known to the general officers as a brave and patriotic woman. She was called Sgt. McCauly [sic] and was wounded at some battle, supposed to be the Brandywine, where her sex was discovered. . . . "[45]

This sole contemporary reference to Mrs. McCauley's role in the war adds the observation, "It was not an unusual circumstance to find women in the ranks disguised as men, such was their ardor for independence," and "It would be interesting to collect anecdotes of the services rendered by women during the revolutionary war."[46]

The image of Molly Pitcher has never been that of a woman in male dress. Indeed, the early versions of the story from Landis, who was sensitive to Victorian sensibilities, insists that she was not even a true camp follower but merely a loving wife who happened to be visiting her husband at the time of the battle.

The Patriotic Order of the Sons of America did not stop with marking the McCauley grave. Once the local woman was formally identified with the Molly Pitcher heroine, fictionalized documentation proliferated. A cannon appeared by the grave in 1905, a supplement to the display purchased by the Patriotic Order from the Watertown Arsenal in Massachusetts; it was soon assumed to be Molly's cannon at Monmouth. During World War I, the Commonwealth of Pennsylvania paid for a much larger monument, topped by a statue of a woman holding a ramrod. And a huge monument erected at the Monmouth battlefield has a bronze bas-relief on the base showing Molly at her cannon. Ponderous debate continues to this day about the precise location of the well or stream from which she procured the water. Someone even contributed an elaborately decorated Victorian pitcher to the Carlisle historical society, declaring that it had belonged to Mary Hays McCauley and was presumably the actual vessel used by her on the battle-field.[47]

Exposing the weak historical basis of the McCauley myth should not be taken as proof that there were no women at the June 1778 Battle of

Monmouth or that no American woman served with artillery during that battle. Two men present at Monmouth mentioned women in combat during the battle: one was observed helping to pass ammunition at an artillery position, and the other stepped into her husband's place in an infantry formation.[48]

There is firm evidence placing another woman, Margaret Corbin, at an artillery position at the Battle of Fort Washington in Manhattan in November 1776. Both the state of Pennsylvania and the Continental Congress awarded her pensions for that service in 1779, although these documents did not become generally known until the twentieth century. Corbin died in about 1800, although it is not certain where. There is some evidence suggesting that she died in Westmoreland County in Pennsylvania; others believe she ended her life in Highland Falls, New York. The unmarked grave in New York was identified by the Daughters of the American Revolution during the sesquicentennial of American Independence in 1926. The patriotic Daughters arranged for reinterment of the remains at West Point. The marker honors Margaret Corbin, who was a real Revolutionary War military heroine, but the remains beneath the stone may be those of a different army woman.[49]

Neither Margaret Corbin nor any of the other real women who fought in the American Revolution became as famous as Molly Pitcher. Other nations have based their symbols of female heroism on real historical figures. Americans created theirs from artifacts of popular culture. Perhaps that was just as well, for those who recorded recollections of women serving with the revolutionary armies recalled some details not likely to inspire later generations. For example, the early collector of Revolutionary War oral histories, Benjamin F. Lossing, presented a version of the Molly Pitcher story in which he associated the heroine of Monmouth with "Dirty Kate," who lived near Fort Montgomery in New York after the war and "died a horrible death from the effects of a syphilitic disease."[50] The "Captain Molly" who died in New York was remembered as a disagreeable eccentric, wearing a cast-off soldier's coat and living on public charity.[51] Mary McCauley was no Victorian heroine either. Peter Spahr, an elderly citizen of Carlisle, said she was "a very masculine person, alike rough in appearance and character; small and heavy with bristles in her nose, and could both drink whiskey and swear." Wesley Miles wrote that she was "prone to indulge in passion and profanity," and her granddaughter remembered that "she drank grog and used language not the most polite." Harriet Foulk recalled, "[She was] a vulgar profane, drunken old woman. . . . I was afraid of her; she was so uncouth, really vulgar, very profane, was homely, yes ugly and gray."[52] The Molly Pitcher legend presents a much prettier picture for schoolchildren being introduced to the topic of women in war.

THE FRENCH REVOLUTION

THE SIGNIFICANCE OF THE American War of Independence for military history lay in the heavy dependence on guerrilla tactics. The importance of this innovation, however, was not obvious at the time; even George Washington was more embarrassed than gratified by the unconventional activities of American "militia." Immediately apparent, however, was the ideological importance of the war. Although the ideas of European as well as English philosophers had influenced the development of the colonial perspective on "self-evident" truth, it was the Americans who first acted on the abstract arguments to overthrow the government. As Lafayette and other European volunteers returned home, the experience they had with the Americans' successful application of the doctrines of the "rights of man" and government legitimized by "the consent of the governed" went with them. As a French secret agent in England before his gender switch, the Chevalier d'Eon helped arrange for the king of France to send secret assistance to the American rebels. Scarcely a dozen years later, revolutionary ideas ignited the French people. They rose up and toppled the monarchy.

The hereditary rulers in the rest of Europe watched in horror and then declared war on the French Republic to halt the spread of its political perversion. The Revolution grew increasingly radical. The execution of King Louis XVI and Queen Marie Antoinette was followed by the executions of other French aristocrats and then counterrevolutionaries, many of whom had supported the Revolution before the bloody Reign of Terror. Continuing political upheaval and war brought Napoleon Bonaparte to power. He then revolutionized warfare as thoroughly as American thinkers had revolutionized political ideology.

The French celebrate July 14, 1789, as the start of their Revolution. On that day Théroigne de Méricourt, a singer and wealthy courtesan, put her theatrical talents into the service of the popular cause, dressing as an Amazon and leading a mob in storming the infamous Bastille. Only a few women participated in that action, although once the crowd was victorious, "an inconceivable number of women, children and old people . . . seemed to burst out of the houses, crying 'there they are, the villains, we've got them.'"[53]

But if women were peripheral on July 14, they were the center of the action during the October Days three months later. The trouble began on the morning of October 5, 1789, when, according to a newspaper account, a young market woman began beating a drum in the streets and crying out about the scarcity of bread.[54] A crowd of fishwives, shopkeepers, and peddlers assembled, and children were sent with a bugle and a bell to round up more. Those who turned out were like most women volunteering for military activity, either very young or over fifty; mothers of young children did not think it right to put themselves at risk if it could be avoided. Soon thousands of women were marching in a driving rain to the royal palace at Versailles. The women were armed: some with knives and swords strapped over their skirts, a few with pikes or muskets, but most carrying brooms and kitchen tools. They also dragged two cannons, although they had no ammunition for the pieces, and a soldier from the National Guard was persuaded to march at their head to demonstrate their serious intentions. The National Guard itself followed at a distance. The goal of the marchers was to force the king to return to Paris, and in this they succeeded, returning in a triumphal procession with the heads of two of the king's bodyguards on pikes and loaves of bread on staves.

As the rebellion spread, groups of women continued their aggressive activity. It is important to avoid the temptation to conflate all women into a single group. Even among Parisian women supporting the Revolution, there was considerable variety based on class rather than gender. Those women of the Third Estate practicing specialized trades—dressmaking, embroidery, and millinery—petitioned the king, wanting most of all free education as acknowledgment that women were not intellectually inferior and the stigmatization of prostitutes:

> We would wish this class of woman [prostitutes] to wear a distinctive emblem. Since nowadays they even go so far as to ape the modesty of our garb, and since they mingle with us, wearing any and every kind of dress, we often find ourselves being confused with them; some men have been mistaken and their error has caused us to blush. We ask that these women be obliged

always to wear this emblem, under pain of being forced to work in the public workshops.[55]

The prostitutes did not pen petitions, but they took political action. In a famous episode a band of Parisian prostitutes used weapons and sex in an effort to turn the loyalty of a detachment of royal cavalry. Brandishing pistols, they ordered the soldiers to cry "Death to the king!" and added, "We're all yours if you join the Revolution!" When the soldiers refused, an eyewitness described how a young girl of no more than sixteen began to dance before the troopers in the street:

She had bared her breasts and was holding them in the palms of her hands, while she deliberately waggled her posterior like a duck. The other women immediately made a rush at her and lifted up her clothing, revealing to the blushing cavalrymen the prettiest figure imaginable, at the same time exclaiming, "If you'd like a taste of that, just shout 'Death to the King!' first!"[56]

The disorder in France alarmed monarchs in the rest of Europe. As the threat of intervention by foreign armies developed, Frenchwomen looked to their opportunities for self-defense. Pauline Léon, who would lead the Society of Revolutionary Republican Women, and two hundred other women signed a petition asking for the establishment of a women's militia. "We only wish to defend ourselves the same as you," she told the male members of the National Assembly. "You cannot refuse us, and society cannot deny the right nature gives us, unless you pretend the Declaration of Rights does not apply to women, and that they should let their throats be cut like lambs, without the right to defend themselves." Women also had a right to share in the honor and glory of a righteous war, she insisted, and "of making tyrants see that women also have blood to shed for the service of the fatherland in danger."[57]

A year later, Méricourt proposed establishing a women's battalion, a company of amazons. She saw this as the only way to assure extension to women of full rights as citizens. Now, she said, was the time "for women to break out of the shameful incompetence in which men's ignorance, pride, and injustice have so long held us captive."[58] In April 1793, the French National Convention ruled against women soldiers. Although, as we shall see, individual women managed to serve anyway, formation of an all-female force with formal recognition of women as capable of bearing arms as a duty of citizenship was denied.[59]

Nevertheless, this would have been an appropriate time to open military service to women. The French revolutionary army was a new kind of organization. In place of the professional standing armies of the past, France developed a national army based on conscription. Citizen Carnot, speaking for the Committee of Public Safety, which was responsible for enforcing the draft, wrote, "Henceforth, the Republic is a great city in a state of siege: France must become one vast camp and Paris its arsenal." The law mobilized everyone, including women and children. But all women, whatever their physical abilities or preferences of service might be, were drafted only to "make tents and clothing and work in hospitals." Children were to "turn old linen into bandages."[60]

Not all of the French king's former subjects were enthusiastic about revolution. Indeed, for more than two years beginning in March 1793, there was violent insurrection in the western part of France known as the Vendée. In the eighteenth century, this was an isolated region with undeveloped roads and an undeveloped economy. The peasant population was conservative, and the conscription decree combined with the atrocity of the king's execution roused them to a revolution of their own directed against the Republic. What followed was a bloody internal conflict.

Tens of thousands of Vendéans formed separate armies led by a handful of generals, whose early victories against the French national army brought murderous retaliation. On August 1, 1793, the Convention decreed that the Vendée should be destroyed, a decree of genocide. The war that followed saw the murder of civilians, rape, and bayoneting of children to save gunpowder. Republican soldiers slaughtered livestock, cut down trees, and razed villages so that tens of thousands of people were left homeless. The people fought back—all of the people. When the fighting was over, some women wanted to downplay their involvement. Mme de la Rochejaquelein wrote in her memoirs that women were seen "rallying, encouraging the soldiers, but not fighting." Women and children threw stones at Republican soldiers and were then taken prisoner and killed, but that, she asserts, "is very different from the rumor spread by the enemy that we marched, like new Amazons, to the war."[61] But elsewhere in her memoirs she gives a different picture. Some women did, in fact, fight and did so mounted astride on horseback (*en amazone*). Others fought on foot with rifles and swords as well as with farming implements and other makeshift weapons. Women were active as messengers, guards, jailers, and munitions carriers. And, as always, they were nurses and sutlers.

But Mme de la Rochejaquelein had also seen Renée Bordereau, who served in the cavalry and whose "unbelievable courage was celebrated throughout the whole army." La Rochejaquelein remembered her as "of ordinary height and very ugly." Those who pointed her out said, "See that soldier who has sleeves of a color different from his coat. That's a girl who fights like a lion."[62] After the war Bordereau, who was illiterate, dictated her memoirs, which were published as a pamphlet. She bluntly explains her motives for going to war at the age of twenty-four: "I saw forty-two of my relatives perish successively; but the murder of my father, committed before my very eyes, filled me with rage and despair. From this moment on, I resolved to sacrifice my body to the King, to offer my soul to God, and I swore to fight until death or victory."[63] There are some grounds for believing that women were the special targets of Republican forces during this genocidal war. Bordereau was sensitive to the situation of women and was proud to act as their protector. She recalled one incident in which she led a force to a town: "[There] the enemy was going to massacre 800 women at 8:00 in the morning; we arrived at 7:30, delivered all of those unfortunate women from destruction, and won a total victory." Remembering this day's fighting, Bordereau said, "I declare that I never fought with such ardor. . . . [T]he republicans' ferocity had transported me with rage, and I killed two of them at the same time, one with a pistol shot and another with a blow from my sword."[64]

THE NAPOLEONIC WARS

IN SOME PLACES THE Vendéans continued to resist the French until July 1796. By this time the French revolutionary government had passed through a period of terror in which many of the early revolutionary leaders died and the government known as the Directory was in power. By this time, too, Napoleon Bonaparte, who became one of the greatest military leaders of all time, was leading French troops against Italian and Austrian armies. Two years later he led an attack on Great Britain's Indian empire by way of Egypt. Before the century closed, the Ottoman Empire of the Turks and Russia and Great Britain together with Austria, Naples, and Portugal were allied against

France; and in December 1799 the French form of government changed yet again. Napoleon, with the title first consul, became the dictator of France.

Napoleon was born in Corsica, where custom sanctioned the participation of women in war.[65] His mother had been active during a Corsican revolt against Genoa led by Pasquale Paoli. She spoke freely of her wartime exploits to her sons, dwelling particularly on the retreat to Monte Rotondo after the final Corsican debacle at Ponte Novo in May 1769. Six months pregnant with Napoleon, with a year-old child in her arms, they had a hard ride through rugged, barely inhabited country. She used to tell Napoleon that she had been prepared to give birth to him in a cave.[66]

Under Napoleon the French army swelled to a strength of over half a million. An armed force of this magnitude had not been seen in Europe for centuries. An uncounted number of women marched, as usual, with the troops. Americans who read the war news from across the Atlantic learned of the great battles and famous generals, but the newspapers paid no attention to the camp followers who suffered and endured infinitely more in these years than the survivors of Saratoga who had so disgusted the women of Boston two decades earlier.

French military regulations, like those of all European armies, attempted to maximize the work contributions of camp followers while minimizing the drag on the baggage train. An ordinance of 1801 reads, "No women shall accompany the corps except those employed as washerwomen, vendors of victuals and drink. The number of women accompanying each battalion may not under any pretext whatsoever, exceed four, with two for each squadron." Since under such strict quotas, not every soldier could bring his wife, the commander of the brigade was to choose from those married to petty officers or soldiers' wives who would be "most agile and useful to the corps" and "whose conduct and morals are known to be most regular." This drawdown of the baggage train forced many women to leave their husbands while in the middle of a war zone. The army gave them twenty centimes per mile to return home, and they were forbidden to approach within four miles of the army. Those authorized to remain received certificates and identification cards that they wore on their chests. The upper margin bore the name of the army, for instance, "Armeé d'Allemagne." On the second line, the woman's occupation was inscribed, and at the bottom of the badge was a registration number.[67]

Napoleon's army suffered its greatest hardship in 1812 when his attempt to invade Russia ended with a miserable winter retreat across icy fields. One soldier's memoirs described women fainting from hunger, fighting over a piece of horsemeat, and their desperation during the crossing of the Beresina River as they rushed after their drowning children, holding them tightly until both mother and child sank under the water. A German military surgeon recalled that the Russians captured three hundred women, girls, and children during that crossing and lodged them together in a filthy deserted building. The building caught fire, and most of the occupants burned to death.[68]

France's defense of its revolution early turned into campaigns of aggression. In the face of French invasions, civilian populations outside of France resisted, just as the Vendéan rebels had done. Between 1808 and 1814, the British fought the French in Portugal and Spain in what was called the Peninsular War. It was during these campaigns that the Spanish gave the name guerrilla warfare to the technique of small-scale fighting in which civilian combatants take up arms.

Napoleon sent one hundred thousand troops into Spain in March 1808, and by June only the town of Saragossa stood against him. The siege of that city produced a heroine, who quickly became famous both in Europe and in America. Ellen C. Clayton, who produced a two-volume compendium of military women in 1879, wrote of her, "Next to Joan of Arc, the Maid of Saragossa is the most famous female warrior that ever lived."[69] Unlike Molly Pitcher, who was frequently compared to her by Americans, the heroism of Agostina at Saragossa is thoroughly documented. It was witnessed by a great many people and recorded by many contemporary writers. The poet Lord Byron and the artist Francisco Goya took her as a subject. The woman herself lived a long life during which she was acclaimed and praised by both Spaniards and their British allies, and when she died she was buried with military honors in a clearly marked grave.

Agostina did not seek fame but reacted to circumstances when her town was besieged. Saragossa faced an army of 12,000 with only about 220 soldiers to defend it. A poorly constructed wall, intersected by private dwellings and ten ancient artillery pieces, was all that stood between the people in the town and the French attackers. The women of Saragossa turned out to play their customary roles in defending against siege, forming companies of two or three hundred each and supporting the soldiers at the guns by carrying wine to the men and water to swab out the cannon.

The French broke through the wall on June 28 and killed all the men at artillery positions. Both Lord Byron and Robert Southey, the English poet laureate, assumed that one of the men at the cannon had been Agostina's lover, but that touch was probably poetic license. At any rate, the people saw her go to the ramparts, take a lighted match from the hand of a fallen soldier, and fire the artillery piece he had failed to set off before he died. Not stopping there, she reloaded the cannon and fired again. Her example inspired others. They put up such a good fight that the French decided not to storm the town but to keep up their bombardment and the siege for a few days. Eventually they made a second attempt, and the civilians resisted them in street fighting. Agostina was in the thick of the action. Finally, after eleven days, the French gave up.

General Palafox, the duke of Saragossa, asked Agostina to choose her own reward. She asked to continue as an artillery captain, with the pay and pension and right to wear the uniform, and to be permitted to wear the arms of Saragossa and to take the name of the town as her surname. The general gave her what she asked for, plus a number of medals.

Sir John Carr met the Maid of Saragossa the following year. He wrote,

> *The day before I was introduced to this extra-ordinary female, she had been entertained at dinner by Admiral Purvis on board his flagship. . . . The admiral considered her as a military character, and much to his credit, received her with the honors of that profession. Upon her reaching the deck, the marines were drawn up and manoeuvred before her. She appeared quite at home, regarding them with a steady eye, and speaking in terms of admiration of their neatness, and soldier-like appearance. Upon examining the guns, she observed of one of them, as other women would speak of a cap, "My gun," alluding to one with which she had effected a considerable havoc among the French at Saragossa, "was not so nice and clean as this."*[70]

Although Agostina was the most famous heroine of the Peninsular War, women fought in defense of all the Spanish towns besieged by the French, just as women had fought in all nations. The best known, for obvious reasons, are those like Agostina who might wear male clothing but were not actually attempting to conceal their gender. Others are known who tried to conceal their identities, failed, but continued in the service anyway. Still others died with the secret intact and became noteworthy only because their death in battle revealed their sex. In *Swords Around a Throne*, John R. Elting writes, "Probably every major battle of these wars left women sprawled among the casualties."[71] Those who kept their secret out of public record and returned to a female identity after the wars are impossible to trace.

An example in the first category, a woman who served openly, is Angélique Brûlon, who campaigned in Corsica from 1792 to 1799. She wore male clothing, but she was known as a soldier's daughter, a soldier's sister, and a soldier's widow. She demonstrated competence as a soldier, so there was no attempt to discharge her on grounds of gender. She advanced in the service from fusilier to corporal, lance corporal, and sergeant major. Brûlon retired in 1799 only after being badly wounded at the siege of Calvi. The soldiers called her Liberté the Fusilier, and those under her command composed the following tribute: "We the garrison at Calvi certify that Marie-Angélique Josephine Duchemin veuve Brûlon, acting sergeant, commanding the attack of Fort Gesco, fought with us with the courage of a heroine." They went on to praise her skill in hand-to-hand combat, noting that when she took a sword cut on her right arm she continued to fight with a dagger in her left hand. The wound put her into the Invalides, but in 1822, at the age of fifty-one, she was promoted to the rank of lieutenant on the retired list. Napoleon III awarded her the red ribbon of the French Legion of Honor, and she proudly wore her uniform until her death in 1859.[72]

Only one woman who served openly as a French soldier during the wars is known to have preserved her own story. Thérése Figueur, like Renée Bordereau, dictated her memoirs because she could not write. In 1793, she enlisted as a dragoon and continued in service until 1815. Her fellow soldiers knew she was a woman, but because they respected her as a soldier no attempt was made to discharge her. She was wounded half a dozen times and taken prisoner once, but after the wars she could not get care in military hospitals, and petitions for award of the Legion of Honor were denied her because of her sex.[73]

Examples of women who attempted to maintain a disguise and failed are Félicité and Théophile de Fernig, whose father was commandant of a National Guard unit. Félicité was twenty-two, and Théophile was seventeen. With the help of other soldiers, they dressed in uniform and joined their father's unit. The disguise held for only a few days because General de Beurnonville, a friend of their father's, suspected them. Then despite faces smeared with smoke and lips blackened by bullet cartridges torn open with their teeth, they had to confess their deceit. De Fernig made a command decision; his daughters stayed on duty. As a home guard unit, de Fernig's force fought invading Austrians with rusty sabers and old-fashioned blunderbusses. Félicité's greatest moment came when she rode in a cavalry charge by the side of the duc de Chartres: Théophile's most significant achievement was capturing a Hungarian major. According to General de Beurnonville, "The Fernig girls were very capable of killing their men."[74]

Those women who were taken for men until their last days usually left no trace beyond their burial markers. A Prussian woman who served in a rifle unit is memorialized thus: "Ellonora Prochaska, known as one of the Lutzow Rifle Volunteers, by the name of Augustus Renz, born at Potzdam on the 11th March, 1785, received a fatal wound in the battle of Göhrde on the 15th September, 1813, died at Dannenberg on the 5th October, 1813. She fell exclaiming:—'Herr Lieutenant, I am a woman!'"[75]

Generally the women who served in the ranks were good soldiers, and had they been male, they would have been unremarkable. Common soldiers do not go down in history when they merely do their duty. Officers are a different matter; their lives leave traces in permanent records whether they like it or not. A Russian woman who served in the wars against Napoleon for nine years performed even greater service a quarter of a century later when she wrote her memoirs based on journals she had kept during her military career.

Nadezhda Durova published *The Cavalry Maiden* in 1836. One of the first autobiographies published in Russia, her book tells how she ran away from home disguised as a boy and joined the Russian cavalry using the name Aleksandr Sokolov. She did so, she later wrote, to escape the "sphere prescribed by nature and custom to the female sex."[76] Her disguise was not very convincing, and the discovery that Sokolov was female resulted in a report to Tsar Alexander I, accompanied by her service record and a strong recommendation from the general in command of her regiment:

> *Major-General Kachowski, praising his willingness to serve and the diligence and promptness with which he carried out all the tasks at hand while taking part in many battles with the French army, earnestly requests that he be left in the regiment as the kind of noncommissioned officer who gives every hope of becoming with time a very good officer; in addition Sokolov himself has expressed a most decided desire to remain always in the army.*[77]

Durova also had the opportunity to make her appeal directly to Alexander, "hugging the emperor's knees and weeping" as she begged him not to send her home. She wrote,

The emperor was moved. He raised me to my feet and asked in an altered voice, "What is it you want then?"

"To be a warrior! To wear a uniform and bear arms! That is the only reward you can give me, sire! For me there is no other. I was born in an army camp. The sound of trumpets was my lullaby. From the day of my birth I have loved the military calling; by the age of ten I was devising ways to enlist; at sixteen I reached my goal—alone, without help from anyone! I held that glorious post through my courage alone, without patronage or subsidy from anyone. And now, Your Majesty, you want to send me home! If I had foreseen such an end, nothing could have prevented me from seeking a glorious death in the ranks of your warriors." I said all this with my arms crossed as if before an ikon, looking at the emperor with tear-filled eyes.

The emperor listened to me, trying in vain to conceal how moved he was. After I finished speaking, he spent a minute or two in evident indecision; at last his face brightened. "If you presume," said the emperor, "that permission to wear a uniform and bear arms is your only possible reward, you shall have it!"[78]

The young soldier went back to her regiment.

Years later, one of the men who served with her recalled, "There was talk at the time that Aleksandrov was a woman, but only in passing. After all, there was a war going on and more important things to think about. I saw her at the front . . . in all the difficult duties of the time, but I didn't pay much attention to her; there was no time to worry about whether she was of male or female gender. That grammatical category was forgotten about then."[79]

CHAPTER SIX

NINETEENTH-CENTURY WARFARE

C HANGES IN WARFARE IN the era of the American and French revolutions may have astounded contemporaries, but they were dwarfed by what would come in the following decades. The armies of Napoleon resembled those of Alexander the Great more than those that fought the American Civil War. The industrial revolution followed the political revolutions, and the American inventor Eli Whitney pioneered techniques for mass-producing interchangeable parts to produce firearms. Improvements in the sniper rifle of the American Revolution made it a standard infantry weapon that took over the battlefield and made Napoleonic tactics obsolete.

Tragically, military doctrine did not keep pace with military technology. Hard lessons were learned slowly as the great slaughters, first in the Crimea and then on Civil War battlefields, demonstrated that mass frontal attacks and shock weapons like bayonets and sabers were less useful than they had been formerly. Infantry with rifles had tremendous effective firepower, giving the defensive position a great advantage. For centuries soldiers had cultivated the virtue of courage, enabling them to advance to meet the enemy head on. Such courageous advances now led not to victory but to inglorious suicide.

The transportation revolution also changed traditional assumptions about time, distance, and logistics. Soldiers still marched, but in many cases they could ride instead, resting and even sleeping instead of exhausting themselves and draining their energy weeks before there was any prospect of meeting an enemy. Railroads and steamships could also supplement the baggage train; supplies could be carried more rapidly and in greater quantity in these conveyances than in wagons and on the backs of camp followers. In the course of the nineteenth century the number of camp followers dwindled as their work was taken over by the military organizations themselves.

THE CRIMEAN WAR

FOR ALMOST FOUR DECADES following the defeat of Napoleon at Waterloo in 1815 there were no conflicts on the European continent between major powers. Then, for three years, from 1853 to 1856, Great Britain, France, Turkey, and Sardinia fought the Russians in a remote, undeveloped region on the Crimean Peninsula on the Black Sea. The dispute that triggered the conflict was a religious matter that arose when Tsar Nicholas I of Russia demanded the right to protect Christian shrines in Jerusalem, then held by the Turks. His invasion of the Turkish Balkans brought the other nations into the conflict. The main action was a siege of Sevastopol. Outside the walls, French and British troops died of disease; inside, Russians also died of disease and suffered the deadly effects of artillery bombardment as well. There were a few bloody battles, including one at Balaklava memorialized by Alfred Tennyson in *The Charge of the Light Brigade,* in which stupidity and courage made a striking, if not edifying, combination.

Western journalists covering the war took note of the Kurdish women combatants. The horse people of the steppe still continued their ancient practice of including recognizably female soldiers in their units. A German newspaper reported early in 1855, "Among 600 Kurdish mounted troops who are at Tulcha along with 200 Turkish guards hussars, there were many women armed and dresed like the men, except that instead of fezes, their heads were covered by a red or yellow scarf, while another scarf covered the lower part of the face up to the nose." Earlier, the *Illustrated London News* carried stories about a Kurdish woman chieftain who led her tribal levies to the Turkish army.[1]

The Kurdish fighting women, however, were just a sidelight to the major news. Historians remember the Crimean War primarily for displays of military and medical incompetence on all sides. The mass of casualties pouring into military hospitals in the Crimea overwhelmed traditional facilities.

Shortages of fuel, clothing, food, and basic supplies added to the suffering of the wounded. For centuries armies had relied on camp women to care for the sick and injured. Now citizens, informed of the horrors at the front by war correspondents, demanded something better for their troops. Soldiers' wives might be good-hearted, hardworking and well meaning, but they were plain, uneducated women.[2] They became field medics and nurses by learning on the job. Having less status than anyone else in the army, they were helpless when faced with problems created by officers and military bureaucracy. All the combatants in the Crimea found the same solution: women nurses who ranked socially well above both the average soldier's wife and the average soldier.

After 1840, the French no longer permitted camp follower wives to deploy with their armies. Instead they hired unmarried women as *vivandières* (daughters of the regiment) who wore uniforms and were assigned duties doing non-nursing women's work. For nursing, they called on women in Catholic religious orders.[3] As journalists published reports of horrors in the British military hospital at Scutari, a piece in the *London Times* went so far as to praise the French hospitals: "Here the French are greatly our superiors. Their medical arrangements are extremely good . . . and they have the help of the Sisters of Charity. . . . These devoted women are excellent nurses." In response, a letter to the *Times* demanded: "Why have we no Sisters of Charity?"[4]

The English did have the equivalent within a few weeks. Florence Nightingale won official approval to take thirty-eight women nurses—secular sisters—to the hospital in Scutari where she did some nursing and a great deal of political combat. At first doctors refused to allow Nightingale's nurses to do anything more than feed the patients. But after the Battle of Balaklava there was too heavy a load to enforce gender restrictions in the hospital. Even so, battling bureaucrats continued to occupy most of Nightingale's time. While grateful soldiers remembered her as "the Lady with the Lamp," others dubbed her "the Lady with the Hammer" following her attack on a locked storeroom when she needed nursing supplies. England hailed her as a national heroine.[5]

The Russians also created a new women's nursing service. Grand Duchess Elena Pavlova called for volunteers to join the Order of the Exaltation of the Cross. Although the women were asked to join for only one year, they were called "sisters" and served without pay. Like

Nightingale, the Russian nurses fought corruption in the medical establishment as they tended their patients. Unlike Nightingale's recruits, the Russian nurses carried out much of their work under fire. Bombs, cannonballs, bullets, and rockets landed on the first-aid stations in Sevastopol. Baroness Budberg, who headed one section of sisters, described the scene at a station she visited in the spring of 1855: "Righteous God! What I saw! All the buildings were without windows, the roofs were torn from some of them, the courtyards were dug up by bombs and strewn with fragments; explosions, like claps of thunder continued unceasingly."[6] In the operating room she found one of her nurses very pale but still at her post; a bomb had just torn out a corner of the room. By the end of the year, seventeen of the one hundred sixty Russian nurses were dead.

Although Florence Nightingale became world famous crusading for cleanliness and good food for soldiers, she was not the only one devoted to the practice of preventive medicine. Dr. James Miranda Barry[7] of the British army's medical service, who had recently been promoted to the rank of deputy inspector general, had been battling for better conditions in military hospitals in such challenging postings as South Africa and the West Indies long before Nightingale was born. When the Crimean War began, Barry was serving in Corfu and immediately volunteered for duty in the Crimea but was not transferred because no slot existed for an officer at the rank of deputy inspector general there. For the duration of the war, however, casualties from the Crimea sent to Barry's hospital at Corfu had the highest recovery rate of any in the sorry Crimean campaign.[8]

Two factors explain the eclipse of Dr. Barry's reputation as a pioneer of preventive medicine. First, Florence Nightingale was convinced that only she had considered the diet and living conditions of the troops and that the senior medical officers of the British army were responsible for the scandalous conditions she had gone to the Crimea to correct. Dr. Barry retired in 1859 after forty-six years of military service and was on Hart's Army List as the most senior of Her Majesty's inspectors-general of hospitals, a rank equivalent to major general. Nightingale's influence with Queen Victoria halted Barry's expected award of a knighthood. The second factor was the doctor's gender. When history remembers Dr. Barry at all, it remembers only that "he" was a woman.

Dr. James Miranda Barry lived disguised as a male from the age of ten until her death in 1865 at the age of sixty-six. The disguise was maintained first because the girl had powerful friends and later because of the loyalty of fellow officers.

Dr. Barry was always deliberately vague about her birthdate and parentage. Yet she took the name of her uncle, James Barry, a prominent if eccentric painter with a wide circle of distinguished friends, including Samuel Johnson, Edmund Burke, and a circle of literary ladies known as bluestockings. Barry's closest friend was Gen. Francisco de Miranda, a cosmopolitan soldier and scholar whose lovers included Catherine the Great of Russia and the bluestocking Madame de Staël. Miranda was an ardent feminist, named women as his literary executors, and published an impassioned plea for female education a year before Mary Wollstonecraft published her famous *Vindication of the Rights of Women.*

When Barry died suddenly of a heart attack in 1806, his friends took his niece under their protection. This younger daughter of Barry's sister was obviously brilliant, but as a girl she would never have the opportunity she deserved. So Miranda dressed her in boy's clothes and arranged for her to matriculate in medical school at the age of ten (only slightly precocious by the standards of that age). At the age of thirteen, Dr. James Miranda Barry joined the army. When she appeared at the hospital of the Plymouth garrison, a tiny childlike personage dwarfed by her large sword, her small, narrow face overpowered by an enormous cocked hat with tassels and feathers, the medical officer in charge protested. He was told bluntly that "it was not wise to agitate the question."[9]

In both appearance and behavior Barry was always more woman than man. From her earliest days in school friends noticed that Barry dressed oddly, wearing a long coat while the other students wore shooting jackets. When a friend tried to teach her to box, "James Barry would never strike out but always kept his arms over his chest."[10] She was always physically small despite wearing boots with three-inch thick soles and elevated heels and stuffing cotton wool into the shoulders of her uniform. Her voice was high pitched, her skin smooth, her hands tiny, and she doted on children and small animals. Throughout her life, there was constant gossip about the brilliant physician's odd appearance and personality. A great many people suspected the truth and after her death recalled incidents in which Barry's disguise was particularly unconvincing. But no one was willing to create a scandal by exposing her during her lifetime. The person who finally did so was no gentleman.

Barry's death certificate was signed by D. R. McKinnon, an army surgeon who had treated Barry for many years and unhestitatingly entered the
sex as male without examining the body. Barry had always objected to physical examinations. The certificate was witnessed with an X by one Sophia
Bishop, a charwoman who laid out the body. Discovering that the corpse was
female, she attempted to blackmail McKinnon. "She seemed to me," he
wrote, "to think she had become acquainted with a great secret and wished
to be paid for keeping it. I informed her that all Dr. Barry's relatives were
dead and it was no secret of mine."[11] Soon the newspapers had the story, and
the scandal spread. The army, however, never ordered a postmortem.
Officially, Dr. James Miranda Barry remained the man she pretended to be.

THE AMERICAN CIVIL WAR

THE AMERICAN CIVIL WAR represents a transition between the old ways
of war that had endured for millennia and the new ways, which fueled by
developing technologies have been evolving at an increasingly rapid rate ever
since. When the war began, both North and South and both men and
women behaved as tradition suggested. Men enlisted to prove their courage,
not realizing that courage was no longer the virtue it had been in days of old
when knights wore shining armor and carried lances. Devoted wives, daughters, and sisters followed their men to camp expecting to do traditional
women's work—making a home in a tent, washing and nursing—not realizing that the army now hired laborers for most of these duties and too many
families just got in the way. Many women, having heard of the exploits of
Florence Nightingale, resolved to follow her example and became army
nurses of a new kind, not soldiers' wives but professionals required to be
unmarried and celibate as a condition of employment. Some women organized all-female home guard units, though none of those in the North saw
action. Some women served the cause of their choice by becoming covert
operatives engaged in espionage, smuggling, and sabotage. Some women put
on pants and enlisted as soldiers.

WOMEN AS SOLDIERS

As recently as the mid-1980s, women soldiers of the Civil War were virtually unknown. A few scholars realized that they existed but thought of them

as a bizarre phenomenon that was more a dirty joke than fit matter for a history book. The expansion of roles for American women in the military, which began in the early 1970s and coincided with the birth of women's history, encouraged and legitimized interest in women soldiers of earlier times. Gay and lesbian historians, taking cross-dressing and assumption of a non-traditional role to be sufficient proof that a woman was homosexual, added their search for "roots" to the stream of research. That interest in women soldiers in the United States focused on the Civil War rather than the Revolution was only natural; the war in which both sides were Americans is the conflict that more than any other defines the American experience of war.

The first stage for recent students of women's military history during the Civil War has been simply to prove that women soldiers existed. Several researchers are now pooling their efforts to piece together the documentary evidence.[12] So much material survives from the Civil War era, much of it still in private collections, that combing it thoroughly for reports of women soldiers is a task that can continue indefinitely. The data are so slight for some soldiers that tracing down the official military record of an individual will be impossible. Another complication was the tendency of many camp followers to wear male clothing and move in and out of combatant roles without formal enlistment. Their comrades might recognize them as a company laundress, but should they be captured, the revelation of gender would be a surprise.

Still, even at a relatively early stage in research, one conclusion has become apparent: for Civil War soldiers, finding a woman in the ranks was no call to action. It came as a surprise to some, a shock to others, but it did not create bureaucratic pandemonium up the chain of command. Thus few records exist, and these document discoveries made by officers. Soldiers did not tattle. For most of the individual cases currently known, only one or at most two references have been found. Even when more than one soldier has left evidence of the same incident involving a woman in uniform, the reference is usually buried somewhere deep in the text, reported casually as an interesting curiosity, something to break the boredom of camp life. For instance, Henry Besançon, who served as a musician in the 104th New York Infantry, noted in his diary on May 26, 1864, that it was raining and that someone had stolen his overcoat. Then he added, "a female dressed in Rebel uniform was taken this morning," and went on to something else. A few days later, A. Jackson Crossly, serving in Company C of the U.S. Engineers, wrote to a friend about a woman prisoner brought to federal army headquarters: "She was mounted just like a man and belonged to cavalry though she was taken as a spy."[13] Henry Schelling of the 64th Illinois Volunteers contributed an isolated report in a letter to a male friend after describing a tedious muddy march during which he and some buddies "got hold of some corn liquid [and] got slightly inebriated." Only then does he add, "We enlisted a new recruit on the way at Eastport. The boys all took a notion to him. On examination, he proved to have a Cunt so he was discharged."[14]

There is also evidence of cases in which a woman's sex was known but deliberately kept secret. Nurse Harriet Whetten was introduced to a "curiosity" by another nurse:

A little figure appeared, looking like a small Laplander, in a sort of uniform. "She is a woman," said Mrs. H, "and has been with her husband in the regiment." She is obliged to go home for a womanly reason. . . . The whole regiment knew that she was a woman and she dressed as a man by the advice of the Colonel and Adjutant. I never saw such a funny figure as she is her little feet and hands look womanish—otherwise I never should have suspected it.[15]

A British observer who met a Southern woman who had served as a soldier was told by the men that "her sex was notorious to all the regiment, but no notice was taken of it so long as she conducted herself properly. They also said that she was not the only representative of the female sex in the ranks."[16]

The most dramatic way a woman in the ranks might reveal her sex was to go into labor. Like the heroines in the women warrior ballads so popular in early modern Europe, which were still sung and sold as broadsides in the United States during the Civil War, the women who combined maternity with soldiering seem the most extraordinary. Col. Elijah H. C. Cavins wrote home in January 1863, telling how "a corporal was promoted to sergeant for gallant conduct at the battle of Fredericksburg since which time the sergeant has become the mother of a child." The battle of Fredericksburg took place on December 13, 1862, when the gallant corporal was in her seventh month of pregnancy. Herman Weiss wrote to tell "something very romantic" to his wife, Adeline, in February 1865:

We had a very good looking corporal in our regiment he belonged to Com K, he was on picket the other day and did not feel well so he asked the officer

if he could go to camp . . . and nobody thought anything of it but what was
our surprise when coming into camp we heard that the corporal had been
taken very sick so that the doctor had send him right off to the division hospi-
tal and that then and there this same good looking corporal had been relieved
of a nice little boy and that the corporal and the boy was doing first rate.[17]

Adeline Weiss replied:

I think it was quite a grand thing about that corporal what a woman she
must have been. I cant contrive how she hid it. I should think her tent mates
would have known it. . . . The idea of her being on picket when she was taken
sick. She must have been more than the common run of woman or she could
never stood soldiering especially in her condition.[18]

Herman Weiss helpfully responded with the answer to his wife's question,
one that regularly occurs to modern readers:

You ask how long that woman was in our regt. she was in it pretty near
from the time it came out and it is no wonder at all that her tent mates did not
know that she was a woman for you must know that we never undress to go to
bed on the contrary we dress up as we go to bed with boots overcoat and all
on and she could find chances enough when she would be in the tent alone to
change her clothes and as for hiding her appearance was easy enough for you
know there is a great many women that dont show much anyway and then
soldier clothes dont fit very snug to the body the only remarkable thing is that
she could stand it so to the very last day.[19]

Scholars studying women soldiers suspect that disguised women in the
Civil War, like those in the armies of early modern Europe, had informal networks that helped them to conceal their female identities. Perhaps women
were keener at identifying each other than the men were. Gen. Philip
Sheridan learned that a teamster in the division wagon train and a private in
a cavalry company had discovered a cache of liquor while on a foraging mission. They became so drunk that they fell into a river and required resusci-
tation, at which point their disguises were exposed. Sheridan made them put
on women's clothing and sent them away. "How the two got acquainted, I
never learned," he wrote in his memoirs, "and though they had joined the
army independently of each other, yet an intimacy had sprung up between
them long before the mishaps of the foraging expedition."[20] A woman from

Pennsylvania who was mustered out of the service after being wounded at Murfreesboro and reenlisted in a Michigan regiment said she had "discovered a great many females in the army, and was intimately acquainted with one such a young lady holding a commission as Lieutenant in the army. She had assisted in burying three female soldiers at different times, whose sex was unknown to any but herself."[21]

In general, however, women not in the ranks themselves were not sympathetic to women in uniform. Nurses who discovered them tried to convince them to go home. Pvt. James H. Guthrie of the First Iowa Infantry described an incident aboard a Mississippi River steamboat as his regiment went south:

> *We have a boy on board with very long hair and the most feminine appearance I ever saw. It was an easy job to make the women on board believe it was a woman in soldier's clothes. It created quite a sensation and lots of fun. One of the women got so high that in distributing pocket handkerchiefs she gave all but our supposed woman one and would not even speak to her. I slipped the boy one and posted him where he played the joke finely. The women went to the Doctor to get him [to] make an examination and if a woman to put her overboard. One of the women said "look at the shape of her ankles, legs and hipps [sic] which proves her to be a female."[22]*

Both Guthrie and the effeminate soldier found this charade amusing; it was the women nurses who were outraged.

Newspapers published during the war and obituary notices years later contain sketchy accounts about scores of women soldiers, usually so sketchy that they cannot be verified by comparison with military records. But Americans knew there were women fighting and dying. Fazar Kirkland wrote in *Reminiscences of the Blue and Gray*, published the year after the war ended, that "accounts presented themselves almost daily to the eye, of the valorous deeds of females fighting in the ranks for months, without their sex being divulged."[23]

Current cautious estimates put the number of women soldiers serving in the Confederate forces at about two hundred fifty and the number in the Union armies at about four hundred. There were probably far more, particularly since many of those who fought were not regularly enlisted. Those estimating the number of women who fought for the Union regularly cite Mary Livermore, a Union nurse, who wrote in her memoirs:

Some one has stated the number of women soldiers known to the service
as little less than four hundred. I cannot vouch for the correctness of this esti-
mate, but I am convinced that a larger number of women disguised themselves
and enlisted in the service, for one cause or other, than was dreamed of.
Entrenched in secrecy, and regarded as men, they were sometimes revealed as
women, by accident or casualty. Some startling histories of these military
women were current in the gossip of army life.[24]

Some startling histories were published after the war, too, which is hardly surprising since Americans had already demonstrated that they had an
appetite for books describing the adventures of plucky women adventurers
even if these were pure fiction. Deborah Samson's semifictionalized autobiography was still in print as the war began. At the end of the War of 1812,
America's three-year participation in the Napoleonic Wars, a Boston publisher named Nathan Coverley, Jr., put out several volumes, under various
titles, purporting to be the first-person narrative of one Lucy Brewer who
had served as a marine aboard the USS *Constitution* during the war. Despite
a number of efforts, no evidence has been found to corroborate this story,
and most of the action scenes were plagiarized from newspapers. Milking
the market, Coverly issued a book said to be written by the owner of a brothel that employed Lucy before she went to sea and a few years later published
The Surprising Adventures of Almira Paul. This woman also went to sea, in
a ship with the peculiar name *Revenue Cutter,* which did battle against the
USS *Constitution.* Bostonians apparently liked to read about the old
frigate's victories in any context.[25]

By the 1840s swashbuckling women heroines multiplied. In 1845,
Maturin Murray Ballou published *Fanny Campbell, the Female Pirate
Captain,* the fictional biography of a woman privateer of the American
Revolution. His heroine was not limited to nautical skills: "Fanny could row
a boat, shoot a panther, ride the wildest horse in the province, or do almost
any brave and useful act." *The Female Volunteer,* published in 1851, presented a protagonist who donned male clothing and fought in the Mexican War,
surviving a series of dangers that would satisfy any reader of modern
thrillers. Publishers kept churning out these pamphlet novels during the Civil
War. In 1862 *The Lady Lieutenant: The Strange and Thrilling Adventures of
Madeline Moore* appeared, and in 1864 *Dora, . . . The American Amazon*
was published.[26]

The two real women soldiers who published memoirs of Civil War experiences were aware of this literary tradition. Indeed, both were inspired by books they had read. Sarah Emma Edmonds remembered reading *Fanny Campbell* and feeling "as if an angel had touched me with a live coal from the altar." When she came to the part where the heroine cut her hair, dressed in male clothing and "stepped into the freedom and glorious independence of masculinity," she threw her hat in the air and vowed that some day she would do the same.[27] The story Edmonds told in *Nurse and Spy in the Union Army*,[28] while not entirely candid, has been substantially corroborated by other evidence.

Loreta Janeta Velazquez, who told her story in *The Woman in Battle*, provided engravings of herself in women's dress as well as one of her male persona, Lt. Harry T. Buford, CSA. Velazquez claimed Saint Joan as her inspiration: "The story of [the] siege of Orleans, in particular, I remember, thrilled my young heart, fired my imagination, and sent my blood bounding through my veins with excitement." Her reading fueled her fantasy life: "Joan of Arc became my heroine, and I longed for an opportunity to become another such as she. I built air-castles without number, and in my day-dreams I was fond of imagining myself as the hero of the most stupendous adventures. I wished that I was a man."[29] Unfortunately, writing for publication encouraged Velazquez to exercise her powers of imagination once more. *The Woman in Battle* includes so many extraordinary stories that it seems impossible for a single individual to have experienced all of them. Consequently, her entire history was suspect. Gen. Jubal Early called her a fraud and doubted that she was even the Southern woman she claimed to be. But Gen. James Longstreet believed her, and her story definitely has a core of truth.[30]

A unique insight into the reality of the experience of a woman serving in the ranks has been provided in a remarkable set of documents: the letters of Sarah Rosetta Wakeman, who served in the 153d Regiment, New York State Volunteers. She faithfully wrote home to her family from the time she enlisted in August 1862 until her death in June 1864. Never imagining that her writing might be published, she had no reason to embellish the facts. Possible discovery of her biological sex never seems to have worried her. She inquired about men from home who had enlisted, asking for their regiments and companies so she could contact them. She found two of them and wrote home, "They knew me just as Soon as they see me. You better believe I had a good visit with them."[31] She sometimes signed her letters with a male name, but more often she signed them "Rosetta Wakeman," and sometimes

"Miss Rosetta Wakeman." In a letter directed to two of her younger siblings, she signed herself "your affectionate sister, Sarah Rosetta Wakeman." When she purchased a ring of a type soldiers bought for identification if they fell in battle, the inscription inside read "Rosetta Wakeman / 153rd N.Y. Vol. / Co. H." Whoever did the engraving knew her real name.

Wakeman was the oldest child in a farming family, and her persistent interest in farm business suggests that she was brought up to work in the fields, probably wearing pants as Sarah Edmonds had done for farm chores. She left home at the age of nineteen to look for work in Binghamton, knowing she would make much more money doing man's work than she could make as a domestic. She was a manual laborer on a coal barge when army recruiters showed up offering a bounty of $152. This was a fortune—more than a year's pay on the barge. She assured the recruiter she was over twenty-one and that her name was Lyons Wakeman. The regimental roll described her as five feet tall with a fair complexion, brown hair, and blue eyes.

Wakeman's war experience was not extraordinary. She was not at Gettysburg or Antietem. Her unit spent much of its time on guard duty to protect Washington from expected attacks. They once spent fourteen consecutive nights in the field behind temporary defenses—anxious work, but the enemy never appeared. Then she stood guard at Carroll Prison in the District of Columbia. One day in 1863, after sending home a series of letters in which she says "I can't think of anything more to write" and falls back on describing the weather, she begins a letter with a little more to say:

> I have just thought of something new to write to you. It is as following.
> Over to Carroll Prison they have got three women that are confined in their rooms. One of them was a Major in the union army and she went into battle with her men. When the Rebels' bullets were a-coming like a hail storm she rode her horse and gave orders to the men. Now she is in prison for not doing according to the regulations of war.
> The other two is Rebel spies and they have catched them and put them in prison. They are smart looking women and [have] good education.[32]

The Rebel spies were probably Belle Boyd and a woman courier known as Ida P. The major was Annie E. Jones, who created quite a scandal. Although she wore a uniform she insisted she "was never anything but a companion to various commanding officers," including "the young and gallant [George Armstrong] Custer." Several officers testified that she had been "a guide, scout, spy or hospital nurse."[33]

The 153d did not go into the field until February 1864. Wakeman finally faced the enemy in battle on April 9, 1864, at Pleasant Hill, the second engagement of the ill-fated Red River Campaign. She told her family, "I was under fire about four hours and laid on the field of battle all night. There was three wounded in my Co. and one killed."[34] Some years later, a lieutenant of the 153d reminisced with other veterans about this campaign, which took the unit from Franklin, Louisiana, west of New Orleans to Alexandria, Louisiana: "No tongue can tell nor pen indite the hardships you endured on that march of over seven hundred miles through an enemies country, where with a scarcity of water, any slough was sought for with eagerness, and though animals partly decomposed and reeking with their millions of parasites were floating upon its surface, you were obliged to drink its waters to allay the thirst caused by that southern sun."[35]

The 153d faced the enemy once again at Monett's Bluff before reaching Alexandria. Like many others who had been drinking polluted water, Wakeman contracted dysentery. She reported to the regimental hospital on May 3d, was transferred to Marine U.S.A. General Hospital in New Orleans on May 7, and died there on June 19, 1864. Despite the ring she wore and despite the nature of her illness, no evidence of any kind exists outside her own letters to suggest that Private Wakeman was a woman. Those who knew, and some medical personnel must have known, were decent enough not to put anything in the official records. And if there was any gossip, it has left no trace in any letter or diary yet discovered.

Hospitals were a likely place for women to be identified. As a result, some avoided them even at the cost of great suffering. When Sarah Edmonds, serving as Franklin Thompson, was injured while carrying mail for the 2d Michigan Infantry, she did not seek treatment:

Had I been what I represented myself to be, I should have gone to the hospital and had the surgeon make an examination of my injuries, and placed myself in his hands for medical treatment—and saved years of suffering. But being a woman *I felt compelled to suffer in silence and endure it the best I could, in order to escape detection of my sex. I would rather have been shot dead than to have been known to be a woman and sent away from the Army under guard as a* criminal.[36]

When Edmonds contracted malaria in April 1863, she deserted rather than risk exposure. A twelve-year-old girl who was a drummer in a Pennsylvania regiment did not, or could not, choose that option; after living through five battles, she was discovered after contracting typhoid.[37]

Albert D. J. Cashier (born Jennie Hodgers) served in the war and maintained a male identity for another half century until a freak automobile accident in 1911 sent the old soldier to the Soldiers' and Sailors' Home. Physicians there promised to keep her secret, and nothing was put in writing. Gossip was another matter, and two years later a Washington newspaper reporter who got wind of the story exposed her. Then some of her old comrades came to visit. "I left Cashier, the fearless boy of twenty-two at the end of the Vicksburg campaign," said the former 1st sergeant Charles W. Ives. "When I went to Watertown I found a frail woman of 70, broken, because on discovery, she was compelled to put on skirts. They told me she was as awkward as could be in them. One day she tripped and fell, hurting her hip. She never recovered." Cashier had no regrets. She told Ives, "Lots of boys enlisted under the wrong name. So did I. The country needed men, and I wanted excitement."[38]

WOMEN AS NURSES

Most women who wanted to share the excitement and serve their country chose the option of military nursing.[39] Exactly how many women nursed will never be known. The best estimate puts the figure at more than ten thousand for the North and the South combined.[40] The destruction of the Confederate surgeon general's records during the fall of Richmond in April 1865 complicates the search for Southern nurses, and in the North about 4,500 women went to nurse at the front without formal approval. Thousands of nurses are known only because of their requests for pensions after the passage of the 1892 Nurses' Pension Act. Presumably, many who would have qualified for pensions had died by that time. About six hundred Catholic nuns from twelve religious orders performed nursing services for both sides. Most difficult of all to identify are black women nurses—slave, free, and contraband—who left little written record themselves and were usually ignored by white chroniclers.

For all its horror, many Civil War nurses found exhilaration in their wartime service and would treasure the memory of the war years as ardently as any male veteran.[41] After joining the hospital staff at Louisville, Mary Shelton wrote, "Never enjoyed anything half so much before. How unimportant everything at home seems." Her sister Amanda wrote, "I have lived more myself and seen more of life than in all the former years." A nurse at the Paducah hospital, which several times came under attack, wrote "I love to *live* full earnest *real* life, not real in the sense we sometimes speak either . . . but a real life of heart and soul, yes I love it and sometimes I so earnestly & ardently desire it."[42]

The flood of casualties that overwhelmed the hospitals meant that nurses often worked knee deep in blood and filth. A few wore pants,[43] certainly more practical than trailing skirts for such work, but most would never think of abandoning their usual clothing and took the inconvenience in stride. Annie Turner Wittenmyer, who tended the casualties from Shiloh, later remembered, "My clothing was wet and muddy to the knees, but I did not see it." Another nurse on the hospital transport Vanderbilt wrote in her diary, "wet through and through, *every garment* saturated. Disrobed, and bathing with bay rum, was glad to lie down, every bone aching, and head & heart throbbing, unwilling to cease work where so much was to be done, and yet wholly unable to do more. There I lay, with the sick, wounded, and dying all around, and slept from sheer exhaustion, the last sounds falling upon my ears being groans from the operating room." Even the luxury of a sponge bath was not always possible. Kate Cumming at the Confederate camps in Corinth, Mississippi, noted in her diary that she had not changed her clothes since her arrival nine days before.[44]

Women who had been bred as ladies in middle-class respectability learned to endure loathsome sounds, sights, and smells. Nurses' descriptions of Manassas, Antietam, and Gettysburg include the odor of decaying horseflesh and the sight of heads and limbs of human corpses sticking out of shallow graves. One nurse wrote in her diary, "[Even in the hospital ward] the wounds smelled so bad that I almost vomited."[45] Sophronia Bucklin told of her experience following the battle of Cold Harbor:

Men lay all around me, who had been left for days on the battleground, wet with the dews of night, disfigured with powder and dirt, with blood oozing from their torn flesh, and worms literally covering the festering wounds— dying with thirst, starving for food, unable to attend to nature's wants, groaning in delirious fever, praying to die. . . .

The field was one vast plain of intense mortal agony, tortured by the sun, and chilled by the night dews. Everywhere were groans and cries for help; everywhere the pleading and glassy eyes of dying men who were speechless in the delirium of death. It was a scene to appall the stoutest of hearts, but the excitement nerved us to shut our senses to everything but the task of relieving them as fast as possible. The dead lay by the living; the dying groaned by the dead, and still one hundred ambulances poured the awful tide in upon us.[46]

Nurses often came under fire. Harriet Eaton made ambulance runs up to one-half mile from the fighting at Fredericksburg, and the house serving as a hospital was itself hit. "Two shells struck the house while we were in it," she wrote, "and the noise of the musketry and the cannon's roar and flash was perfectly terrific." While Vicksburg was under siege, Annie Turner Wittenmyer rode on horseback on the only access road to the hospital, which was under constant bombardment. Thirty years later, she still remembered the crippling effects of the continuous shelling.[47]

Many nurses died in service, some from wounds and many more from disease. Arlington Cemetery has a section dedicated to them; the old markers read "Army Nurse." Although nurses were not officially recognized as military personnel in the United States until the twentieth century, the Union army established a civilian nursing corps in June 1861. It was under the stern command of a superintendent of army nurses, fifty-nine-year-old Dorothea Dix, who was known for her work with the mentally ill. The forerunners of the Navy Nurse Corps were black women listed as "nurse" on the crew rosters of the USS *Red Rover*. They were later joined by Sisters of the Holy Cross who nursed but were not listed as part of the crew.[48] Eventually the U.S. Sanitary Commission sent about five hundred women as well as a few men to staff hospital steamers.[49]

Dix was an admirer of Florence Nightingale. Like her, she denounced camp followers as dirty, uneducated sluts. She was out to recruit women the nineteenth century called "spinsters"—unattractive, middle-aged women who wore plain clothing without hoops. Mary Livermore wrote after the war, "Many of the women whom [Dix] rejected because they were too young and too beautiful entered the service under other auspices and became eminently useful. Many women whom she accepted because they were sufficiently old and ugly proved unfit for the position and a disgrace to their sex."[50]

Two women surgeons, Esther Hill Hawks and Mary E. Walker, offered their services, but Dix rebuffed them. Both, she thought, were too young and too pretty. Furthermore, she thought it unwomanly for a female to train as a regular physician and practice medicine like a man. Hawks then went with her surgeon husband to Beaufort, South Carolina, and took his place during his frequent absences.

Walker was an independent thinker and not easily discouraged. She believed female clothing was unhealthy and wore trousers and a suit coat even on her wedding day in 1855. Of course, she kept her maiden name for professional use. She tried early in the war to obtain a commission as a surgeon. When that was denied, she practiced medicine without official approval, as did several other women. Walker joined Gen. Ambrose Burnside's forces in Virginia as a volunteer surgeon in the summer of 1862. Following the battle of Fredericksburg, the general recommended that Walker be commissioned, and there was hot debate on the proposal in the War Department. She was appointed acting assistant surgeon for the 52d Ohio Infantry and was with the unit at Chickamauga.

From late in 1863 until April 1864, Walker worked as a contract surgeon for the 52d Ohio, treating civilians in heavily Confederate territory in Chattanooga for a salary of $80 a month. On one occasion she took a wrong turn and ended up behind enemy lines where she was captured and sent to Richmond as a suspected spy. She was there for four months, until the federal government arranged for her exchange in August 1864. Her arrest brought this reaction from Confederate Capt. B. J. Semmes:

> *This morning we were all amused and disgusted too at the sight of a thing that nothing but the debased and the depraved Yankee nation could produce, a female doctor. She was taken prisoner yesterday and brought in by the pickets this morning. She was dressed in the full uniform of a Federal Surgeon, boots hat & all, & wore a cloak. . . . She was about 25 or 28 years old fair, but not good looking and of course had tongue enough for a regiment of men. I was in hopes the General would have had her dressed in a homespun frock and bonnet and sent back to the Yankee lines, or put in a lunatic asylum.*[51]

After her release from the Confederate prison, she was again appointed acting assistant surgeon but denied work in the field. She became surgeon at the women's military prison in Louisville and then superintendent for a refugee home in Clarksville, Tennessee. In 1865, she received the Congressional Medal of Honor, an award that was revoked in 1917 when Congress decided retroactively to make noncombatants ineligible. But she refused to give it up and wore it for the rest of her life. In 1977, decades after her death, Congress retroactively restored it to her. To this day, she is the only woman to have received that decoration.[52]

Clara Barton, the most famous of the Civil War nurses, was asked to work with Dix's battalion of army nurses, but she turned down the offer. Barton chose to nurse independently, avoiding military discipline and bureaucratic ties in order to go where she felt she was needed most. Shocked by the lack of simple first-aid facilities at the first Battle of Bull Run, she collected food, medicine, and bandages at her own expense. In the summer of 1862, she and a few friends used a mule team to distribute these supplies to the battlefields. She wrote home, "I wrung the blood from the bottom of my clothing before I could step, for the weight about my feet."[53]

Barton remembered Antietem as her baptism of fire: it was the first time she removed a bullet from a patient on the battlefield and the first time a patient was shot to death as she held him in her arms to give him water. It was she who often remarked after the war that if this sort of activity seemed "rough and unseemly for a *woman,* it should be remembered that combat was equally rough and unseemly for *men.*" Barton never received pay or official recognition of any kind for her battlefield nursing, and she always insisted that there were hundreds of women like her at the front. After the war, Barton took on a mission to locate graves of soldiers missing in action and to report these sites to their families. In 1881, she founded and became president of the American Association of the Red Cross.

CAMP FOLLOWERS

While nurses went to the front as professional medical workers, thousands of women went to the front in the traditional role of camp follower. The Articles of War, which had most recently been revised in 1846, recognized this group of civilians: "*camp followers* entering into a new society, having peculiar laws of its own, by their own voluntary act, must conform to those laws, as such is an understood condition of their admission." As part of the military establishment, members of military families and civilian employees of the military could face court-martial.

They are therefore liable to receive the orders of their military superiors, and are to act in conformity thereto, though rather in a civil than in a military capacity. These persons cannot be called upon to perform military duty; but in all that relates to the maintenance of the peace and order of the camp . . . they are as liable to military command, and punishment for the non-observance of the same, as the enlisted soldier.[54]

No count of civilians in the camps was kept, but one visitor who spent several winters with the Army of the Potomac said that the camps were "teeming with women."[55] Georgia Augustus Sala, a British journalist, observing the numbers of women in the camps of both armies, concluded that never before in history had there been a conflict that was as much "a woman's war."[56] And generally they were not a threat to good order and discipline but contributed to the welfare of the force.

As was the case in the American Revolution, the best-regulated camps seemed to be those with the greatest number of women. Soldiers appreciated their presence, and officers felt that they brought moral stability through their efforts to make the camps more homelike. As they had done in their drawing rooms at home, women sang and played the guitar to entertain the troops. Sometimes professional entertainers were also invited to perform. Gen. P. G. T. Beauregard persuaded the Confederate belle Constance Cary to sing to encampments around Fairfax Station in August 1861. The next spring, the vocalist Kate Dean toured Union camps in Virginia, "to dissipate the *ennui* of camp life, [and] to stir up those patriotic impulses which inspire the heart."[57] One camp had trouble with a spiritualist whose psychic ability to commune with the dead caused so much disruption that the officers "could not tolerate it and expelled her from camp as a dangerous fanatic."[58]

Women from different social classes lived in the camps. The officers' wives who were simply visiting might be resented by hardworking nurses and camp women who were offended by their idleness. Nurse Cornelia Hancock complained about the number of "ladies" at Brandy Station, Virginia, and said the government ought to ban them, and nurse Harriet Whetten was exasperated when the medical director of her hospital transport brought aboard his nineteen-year-old daughter. Whetten reported that the young lady "appeared the next morning in a pink muslin morning dress and embroidered petticoat and has never done anything since she came on board but flirt with one of the medical cadets."[59] But many visitors ended up doing useful work. One wife began nursing and also opened a camp school to teach reading and writing to former slaves.

Nadine Turchin, wife of the colonel of the 19th Illinois Infantry, joined her husband at the beginning of the war and found plenty of tasks to occupy her time. She and her husband came from Russia and understood war from a European perspective. When her husband became ill, she took over at the head of the regiment. The soldiers had such confidence in her military knowledge and leadership that they gave her "implicit and cheerful obedience," which enabled her to "le[a]d the troops into action, fac[e] the hottest fire, and f[i]ght bravely at their head." An Ohio senator, a member of Turchin's brigade, testified in support of Madame Turchin's pension application that "every man who belonged to his brigade admired her as much as they admired the General. She was with him constantly in the field, shared with him all the privations of the camp and all the dangers of battle."[60]

As always, an enormous social gap existed between officers' ladies like Madame Turchin and the wives of common soldiers. Some of the soldiers' wives had been camp followers in European armies before emigrating to the United States, and they considered themselves fully part of their regiments. Their place during battle was in the thick of the fighting, carrying ammunition and water, and at least some of them were acquainted with the use of weapons and capable of taking a place in the line. As the term "camp follower" had disagreeable overtones, however, Americans called to the women working for pay as sutlers and laundresses vivandières.

The best known of the women who enlisted without concealing their gender is Kady C. Brownell, whose honorable discharge papers from her Rhode Island regiment are on display in the permanent Women's Corridor exhibit at the Pentagon. Thirty years after the war a newspaper reporter called on her for an interview. "She displayed a modest aversion to discussing her war record, but she prompted her husband, Robert S. Brownell, as he told the story, which was supported throughout by original documents," as follows:

She and I were married in Providence just as the war broke out. Three days after came the first call for three months' volunteers. I was a member of the Mechanics' Rifle corps, and of course I enlisted right away. I went to Washington with the first detachment of my company, and as the ship was leaving the dock my wife called to me, "I won't be far behind you!" The next day she went to Governor Sprague and told him she wanted to join me. He finally agreed that she should go to Washington with the second detachment, and he introduced her personally to the boys as the daughter of the regiment. When she got to Washington, I told her the best thing she could do was to go home. I told her one woman wasn't safe among a thousand men. "A woman could be good in hell if she wanted to," was her reply, and that settled it.

She had a uniform made very much like that worn by the men, consisting of a blue blouse, a red skirt to the knee and gray trousers under that. She wore a sword and had her hair cut short, and as she was only about 18 half of the people thought she was a boy, and the rest wondered what on earth she was. Whenever we turned out, she marched by my side, and as she always carried a flag she was generally regarded as the color bearer. When we were mustered in and took the oath, her name was called off with the rest of them, and nobody noticed that she was a woman.

She carried the colors and suffered a minor wound at the First Battle of Bull Run and was in other actions as well. Thirty years later her husband's pride in her soldierly skills is unabated. "While she was in the army my wife naturally got a good deal of practice with both gun and sword," he told the reporter. "She is a splendid shot now, and with gun and bayonet she can disarm a clever swordsman in a few minutes."[61]

Postwar writers praised women like Annie Ethridge, Briget Divers ("Irish Biddy"), Marie Tepe Leonard ("French Mary"), and Kady Brownell for their patriotism and coolness under fire.[62] Here is one soldier's description of "Dutch Mary," who served with the 17th Maine Regiment:

A division drill by General Birney on the Brooks Farm. We were out two hours, and for those who like this kind of thing, it went well. On this occasion we had with us old "Dutch Mary," a female whose adipose tissue is quite remarkable, as is her agility. She is the "frau" of a Zouave, who persists in eating her sauerkraut mit hans and in drinking her schnapps. She cooks and washes for the officers, thereby earning an honest penny.

When a battle rages, she is on hand to minister to the needs of the wounded. When in camp, she sometimes drills with the men, as today, and she can go through it as well as any. The way her legs fly when executing a wheeling operation reminds me of some swift-moving insect. . . . With her tight Zouave suit on, she looks like a man. One private, thinking to have a little sport at her expense, once came up behind her as she was washing some clothes at the brook, and kissed her. She seized a wet shirt and belabored him right and left, pursuing him out of camp, to the great amusement of his comrades and chagrin of himself. When next he felt in a jocose frame of mind, no doubt he didn't take Dutch Mary as the object of his mirth.[63]

Black women, who worked for armies on both sides, had race as well as class against them; they are not praised by the chroniclers. An "Anglo-

African" woman, disguised as a boy, was discovered serving as body-servant to a captain in the 12th Rhode Island Infantry,[60] but so far no evidence has been found of black women serving in the ranks with black troops before the end of the war. One who served in a woman's role with the 33d U.S. Colored Troops, however, described duties that gave her hands-on experience with infantry armament. Susie King Taylor was enrolled as company laundress, but she did very little washing, she explains, "I was always busy doing other things through camp."[65] One of the things she did was train with weapons: "I learned to handle a musket very well while in the regiment and could shoot straight and often hit the target. I assisted in cleaning the guns and used to fire them off, to see if the cartridges were dry before cleaning and reloading, each day. I thought this great fun. I was also able to take a gun all apart, and put it together again."[66] Like the white women in the regiments, black women considered themselves part of the unit. Martha Gray, who was with the 54th Massachusetts Infantry wrote, "I consider myself a worn out soldier of the U.S. I was all around the South with the regiment administering to the wants of the sick and wounded and did have the name of the Mother of the Regiment."[60]

Black women in the South were under peculiar pressure to join the armies. Black men who left the plantations to join the Union army left their families vulnerable. Slave owners might evict these women and children from the slave quarters, leaving them without food or clothing. One slave woman wrote to her husband, "I have had nothing but trouble since you left. [T]hey abuse me because you went & say they will not take care of our children & do nothing but quarrel with me all the time and beat me scandalously the day before yesterday—Oh I never thought you would give me so much trouble as I have to bear now."[68]

Some women took the initiative in leading their families to freedom. In one case a seventy-year-old grandmother took command of a daring escape expedition, leading her twenty-two children and grandchildren forty miles down the Savannah River on a flatboat until they found a federal vessel. But families who followed their men into Union lines were not necessarily better off than those who stayed on the plantation. Union army officers did not welcome an army of contraband camp followers marching behind the troops. Newly freed black women and their children who joined soldier husbands faced economic pressures as great as those endured by camp followers in the armies of the Thirty Years War. Black soldiers were not paid for their first eighteen months of service, leaving women to be the sole support of their families by doing laundry and selling baked goods. Living in squalid settlements around the camps, hundreds died of malnutrition and disease, and military officials, who viewed them as a nuisance, sometimes evicted them even from these poor shelters.[69]

Black women were also especially vulnerable to abuse by soldiers on both sides who would do to a black female what they would never do to a white one. Esther Hill Hawks, a surgeon in a hospital for black soldiers in Beaufort, South Carolina, wrote in her diary in October 1862:

> *During the first year of our soldiers coming the blacks probably suffered more from their tyranny and insults, than ever in their lives before. It is a sad comment on humanity, but I believe in* this *case, a true one! No colored woman or girl was safe from the brutal lusts of the soldiers—and by soldiers I mean both officers and men. The 55th Penn Reg would, no doubt bear off the palm in these affairs, if they could have their just dues. The col. [Colonel White] for a long time, kept colored women for his especial needs and officers and men were not backward in illustrations of his example. Mothers were brutally treated for trying to protect their daughters, and there are now several women in our little hospital who have been shot by soldiers for resisting their vile demands. One poor old woman but a few months since, for trying to protect her daughter against one of these men was caught by her hair and as she still struggled, shot through the shoulder. She is still in Hospital. No one is punished for these offences for the officers are as bad as the men.[70]*

PROSTITUTES

Soldiers and officers might also have their "especial needs" met by professional prostitutes. Prostitution flourished in American cities during the nineteenth century on both sides of the Mason-Dixon line. Low wages for most women's work tempted poor girls to sell the only service they could offer that would bring in a decent income. Distress and dislocations caused by the war increased the pressure. One student of Civil War prostitution claimed to have seen a diary kept by a prostitute who was only fourteen when she began "catering to the finest carriage trade" in Richmond. She amassed a fortune in this line of work and after the war married into a "prominent" family in Richmond.[71] Most stories probably did not have such happy endings. Indeed no other first-person account by a prostitute from this time is known to exist.

Washington and Richmond were equally notorious for their large population of prostitutes. Before the war, there were about five hundred prostitutes working the nation's capital, a number that grew to five thousand, not counting those in Georgetown and Alexandria. Whole blocks south of Pennsylvania Avenue, Lafayette Square as well as parts of Twelfth and Thirteenth streets, were notorious for their bawdy houses and streetwalkers. Soldiers looking for a good time could visit Hooker's Division, the Haystack, Madam Russell's Bake Oven, or dozens of other establishments catering to the military.[72]

Business was just as good in the Confederate capital. Richmond's mayor, Joseph Mayo, repeatedly ordered raids on houses of prostitution, without much profit except for himself. After one madam had seven of her houses raided by police in one evening, she sent $50 "in metal" to "Rednose Mayo's" headquarters and dared him to interfere with her business any further. Indeed, prostitution flourished in all the cities of the South, where selling sex to soldiers might be the only profitable business remaining. Personnel from both sides partook, and both suffered from venereal disease.

From a strictly medical perspective, the best solution for avoiding the spread of venereal disease is for every soldier to be monogamously mated and to keep that mate close by. That was the solution preferred by all armies until new technology made it impossible to guarantee every wife a paying job with the army. Only a limited number of men could bring wives to camp, and unmarried men as well as husbands with roving eyes faced temptation. The medical solution was to license prostitutes and to forbid interaction with any other women.

Confederate officers were reluctant to wage war on amateur prostitutes, partly because it was not gentlemanly and partly because the women were mostly from the South, although a surprising number of New England women were in the trade as far south as Portsmouth and Norfolk, Virginia. After the federal occupation Memphis became a magnet for professionals from Northern cities. The Memphis *Bulletin* charged on May 1, 1863, "When a woman could 'ply her vocation' no longer in St. Louis, Chicago or Cincinnati, she was fitted up in her best attire and shipped to Memphis, and in more cases than one to prevent the 'package' from being miscarried, was accompanied by gentlemen (heaven save the mark) with insignia of rank."[73]

Union army surgeons, however, faced the problem unblushingly and successfully regulated prostitution in Memphis and Nashville. A license to practice in the form of a certificate was issued to prostitutes who registered and submitted to periodic examinations. In Nashville, fees paid by the prostitutes supported a special hospital for diseased women, and the surgeon in charge was chiefly concerned with keeping soldiers from infecting his patients rather than the other way around.

Unfortunately, the women most likely to spread disease among soldiers were the same ones most likely to become pregnant: amateurs, nice innocent girls seduced by some soldier's sweet talk and giving him a little love before he went off to face the foe. Once abandoned, the former innocent, having no sophisticated madam to advise her, became a freelance sex worker able to protect neither herself nor her clients from infection. Surgeons had no sympathy for them. In 1863, faced with an excess of prostitutes, the post commander in Nashville loaded approximately one hundred fifty of them on a boat and sent them up the river. But authorities in Louisville and Cincinnati protested so vigorously that the expulsion order was revoked and the prostitutes returned on a government steamer.[74]

The study of military prostitution is clouded by the tendency of older historians to absorb nineteenth-century views of morality and characterize as a whore any woman who was sexually active or who might have had an opportunity to be sexually active and was not married. Women soldiers, vivandières, and camp followers were casually dismissed as "morally loose." It did not take much for a woman of the Victorian age to compromise her reputation. Indeed, Gen. Benjamin Butler declared any Southern woman who behaved disrespectfully toward a member of the occupying army to be a prostitute. In his "Woman Order directed to any New Orleans female [who] shall show contempt for any officers or soldiers of the United States," he decreed that any such would "be regarded and held liable to be treated as a woman of the town plying her vocation."[75]

CIVILIAN WOMEN IN WAR ZONES

"Woman of the town" was hardly the worst of the epithets directed against Southern women. In 1867, the authors of *Women's Work in the Civil War* made it plain why they would not include the women of the Confederacy:

> *Indeed it would be difficult to find in history, even among the fierce brutal women of the French revolution, any record of conduct more absolutely*

fiendish than that of women of the South during the war. They insisted on the murder of helpless prisoners; in some instances shot them in cold blood themselves, besought their lovers and husbands to bring them Yankee skulls, scalps and bones, for ornaments, betrayed innocent men to death, engaged in intrigues and schemes of all kinds to obtain information of the movements of Union troops, to convey it to the enemy, and in every manifestation of malice, petty spite and diabolical hatred against the flag under which they had been reared, and its defenders, they attained a bad pre-eminence over the evil spirits of their sex since the world began.[76]

Obviously, these writers did not know much about women's military history. But their outrage also demonstrated a victor's perspective on the war.

Whatever the moral "rightness" of Union and Confederate causes, the Union was obliged by the nature of the Southern challenge to undertake an invasion of the South. Furthermore, as the war dragged on, the goal of Union strategy became the destruction of the Confederate will to resist by taking the war to civilians who supplied the soldiers with food and other support essential for military operations. The Civil War was a "total war," and in that context the North abandoned standards of "proportional response and discriminating protection of civilians," that had been dictated by international law since the end of the Thirty Years War. Such strategy inevitably targets women and children, and the victims always fight in self-defense.[77]

All-female home guard units were common in the Confederacy and did not require official sponsorship of any kind. One formed in Gainesville, Alabama, very early in the war,[78] as did the one in LaGrange, Georgia, called the Nancy Harts in honor of the Revolutionary War heroine. Beginning in May 1861, forty women drilled regularly and actually formed a line in the last days of the war to face a party of Union soldiers. In Bascom, Georgia, nine women met every Wednesday and Saturday for target practice so that they would be ready if the Yankees came. One of the group wrote to a friend, "You know how nervous and timid Millie was. Well now she can load a gun and fire and hit a spot at a good distance."[79]

Other women, however, did seek official endorsement. In April 1861, students at a finishing school sent a letter addressed to President Jefferson Davis and his secretary of war: "If you cannot obtain sufficient gallant men to sustain you in your righteous cause, we, a portion of Young Ladies of a

Female School in this place, tender our services to you. We have organized a military company and desired, if our Fathers and Brothers should not take up arms to pledge ourselves to do all in our power to advance you in your cause." In the early days of the war such encouragement was sufficient to bring the fathers and brothers to the recruiting office, but there is no doubt that many Southern ladies were as eager for battle as the gentlemen. "O! If I was only a man!" wrote Sarah Morgan Dawson. "Then I could don the breeches, and slay them with a will. If some few Southern women were in the ranks, they could set the men an example they would not blush to follow. Pshaw! there are *no* women here! We are *all* men."[80]

In December 1864, now disillusioned with the ability of the Confederate forces to protect them, twenty-eight women wrote to the Confederate secretary of war for authorization to raise a regiment:

> We the undersigned true and Loyal citoyennes of the Confederate States propose to organize a volunteer regiment for purposes of local defense. . . . [W]e suggest that the right to bear arms in defence of our homes be delegated to certain of the fairer portion of this ill starred confederacy. With the permission of the War Department we will raise a full regiment of ladies between the ages of 16 and 40 armed and equipped to perform regular service. . . . We have been subjected to every conceivable outrage and suffering and this we believe is owing to the incompetency of the Confederate Army upon which we depend for our defense. Therefore . . . we propose to leave our hearthstones to endure any sacrifice any privation for the ultimate success of Our Holy Cause.[81]

The secretary of war declined the offer.

In the border states the Civil War was fought by guerrillas on both sides. Sardinius Smith, a Union private, observed the muster of integrated companies: "I have seen at an early hour they began to assemble in squads women as well as men and the place was soon full of men and women of all ages and descriptions."[82] The nature of guerrilla warfare makes small units, even individual operatives, particularly effective. In June 1864, Mrs. Gibson and her daughter were caught cutting telegraph wires. Another mother-daughter team confessed to destroying several bridges in Tennessee to slow the Union advance. And, said Mrs. Hunter, they would do it again if they got the chance. Kate Beattie and her landlady were imprisoned for helping prisoners escape and burning federal boats and warehouses. Sarah Jane Smith, described by one journalist as among the "most aggravating" nuisances of the Civil War, began her activities at the age of fourteen. She was sentenced to hang after she cut four miles of telegraph wires in Missouri; Gen. William S. Rosencrans commuted the sentence to imprisonment.[83]

Although Union sources emphasize the violence of Confederate women, Union women could be just as fierce. Private Smith wrote, "If [Southern guerrilla women] are warlike, union women are about equally so, and the old lady with whom I supped once stood between her husband and a Secesh with a loaded gun who was trying to shoot her husband and actually kept him out."[84] Sarah Edmonds, while on a foraging mission as a nurse, described her own brutal behavior toward a Confederate woman who had lost her father, husband, and two brothers within the previous three weeks. The widow not only refused to "donate" supplies to the Union but took a shot at Edmonds as she turned to leave. Edmonds pulled her own revolver, wounded the "wretch," and then tied her up to her horse and dragged her along the ground for a mile until she fainted. Next Edmonds forced her to swear an oath of loyalty and promise to nurse Union soldiers. Edmonds clearly enjoyed herself. "Soon after this conversation," she wrote, "we started for camp, she weak and humbled, and I strong and rejoicing."[85]

As always, women excelled in covert operations. Early in the war many young women rode out to the camps to watch the soldiers drill and to offer their services as scouts or couriers, believing their knowledge of the neighborhood would be useful. Indeed, many women became valuable intelligence sources simply by keeping their eyes and ears open in their own neighborhoods, which gave rise to all sorts of rumors and charges of espionage. A Confederate nurse, Phoebe Pember, caught the atmosphere of distrust and suspicion in her description of Rose O'Neal Greenhow's activities in Richmond after she had spent some time in prison for spying for the South. Pember wrote that there was speculation that Mrs. Greenhow was now being paid to watch a Mrs. McLane, who was suspected of espionage even though her husband was a Confederate officer. "The report says that Lincoln pays Mrs. McLane for her information and Jeff Davis pays Mrs. Greenhow for watching her," she wrote. "Mrs. G is also paid by the Federals for not seeing too much and lastly that the two ladies are in collusion and divide the spoils."[86]

Since secrecy and deceit are essential for effective agents, many of the stories told of female spies cannot today be either proved or disproved. But the women were undoubtedly valuable to their employers and dangerous to their enemies, and their histories make racy reading. Loreta Velazquez described a conversation she had with a Northern "spy-catcher," a man pretending to be a Confederate sympathizer to trap Confederate spies. At the time, she had been posing as a double agent, a Confederate spy working for the Union. She knew who he was, but he did not recognize her and gave his frank opinion of women covert operatives: "It don't do to show any mercy to these she-devils, they give us more trouble than all the men together." [87]

Women also excelled at smuggling. Most of them merely hid a few things on their person. "False hair . . . is searched for papers," wrote the Confederate Mary Chesnut. "Pistols are sought for with crinoline reversed, bustles are suspect. All manner of things . . . come over the border under the large hoops now worn. . . . Not legs but arms are looked for under hoops, and sad to say are found." [88] Some women, however, supervised smuggling of large quantities of goods. One woman on a steamer was intercepted with an assortment of contraband, including uniforms for Confederate officers. Mary Walker Roberts, a nurse in Richmond, went all the way to Canada to obtain hospital supplies. Her cargo was hauled on sleds for five hundred miles down the frozen St. Lawrence River, then stowed on a ship that went from Canada to Cuba, and finally arrived safely in Galveston. [89]

The outstanding covert operative on either side during the war was Harriet Ross Tubman, [90] born a slave in Maryland. She worked hard from childhood. In addition to doing women's work as a maid, child's nurse, and cook, she was a field hand and a woodcutter. But she was never a good slave. Her owners constantly complained about her performance, and when she was about thirteen, an overseer struck her in the head with a two-pound weight and fractured her skull. In 1849, she made her break for freedom and escaped to Philadelphia. But Tubman wanted more than her own liberty. In 1850, she returned to Maryland and helped her sister and two children to escape. The next year she went back twice, bringing out two brothers and their families and a number of other people. During the next decade Tubman made nineteen trips back into Maryland and may have liberated as many as three hundred slaves. At one time the rewards for her capture rose to $40,000.

Northern abolitionists supported Tubman's efforts, and she was well known among them. Her influence was national; before the war she advised and encouraged John Brown, who referred to her as "General Tubman," and in 1860 she led a crowd in Troy, New York, which freed a fugitive slave, enabling him to escape to Canada. When the war began, she went to South Carolina with an endorsement from the Massachusetts governor, John A. Andrew, and offered her services to Maj. Gen. David Hunter, commander of the Department of the South. He gave her a pass to travel on government transports but no pay; she supported herself by selling chickens and eggs. For a few months in 1865, she worked as a nurse in a freedmen's hospital.

Her real work, however, was as espionage agent and guerrilla leader. Under the command of Col. James Montgomery of the 2d Carolina Volunteers, Tubman led black troops on expeditions deep into Confederate territory. Her most famous mission began on the night of June 1, 1863, up the Combahee River with three Union gunboats under her command. Her raiders destroyed a bridge, gathered vital intelligence, and brought more than 750 slaves up the river to freedom.

In 1869, Sarah Bradford published a sketch of Tubman's life, entitled *Harriet Tubman: The Moses of Her People.* She gave the proceeds to Tubman to pay off the mortgage on her farm where she was caring for her parents and several other elderly blacks and orphans. At the same time Tubman petitioned for compensation from the government for her wartime service. But, despite the backing of many prominent people, including William H. Seward, who had been Lincoln's secretary of war, she was not successful. In 1897 she tried again, asking for $1,800 for "three years' service as nurse and cook in hospitals and as commander of several men (eight or nine) as scouts during the late War of Rebellion." Congress finally voted to give her a pension of $20 a month, which she collected until she died in 1913 in her late nineties. Over time, memory of Tubman's military service faded, as did, indeed, memory of all the women who bore arms and provided other useful services during the greatest of American wars. As a recent writer says, "Harriet Tubman was an extraordinary human being, and probably the most underrated and underappreciated person, of either sex or any race, from the Civil War period."[91]

Assyrian bas reliefs discovered in the nineteenth century are older than written records. Here we see bearded and beardless soldiers in battle (above) and in camp (below). From Austin Henry Layard, *The Monuments of Nineveh* (London: J. Murray, 1853). (The George Peabody Library of the Johns Hopkins University)

The classic feminine role for women in war is that of victim. Above, painting by unknown artist, the *Massacre of Jane McCrae*. The event inflamed New Yorkers against the British and their Indian allies during the American Revolution. (Chicago Historical Society)

Allied propagandists drew on the same powerful symbol of woman as victim to stir passions against Germany and Japan during World War II. Poster by Gordon K. O'Dell, 1942. (National Archives of Canada/c-90883)

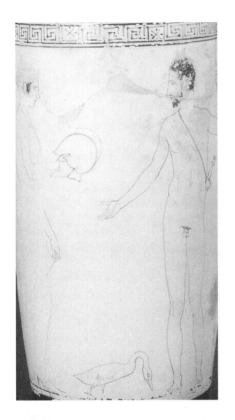

Women as instigators encourage men to fight. Left, an Athenian vase from about 440 B.C. (The British Museum) Below, New York City women from uptown Manhattan register immigrant men from the Lower East Side for the draft during World War I. (National Archives/165-WW 480 B-39)

Military wives brought comforts of home to soldiers' lives. Above, an early nineteenth-century drawing depicting a domestic scene in an English army barracks. (Courtesy of the Director, National Army Museum) Below, a military family's quarters during the American Civil War. (Library of Congress)

Women with a marching army carried their children along with spare clothing for the men, cooking equipment, firewood, and other articles. This drawing of an English scene dates from the early nineteenth century. (Courtesy of the Director, National Army Museum, London)

No. [ ]

Office of Provost Marshal,

Nashville, Aug. _____ 1863.

License is Hereby Granted to Anna Johnson a Public Woman to pursue her avocation in the City of Nashville, Tenn., she having received a Surgeon's Certificate of soundness.

If found plying her avocation without such License and Certificate she will be imprisoned in the Work=House for a period of not less than thirty days.

Residence _____ Street.

Geo. Spalding
Lieut.-Col. & Provost Marshal.

Sex workers have been recognized officially or unofficially by most military organizations. This license, issued by the U.S. Army in Nashville, was carried during the American Civil War by Anna Johnson. It identifies her as a "public woman," certified free of disease, and bears the signature of Provost Marshal Lt. Col. George Spalding. (National Archives)

Virago roles require masculine boldness and daring but do not challenge gender identity. These paintings represent nineteenth-century women who stepped into male roles. Above, Agostina of Saragossa is depicted in feminine dress rather than the tunic of an artillery captain that she actually wore. She won international recognition for her role in defending the Spanish town of Saragossa during a three-month siege in 1808. (Corbis) Below, an 1854 painting by Dennis Malone Carter, *Molly Pitcher at the Battle of Monmouth,* depicts the legendary heroine of the American Revolution, who first appeared in an 1849 engraving and was compared to the "Maid of Saragossa." (Courtesy of Fraunces Tavern Museum, New York City)

Guarding the rear is a virago role approved for women because it is related to the duty of a mother to defend her children. Above, Japanese women and girls were mobilized for defense during the Russo-Japanese war in 1905. (Library of Congress) Below, an Afghan militiawoman guards a guest house in Jalalabad for families returning from refugee camps in Pakistan in 1989. (AP/Wide World Photos)

Women's combat support roles bring them under fire. Above, woman's place during battle on an early nineteenth-century British man-of-war. Women carried powder to the guns and cared for the wounded. (National Maritime Museum, London)

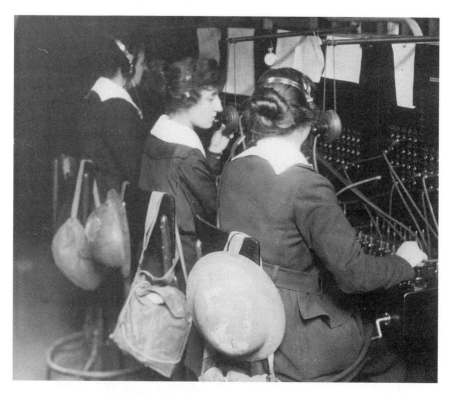

Women recruited for service in the U.S. Army Signal corps during World War I kept helmets and gas masks at hand as they worked the telephone switchboards at Scuilly during the Argonne drive. (Liberty Memorial Museum)

The earliest Amazons known to history were Amazigh from Libya. *Gorgon/Medusa*, left, is a reconstructed image of an African warrior woman based on a sixth-century B.C. marble relief from the Temple of Artemis at Corfu. The photograph appears in the JBL Devotional Statues catalog. (Courtesy JBL Statues, Crozet, VA 22932)

This representation of a Scythian Amazon adorns the rim of an Etruscan bronze mixing bowl from Campania in southern Italy, ca. 480 B.C. (The British Museum)

The Amazonomachy, the war between Greeks and Amazons, is depicted in a fragment of frieze from the Mausoleum at Halicarnassus, about 350 B.C. (Corbis)

The Amazons of Dahomey were first described by an English writer in 1727. Here they appear in a late nineteenth-century photograph. (Peter Newark's Historical Pictures, Bath)

Twentieth-century Amazons. Members of a Russian women's battalion of death train in Petrograd during World War I. (Trustees of the Imperial War Museum, Q106250)

Iranian women train in a segregated camp in 1986 during the Iran-Iraq war. (Farnood/Spia Press)

Individual women have served as androgynous soldiers throughout history by wearing male clothing and passing as men. In the last years of the twentieth century the integration of women as full members of the military has become a symbol of equality in the United States. Meanwhile, in Third World nations wartime conditions force all individuals capable of bearing arms into combat roles. Left, a lesbian army veteran demonstrates at the Pentagon. (© 1997, Washington Post Photo by Larry Morris, Reprinted with permission) Below, a girl soldier in Chechnya armed with an assault rifle shares guard duty with an adult male. (Agence France Presse)

CHAPTER SEVEN

THE AGE OF IMPERIALISM

Aᶠᵗᵉʳ ᵗʰᵉ ᶠᵃˡˡ ᵒᶠ Rome, Europe had been subject to attacks from other empire builders, Asian and African. But by the end of the fifteenth century, the Mongol advance had halted, Isabel of Castile and her husband, Fernando of Aragon, had conquered the Moors in Spain, and new lands had been discovered across the Atlantic Ocean. Rather than experience invasions by others, European nations were now building empires around the globe and fighting with each other over the spoils.

THE NEW WORLD

ᵂᴱ ˢʰᵒᵘˡᵈ ⁿᵒᵗ ᵇᵉ surprised that European explorers discovered women warriors throughout North and South America. The great Amazon River got its name when Indians in the region told the Spanish conquistador Francisco de Orellana that they were ruled by a tribe of women warriors who lived alone and raided other villages in search of mates.[1] Besides these all-woman armies, the Spaniards found many examples of men and women fighting side by side from the very earliest contacts.[2]

Nor were all the female combatants on the American side. Among the flamboyant conquistadors was Catalina de Erauso, known as La Monja Alferez, or the Nun Ensign, who wrote her autobiography at the end of her bloody career in the first half of the seventeenth century. She got her nickname when she ran away from a Spanish convent to which she had been sent at the age of four. It was expected that she would become a nun, but at fifteen she stole some money, a pair of scissors, and a needle and thread. Turning her bodice and petticoats into a doublet and breeches, she began a life of her own. Earning her passage to Central America, she swashbuckled her way through Mexico, Peru, and Chile. She wore male clothing, but this could hardly have served as disguise; in her Chile adventures she served under the command of her own brother. When she returned home, Pope Urban VIII gave her special permission to continue to wear men's clothing and Philip IV gave her a pension for her service in defense of the Spanish empire.[3]

The Spanish and Portuguese divided South America between them. In Central America and the Caribbean, the French, English, and Dutch joined the Spanish in claiming colonial rights. In North America, Swedes and English added their claims to those of the other empires. All of the indigenous inhabitants of what the Europeans called the New World felt the deadly impact of the invasion. The Indians of North America were so weakened by disease and ecological disaster caused by the introduction of European life-forms, including humans, that the dominant culture of the continent became that of the conquerors. The Europeans took elements from the cultures they destroyed and made them their own, but as had occurred many times before in Europe and Asia, entire civilizations lost their identities and even their languages.

The roles of women in indigenous American cultures varied at least as widely as in different cultures in Europe. Their roles in warfare included the tasks of motivating warriors, supporting them logistically and morally, following them to war, and occasionally becoming combatants themselves, as had Awashonks and Weetamoo during King Philip's War.[4]

Probably the best known of Indian women warriors is the Cherokee Nancy Ward, whose name is an Anglicized version of her real name, Nanye'hi, combined with the name of her second husband, who was a white trader. She was born at Chota, a village on the Little Tennessee River, and first became prominent in 1775 when she fought alongside her first husband, Kingfisher of the Deer clan, at the battle of Taliwa, a skirmish between Cherokees and Creeks. Her original role in this engagement was combat support; she crouched behind a log next to her husband and chewed the musket balls so they would make more deadly lacerations if they hit a target. When he fell, she took his place on the firing line, fighting so well that she was credited with securing the Cherokee victory. As a reward for her valor, she became Agi-ga-u-e (or Ghigua), or Beloved Woman, the title given to women who distinguished themselves by warlike deeds.

Among the ceremonial duties of the Beloved Woman, a rank that had judicial and spiritual as well as military aspects, was preparation of "the black drink" given to warriors leaving for battle. Nancy Ward did not fight again, but she continued as a leader of her people as they resisted encroachment on their lands. There were no permanent Indian victories against the European onslaught, and like so many other gallant fighters, Nancy Ward died in exile. According to her great-grandson, at her death in 1822 a light rose from her body and flew out toward Chota. Thirteen years later the Cherokees gave up all claim to their historic homeland and were removed by government decree to new territory in the Southwest.[5]

Wars continued, and armies of the United States fought tribal warriors as the frontier was pushed west mile by mile. In 1845, during an expedition on the Klamath, American soldiers frequently saw women fighting or found their bodies on the battlefield. Sometimes the women fought in separate units: "One day the savages came suddenly upon them . . . filling the air with a perfect shower of arrows. But not a male barbarian was in sight. Before them, in serried line of battle, their women were moving to the charge, while the warriors slunk behind them, discharging their arrows between the women."[6]

In the years following the Civil War, Americans finished the job of "winning the West." The Indians of the Great Plains had a form of warfare still rooted in the traditions of primitive war but adapted for combat with white soldiers. Despite the new rifles, Indian warriors could hold their own against the U.S. Army. What they could not survive were epidemic disease and the destruction of their food staple, the buffalo.

Male keepers of tradition among the Indians, like those of Europe, sang of "arms and the man"; the women's war songs are muffled. A poignant illustration comes from the memory of Pretty-shield, a Crow medicine woman, who told her story to Frank B. Linderman, a collector of oral traditions, more than sixty years ago. After repeatedly assuring Linderman that, as a woman, she knew nothing of battles except what she learned from her husband, he recounts:

Pretty-shield paused, a quizzical look in her eyes. Leaning toward me she asked in a half whisper, "Did the men ever tell you anything about a woman who fought with Three-stars [Gen. George Crook] on the Rosebud?"

"No," I replied, wondering.

"Ahh, they do not like to tell of it," she chuckled. "But I will tell you

about it. We Crows all know about it. I shall not be stealing anything from the men by telling the truth.

"Yes, a Crow woman fought with Three-stars on the Rosebud . . . . [S]he was a wild one who had no man of her own. She was both bad and brave, this one. Her name was The-other-magpie; and she was pretty. . . .The woman, I remember, wore a stuffed woodpecker on her head, and her forehead was painted yellow. Her coup-stick was big medicine that day, and she rode a black horse. She went to war because her brother had lately been killed by the Lacota. She wanted to get even, and she did. Riding straight at the Lacota, with only her coup-stick, she spat at them: 'See,' she called out 'my spit is my arrows,' She rode against a Lacota's horse, even struck the Lacota with her coup-stick, counting coup on him. . . . The-other-magpie took his scalp. She was waving it when I saw her coming into the village with the others. Yes, and I saw her cut this scalp into many pieces, so that the men might have more scalps to dance with."

Pretty-shield had been speaking rapidly, her dark eyes snapping. Now she leaned back in her chair. "Ahh," she said a little bitterly, "the men did not tell you this; but I have. . . . and I hope that you will put it in a book, Sign-talker, because it is the truth."[7]

THE INDIAN WARS

The Indian Wars of the late nineteenth century meant virtual extermination for the original inhabitants of the continent, but they were not very bloody for the U.S. Army. Especially in contrast to the Civil War, the pacification of the West scarcely seemed like a military operation at all. Gen. Tasker H. Bliss observed that it was a common saying in the regular army at that time that military surgeons at the western forts "had nothing to do but confine laundresses [in childbirth] and treat clap."[8]

The "laundresses" were what was left of the old institution of camp followers.[9] The gap in status between officers' ladies and working women loomed even larger in the West where common soldiers could not bring wives and often took Mexican or Indian women as partners. Most soldiers, however, were forced to seek female company off-post since the army had a strict quota for laundresses. At the beginning of the nineteenth century, Congress authorized women to accompany the troops at a ratio of four laundresses for every one hundred men. Over the years, as other forms of work for camp followers disappeared, the ratio became slightly more liber-

al: one laundress for every nineteen and one-half men. The company commander decided which women would get the limited number of jobs. One
officer explained, "It is the captain's privilege to make or unmake them
[laundresses], it is sort of a right of appointment that he has in common
with the right of appointing his first sergeant."[10]

Army laundresses were given quarters, fuel, one daily ration, and the
services of the post surgeon. Enlisted men and officers paid them for washing at fixed rates, and the laundry bill was deducted from their pay. As camp
followers, laundresses served at the captain's pleasure; he could fire them at
any time, and they were subject to military law. Domestic quarrels were not
private, and military justice was severe. One laundress in distress wrote to
Maj. L. H. Marshall at Fort Boise, Idaho, describing how she had been
arrested, charged as a murderess, and confined in the guardhouse for hitting
her husband with a tin cup that he claimed was an ax. She appeared before
an officer who sentenced her to be drummed off the post under force of fixed
bayonets. After that, she and her three children had to live in a cold house
without the food ration they depended on. A sergeant once threatened her
with flogging or death because during a march she put two of her children
in an ambulance.[11]

Even without this sort of trouble life was hard for military women. At
some posts the officers condoned polyandrous arrangements, with three or
four men claiming the same woman as wife. It was assumed, however, that
laundresses would be legally joined to enlisted men; the *Regulations of 1863*
specifically connected the number of married enlisted men with the authorized number of laundresses.

Army wives provided much more than sexual service. Hardworking Mrs.
Nash of the 7th Cavalry attracted the attention of Elizabeth Custer, the general's wife. "Old Nash," according to Mrs. Custer, not only worked as a company laundress but retailored soldiers' uniforms and baked pies. She managed
to accumulate a tidy nest egg, which her first soldier husband took from her
and then disappeared. She did not get a formal divorce but married another
soldier and went with the regiment to Dakota. He was no better than the
first, also stealing her money and deserting. Her third consort was an enlisted man, serving as Capt. Tom Custer's servant, and proved a better match.

Old Nash was popular with both the women and the men of the
regiment because in addition to her washing, sewing, and baking, she was a
skillful nurse and midwife and just plain fun to have around. Mrs. Custer
described a company ball at Fort Abraham Lincoln organized by the com-

pany first sergeant. Officers and their ladies attended. Although they danced on their own side of the room, they could see the enlisted men and their wives enjoying themselves on the other. The women put their babies on the first sergeant's bed as they went to dance. Mrs. Nash wore a "pink tarleton and false curls," and she "had constant partners."[12]

By 1878, Mrs. Nash had a fourth husband, a corporal at Fort Meade in the Dakota Territory. While he was off campaigning, Mrs. Nash became gravely ill. Aware that she was dying, she begged the women attending her to disregard the last rites and bury her as soon as she was gone. But the women felt Mrs. Nash deserved a decent funeral and laid out the body as Mrs. Nash had laid out those of so many others over the years. And so they discovered that Mrs. Nash had a secret: she was biologically male.

Although most laundresses doubtless were equipped to meet a husband's sexual needs in the expected form, too few of them were available for every man to claim one as a wife, and many soldiers were jealous and would not even allow their wives to dance with others. In 1881, President Rutherford B. Hayes made it illegal to sell liquor on a military base, so army men looking for any kind of good time went out to the "hog ranches" where "watered whiskey and wayward women" were available for a price. These establishments were outside the post, unregulated and unsupervised. By contrast, the laundresses' shacks were models of propriety.[13]

In 1876, when Congress moved to abolish the position of company laundress, many senior officers spoke up in their defense, pointing to the good influence they had on the men. Gen. George Sykes said that just seeing and talking to the women made the troops "more contented." Gen. J. C. Kelton declared, "It had been discovered ages ago that no community of men can prosper where there are no wives and children." The army wives, he said, were superior women and their offspring "just as neat and charming as may be found in any community." He firmly believed that the "influence of these women and their helpless families [was] of incalculable advantage to the men of the garrison, cut off for years from home influences." Maj. Gen. E. O. C. Ord even recommended increasing the number of laundresses and doubling the quota for companies of black soldiers, who, he said, "[were] domestic in their attachments, [and] . . . miss[ed] the society of women." He said that in his experience laundresses were good honest married women, wives of his best soldiers. He warned Congress that discharging the laundresses would result in mass resignations because the low wage enlisted men received required that their wives have an opportunity for paid employment.[14]

But other officers thought enlisted men could do without wives and the problems of base housing and moving goods that they caused when troops changed stations. Said one colonel, "All these little tribes have to be provided with shelter, cooking stoves, etc. and when troops were reassigned, the "transportation of all the laundresses' paraphernalia, children, dogs, beds, cribs, tables, tubs, buckets, boards, and Lord knows what not, amounts to a tremendous item of care and expense." He urged Congress to permit no women except hospital matrons to live on the posts. Capt. Henry G. Thomas said flatly, "Get rid of them!" In his opinion the men married to the laundresses were the worst, not the best, soldiers—because when children became ill, they had to care for them so that their wives could do the company wash.[15] These critics represented the wave of the future. Congress estimated the government could save several hundred thousand dollars a year by establishing post laundries and discharging the women. General Orders No. 37 of 1878 abolished the position of laundress in the American army.[16]

AFRICAN WARRIOR WOMEN

AT THE SAME TIME that Euro-Americans completed their conquest of the North American continent, the European nations divided Africa among themselves. By 1914, maps of what was once called the Dark Continent showed in bright colors the colonies of Great Britain, France, Germany, Italy, Portugal, Belgium, and Spain.

The original inhabitants of Africa did not die off as the indigenous people of North America had. For one thing, African microbes were more deadly to Europeans than anything the Europeans brought with them that might weaken the Africans, the reverse of the situation in America. And despite their less sophisticated technology, the African armies resisted the invaders much longer.

Powerful warrior queens ruled in Africa from the days of the Libyan Amazon empire,[17] and when Europeans rediscovered the continent in the fifteenth and sixteenth centuries, they encountered them again. Queen Amina (or Aminatu) ruled the Hausa empire of west and central Africa from about 1536 to 1573 and expanded its boundaries to the Atlantic. She led her army of 20,000 soldiers, built fortifications and cities, and established trade routes into North Africa. Her capital city was in Zazzau, which was later renamed Zaire after her youngest daughter. Farther south, in Nigeria, Bazao-Turunku was queen of a warrior tribe. But the most celebrated of the African queens was Jinga Mbandi (or Nzingha Mbande, or Zinga).

Jinga became queen of Ngola (today Angola) in 1624, shortly after the Portuguese had founded Luanda as a base for their slave trade. African rulers were willing participants, selling members of other tribes, but they wanted to control the trade and, of course, to keep their own independence. Before she became queen, Jinga had handled negotiations with the Portuguese for her brother, but when she succeeded him, the Portuguese declared war.

Through alliances and conquests, Jinga built a powerful African coalition to oppose the Portuguese. Her armies, which included many women, helped the Dutch slave traders take Luanda from the Portuguese. A few years later the Portuguese took it back, but they decided it would be more profitable to negotiate with Jinga than to continue fighting her. A peace agreement made in 1656 lasted until Jinga's death seven years later.

Despite their cooperation in slave trading, Jinga's people had many habits that the Europeans, both Dutch and Portuguese, found distasteful. They practiced infanticide much more openly than Europeans, for one thing, and they also consumed human flesh. A Dutch captain named Fuller, who commanded sixty Dutch troops who were in the queen's service for several years, described Jinga's performance of a ritual sacrifice. She wore "man's apparel" for this occasion with "the skins of Beasts, before and behind." A sword hung around her neck, an ax was belted around her waist, and she held a bow and arrows in her hand. The queen, who was well over sixty at the time, then began to leap "according to the custom, now here, now there, as nimbly as the most active among her attendants" as she struck two iron bells. "When she thinks she has made a show long enough, in a masculine manner," wrote Fuller, "she takes a broad feather and flicks it through the holes of her bored Nose, for a Sign of War." Jinga then chose the first sacrificial victim, cut off his head, and drank "a great draught of his blood." Captain Fuller grew accustomed to the queen's eccentricities, and despite her "Devilish Superstition and Idolatry," he came to respect her. She was, he wrote, "a cunning and prudent Virago, so much addicted to arms that she hardly uses other exercises; and withal so generously valiant that she never hurt a Portuguese after quarter given, and commanded all her slaves and soldiers alike."[18]

Jinga was not the only African ruler to have women soldiers in her armies. Almost one hundred years earlier a Portuguese official named Duarte Barbosa described a central and south African state where the king "always [took] with him into the field . . . a great band of warriors, and five or six thousand women, who also [bore] arms and [fought]." A book entitled *Report on the Kingdom of Congo,* published in 1591, described an emperor who ruled a huge territory with massive armies divided into legions. Of these, the book tells us, "those most renowned for bravery, are the female legions, greatly valued by the Emperor, being the sinews of his military strength." The women soldiers were not merely strong but also tactically clever:

> *In battle they resort to very warlike maneouvres, retiring at times as if put to rout, and taking flight, yet turning around to assail their adversaries with arrows; and, on seeing the enemy elated with victory, already beginning to disperse, they suddenly turn and repulse them with great slaughter. So that on account of their wiles and cunning as well as rapidity of action in battle, they are held in great dread in those regions.*[19]

THE AMAZONS OF DAHOMEY

In 1727, Captain William Snelgrave discovered women warriors in West Africa who would become famous as the Amazons of Dahomey. Because Snelgrave was a slaver, he was interested in developing his contacts with African rulers. He accepted an invitation to visit the king of Dahomey in what is modern-day Benin. The English party found him sitting on a gilt throne surrounded by his female bodyguards. They were naked from the waist up, carried flintlock muskets on their shoulders, and wore gold rings around their arms and beads around their necks and in their hair. On another visit a few years later, Snelgrave heard that the Dahomean king had lost a great many men in the wars he fought to capture slaves and, as a result, had expanded his army of women. Snelgrove reported, "He ordered a great Number of Women to be armed like Soldiers and appointed Officers to each Company, with Colours, Drums and Umbrellas, according to the *Negroe* Fashion. Then ordering the Army to march, the Women Soldiers were placed in the Rear, to prevent Discovery."[20] This first account of the Amazons of Dahomey in battle appears to be an example of the ancient tactic of using women in disguise to make an army look larger than it really was. But they soon become a fighting force in their own right.

By 1850, England had repudiated the slave trade and was hunting slavers as pirates. Frederick Forbes was an antislaver, who made two visits to the court of Dahomey to learn more about the slave-hunting wars. He gave his impressions of the king's elite brigade:

> *The amazons are not supposed to marry, and, by their own statement, they have changed their sex. "We are men," say they, "not women." All dress*

alike, diet alike, and male and female emulate each other: what the males do, the amazons will endeavour to surpass. They all take great care of their arms, polish the barrels, and except when on duty, keep them in covers.[21]

In 1856, John Duncan, formerly of the British Life Guards, wrote of them:

> *They seem to use the long Danish musket with as much ease as one of our grenadiers does his firelock, but not, of course with the same quickness, as they are not trained to any particular exercise, but on receiving the word, make an attack like a pair of hounds, with great swiftness. Of course they would be useless against disciplined troops, if at all approaching to the same numbers. Still their appearance is more martial than the generality of the men; and if undertaking a campaign, I should prefer the females to the male soldiers of this country.*[22]

Duncan described their uniforms as consisting of "a blue and white striped cotton surtout, the stripes about one and a half inch wide, of stout native manufacture, without sleeves, leaving freedom for the arms. The skirt or tunic reaches as low as the kilt of the Highlanders. A pair of short trousers is worn underneath reaching two inches below the knee."[23]

Sir Richard Burton, British consul at Dahomey from 1861 to 1865, left detailed descriptions of the Amazons, as did J. A. Skertchly, an insect collector who spent eight months in Dahomey in 1871. The army, these men reported, numbered about four thousand and was divided into three brigades, each of which wore a distinctive headdress: "The king's brigade, sometimes called the Fanti company, or centre, wear the hair shaved *à la turban*, and bound with narrow fillets, with alligators of coloured cloth sewn on them. The right wing have their heads shaven, leaving only a solitary tuft or two, while the left wing wear the hair *au naturelle.*"[24] Within each brigade there were four classes of soldier. The Agbaraya, or blunderbuseers, were the veterans and only went into action as reserves. They, however, were the biggest and strongest of the women, and each was accompanied by a servant who carried ammunition. They wore distinctive blue tunics and carried the most ferocious banners, showing images of an enemy being cut to pieces or blown apart with a musket shot.

A second class of soldier, the Gbeto, or elephant hunters, were known as the bravest troops. They proudly displayed the scars from close contact with wounded elephants. The Nyekplehhentoh, or razor women, carried a hinged sword about eighteen inches long that folded into its scabbard like a razor.

They used the blade to decapitate enemies. The largest class of soldier was the Gulonetoh, or musketeers, who were infantry. Burton noted that they were armed with Tower muskets but had bad ammunition and had to use bamboo fiber for wadding. The elite Fanti company had a fifth type of soldier, the Gohento, or archers, who were young girls armed with bows and poisoned arrows plus a small knife strapped to the wrist. The Gohento served as scouts and porters. "They are savage as wounded gorillas," Burton wrote of the Amazon army, "more cruel far than their brethren in arms."[25]

For most of the time the Dahomey's Amazon army existed, it waged annual slave wars; the king paid the warriors for their captives and then sold them to the Europeans on the coast. But the market for slaves declined in the nineteenth century as slavery was banned in Europe and then in the United States. In the second half of the century, France began expanding her interests along the Gold Coast. When Behanzin, king of Dahomey, attempted to enforce his right to tax a French trading post at Porto Novo in 1890, the French resisted and defeated his army. Behanzin wanted revenge, but he realized that the French had superior weapons. So he purchased machine guns, breech-loading rifles, and artillery from traders and in 1892 invaded Porto Novo with an army of 12,000: 2,000 Amazons, 5,000 male soldiers, and 5,000 armed slaves.

The French commander, Colonel Dodds, had 150 marines, 800 Foreign Legionnaires, 1,500 Senegalese riflemen, and 300 Houssas, under French officers. Together with a company of engineers, a battery of mountain artillery, a few cavalry, a transport and ambulance detachment and a riverboat armed with machine guns, the force totaled just under 3,500. Dodds's orders were to leave enough soldiers to protect Porto Novo and take the rest of this army seventy miles into the disease-ridden forest to attack and destroy Abomey, the Dahomean capital. Their progress across swamp and rain-sodden bush was slow. After two months they reached the River Koto. The king's palace was in sight; so was a triple line of entrenchments and artillery on the higher ground on the other side of the river. As Dodds's force was hacking through the bush along the water, the Amazons attacked, picking off the French as they struggled through the tangled vegetation.

The Gbeto women took the offensive, using new high-powered rifles made even more deadly by the exploding bullets usually used to bring down elephants. Dodds realized that he could not get across the river and that his men were almost out of water. Meanwhile the Amazons continued to advance, using giant anthills as cover. Dodds retreated and waited for reinforcements. Then, unexpectedly, Behanzin offered a truce. The next day, the French crossed the bridge over the River Koto—and met a fusillade of rifle and artillery fire. The French fixed bayonets, and the battle between French and Amazons became furious hand-to-hand fighting from trench to trench. After half an hour the Dahomean line broke, and this was the turning point of the war.

The French advanced toward Abomey, but as Dodds's troops marched the final miles, they heard a series of explosions. Behanzin had destroyed the city rather than let it fall to the French. That was the end of Dahomey; its land and people became part of the French Empire.[26]

INDIA

THE GREATEST OF THE nineteenth-century empires belonged to Great Britain. It was an empire on which "the sun never set," and by the end of the century fully one-third of the British army was stationed in India, halfway around the world from home.[27] The decline in the need for women's services in the army led to a sharp restriction on marriage for soldiers, the same trend that occurred in the United States. Early in the century, general opinion held that it was a great asset to have women follow the flag, not simply because they were companions who made the hard life in the camps more bearable but also because they served as cooks, seamstresses, and above all laundresses. As an officer in the 95th Rifles put it, with no women in the regiment, "the ceremony of washing a shirt amounted to a servant's taking it by the collar and giving it a couple of shakes in the water, and then hanging it up to dry."[28]

Since wives came to have no value except to provide homelike comforts and produce children, the ancient ambivalence toward the baggage train could be resolved. In the nineteenth century, military families were not necessary for a soldier; indeed, they hindered his performance rather than encouraged it. The classic view is expressed by Rudyard Kipling:

> *The bachelor 'e fights for one*
> *As joyful as can be;*
> *But the married man don't call it fun,*
> *Because 'e fights for three—*
> *For 'Im and 'Er and 'It*
> *(An' Two an' One make Three)*
> *'E wants to finish 'is little bit,*
> *An' 'e wants to go 'ome to 'is tea!*[29]

Kipling also coined the adage, "the Colonel's Lady an' Judy O'Grady are sisters under their skins." In practice, there was an enormous social gap between "officers' ladies and wives of other ranks," as there was between officers and enlisted men. In the nineteenth century, however, marriage was discouraged for both classes of soldiers.

Soldiers of all ranks needed permission from their commanding officers if they wished to marry. The commander would decide whether he thought the match was appropriate as well as whether too many men in his command were already husbands. Quotas varied according to the branch of service (more cavalrymen than infantrymen could marry), rank (more noncommissioned officers than privates), and any other factor, like having savings in the bank, that the commander wanted to consider. Generally everything possible was done to discourage matrimony. For instance, in the 1860s the Standing Orders of the 52nd Light Infantry stated:

To prevent the inconveniences that arise from the incumbrance of too many women and children, officers commanding companies must, at all times, make every reasonable exertion to prevent their men from contracting imprudent marriages, as well for the interests of the regiment as of the men themselves.

The regiment cannot furnish employment for more than a few women, consequently any increase of numbers diminishes the means of existence of those already belonging to the regiment. The small quantity of accommodation in barracks, the difficulty of procuring lodgings, the frequency of moving, and inconveniences attending marches and embarkations, are to be urged as dissuasives against imprudent marriages.[30]

Since family connections were useful in obtaining promotion to the higher ranks in the officer corps and since the fortune of a wealthy wife might be useful to a gentleman after his retirement, some grudging approval was given to marriage by officers. As a general rule, it was said, subalterns may not marry, captains might marry, majors should marry, and lieutenant colonels must marry.[31] But many officers thought that no soldier of any rank ought to have a family. One who had married expressed exactly this view to his wife. "The fact is a soldier has no business to be married," Gen. Ian Hamilton wrote to Mrs. Hamilton. "He is no longer whole-hearted in his pursuit of glory." Another man wrote to his sister from the Crimean War, "I have seen by far too much of the folly and misery of a married officer in

Service ever to make me marry as long as I wear a red coat. . . . It is sad to see . . . the sad depression of spirits I have witnessed in more than one married officer—first rate officers spoilt." To his mother, the same officer wrote, "I have seen quite enough of married life in this campaign to prove to me that marriage and soldiering are totally incompatible."[32]

Some men found giving up marriage, indeed giving up sexual contact with women, to be easy. Although they kept overt homosexual activity discreet, Gen. Charles George Gordon, who defended Khartoum during a ten month siege, clearly preferred boys, and Gen. Horatio Kitchener, who led the force that lifted the siege, was fond of young men and allowed no married officers on his staff. Others, including many married officers, were so closely bonded to the men in their regiment that they seemed not to miss feminine companionship. Lady Wolseley wrote to her husband, "You have no time for God or me. I don't say that unkindly, but it is a fact—is it not?" During one seven-year period during his career, Gen. Evelyn Wood spent only fourteen and a half months at home, and most of that time he was off hunting.[33]

Most of the officers opposed to marriage did not object to nonmarital affairs. Two officers were overheard in the mess of the 2d Scottish Rifles discussing the recent marriage of a comrade. "Another good officer lost," one of them said. "Well, they won't catch us—we'll whore it out to the end."[34] Ironically, the army of Queen Victoria, having decided family life was inappropriate for its mission, provided its men opportunities for safe sex with prostitutes.

A joint committee appointed by the war office and admiralty studied the subject of venereal disease and the systems used by European armies to regulate prostitutes, which included compulsory examination of prostitutes and the forced detention of diseased women. Florence Nightingale opposed "regulated" prostitution and influenced the appointment of committee members who made such recommendations as the following: "Soldiers should be encouraged in some handicraft to occupy their time in barracks. A greater number should be allowed to marry."[35] But the military establishment ultimately got its way, and the first Contagious Diseases Act was passed in 1864 and then expanded in 1869. This legislation identified eighteen garrison and seaport towns in which, henceforth, any plainclothes policeman could arrest any woman he had "good cause to believe" to be a "common prostitute" and order her examined in a certified hospital. If she was found to have a venereal disease, she could be confined in the hospital for up to six months. The law also established a system of registration for prostitutes, and a justice of the peace could order a woman to report for medical examinations twice a month for as long as a year. A woman who refused to be examined could be sent to prison for two months.[36]

The Contagious Diseases Act seemed to be common sense to the military, but it outraged civilians, especially civilian women. Throughout the sixties and seventies reformers published hundreds of pamphlets and leaflets with arguments such as this one:

If we rely for our security upon a celibate army, and upon the sanitary benefits which are supposed to accrue from the Acts, we shall assuredly lean upon a broken reed, and one day discover that immorality, whether legislative or personal, inevitably leads to national decay. . . . At present the soldier is only valued as a fighting machine. He is compelled to live in a state of laborious idleness. He is practically shut out from preferment beyond a certain inferiour grade, by the aristocratic exclusiveness with which the army is officered. In his barrack-room he enjoys none of the comforts of domesticity—he is there compelled to herd indiscriminately with men whose bad example may exercise a pestilent influence on his own character.[37]

The army outside of England suffered less interference from critics, and officers proceeded to provide for the "needs" of their men by making arrangements with sex workers and giving them suitable housing and supplies. To prevent conflict with local patrons, the army brothels, called "rags," were for English troops only and soldiers were forbidden to patronize any others. Medical officers examined the prostitutes several times a week. Local commanders made their own arrangements. For instance, the brothels at Agra had about forty women and girls, ranging in age from twelve to thirty. They were required to have towels, vaseline, Condy's fluid, and soap and were fined if an inspection showed any of these to be lacking.

In 1904, Lt. Col. Patrick Mantell, commander of the 1st Welch Fusiliers in Burma, took action against the spread of venereal disease by pulling down the huts of the Chinese and Burmese prostitutes around the camp. Then he built new huts and imported twelve Japanese prostitutes. A private in the battalion proudly said, "During the fifteen months I served in Burma there was never a case known of a man contracting venereal with the Japs in the rag."[38]

In many parts of the world, prostitution was a traditional occupation, and everywhere freelance prostitutes congregated around army camps. The military simply offered them a formal arrangement. Regimental Sgt.-Maj. John Fraser of the Northumberland Fusiliers expressed the general opinion when he said, "An army, especially an army in a hot, tropical country—without prostitutes available, is likely in a very short time to become a menace rather than a safeguard."[39]

Perhaps if there had been no wives at all with the armies abroad, this neat military solution could have continued without criticism. As it was, the small quota of soldiers' wives and the "memsahibs" of the officers did not share the same perspective on military brothels. What some soldiers and others called "the Shrieking Sisterhood" joined the critics of the Contagious Diseases Act at home. There, members of Parliament heard testimony from the Baptist Missionary Society and other reformers, who provided detailed descriptions of the army's system of prostitution, as did a Mr. Dyer:

> *In an official report a boastful emphasis was laid on the fact that the "women in Sitapur are well kept." In a camp at Lucknow, thirteen tents were erected for the accommodation of prostitutes who accompanied the brigade and who stood under the orders of the generals. Likewise, the Lucknow barracks were given quarters for public prostitutes who occupy 72 apartments located on both sides of a street; these quarters built by British authorities from funds reserved for the army, are better furnished than the homes of the natives. . . . The commanding officer of a regiment in passage from Bombay to a distant camp, personally requisitioned a number of prostitutes who were to follow the soldiers from one halting-place to another, and to the provost of the field chaplain he said he had orders from higher up. At each halting-place, a flag was run up over the camp of the prostitutes to let the soldiers know where to go.*[40]

In 1888, the opponents of the Contagious Diseases Act triumphed; they succeeded in closing the rags, at least officially. Within a few years, however, a soaring rate of venereal disease led the military authorities to return to the system of regulated prostitution "so successfully practiced in the French and German armies in Europe."[41]

Because such a large proportion of the army was in India, even with the quota system more soldiers' wives lived in India in the nineteenth century than anywhere else outside Great Britain, and this was the case until India finally won independence after World War II. Soldiers stationed far from home were permitted to marry native women, and many did. Although the marriages were sanctioned, these women received a wife's allowance only half that given to European women because, as the regulation put it, having "been born in India and habituated to live chiefly on rice, the wants of half-caste women are much less than those of European women."[42] Regiments might remain stationed "east of Suez" for many years. Soldiers who could not get permission to marry took mistresses. Children were born, and, as had been the case for the Roman legionnaires centuries earlier, the fathers had de facto families. One battalion of the Green Howards remained in Ceylon for twenty-five years, but when they were ordered to move on, only women officially "married on the strength" could follow the men. The government recognized no responsibility, and neither the soldier nor his mistress-wife was ever likely to have enough money to pay for the passage that could reunite them.

The original involvement of Great Britain in India came about through the commercial dealings of a private corporation, the East India Company, and India did not became a Crown colony until 1858. Although the company faced charges of inefficiency and corruption for decades, it managed to survive criticism. But the last straw, as far as Parliament was concerned, was the Indian Mutiny of 1857, in which a young woman, Lakshmi Bai, the rani of Jhansi,[43] was a leading actor.

Unlike the practice in North America, the colonial powers in India did not replace the indigenous population with their own settlers. Consequently, friendly relationships and treaties with ruling families were essential to the conduct of business. Until 1853, relations between Jhansi and the British had been very good. An English officer who spent many years stationed at the Jhansi court wrote, "I have always considered Jhansi among the native states of the Budelkhand as a kind of oasis in the Desert."[44] Difficulty arose when the ruler, Gangadhar Rao, failed to father an heir. His first wife died childless. His second wife, Lakshmi Bai, did bear a male child, but the infant unfortunately died within a few months of his birth. When Gangadhar Rao became ill, he adopted an heir, a five-year-old boy named Damodar Rao, a relative who was a member of the royal line. Then Gangadhar Rao died. The governor general of India refused to recognize the rights of the rani and the adopted heir, declaring that Jhansi was now the property of the East India Company.

The governor had already annexed other territory on the same grounds—that an adopted son was not an heir under the terms of the treaties with local rulers. Not only did Indians resent these annexations, but the assumption of illegitimacy of an adopted son also struck at an important tenet of the Hindu religion. The sacrifices of a son kept a deceased father from suffering punishment in the afterlife, and an adopted son was capable of performing these religious duties. The rani drafted petitions to the British authorities and retained an English lawyer, who advised her to take her appeal to London. When these appeals failed, she retired into private life—temporarily.

Meanwhile, British insensitivity toward Indian customs and religious beliefs sparked a revolt of supposedly loyal Indian troops. The soldiers were horrified to learn that they had been issued rifle cartridges, which they would have to tear open with their teeth, that had been greased with pork fat, a substance abhorred by the strictly vegetarian Hindus. As the mutiny spread, the English turned to the rani for help. She was asked to "take your kingdom and hold it, along with the adjoining territory, until the British authority is established."[45] Because she tried to oblige, she was also threatened by the mutineers, who found her overly tolerant of foreigners. They besieged City Fort in Jhansi and killed the Europeans who had taken refuge there, most of them women and children. Then despite the British request that the Rami hold the territory, they sent no official confirmation of her jurisdiction over Jhansi. Instead the English suggested that she had supported the mutineers who massacred Europeans at City Fort, and when another massacre occurred at Cawnpore, they blamed her for that too.

The memory of the events at Cawnpore on July 15, 1857, would poison relations between Indians and Europeans for almost ninety years, until the British finally left the continent. The slaughter of 211 British women and children was followed by ten times that number of Indian deaths as the British soldiers retaliated with a worse atrocity. Then they went after the rani. Her father was captured and hanged. Clearly, whatever her wishes, the rani was now obliged to fight. She recruited an army, strengthened the defenses of the city of Jhansi, and prepared to resist a siege.

The British were surprised by the quality of Jhansi's defense. The male troops worked more energetically than they ever had under British officers and the women organized by the rani not only carried food and ammunition to the soldiers but also worked the gun batteries.[46] Lakshmi Bai was constantly visible and fired on the enemy herself. When the British made their assault on the city, she was in the thick of fighting that left an appalling number of casualties. British histories place the number of casualties at four thousand or five thousand and say that civilians were spared. But a priest from Bombay who was present remembered four days of burning, looting, and murder. The rani escaped, but troops vented their frustration by destroying her home. Dr. Thomas Lowe, a British medical officer, described her lovely apartments with their plate-glass doors, mirrors, chandeliers, velvet and satin beds, cushioned chairs, silver bird cages, ivory footstalls, "and a thousand other things such as a luxurious woman would have." Unable to get their hands on the rani, "the soldiery went to and fro tramping over and through these things and kicking them about as they would any heap of rubbish."[47]

The rani joined forces with Rao Sahib, another Indian ruler. Together, they seized the fortress at Gwalior, and when the British attacked, she was there in charge of the eastern side of the defense. She wore armor, a sword with a jewelled scabbard, and a fabulous pearl necklace taken from the Treasury at Gwalior. According to tradition, she told her troops, "If killed in battle we enter the heaven and if victorious, we rule the earth." At some point in the fighting that followed the rani was killed. The private journal of Lord Canning contains the entry: *"Ranee of Jhansi*. Killed by a trooper of the 8th Hussars, who was never discovered. Shot in the back, her horse balked. She then fired at the man and he passed his sword through her."[48]

Once she was dead, the British could afford to be generous to her memory. Sir Hugh Rose's report on the final action said, "The Ranee was remarkable for her bravery, cleverness and perseverance; her generosity to her Subordinates was unbounded. These qualities, combined with her rank, rendered her the most dangerous of all the rebel leaders." The regimental history of the 8th Hussars says, "In her death the rebels lost their bravest and best military leader." For the Indians, she became a symbol of resistance to British rule. A study published at the centenary of the Indian Rebellion states, "The Rani's noble example and supreme sacrifice have blazed the path for countless sons and daughters of India to join the freedom struggle. She is one of the immortals of our national movement."[49]

THE BOER WAR

THE LAST OF THE nineteenth-century wars of Western imperialism was fought in South Africa. The first European contact with that part of the world had been Portuguese; Vasco da Gama rounded the Cape of Good Hope in 1498 and described his encounter with the yellow-skinned Hottentots who were then the only inhabitants of the region. Although other voyagers followed da Gama, the first permanent settlement was not established until 1652. In that year Johan van Riebeck of the Dutch East India Company brought four women and about one hundred men to the tip of Africa to create a supply station for company ships on the way to India.

After building a fort and planting crops, van Reibeck wrote home to demand an additional shipment of "lusty farm wenches."[50] With their arrival, the population began to grow.

For a few decades the Hottentots fought with the Dutch colonists, but they were finally defeated and began working for the white farmers. Then, in 1688, another group of European immigrants joined the colony: a group of about 175 Huguenots who were religious refugees from France. Like the Dutch colonists, the new arrivals pushed fertility to biological limits. Although the French soon lost their cultural roots and adopted the language, religion, and lifestyle of the Dutch community, large numbers of French surnames survived. Soon after that, a number of German peasants arrived, tempted by the offer of free land in the colony. They, too, were assimilated, and the Dutch-French-German settlers became a distinct people who called themselves Boers, a word meaning *"farmers,"* and spoke a variation of seventeenth-century Dutch, now known as Afrikaans.

The Boers liked large farms, situated well apart from their neighbors, and the rapidly growing population pushed the boundaries of the colony to the northeast. Eventually, the Boers collided with the Bantu, and for more than a century the two groups battled for control of the rich grazing lands known as the veldt. By the mid-nineteenth century, the Boers had forced the Bantu into submission; they became servants of the white farmers.

Although the Dutch East India Company founded the settlement, the Boers were never docile colonists. They were fiercely independent and devoted to republican principles that eschewed all hierarchy. During the Napoleonic Wars, British troops occupied the strategic territory at the cape and afterward bought the colony from Holland. The Boers thus became British subjects without consultation or consent. Even worse, the English passed laws that seemed to be aimed at destroying Boer nationality. The burgher councils by which citizens had governed themselves were abolished, the Dutch legal system was eliminated, and English was made the official language in the courts.

The last straw was the emancipation of black workers. The Boer economy was based on black labor, and the Parliament, seemingly unconcerned with that reality, announced from far-off London that the labor system was slavery and that all black workers would be freed on December 1, 1834. The Boers, with their seventeenth-century attitudes toward race, could no more make this rapid adjustment than slaveholders of the American antebellum South could have done. The emancipation date, set just at the time of the wheat harvest, meant ruin for most farmers. Although Parliament promised compensation, the payment had to be collected in London and would in no way make up for the loss.

The Boer response to English attempts to govern them according to British notions of right and wrong was the Great Trek, a mass exodus from the Cape Colony. Boer families, together with their herds of animals and their black workers, moved in two directions. Some went north onto the high veldt; others moved northeast into Natal. They traveled slowly in ox-drawn wagons at the pace set by the animals, the women giving birth in wagon beds or on the bare ground and the men and boys guarding the train to protect the company from animals or hostile humans. In the end, they settled in new homes and established two independent Boer states, the Transvaal and the Orange Free State.

The British made several attempts to annex the new Boer land, especially since it soon became much more valuable for its underground wealth than for its grassy plains. In 1867 diamonds were discovered near the Orange River in 1867, and in 1886 gold was discovered in the Transvaal. The gold rush attracted thousands of foreigners, whom the Boers called "Utlanders." Although these people came from all over the world, most of them were British citizens who expected England to defend their demand for equal rights. The British representative, Sir Alfred Milner, insisted that all Utlanders who had lived for more than five years in the Transvaal should have voting rights. The president of the Transvaal, Paul Kruger, realizing that the new voters would outnumber the Transvaal burghers, protested, "It is our country you want."[51] Milner abruptly terminated the negotiations, and the Boers went to war.

The English did not expect to have much difficulty defeating a small nation of farmers, yet the war that began in October 1899 did not end until May 1902 and then only after the Dutch government helped to mediate a peace. By the end of the war, the British had sent 300,000 troops to deal with approximately 60,000 to 75,000 Boers. During the first few months, despite the modern weapons used by both sides, the fighting resembled eighteenth-century warfare, with formal battles, individual heroics, and civilian spectators. The last eighteen months, however, resembled wars of our own time, with guerrilla combatants and appalling numbers of civilian casualties.

Neither the Transvaal nor the Orange Free State had a conventional standing army. Instead, they had a citizen army; all able-bodied male citizens between sixteen and sixty were expected to report for military duty when needed, an exercise known as "going on commando." Each farmhouse was a supply station, since every man going to war was expected to bring a horse, rifle, ammunition, and provisions for eight days in the field. Wives packed up the rations, which consisted of biscuits and dried meat called *biltong*. Although burghers had to take up arms when called to commando, they did not owe unconditional obedience. In republican style, soldiers dressed in civilian garb with no distinguishing badges or medals, even for officers. Generals and ordinary soldiers slept in the same tent. Commanders had to persuade rather than order their troops; tactical decisions were made by consensus of commanders, and individual commanders or soldiers could refuse to participate in an engagement if they disagreed with the plan. In some of the early major battles, the British could see armed burghers, sometimes accompanied by their wives, watching the action from a vantage point off the field.[52]

By September 1901, the large British force had invaded and overrun both Boer states. President Kruger, however, did not surrender; he fled to Europe to try to win support for his people's cause while the Boer commandos continued to wage guerrilla warfare. Kruger soon had plenty of ammunition with which to appeal to the conscience of the world, for as guerrilla campaigns replaced conventional warfare, Gen. Horatio Herbert Kitchener, the British commander in chief, adopted a strategy targeting women and children. In Europe, America, and even on the floor of the English House of Commons, the campaign in South Africa was now denounced as a war of genocide.

Kitchener's strategy of land clearance was designed to deny the Boer enemy the refuge and resupply provided by their families. He did this by burning down their farmhouses, killing their livestock, and carrying the homeless civilians to concentration camps. For him, it was a simple matter of military necessity. Kitchener was a man of cold, logical temperament. He never courted a woman, had no intimate friends, and took pride in his ability to make unemotional decisions. He envisioned the concentration camps as places where the displaced civilians would be fed, housed, and protected. There is no evidence of deliberate cruelty; those in charge of the camps did the best they could under the circumstances. But the end result was the death of more than twenty-six thousand women and children. Since the entire population of the two Boer states was less than four hundred thousand, these deaths represented a catastrophic loss. *Genocide* is not too harsh a word.

The soldiers ordered to carry out the land clearance did as they were told. Capt. L. March Phillips gave this description:

The men belonging to the farm are always away and only the women left. Of these there are often three or four generations: grandmother, mother and family of girls. The boys over thirteen or fourteen are usually fighting with their papas. The people are disconcertingly like English, especially the girls and children—fair and big and healthy-looking. These folk we invite out onto the veldt or into the little garden in front, where they huddle together in their cotton frocks and big sun-bonnets, while our men set fire to the house. Sometimes they entreat that it may be spared, and once or twice in an agony of rage they have invoked curses on our heads. But this is quite the exception. As a rule they make no sign, and simply look on and say nothing."[53]

Phillips described one child who did the only thing she could to protest the destruction of her home:

At another farm a small girl interrupted her preparations for departure to play indignantly their national anthem at us on an old piano. We were carting the people off. It was raining hard and blowing—a miserable hurried home-leaving; ransacked house, muddy soldiers, a distracted mother saving one or two trifles and pushing along her children to the ox wagon outside, and this poor little wretch in the midst of it all pulling herself together to strum a final defiance.[54]

Both officers and soldiers sometimes looted the houses before they burned them, and the soldiers sometimes destroyed things just for the fun of it. Captain Phillips wrote,

Soldiers as a class (I take the town bred majority) are men who have discarded the civil standard of morality altogether, they simply ignore it. . . . Looting, for the sheer fun of the destruction; tearing down pictures to kick their boots through them; smashing furniture for the fun of smashing it, and maybe dressing up in women's clothes to finish with, and dancing among the ruins they have made. To pick up a good heavy stone and send it wallop *right through the works of a piano is a great moment for Tommy.*[55]

The Kitchener plan entailed establishing concentration camps near railroad lines for the civilians made homeless by his land clearance so that they could be easily supplied and defended. Eventually there were about fifty of these camps with a total inmate population of about 120,000. The largest, Potchefstroom camp, housed 7,400 people, and the smallest, Waterval North camp, held only 8, 2 men, 3 women, and 3 children. Conditions in the camps and their death rates varied considerably, with the worst in the camp at Merebank.[56]

Kitchener never visited a camp himself, but he assured members of Parliament that the people there had "a sufficient allowance and were all comfortable and happy." He had a subordinate make a tour and was confident in the report he received that the people were "well looked after and completely satisfied with all [they were] doing for them."[57] The truth was quite different, but it took a strong-minded Englishwoman named Emily Hobhouse to ferret it out and make the facts public.

Emily Hobhouse was born in the rectory of St. Ives, a village in eastern Cornwall. After her mother's death, she cared for her domineering father, who was a chronic invalid. When she fell in love with a farmer's son, her father broke up the match and the young man departed for America. Finally, when she was thirty-five, her father died. Hobhouse, now free, left the village and went to America. She spent two years in a mining town in Minnesota. She had a romance with the mayor, who also owned the general store, and followed him to Mexico when financial difficulties made it advisable for him to leave town suddenly. After Hobhouse's money ran out, he deserted her, and she returned to England. Hobhouse did not, however, return to St. Ives. She was no longer a submissive village girl but a woman of the world. When the Boer War began, she decided, like many others, to go to South Africa to have a look.

Not since the Crimean War half a century earlier had there been such an interesting opportunity for English travelers to inspect a war zone. Within a few months, organized Cook's tours included stops at battlefields. Other tourists set out on their own. Sir Claude and Lady de Crespigny took the opportunity to visit their three sons who were serving in South Africa. Since one son was ill, Lady de Crespigny spent some time nursing him in the hospital while her husband attached himself to a military unit for a few weeks. Many young officers whose regiments remained in England requested leave so they could go to see a real war, and many young ladies went as well. Lady Edward Cecil, who was one of those, waxed nostalgic in her memoirs: "Nobody in those free and spacious days objected to women who came out to see their husbands or brothers, but there were plenty of others, some of whom were even mischievous."[58] One officer whose wife wanted to join him told her to stay home because she would not be able to find lodging in Cape Town where, he said, "every hole and corner is crammed with ladies who alternate squabbling among themselves with the washing of officers' faces."[59]

Queen Victoria did not approve of such visitors. Sir Alfred Milner, the governor of the Cape Colony, received a letter in April 1900 in which he was told, "The Queen regrets to observe the large number of ladies now visiting and remaining in South Africa." The governor passed this remark on to Field Marshal Lord Roberts, whose wife and daughter were then on their way to join him at Bloemfontein. Lord Roberts was sure there could be no objection to his relatives and so replied to the queen, "I understand that Your Majesty does not approve of ladies coming out of South Africa from mere curiosity. I am forbidding any to enter the Orange Free State, except those who have a son or husband in hospital, or whose husband is likely to be quartered in Bloemfontein for some time."[60] But a few months later, Emily Hobhouse was in Bloemfontein.

In December 1900, Hobhouse sailed to Cape Town. She had already been active in humanitarian war work back in England, raising funds for the South African Women and Children's Distress Fund. Until she arrived on the scene, she had never heard of the concentration camps. Within a few days, however, she contrived permission to visit the camp at Bloemfontein to distribute food and clothing paid for by the Distress Fund. She traveled on a military train and made a minute inspection of the camp with a Boer woman serving as her guide. She not only inspected, she talked to the inmates as well, bringing a sympathetic ear to their reports. She heard dozens of stories, each refugee having some homely detail making her narrative unique—the death of a lame chicken kept as a child's pet, a description of soldiers digging up the grave of a newly buried infant on the assumption that it was an arms cache, and always the repeated themes of a loved home left in flames, of cold and hunger, and of watching children suffer and die.[61]

Two days after her visit, Hobhouse had a blistering report for the Distress Committee. Conditions were abominable: soap and water were scarce, many people were sleeping on the bare ground, the camp was infested with flies and vermin. In one tent, she found a venomous puff adder, which she beat to death with her parasol after the Boer woman who was her guide fled. In conclusion, she told the committee: "I call this camp system wholesale cruelty. It can never be wiped out from the memories of the people. It presses hardest on the children. . . . To keep these camps going is murder for the children. Of course by judicious management they could be improved; but do what you will, you can't undo the thing itself.[62]

While the Boer men were at war, Bantu workers continued to sow and harvest the crops, and the black villages on the farms fed and gave refuge to Boer commandos. Kitchener's soldiers applied the land clearance policy to them as well. By the end of the war, more than fifty concentration camps for Africans housed an estimated eighty thousand inmates, most of them women and children. The mortality rate in these camps was also high, but no one ever investigated them and no reliable statistics exist. In her book, *The Brunt of War and Where it Fell*, Emily Hobhouse stated that 13,315 Africans died in the camps, but she never visited one, and her figures probably underestimate the actual number.[63]

Hobhouse now had a mission. She wrote home, "The authorities are at their wits end, and have no more idea how to cope with the one difficulty of providing clothes for the people than the man in the moon. Crass male ignorance, stupidity, helplessness and muddling. I rub as much salt into the sore places of their minds as I possibly can because it is good for them."[64] In May, she returned to England and publicized her findings, creating an uproar further fueled by vehement counterstatements from British South Africans. A Presbyterian minister wrote, "I have walked through every department of the camp at Johannesburg and have seen nothing to suggest hardship and privation. Everywhere there is evidence of cheerfulness and contentment."[65]

The British government hit on an unusual tactic to deal with the situation: they appointed a committee, called the Ladies Committee, to go to South Africa and investigate. Hobhouse asked to join but was told that the committee was to be impartial and she was obviously biased, so in October Hobhouse returned to South Africa by herself. While she was at sea, martial law was proclaimed in the Cape Colony, and on her arrival, Kitchener ordered her deported. She did not cooperate; soldiers wrapped her in a shawl and carried her onto a troopship for the return trip.

The Ladies Committee corroborated Hobhouse's findings, and there was an attempt to improve conditions. But the deaths of children from epidemic disease and malnutrition continued. After the war, Hobhouse returned to South Africa and helped in Boer resettlement. To the Boers she was a venerated heroine. She was buried in Bloemfontein next to the memorial honoring the women who died in the camps. This was also the burial place for Marthinus Theunis Steyn, the president of the Orange Free State Republic, and of Gen. Christiaan Rudolf de Wet, the commander in chief of the Orange Free State guerrilla force during the war. Burial at Bloemfontein was the highest honor that could be bestowed by the Afrikaans nation.

The pathetic conditions in the camps tempt us to remember the Boer women only as victims. But despite their misery, they remained defiant. In one camp, a demonstration was held on President Steyn's birthday; women and children marched through the camp waving Transvaal and Orange Free State flags and singing patriotic songs. When, late in the war, volunteer teachers came to the camps to teach the children English, one girl explained the value of the lessons thus: "I will try to learn English that I can say to the Kakky, hands up. I am twelve years old. This is my first English writing."[66]

Camp inmates could occasionally provide more active support for the Boer struggle. Some women saved up their rations and tried to smuggle food out to the guerrillas. A few women escaped from the camps and joined the commando bands themselves. Capt. Francis Fletcher Vane captured a woman guerrilla and was sufficiently interested in her history not only to record it but also to visit her family after the war. Ella Jacobs had been confined with her mother at the concentration camp at Springfontein. She and another girl escaped and went in search of Jacobs's two brothers. When she was captured, together with five other Boers, Jacobs was wearing male clothing and carrying a rifle and bandolier. She said she had been fighting with the unit for six months. She was quickly dubbed the "Boer Joan of Arc" but downplayed her combat service. She lived to be eighty-five years of age and in her later years referred to her military experience as "the follies of [her] youth."[67]

There is no way of knowing how many women may have worn male clothing to fight alongside the Boer burghers. But many women in skirts traveled with the commandos, enough so that the Boers were accused of using the tactic of firing from behind women. These women were refugees who, rather than wait for the British to burn their homes and carry them off to concentration camps, packed up their children and a few chickens and cows and drove their ox wagons out to the veldt. They only superficially resemble traditional camp followers. Rather than carry supplies and give logistical support, the women were a drain on the meager food and clothing the guerrillas could find on the veldt or steal from the British.

Eventually so many women were following the commandos that women's camps known as *lagers* sprang up. President Steyn had a report on conditions, which were as bad as anything in the camps, preferable only because the people living there were still free. According to the report, "The women and children, suffering almost every one from malaria, fever and other diseases in consequence of privations and bad food, without physicians, without medicines, without any consolation in this world, almost without any clothes, and after hostile raids, without any food at all."[68] General De la Rey's wife spent eighteen months in a women's lager with six of her children and three Bantu servants. Food and clothing were scarce. Captured British blankets were prized possessions, and the general's wife used captured British flags to make dresses for her daughters.

Eventually the British extended their activity against Boer families by incarcerating not only those burned out of their homes but also those following the guerrillas or camped in the veldt. They considered this a humanitarian act, for the people brought into the camps were usually in a pitiable state. Dr. Pratt Yule, a British medical officer in the Orange Free State, wrote, "Those who followed the commandos were in miserable condition. They were worn out, half clad, riddled with disease. At Kroonstad one batch brought in eight moribund and three dead. Many had lost from one to four children on commando."[69] Dr. T. N. Leslie wrote in his diary of women and children who were "ragged and unkempt and looked half-starved. . . . They wore a haunted look and their fragile bodies, worn down with the long privations and hardships they had shared with the men, were in striking contrast to the old-time buxom Boer vrow whose size and capacity was so long a byword throughout South Africa."[70]

The Boer women were in the war zone because that was their homeland. English ladies came to be with family members or out of curiosity or, like Emily Hobhouse, with the hope of doing some good. One other group of women spent the war years in South Africa: the women serving in the British Army Nursing Service. Although female nurses had been part of the regular establishment of the army since the Crimean War, only fifty-six nursing sisters and one "lady superintendent" were in service when the Boer War began. Fifty years after Florence Nightingale, army doctors were still prejudiced against women serving in their hospitals. It seemed unsuitable to have females treating soldiers with venereal disease, which made up a large proportion of the military hospital cases in peacetime, and it seemed unsuitable in wartime to have women go to the savage lands where the British army campaigned. In March 1900, when there were 207,000 troops in the war zone, there were only eight hundred nurses.[71] Sir William Wilson, the principal medical officer in South Africa, explained why there was a shortage: "We can get any amount of good trained nurses. . . . [T]he great difficulty is to get accommodation for them. A woman or a lady will always require a certain amount of accommodation: she must have all the bedroom equipment and everything else, and she must have servants. It was absolutely impossible to get female servants in South Africa as they are not to be had."[72]

The treatment of surgical cases had vastly improved since the scandals of the Crimean War, but the primary medical problem in South Africa was not wounds but disease. Doctors had no cure for such killers as enteric fever, and the only hope for patients was good nursing care, which might allow the sufferers' own immune systems to heal them. The shortage of nurses continued throughout the war, and convalescent patients were pressed into service as orderlies; yet, when criticized, two highly respected medical authorities insisted that the care given soldiers was excellent in spite of "a plague of flies and a plague of women."[73]

Although generals and physicians might not appreciate the quiet heroism of the nursing sisters, Queen Victoria did. The regular nurses of the Royal Army Medical Corps did not seek notoriety, and their public statements were always carefully phrased and emphasized how brave and uncomplaining their patients were. Still, Queen Victoria was so impressed by the work of the nurse Frances Bell that she personally handed her the Victoria Cross. Even though the award was named for the queen, Victoria had no authority to bestow it on a woman, and the honor was not officially gazetted.[74]

AMERICAN OVERSEAS IMPERIALISM

IN THE LAST YEARS of the nineteenth century, the United States, having "won the West," entered the competition for overseas colonies. The new steam-powered warships created a demand for coaling stations around the world, and before the end of the century, the United States acquired several tiny islands in the Pacific—Johnston Island, the Swan Islands, Wake Island, Midway Island, and Palmyra Island—plus exclusive rights to a naval station at Pago Pago in Samoa. In 1893, U.S. marines helped American revolutionaries overthrow the Hawaiian government of Queen Liliuokalani. In many parts of the Pacific, including Hawaii, New Zealand, New Guinea, and Malaya, women traditionally fought alongside men. In the Ladrones (now known as the Mariana Islands), they fought amazon style under female leaders.[75]

In North America, the United States purchased Alaska from Russia in 1867. Later the United States supported a revolution by the inhabitants of Cuba directed against Spain, which had claimed that island since the fifteenth century. After the Spanish-American War that followed in 1898,

American opponents of imperialism prevented the grab of Cuba, but the United States, as a result of the war, ended up in control of the Philippines, Puerto Rico, and Guam. Two months after the Spanish-American War ended, the people of the Philippines, who had expected independence as the reward of victory, rebelled against their new foreign rulers. For the next three years sixty thousand American troops engaged in guerrilla warfare in those faraway islands.

As a modern world power, the United States adopted policies with regard to women similar to those of the European nations. The army regulated prostitution in the Philippines for the "protection" of its soldiers,[76] and soon afterward recognized American women nurses as part of the military establishment. For the twenty years following 1878, when the army eliminated the position of laundress, no women, except those who may have been disguised as men, served in the American military. As soon as the Spanish-American War began, however, it was clear that the military could not do without them. In particular, the new profession of nursing was dominated by women as the army discovered when an epidemic of typhoid fever swept the camps. An attempt to recruit six thousand men for patient care failed. The surgeon general appealed to Congress for authority to appoint women nurses, which was granted with the understanding that these nurses would be *civilian* contract workers not to be confused with those men in the army who cared for the sick and were *soldiers*.

Meanwhile Clara Barton's American Red Cross nurses, following the Civil War tradition, did not bother to wait for an invitation but were in Cuba even before the declaration of war. A woman physician, Anita Newcomb McGee, devised a method whereby women nurses could serve the army without being *in* the army.

McGee was born into a prominent family in Washington, D.C., and earned a medical degree from Columbian (now George Washington) University before taking additional training in gynecology at the Johns Hopkins University. She practiced medicine for just a few years, however, since her great interest was making contacts and organizing. Her position in Washington society gave her access to government leaders. When McGee heard of the need for women nurses, she spoke to the surgeon general, George M. Sternberg, and got his tentative approval for her plan to screen applicants for wartime nursing positions. Then she presented the plan to a national executive meeting of the Daughters of the American Revolution

(DAR). They named her chairman of a DAR hospital corps. With this credential she went back to the surgeon general and he appointed her acting assistant surgeon general.

The Spanish-American War was finished very quickly, and casualties were light. But fifteen hundred American women served as nurses under contract to the army and navy in the United States, aboard the hospital ship USS *Relief*, and in Cuba, Puerto Rico, Hawaii, and the Philippines as well as in Japan and China. Dr. McGee, encouraged by this success, drafted legislation that would establish a permanent nurse corps and the regulations that would govern it in the Army Reorganization Act of 1901. When the legislation passed, however, Dr. McGee lost her job; the corps would be directed by a graduate nurse, not by a physician.

Dr. McGee found other ways to keep busy. She organized the Society of Spanish-American War Nurses, of which she served as president. During the Russo-Japanese War of 1904–5, she offered this group's services to the government of Japan, and she and nine veterans of the Spanish campaigns spent six months working alongside Japanese nurses. William C. Braisted, a navy surgeon, who was also in Japan during the war, admired the Japanese nurses. He said, "The Japanese woman has occupied so long a position so subordinate and has been trained to an ideal of obedience so absolute that they are specially fitted for service in military establishments."[77]

Such docility was not, however, required of the American Dr. McGee. The Japanese gave her the title "supervisor of nurses" and military rank. She visited hospitals in Japan, Manchuria, and Korea and wrote reports on their operations. At the end of the war, the Japanese awarded her the Imperial Order of the Sacred Crown and other military decorations. Although she would never hold military rank in her own country, McGee was buried with military honors in Arlington National Cemetery when she died in 1940.[78]

CHINA

CHINA CLAIMS A SPECIAL place in the history of Western imperialism, although it never became a European colony. The wealth and splendor of China, described in seductive detail by Marco Polo, fired the imaginations of Europeans from kings to cabin boys, and for those who made the first voyages to open trade routes, it was the mysterious promise of the Orient that jsutified the great risks and enormous suffering.

China was a quasi-mythical land at the dawn of the age of exploration, but Chinese history is still a mystery for most Americans today. Even Africa, once know as "the Dark Continent," has received better coverage in American schools. Yet China has a longer tradition of written history than the West. According to Xiaolin Li, the foremost scholar of Chinese women's military history, "The history of women's involvement in military activities in China is probably longer and more continuous than that of any other country in the world."[79]

The earliest known Chinese woman soldier was a general named Fu Hao, who lived about 1200 B.C., four hundred years earlier than the Assyrian Summuramat whose history was recounted by Herodotus. A written record of her military activities and favored strategies and tactics inscribed on bones and tortoise shells dating to the middle and late Shang Dynasty (16th century B.C. to 11th century B.C.) was discovered by Wang Yirong, a Chinese epigraphist, in 1899. Thirty years later the inscriptions were translated, and the excavation of her tomb in 1976 was a major archaeological event.[80]

Chinese history based on written sources extends farther back than Western history. Chinese scholars long before Herodotus kept local annals of significant events. According to Li, each of the approximately three thousand counties in China has an archive, some of which date back more than five thousand years. In addition, there is a thousand-year-old literary tradition, begun by the scholar Liu Xiang, which is devoted to recording lives of "exemplary women." Only scratching the surface of this rich collection of resources, Li has gathered a database of more than two hundred individual military women, most of them famous in China.[81]

The most famous is Wei Hua Hu (also known in legend as Hua Mulan), who lived in the third century A.D. She was the daughter of a sergeant. Raised in a military family, she received military training from her father. When he was called to active duty after his retirement, he was too old to serve, and his son was too young. Hua therefore put on male clothing, purchased a horse and saddle, and reported for duty. She was stationed in Wan county, and the local annals, as well as later scholars, record her history.

Hua served in the imperial army for about twelve years, receiving promotions and rewards for her military skill. The sources say that in all this time, no one realized that she was a woman. At the end of her long service, the emperor wished to reward her by making her a general, but she refused. She asked only that she be given a camel to return to her home. The emperor gave her the camel but also an honor guard as an escort, and her return to her home revealed the secret she had kept for so many years. There are two versions to the end of this story. In one, she married a general and settled into a conventional woman's role. In the other, which Li believes to be more credible, the emperor ordered her back to serve in the imperial court as his concubine.

The first all-woman army known in Chinese history was formed by Princess Ping Yang, who died in A.D. 623 or 624 at the age of twenty-three after a considerable military career. She, like Hua, wore male clothing when she raised troops to battle the enemies of her father, the emperor of Tang. After conquering several neighboring counties, her army had grown to seventy thousand. She married a famous general named Chai Shao. She and her husband had separate headquarters, and the princess created a segregated women's unit. An area in Shanxi Province was renamed Women Pass to memorialize the all-female army that was stationed there.

Princess Ping Yang is not the youngest of China's military heroines. That distinction belongs to Xun Guan, who, like Wei Hua Hu, came from a military family and received military training from her father. Her fame rests on an exploit, carried out when she was only thirteen, while her father's city was under siege. She broke out of the encirclement in a daring midnight mission at the head of several dozen soldiers.

Li's collection of Chinese women soldiers includes women "commanders in chief, who won many military victories, as well as female laborer/defenders, who participated in one battle of hometown defense. Chinese women fought in segregated units, in militia organizations, in large-scale campaigns, and in defense of a single farming estate or village."[82] And they appear in all time periods.

Although China never became a European colony, the British did manage to seize Hong Kong in the nineteenth century and to force acceptance of British traders in China's major port cities. In the last decade of the century, China was defeated in the Sino-Japanese War, after which Russia, Germany, and France also scrambled for concessions. In 1899, when Italy demanded a Chinese port, Tzu Hsi, the empress dowager of China, was able to drive them off, and shortly after that militia forces, known as Boxers, organized a movement designed to drive out all foreigners. But the Boxer Rebellion ended with defeat in 1900 and further concessions to the dozen Western nations that were asserting their interests in China.

Still, the empress Tzu Hsi remained in power. The Manchu dynasty was not overthrown by foreigners but by a movement organized in Japan by

Chinese students under the leadership of Sun Yat-sen. Revolution broke out in October 1911, Sun Yat-sen became president of the United Providences of China in December, and the following year the boy emperor of China abdicated.

Throughout this period of turmoil, women were conspicuous actors. In the mid-nineteenth century, a peasant uprising known as the Tai Ping Tian Guo Movement involved thousands of women officers and soldiers organized in segregated amazon battalions. They carried out a range of military assignments including combat, and individual women are remembered for participation in the revolutionary movements at the turn of the century. Qui Jin, who organized an unsuccessful uprising in Shaoxin, Zhe Jiang Province, was prominent in the final overthrow of the dynasty. She was captured and executed.[83]

Chinese women continued in active military roles in the early years of the Chinese communist movement. About 3,000 participated in the famous thirteen-month Long March in 1934–35, which covered more than 12,500 kilometers and had more than 500 military engagements. They continued to be visible through World War II and the Liberation War (1945–49) when the communist forces became officially known as the People's Liberation Army (PLA).

CHAPTER EIGHT

THE GREAT WAR

URING THE CENTURY BETWEEN the defeat of Napoleon at Waterloo in 1815 and the assassination of the archduke Francis Ferdinand in Sarajevo, which triggered what was known at the time as the Great War, Europeans avoided military actions involving all the major powers at once. In the last decades of the nineteenth century, war was something remote and romantic for those at the center of Western Civilization. Wars were of two sorts. The most colorful wars were fought far from home in Africa or Asia. In Europe armies conducted short campaigns with limited political objectives, most of them involving the nation-building activity of Italy and Germany. The list of these wars, none of which lasted longer than a year, begins with the Franco-Austrian War of 1859 and concludes with the Franco-Prussian War, which ended in 1871.

At the turn of the century, military strategists such as Alfred von Schlieffen and Helmuth Karl Bernhard Moltke fine-tuned plans for action should there be any testing of the stable balance of power the European nations had achieved. These plans called for the largest possible offensives to be launched as rapidly as new technology would allow. Some military theorists believed that growing militarization in the nineteenth century, including enormously lethal weapons, meant the end of wars between major powers on the grounds that no one would be foolish enough to start one. Some confidently asserted that being armed to the teeth was the guarantee of peace in the civilized world.

No one deliberately triggered World War I, although vigorous attempts were made to fix blame after the fact. The original birthplace of war, at the edge of the steppe in eastern Europe, was a tinderbox of ancient hostilities and warlike traditions. A shot fired by an assassin in the Balkan town of Sarajevo set off a chain of preplanned military responses and brought all the major powers of Europe into full-scale war before anyone quite realized what was happening. The first public reaction to the mobilization of huge, well-equipped armies by one nation after another was surprise. Europeans thought they had become too civilized for such activity. The second was the thought that it might be fun and even beneficial for the soft civilized nations to get back in touch with their barbaric roots.

Attitudes toward war in the nineteenth century had become intertwined with three developing ideologies: pacifism, feminism, and "compulsive masculinity."[1] Praise for war and warriors is as old as history. Criticism of war is far rarer. A number of religious sects, notably the Quakers and the German Mennonites, reacted to the slaughter of the Thirty Years War by committing themselves to nonviolence. Those same sects were notable for a commitment to women's equal participation in the religious community. After the Napoleonic Wars the first secular peace groups organized in New York and London. Women activists of the time were prominent in these groups, as they were in the antislavery and early women's rights movements that appeared simultaneously. In 1844, a French feminist, Eugenie Niboyet, published the first pacifist journal in Europe. It was only during the last three decades of the century, however, that a real peace movement appeared and an international feminist movement became strong and visible.[2]

Although most peace activists were feminists, most feminists were not peace activists. During the Civil War, the American women who had been most active in the women's rights movement plunged into war activities. And they did so again during World War I; suffrage marches became war bond drives. Women may have been discouraged from taking up weapons, but there was nothing innately pacifist about them. Those feminists who supported the peace movement saw it as fitting into a broader vision of democracy, egalitarianism, and social justice that would be better advanced by international cooperation than by a resort to arms.

Meanwhile, the feminist movement itself challenged the pattern of masculine dominance that had been part of European civilization since the Roman conquest. It made men, particularly upper-class men socialized in the sadomasochistic tradition of English public schools, extremely uncomfortable. "Compulsory masculinity" was the response to this discomfort, and war proved the ideal metaphor for the qualities these men valued most as being different from women.

From the perspective of the closing years of the twentieth century, the pre-World War I enthusiasm for battle is almost incomprehensible. Nevertheless, it was real, and it was shared not only by men but also by women, who felt that they too could display "masculine" virtues such as courage, stoicism, and even gallantry if only they had a proper stage for action. In the United States, Theodore Roosevelt was the great proponent of war as an ennobling experience. He came close to triggering, single-handedly, the war with Spain, which he called a "splendid little war," and he is a fine source of pro-war quotations. In 1900 he wrote, "If we seek merely swollen, slothful ease and ignoble peace, if we shrink from the hard contests where men must win at the hazard of their lives and at the risk of all they hold dear, then bolder and stronger peoples will pass us by, and will win for themselves the domination of the world."[3] For him, even the fratricidal Civil War was sublime: "We are all, North and South, incalculably richer for its memories."[4]

Roosevelt was hardly unique; similar sentiments appeared in writing from every part of Europe. From Ireland: "Bloodshed is a cleansing and sanctifying rite and the nation which regards it as a final horror has *lost its manhood.*" From Spain: "When a nation shows a civilized horror of war, it receives directly the punishment for its mistake. God changes its sex, despoils it of its common mark of virility, changes it into a feminine nation, and sends conquerors to ravish it of its honor." And Italy: "We are out to glorify war, the only health-giver of the world! militarism! patriotism! The Destructive Army of the Anarchist! contempt for women!"[5]

Somehow this pattern of thought survived even the far from glorious war years in which soldiers huddled for months at a time in muddy trenches threatened by poison gas and artillery shells launched by enemies too far away to see. The literary conventions of the war years carried the mythic heroism of warfare to an extreme. As Mark Gerzon puts it in *A Choice of Heroes,* "The idea of combat was so infused with sexual energy that it became a romantic myth."[6] The language of Sir Walter Scott's medieval fantasies was the staple of popular journalism. Horses were "steeds," the enemy was "the foe." The dead never became corpses or carrion but "ashes and dust." And the dead never died: they "fell." Men also discovered that combat provided a context in which they could experience certain feelings that were taboo in ordinary circumstances: "In the trenches of the First World War, men came to love one another decently, without shame or make-believe, under the easy likelihoods of their own sudden deaths. While Europe died meanly in its own wastes, men loved."[7]

For women to participate in this exalted experience would destroy the attraction of the fantasy. Women were supposed to display their courage and heroism by bearing children and then bravely sending the boys off to battle. Nevertheless, as in every war, women combined other roles with their biological functions. Some were in the war because the war came to them and there was no choice. But many others sought out the experience and went to the front because the thought of battle was for them as seductive as it was for males. An American reporter, Mrs. Mabel Potter Dagett, who went to Europe to research a book called *Women Wanted,* described the attractions and concluded, "I know of no more impressive place to be on the closing days of the year 1916 than here at the front of the terrible world war."[8]

Some women felt so comfortable in the "masculine" roles they took on during the war that they wondered whether they were really "women" at all. The new science of sexology had identified a new gender category, the "sexual invert." With that starting point, some women began to develop a specifically female homosexual category: "lesbian." The war years saw the early stirring of a lesbian subculture in some parts of Europe although it would not reach the United States until after the war.[9] Most women who enjoyed increased freedom and responsibility, as well as the thrill of danger, during the war years believed they were merely "new women." They were independent and competent, even strong and daring, but not "inverts" and certainly not men. They were by no means denying their gender simply because they put on pants and went to war.

WOMEN SOLDIERS

HISTORY GROWS CLEARER AS events come closer to our own times. Cultural conventions are more familiar, and abundant photographic evidence fleshes out the documentary records. Whatever uncertainty or ambiguity exists for women serving as soldiers in wars prior to the twentieth century, it is certain that many women who served in military uniform during World War I were keeping no secret and attempting no disguise.

Women who disguised themselves in order to become soldiers or sailors appear regularly in the relatively quiet century prior to 1914, although in much smaller numbers than they had in the two previous centuries. As always, we only know of those who were discovered and usually very little about them. A clipping from an 1877 issue of the *London Times* reported the death in action at Kaclyevo of a young Russian officer "known now to be a woman, after displaying most brilliant gallantry in rallying the men against the Turks."[10] In Italy, one Sylvia Mariotti served from 1866 to 1879, participating in combat against the Austrians at the Battle of Custozza.[11] In March 1907, a sailor known as John Wilkinson serving aboard the USS *Vermont* was found while taking a bath to be female.[12] And a report in the *Daily Telegraph* described an incident in 1908 in which German twins had joined the French Foreign Legion: the male twin went to the medical examinations twice, and his sister served for six months until the commandant ordered a muster parade for showers and revealed her secret.[13]

The best-known women soldiers of the Great War, however, are well known precisely because they never made any pretense of being anything but what they were: women in uniform. In the Balkans, where the tensions that triggered the war were centered, Amazon traditions had never died and the cultural category "sworn virgins" provided a context for women assuming male roles. In Serbia, northern Albania, and Kosovo, the tribal culture was characterized by blood feuds and a strong patriarchal hierarchy. Women were little more than the property of their fathers or husbands, but they had one alternative to accepting an arranged marriage. By swearing to remain unmarried and renouncing sexual relations with men, a woman might become a sort of honorary male. Such women wore men's clothing and carried weapons, an important gender marker in that society. In a family that did not have a male heir, an infant girl might be declared a "son" and reared as a boy. Or if the male head of the family died, an older girl could swear the oath and replace her father or brother.[14] Sworn virgins had the same duty to fight that biological males accepted, and other women who were celibate and "manly" might join the Balkan armies as well. Serbian peasant women fought in the war between Turkey and the Balkan League in 1912.[15]

Even foreign women might be accepted in the Serbian forces. In 1875, Jenny Merkus, a Dutch social reformer, supported the Herzegovinian revolt against the Turks and joined the Serbian army, but she was never "in disguise." A Serbian writer described her appearance in Belgrade:

She was a young, rich, but far from beautiful Dutch woman. . . . As she dressed like a man and rode horseback, she was known as the amazon of the Herzegovina uprising. All Belgrade seemed to go mad about this female revolutionary. The poet Jura Jaksic sang, "Our Joan, not the one from Orleans, yet her equal, as pure as an angel." On the evening of Palm Sunday a torchlight procession was organized in her honor. Jenny appeared on the balcony with a Montenegran cap on a large mop of blond hair, and this feminine figure with a man's cap . . . caused more enthusiasm than if Peko Pavlovic [leader of the revolt] had turned up in person.[16]

Flora Sandes, an Englishwoman from a middle-class background, became internationally famous as a Serbian soldier during the Great War and wrote books and lectured on her experiences.[17] She went to Serbia in August 1914, just days after the fighting started. She signed on as an ambulance nurse, she later told an Australian audience, "with no more idea of going as a soldier than any other lady now in the hall."[18] But a soldier she became, rising to the rank of corporal in charge of a platoon. She proved she was "man enough" to deserve the respect of her fellow soldiers by enduring the hardships in the field—rain, freezing nights, typhus, and artillery fire—without complaining. She also suffered combat wounds; her right arm and leg were smashed by a grenade. While hospitalized in Solinka, with another woman sergeant named Milunka who had also been wounded, she received the Kara George Star, pinned to her pajamas, and was made sergeant major. In 1919, she became a lieutenant, and in 1926 she was again promoted, to captain. The following year she married a fellow officer, Yuri Yudenitch, who was a former general in the Russian army,[19] For her, as for so many others, the war represented the best years of her life, and she was as nostalgic for the male camaraderie she had shared as any other soldier:

Sometimes now, when playing family bridge for threepence a hundred in an English drawing-room, the memory of those wild, jolly nights comes over me and I am lost in another world. So far away it all seems now that I wonder whether it was really myself, or only something I dreamed. Instead of the powdered nose of my partner I seem to be looking at the grizzled head and unshaven chin of the Commandant, and the scented drawing-room suddenly fades away into the stone walls of a tiny hut lighted by a coupe of candles stuck into bottles and thick with tobacco smoke, where five or six officers and I sit crowded on bunks or camp stools. . . . I return to the prosaic drawing-

room with a start, and the realization that I am a "lady" now and not a "soldier and a man."[20]

We know of only one Englishwoman who served as a soldier in the military forces of her own nation during World War I, and she did not stay on duty very long. In 1915, Dorothy Lawrence disguised herself as Pvt. Dean Smith and joined a British Expeditionary Force tunneling company at the Western Front. After ten days on duty, she confessed the deception to her sergeant, who at first seemed understanding. But as soon as she returned to her work laying mine fuses, a military policeman turned up to place her under arrest for espionage.[21]

The military career of an American woman ended even before she reached France. Hazel Carter stole an army uniform, cropped her hair short, and boarded the troop train carrying her husband, Cpl. John Carter. She got away with the disguise for two days until a suspicious officer put her off the train. She mingled with the crowd of soldiers taking a break at the stop and, when the train started, got back on again. She made it to Hoboken, New Jersey, found the troopship carrying her husband, and again escaped detection for several days. Eventually, because of a rumor that a woman was aboard, her squad was paraded onto the afterdeck for a medical examination, which ended her brief military career.[22]

There is one isolated report of a German woman serving as a lieutenant of the German hussars,[23] and there may have been more cross-dressed women than we now suspect in other European armies. Russia, however, was the only major power to admit large numbers of women to the ranks during World War I. The Amazon traditions of the steppe still endured. Russia's various tribal cultures supported the ancient custom of women following the armies and, when necessary, fighting together with the men. No disguise was involved in such arrangements. Throughout the war women's names appear in Russian lists of new recruits. Some asked for permission to become soldiers; some just showed up on the lines. English and American newspapers found the women soldiers intriguing and carried reports about them, suggesting that despite considerable tolerance for women serving openly, many women soldiers were concealing their gender. In 1915, the *London Graphic* stated that about four hundred women soldiers were serving in Russia, mostly in Siberian regiments, and that about fifty of these were passing as males until death or wounds revealed them to be female.[21]

Russia's easy acceptance of women in the ranks was, in part, related to the conditions in peasant society, where women worked side by side with men in the fields, and the question of whether a female was strong enough for combat duty consequently never arose. By contrast, the hard physical labor performed by working-class women in Britain at this time did not lead to similar acceptance of them as soldiers. But, of course, Britain did not face an enemy on her own soil.

Many Russian women felt they had no choice when they joined the army. Of course, they would go to the front; everyone they knew was going. Rosetta Forbes, an English journalist, spoke to a former Russian Red Army woman who said, "I had to go the front. The whole of my village went. I didn't think about [whether I liked fighting]. I had to do it."[25] Marina Yurlova, who published her memoirs under the title *Cossack Girl*,[26] literally drifted into a military career as she was shoved accidentally into a train filled with Cossack women from her village who were following their men to war. She was only fourteen, but she believed her father was somewhere on the train and was more excited than frightened at the prospect of becoming a camp follower. "As with my companions, so with me it was a blind instinct to follow men to war," she wrote. But when the train reached its destination and the men disembarked, she realized that her father was not one of them and she was in an unknown place separated from her family. She started to cry, which attracted the attention of a "big Cossack" named Sergeant Kosloff. He took her under his wing, gave her regulation trousers, a khaki shirt, boots and a lambswool hat, and said, "All right, synok (sonny), before I die, I'll make a Cossack out of you." For two months, the girl groomed horses, but as the company awaited orders to ship out to Armenia, they cut off her pigtails and gave her a saber and she became one of them.[26]

Even more intriguing to foreign observers than women serving alongside men in integrated units was the Russian creation of real Amazon units: the all-female Battalions of Death. The first battalion was organized in 1917 by Maria Bochkareva, who had been serving in integrated combat units. Her appeal for female volunteers brought out women of all nationalities and social classes: stenographers, dressmakers, domestic servants, factory workers, university students, peasants, and middle-class ladies. Women responded eagerly, with as many as fifteen hundred enlisting in a single night. Enlistments continued to grow rapidly during the summer of 1917, and women's battalions sprang up in Moscow, Perim, Odessa, and Ekaterinodar.[27]

Unlike women recruited for service in women's auxiliaries in other nations during this war, the Russian women soldiers were armed and trained for combat. They were given regulation short haircuts and unadorned men's uniforms with no special gender markers. They were, however, required to take an oath of chastity for the duration, just as were nursing sisters, and special regulations confined them to barracks. Giggling or frivolity was punished with dismissal, and other breaches of discipline with slaps across the face. Bochkareva once personally bayoneted one of her soldiers discovered fornicating.[28]

Maria Bochkareva's call for women to volunteer as soldiers emphasized feminine values. Her forces, unlike the ancient Amazon armies, were subordinate to a military hierarchy and a nation-state controlled by men. Placing women in segegated units emphasized, rather than minimized, gender distinctions. "We women are turning into tigresses to protect our children from a shameful yoke to protect the freedom of our country," she told recruits.[29] Maternal instinct, not a quest for glory or adventure, was what sent them into the trenches. And a significant part of their mission was, by their example, to shame men into greater efforts as the Imperial Russian Army began to crumble under relentless German pressure.

Women soldiers who served in integrated units had no desire to be part of such an amazon corps. Flora Sandes said of the women's battalion, "I'd very much like to see it but I don't think I'd like to be in it." Florence Farmborough, an English Red Cross nurse who attended a woman soldier in a Red Cross station at Illisheysti, found her patient had heard of the Battalion of Death, but "from her curt remarks one could understand that she held them with little respect."[30] Louise Bryant, who interviewed former members of the Battalion of Death in 1918, found that they were disillusioned with the amazon experiment. Anna Shub, who enlisted at seventeen because she believed "the poor soldiers of Russia were tired after fighting so many years and . . . we ought to help them," felt later that she should "die of shame" when she found the Battalion of Death was meant to embarrass the soldiers. Another said that she had enlisted out of patriotism and continued "We expected to be treated as heroes, but always we were treated with scorn." The women Bryant interviewed intended to continue military service, but in conventional male battalions. "There will always be fighting women in Russia," Bryant concluded, "but they will fight side by side with men and not as a sex."[31]

Because it was organized as an independent unit, the Battalion of Death found it impossible to equal the combat readiness of other units. The commander, Maria Bochkareva, was a decorated combat veteran, but no experienced cadre of women noncommissioned officers existed. On July 8, 1917, the women's battalion had its baptism of fire. They broke through the German first, second, and third lines and captured two hundred prisoners. Then they were forced back and took heavy casualties on the retreat.

The unsuccessful defense of the Winter Palace against Bolshevik revolutionaries on October 25, 1917, included the last action of an all-woman Russian military unit during World War I. A detachment of a Petrograd women's battalion stood in defense of the provisional government in power. Fighting against them were women members of the paramilitary units known as the Red Guards.

The civil war that followed found Russian women fighting on every front, from Siberia to the Crimea and from the Baltic Sea to Central Asia. Most of them were integrated into regular fighting units, although a few small, all-woman units of about three hundred members fought in segregated groups. Even the women nurses serving with the Bolshevik military received rifle training.[32]

NONCOMBATANT WOMEN AT THE FRONT

DURING WORLD WAR I, noncombatant women, both those who served at the front and those who never got closer to the war than reading newspaper accounts, were intensely interested, even inspired by, accounts of the all-woman military units. When the English militant feminist Emily Pankhurst watched a regiment of four hundred women pass in review, she declared it "the greatest event in the world's history." An American woman who had been working with other Red Cross volunteers, managing a truck depot for six months, thought of the Russians when the Red Cross sent a group of inexperienced and incompetent male officers to supervise her operation: "Oh [war's] a wretched business, but my fighting blood is up and I'd give anything if I could be a man. . . . I wish I could form a 'Legion of Death.'"[33]

The feeling that women could do good work for the cause if the men would just stay out of their way was shared by many of the thousands of women who went to the front without following one of the armies and without asking permission. Not only English and European women but American women as well went off to the Great War years before the United

States became officially involved. The first of these women made their way to the war zone alone or with a few friends, paying their own way and bringing their own supplies, as Clara Barton had done during the Civil War. They did not ask for assignments but looked for work that needed to be done and did it.

An example of this independent style is provided by a pair of Englishwomen, Mrs. Elsie Knocker and Miss Mairi Chisholm, who came to be known as "The Two."[30] Elsie was a trained nurse and also an expert driver and mechanic in an age when automobiles were still a novelty and horse cavalry the standard for military transport. Although Mairi was only eighteen years old, she, too, could drive an automobile, and she could ride a motorcycle as well. Scarcely two months after the German invasion of Belgium at the start of the war, the women were on their way to the front. On October 5, 1914, they drove in the direction of gunfire near Ghent, then walked three miles to a river searching for casualties in the swamp. Crouching low to avoid bullets, they pulled out injured Belgian soldiers. In the tradition of the Red Cross, they tended German as well as Belgian and French casualties. Sometimes they were so close to the action that they had to run to get out of the way of soldiers charging with fixed bayonets.

Elsie Knocker believed that a first-aid post should be established close to the trenches so that the wounded could rest, get some immediate attention for their injuries, and partially recover from shock before they had to endure the rough, jolting ride to a hospital. Convinced that this arrangement would save lives, the women set up such a post in the village of Pervyse despite official disapproval and a total lack of cooperation. During the first winter of the war, The Two worked at tasks requiring considerable upper body strength, such as lifting unconscious men with all their gear, which was too valuable to leave behind, onto stretchers and carrying them through the mud. Elsie, having had nursing training, treated the more serious cases. Mairi treated boils, sores, swollen feet, septic cuts, and venereal disease. They worked from a post only a couple of hundred yards behind the leading trench, a position from which they could watch the progress of an infantry attack.

Finally, after several months, military authorities acknowledged what The Two were doing and gave them official permission to stay where they were. No other women had permission to be closer than three miles from the front line. The media, which covered the Great War more thoroughly than any previous conflict, naturally discovered them, and newspapers wrote about the "Valkyries in knickerbockers" and "the heroines of Pervyse." They became a major attraction for those touring the battlefront. Officers came to have a look as did the more courageous journalists. Even King Albert and Queen Elizabeth of Belgium came to pay their respect, and the American writer Mary Roberts Rhinehart, well known for her mystery novels at that time, received permission to visit them briefly.

Not surprisingly, because they were in the line of fire, their first-aid post eventually took several direct hits. By this time, however, The Two were too famous to be left sitting in the rubble. The British army built them a new, well-protected concrete post about four hundred yards behind the trenches, and their work continued. In 1917, the women received military decorations: the Military Medal and the Order of St. John of Jerusalem. The awards recognized, among other acts, Elsie's courage in going alone into no-man's land to rescue the pilot of a British plane that had crashed near the German trenches; she had to talk the German officers into allowing her to take the man away. This action was not, however, the most difficult or dangerous of the sorties The Two made to rescue the wounded.

In March 1918, a shell carrying mustard gas and arsenic exploded near the first-aid dugout and signaled the end of their service. Both women were wounded. Elsie's injuries were so severe that she had to return to England for medical treatment. Mairi recovered more rapidly and carried on alone. Then she was gassed again, and learning that Elsie would not be able to return to duty for a considerable time, she reluctantly abandoned the post. That was also the end of Elsie Knocker's system of immediate first-aid. Many other women volunteered to take up the work—but none could get permission.

The greatest number of women who went to the front were primarily caring for the wounded. Nursing, which extended to performing surgery when the nurse was the only medical specialist present, driving ambulances, and burying the dead, remained dirty, dangerous, disgusting, enormously hard and stressful labor. All of this was expected to be accepted as its own reward by good women, as it had been for centuries. But in the Great War, many other possibilities arose for women.

A partial list of jobs filled by American women who went to Europe, compiled by Dorothy Schneider and Carl J. Schneider, includes "physicians, dentists, dietitians, pathologists/bacteriologists, occupational and physical therapists, administrators, secretaries, 'chauffeuses,' telephone operators, entertainers, canteen workers, interpreters and translators, searchers (for soldiers reported missing), statisticians, decoders, librarians, supervisors of rest homes for women munitions makers, directors of recreation, accountants, publicity directors, social workers, distributors of supplies, journalists, peace activists, small factory and warehouse operators, refugee workers, interior decorators, laboratory technicians, and architects."[35] In 1923, Mrs. Ettie A. Rout proudly published the record of her wartime service. She had supervised sanitary regulations in a "tolerated" house of prostitution in Paris, and boasted that not a single case of venereal disease appeared during the year she was in charge, "although the house bore an enormous traffic."[36]

As might be expected, wartime Europe produced plenty of prostitutes, and the European armies continued their nineteenth-century practices of regulating the sex trade. In Ghent and all the large Belgian and French cities occupied by the Germans, approved facilities were clearly labeled, carrying legends over the entrance such as "For Officers Only," "For Officers and Civilians," or "No Admittance for Dogs and Soldiers." In the field, horse-drawn mobile brothels accompanied the troops, again clearly labeled to indicate those who were allowed admission.[37]

Hans Otto Henel described a visit to such a facility in his novel *Love on Barbed-Wire*. The soldiers and noncommissioned officers were marched to the place in companies. They moved along in line, and each soldier was examined for venereal disease by a sanitary noncommissioned officer who gave them a tube of preventive salve. The men were then told to read an announcement explaining rules for intercourse and the price for a ten-minute visit. Then they waited their turns. After a wait of forty-five minutes, someone called out, "Next!" and directed Henel to "Room 6."

Half trembling with confused emotions, he opened the door. A horrible odor of bichloride and patchouli struck his nostrils. That a woman stood in the half darkness of the room with her face to the window, he could see from the contour of her body underneath her black nightgown. Very stolidly and without a word she turned around and simply let herself fall on the edge of the bed, while hiking up her skirt.[38]

English and American officers, coming from societies in which there were more inhibitions about sex, faced a tricky challenge. As military men, they believed they could not enforce celibacy on soldiers the way it was enforced on women enlisted as nursing sisters. Yet celibacy was what their civilian leadership, not to mention civilian wives and mothers at home, expected. They needed to regulate sexual behavior to protect their men from disease, but they could not do so openly. Officers did what they felt was necessary while trying to keep their actions quiet and off the record. It was understood that company commanders were responsible for providing their soldiers with safe sex.

Gen. John Joseph Pershing, who commanded the American Expeditionary Force in Europe, had prior experience with regulated prostitution. He had managed it in the Philippines, and he set up a similar system when he was in command of troops engaged in the excursion into Mexico just prior to the American entry into World War I. A Chinese civilian was authorized to build adobe shacks for prostitutes inside the support camp, where they would not be readily visible to visitors and reporters but would be close enough for easy access. The civilian hired the women and ran the business; the army Medical Corps examined the women for venereal disease and treated them if they were infected. The provost marshal kept order and enforced the rule against alcohol. The soldier got a thirty-minute visit for $2. When America entered the European war a few months later, Pershing was explicitly forbidden to continue the practice of regulation, leaving the soldiers to fend for themselves among the French mademoiselles.[39]

With the enormous hardships war forced on the civilian population, many women all over Europe were willing enough to sell what they had to survive. Having lived through an enemy invasion, many no longer had any "virtue" left to protect. A systematic scholarly investigation of wartime rape has never been attempted, and it would be an extremely difficult subject to study. On one side, war propaganda always magnifies the extent of atrocities, and on the other, the victims try to hide the evidence rather than face public shame. Unsympathetic males are always quick to suggest that a woman who charges rape was actually a willing participant, if not the aggressor, in a sexual contact.

Although impossible to quantify, many women were certainly rape victims during World War I and rape by the enemy was especially horrific for those believing in the theory of telegony. Telegony was a belief, unscientific but widespread at the time, "that all females are impregnated by the man who fecundifies her, in such a way that all subsequent fecundation, whoever the author, will be under the influence of the preceding one, this action manifesting itself by resemblance of physical, intellectual, or moral traits." In other words, even if a woman made pregnant by rape miscarried or aborted the child, any other children she bore later would resemble the rapist.[40]

WOMEN'S AUXILIARIES

GIVEN THE LONG HISTORY of regulated prostitution in European armies, it is not surprising that the new "women's auxiliaries" that accompanied the military forces during the Great War were widely assumed to be another way of providing "clean" girls to meet "soldiers' needs." Even military nurses who enlisted for life and took vows of celibacy became subjects of speculation. Ironically, the civilian women who went to war on their own without chaperones had better reputations than those women who went officially and were paid by the armies. The civilians, who could afford to serve without pay, were of a higher social class than those who accepted salaries. And it was still a novelty for military authorities in Western armies to pay women, other than soldiers' wives, whose "camp follower" status carried its own stigma, for any service other than prostitution.

The British did not establish nonnursing women's services until 1917, and the government sent an official commission to France the following year to investigate complaints of widespread prostitution. The complaints proved groundless. The commissioners concluded that "a vast superstructure of slander had been raised on a small foundation of fact." But the commissioners probably underestimated the contribution to the slander from soldiers' expectations of the women hired by the army. The British commission believed, rather, that "the scandalous tales" were started in "the low-class French *estaminets,* whose custom among British soldiers has suffered considerably, owing to the better type of companionship now available for the men."[41]

The same inhibitions that prevented rape victims from reporting the crime operated to keep "nice girls" from reporting what is now called "sexual harassment." While studies of the English and American women's auxiliaries are based on enough solid documentary evidence and oral history to establish conclusively that their officers were indeed chaperones and not pimps, evidence is less clear for other armies that established women's auxiliaries. Military officers in some armies may indeed have expected their women clerks and telephone operators to perform sexual service as well. Magnus Hirshfeld, the German author of *The Sexual History of the World*

War, described the Austrian female military service, which was established in January 1917. A proclamation calling for female volunteers brought out between 95,000 and 100,000 women.[42]

> *Many women applied for this work because, first, they were assured of good food and, secondly, of a considerable amount of money, between a hundred and a hundred and sixty kronen a month. In addition, many women were impelled by a conscious or unconscious desire for adventure and a yearning for a vague romanticism. What was the destiny of these female auxiliaries of the Austrian army? They were sent out from Vienna to various places where the war raged, including Trieste, Lemberg, Lublin, Belgrade or Bucharest. For the most part nobody worried whether they arrived at their destination or not. When and if they did arrive, they had to ask their way about until they got to the office of the general staff where, after a superficial investigation of their capacities and training, they would be assigned to a certain job. In Trieste, there was a perfect slave market for female auxiliaries. The latter would all congregate in a large room where, seated on benches with their baggage at their feet, they would wait for hours until a gentleman who needed female help would come and select the woman who attracted him the most. Every man who came here knew that the creature he took along with him was hopelessly in his power, a condition of responsibility which transcends the capacities of most men. In many cases the female auxiliaries were assigned to military superiors who exploited their subordinate positions in a sexual way.*[43]

From the beginning of the war until 1917, the warring powers required women's work but kept women out of uniform; that is, they kept lower-middle-class and working-class women out of uniform. Middle- and upper-class women who created their own military assignments also designed and paid for their own dashing costumes. The traditions of military service assumed an unbridgeable social gap between "officers and gentlemen" and "other ranks." The first were respected and admired; the rest were thought to be licentious, if not depraved.

In civilian life the upper classes believed the ignorance and lack of discipline in the lower classes were a threat to society, and even the lower classes felt that ordinary soldiers were morally reprobate. Thus some women might aspire to recognition equivalent to that of military officers, but no British women wanted to be in the ranks. This changed only as the war brought many thousands of "respectable" men into military service.

Within a year after the beginning of the war, England instituted conscription. As of August 1915, everyone, male and female, between the ages of fifteen and sixty-five was to provide personal information to the National Register. By this time, working-class women were already in national service, though not in the military, performing all kinds of hard, dirty work. When men went to war, women filled in in the coal mines, in the sludge pits of glass factories, lifting and carrying timber in shipyards, cleaning firebricks in a gas works, and eventually serving abroad, building huts for British troops in France. Women had done hard physical labor for centuries, but during the war they became visible in heavy industry. The photographs of working women in overalls and trousers, grinning with heavy loads on their backs, was a change from the pretty milkmaids and maidservants or the "brave bonny lasses" in the army or navy depicted in traditional broadsides and picture books.[44]

In work more closely related to the military mission, Englishwomen worked in cartridge factories, putting TNT into shells, where the health hazard became visible when their hands and faces turned yellow from TNT poisoning.[45] They also welded bodies of aerial bombs.[46] Working directly with weapons of war was hazardous duty, and some of them were killed. Women who worked in munitions factories wore triangular brass badges declaring them to be "On War Service." A photograph shows the funeral of one woman whose co-workers clearly believed her to be as much a casualty of war as a soldier dying at the front. Although a civilian, her body lay in a coffin covered with the Union flag, and she was escorted by eight women pallbearers in their working uniform of long coats, pants, and heavy shoes.[47]

In 1915, working-class women were recruited by the Women's Forage Corps to find fodder for horses. Later, the Women's Land Army and the Women's Forestry Corps joined them. These were civilian organizations but officially sanctioned, which meant pay for the volunteers. Only women who were fairly well off could afford to undertake war work without pay. The most successful of the voluntary organizations was the Women's Legion, organized by the Marchioness of Londonderry, who realized that the "officer and gentleman" structure of other groups excluded large numbers of women who wanted to work. Her group still had uniforms and officers but specialized in familiar nonmilitary work with cooking, canteen, ambulance, and agriculture sections. Her success convinced the authorities that an official military unit for women might be workable.

In 1917, the English created two auxiliary services: the Women's Army Auxiliary Corps (WAAC) and the Women's Royal Naval Service (WRNS). These were civilian organizations, but the women who served wore uniforms and received pay. In 1919, the Women's Royal Air Force was formed, drawing recruits from the WAAC and the WRNS. Because the Royal Air Force (RAF) was itself a new service, the women were more closely integrated with the men and served at the RAF Headquarters in Cologne. Despite hope that this women's auxiliary might continue, all women's units were disbanded after the war ended.[48]

Aviation, still in its infancy during the Great War, had already captured the imagination of many women. As early as 1910, a French nurse named Marie Marvingt earned one of the first pilot's licenses granted to a woman, and she urged the French army to create a medical aviation branch. She envisioned special rescue planes that would carry nurses, stretchers, and surgical supplies to the front. She contracted with a civilian factory to construct a prototype, but the contractors went bankrupt before it was completed, and the French military ignored her proposal. She persisted, and during the war a few army units did use planes for emergency medical service. In 1934, the French army finally invited her to organize a civilian ambulance service.[49]

Other women flyers had combat, rather than humanitarian, missions on their minds. Two women flew military reconnaissance missions in the Great War: Hélène Dutrieu in France and Princess Eugenie Mikhalovna Shakhovskaya in Russia.[50] In the United States, Ruth Law was a flyer who wanted a combat assignment. She had earned a license in 1912 and was the best-known woman pilot of her time. Intensely competitive, she did acrobatic flying and strove to set altitude and distance records. In 1916, she set out to better Victor Carlstrom's cross-country nonstop record of 452 miles. She planned a flight from Chicago to New York City and flew as far as Hornell, New York, when her engine began to sputter. Although short of her goal, she had broken the American nonstop cross-country record. At Hornell, a young army lieutenant named Henry H. (Hap) Arnold changed her spark plugs. Arnold became commander of the U.S. Army Air Forces in the Second World War.

Law continued her flight and landed on Governors Island, where she was hailed and celebrated. President and Mrs. Woodrow Wilson, Adm. Robert E. Peary, and Cap. Roald Amundsen attended dinners in her honor and praised her splendid accomplishment. But when the United States entered the war and Law volunteered to fly over the trenches, she was refused permission. "We don't want women in the Army," the secretary of war told her flatly. Instead, she and other women flyers were encouraged to go on recruiting tours and fund-raising flights.[51]

AMERICAN WOMEN IN THE MILITARY

WHEN THE UNITED STATES entered the war in April 1917, the military already had two women's auxiliary services: Nurse Corps (female) in the army and the navy. Although their members did not have military rank, were not entitled to veterans' benefits, and received lower pay than men doing the same work, the nation did not have to go to the Daughters of the American Revolution to recruit nurses when its army went overseas.

The military also put women in other jobs, some of which were not ordinarily undertaken by women in peacetime. Military leaders wanted the services of women but were puzzled about exactly how to fit them into the organization. Capt. Joy Bright Hancock, USN, who would become adviser for women to the chief of the Bureau of Aeronautics in World War II, recalled Secretary of the Navy Josephus Daniels explaining how he confronted the problem:

"Is there any law that says a yeoman must be a man?" I asked my legal advisors. The answer was that there was not, but that only men had heretofore been enlisted. The law did not contain the restrictive word "male."

"Then enroll women in the Naval Reserve as yeomen," I said, "and we will have the best clerical assistance the country can provide." Tremendous gasps were heard, but this was an order, and it was carried out.[52]

The navy created a new rating "yeoman (F)," and enlisted women, who were popularly called "yeomanettes," into the Naval Coast Defense Reserve. The women sailors could not go to sea, but they did more than routine office work; some worked as radio electricians, drafters, fingerprint experts, translators, camouflage designers, and recruiters. Some put on overalls and assembled torpedos. A few got to France on assignment to hospital units, and some worked with intelligence units in Puerto Rico.[53]

Inspired by the navy example, Maj. Gen. George Barnett asked for authority "to enroll women in the Marine Corps Reserve for clerical duty at Headquarters Marine Corps and at other Marine Corps offices in the United

States where their services might be utilized to replace men who may be qualified for active field service." Eventually 12,500 women yeomen and 305 women marines came into service. Unlike nurses, they had full military rank and status, which meant that they received the same pay as enlisted males, although they could not advance to equally high rank. They swore the same oath at enlistment, wore uniforms, had a four-year service obligation, and would be entitled to veterans' benefits.[54]

The U.S. Army also wanted women workers, but the secretary of war would not permit them to be recruited with military status. When the quartermaster general asked for a "Women's Auxiliary Quartermaster Corps" of five thousand women with clerical skills, he got five thousand unskilled enlisted men instead. The chief of engineers, the operations branch of the general staff, and the chief of ordnance all wanted women but failed to get approval. General Pershing got what he wanted by not asking for permission. In November 1917, he took it upon himself to issue a call for women recruits. He wanted experienced telephone operators who could speak fluent French to serve as "women switchboard soldiers."[55] The only authorization he had was from the adjutant general, stating that the Signal Corps could hire *civilians* to do the work. But no one ever drew up a contract or signed one, and Pershing's call for recruits emphasized that he wanted women telephone operators for a military mission. A representative newspaper article of the time stated, "In every respect these young women will be soldiers, coming under military restrictions at all times."[56]

Seven thousand women responded to the call, but the standards were high. Not only must the Signal Corps women be fluent in French, they must also be free of any German connection. And to prevent the possibility of unseemly fraternizing, no woman with a male relative overseas would be accepted. Thirty-three women, ranging in age from nineteen to thirty-five, were in the First Unit accepted for service in the new Signal Corps unit. The Office of the Chief Signal Officer sent them telegrams directing them to go to a notary public or justice of the peace to take the enlistment oath as required by the Articles of War and army regulations. They then reported to New York City, where they were given physical examinations and measured for their uniforms. Just to make doubly sure they knew they were in the army now, they were all sworn into the service a second time.

The uniforms cost about $500, which the women paid for just as officers did, to equip themselves properly for duty in France. The outfit included a summer and a winter suit, black or russet shoes, a hat, an overcoat, a rubber raincoat, and brown army boots. The women wore skirts rather than breeches, but the uniforms had regulation army buttons and insignia on the white brassard worn on the left arm. The women were told to send their civilian clothing home. After two weeks of training at the American Telephone and Telegraph Company, they sailed to France.

Crossing the Atlantic in wartime was no pleasure cruise, and after reaching Southampton and boarding a small cross-channel ferry bound for Le Havre, the First Unit barely escaped alive. Dense fog shrouded the English Channel, and the vessel became entangled in a submarine net, unable to move. It was nearly rammed by a French warship, and there was no way to evacuate, so the women spent two days and two nights on the ferry, sleeping in their clothes on the deck. But in the best army spirit, the women made no complaints. The chief operator remembered, "What good sports the girls were in that First Unit! They took everything in their stride. They were the pioneers."[57] They would have a good deal more to endure.

Because it would have been improper for men and women to share the same barracks, the women often had accommodations that had been abandoned as inadequate for other soldiers. Their first barracks at Ligny was infested with vermin, and the roof leaked. A member of the First Unit recalled how her feet were frozen while she slept in her cot:

> I had been working long hours with very little sleep. Before a drive I seldom had more than two or three hours of rest. Consequently, when I tumbled into the bed at night, I never noticed anything until my feet began to swell and then I discovered that the bed covers were soaking wet from a leak in the roof overhead. It was a long time before I could wear shoes again. Of course, I moved the bed, but, although I moved it several times, I never found a place where there wasn't at least one leak.[58]

Another woman remembered the improvised toilet: a large table with holes in it and seats over the holes and under it a large barrel. Once when stationed at Soully, fire broke out in the barracks housing the main switchboard. As enlisted men and officers tried to bring the fire under control, the women remained at the switchboards, handling calls generated by the battle of Argonne.

Eventually six units, a total of 233 women, would serve in the war zone. Switchboards had to be open twenty-four hours a day and seven days a week.

The largest telephone exchange at Tours employed thirty-five women. Others worked switchboards at Pershing's headquarters and at headquarters of the First and Second armies, moving with the troops. A photograph taken at First Army Headquarters during the St. Mihiel offensive shows them with gas masks and steel helmets ready for use. Although the women there were working forty-eight hour stints, with only brief breaks for sleep, one operator Helen Hill, "found it quite entertaining to sit through the night until dawn."

> *There was always a Wire Chief and soldier-operator on duty in case we needed help. I amused myself, also, by swapping stories over the wire with different soldier-operators when they would call in to test the lines. . . . The officers were getting no sleep and were sometimes impatient to us, but we kept our tempers fairly well and gave every ounce of endeavor that was in us. Nor did it have a marked effect on any of the girls. One could see the dark hollows under their eyes, but not a change in their usual happy voices. . . . I have gained a whole lot of self-control and patience, and am awfully proud of having had such a real part to play in this great salient of St. Mihiel.*[59]

A few operators continued to work with the Army of Occupation in Germany. Some were recalled from leave after the Armistice to work switchboards for Americans in Paris during the peace negotiations. All in all, the Signal Corps' "Hello Girls" had a good war. They were praised in the newspapers and generals pinned medals on their jackets. Brig. Gen. George Van Mosley gave a special Christmas dinner in their honor in 1918. On that occasion he declared that they were "better disciplined than the army itself," and added, "You have nobly performed your duty as part of the Advance Guard of the women of America, the strongest force for good in the world today."[60]

Eventually orders came which took the women home. One woman protested the routing of the travel orders and was told sternly, "Young lady you are still in the Army."[61] Then, without any of them knowing quite what had happened, they were retroactively civilianized. Instead of honorable discharges, the adjutant general sent them "service termination letters." He thought they had signed contracts and were civilian employees. Because General Pershing *should* not have enlisted them, they had never *really* been in the army at all.

Army and navy nurses had not "really" been in service either, but the Army Reorganization Act of 1918 created the new designation Army Nurse

Corps (ANC) and restricted appointments to women. Another reorganization act in 1920 authorized relative officer ranks for the army nurses, though with lower pay than equivalent male ranks. Later, Julia Stimson, superintendent of the ANC from 1919 to 1937, helped to gain veterans' status for the nurses, including retirement pay.[62] No one with that kind of influence was there to battle for the Signal Corps women. Although the American Legion and Veterans of Foreign Wars voted them membership privileges and many states gave them bonuses under the state veterans bonus statutes, they were not awarded federal veteran equivalent status until 1977. By then most of them had died, and the youngest of those alive was close to eighty. To this day, their service is officially classified as having been civilian.

Although army nurses received recognition as veterans, those who joined the Red Cross did not, even though they did identical work. Red Cross nurses enlisted for a two-year term, shorter than the three-year, renewable appointments of the Army nurses. The Red Cross sent about ten thousand nurses overseas during the war. The army had a peak strength of 21,480 nurses in service in 1918, and the navy, about 1,500. After the war, all women in the military except nurses were discharged. The loophole in the Naval Reserve Act that had permitted the navy and Marine Corps to enlist "citizens" was closed; after 1925, those citizens had to be male. Until war came again, nurses would be the only women in the military.[63]

WOMEN REMEMBER THE GREAT WAR

BUT WAR WAS NOT supposed to come again. America had entered the Great War to make it the "war to end all wars." Censorship prevented the full magnitude of the horror that had engulfed Europe from reaching the American public, but what was known was bad enough. In Europe, even with censorship, for those who lived through the Great War, there was no hiding its impact. Aside from direct military damage, famine and disease killed millions of civilians. In Armenia fully one-third of the civilian population, five hundred thousand people, died, many by torture, and an equal number were deported to wander as refugees, surviving if they could.

For some women, choosing to go to the front had been a way to make things a little better, and they found the experience exhilarating. Their memoirs describe the war years as the best of their lives.[64] Other women who went to the front wrote books that stripped away romantic rhetoric to focus on the gritty reality of lice, blood, putrifying wounds, and vomit, of infants and old people dying in their own filth on the roadside. Vera Britain, an English nurse who left her studies at Oxford to enlist as an army nurse and served throughout the war, wrote, "no one now living will ever understand so clearly as ourselves, whose lives have been darkened by the universal breakdown of reason in 1914, how completely the future of civilised humanity depends upon the success of our present halting endeavours to control our political and social passions, and to substitute for our destructive impulses the vitalising authority of constructive thought."[65]

The Great War had been a terrible mistake; surely such a thing could never happen again.

CHAPTER NINE

THE SECOND WORLD WAR

WITH THIS CHAPTER WE reach our own times. People still alive today witnessed the events of World War II, and the sheer quantity of living memory is overwhelming.[1] World War II, with battlefields from Africa to Asia, from Poland to the Philippines, was a war more vast in its impact than any other in history. Civilians in primitive cultures on Pacific islands and in cosmopolitan cities like London and Shanghai were killed, wounded, or made homeless. For the first time since the Thirty Years War, civilian casualties outnumbered those in the military.[2]

World War II ended with the use of nuclear weapons. Unlimited war, as it had been practiced since the time of Napoleon, abruptly became archaic. No war comparable to World War II can ever be fought again because total war between nuclear nations would have no front lines, no home front, and few if any survivors. This makes full preservation of the history of the roles of women in World War II a unique imperative. If their war stories die with the generation that witnessed the events, no comparable war will occur in the future to give hard evidence on this scale against the persistent myth that only men go to war or suffer and die fighting for their country.

For much of Europe, World War I never ended. England and the United States rapidly demobilized, but in Russia revolution and civil war began even before the Armistice of 1918 was signed. Years of famine and political turmoil followed, with constant fear of new wars with Poland or the Baltic states to the west or with China or Japan to the east. Meanwhile attempts to implement the new communist ideology at home resulted in purges and terror that left no one feeling secure. Soviet citizens experienced no real "peace" between the two world wars.

The Paris Peace Conference of 1919, which ended the Great War, created an entity in the Balkans that was later named Yugoslavia. It was made up of six republics with blood feuds based on ethnic and historical differences stretching back hundreds of years. These feuds blended into partisan battles when the next "real" war began and brought German and Allied troops battling in the Balkans.

Spain faced revolts in Morocco and Catalonia, then revolts from within its own military, that led, in July 1936, to civil war.[3] This latter conflict attracted volunteers, men and women, from other nations: fascists from Germany and Italy who supported the insurgent leader Francisco Franco, and communists from the Soviet Union, England, and the United States who fought with other leftists against Franco in international brigades. Ferocious fighting gave the world a foretaste of the power of weapons that would be used soon after on a global scale. It was here, for example, that Hermann Göring's *Luftwaffe* perfected the dive-bombing tactics with which they would later overrun Europe.

BLITZKRIEG

WORLD WAR II BEGAN with the German *blitzkrieg*, or lightning war, launched by Adolf Hitler. One of history's most powerfully charismatic leaders, Hitler embraced a Nazi philosophy that exalted warfare as ennobling. The doctrine of "compulsive masculinity" was carried to a new extreme and found receptive listeners in the nation that had lost, and was therefore blamed for, the horror of, World War I. While the victorious nations in that war moved toward pacifism, the defeated Germans saw another war as the best way to restore their national pride.

On September 1, 1939, columns of fast-moving tanks, supported by Stuka dive-bombers rolled over Poland, overwhelming the country's defenses in just ten days. That assault aroused the peace-loving nations to action, and Britain and France declared war on Germany. In April 1940, Germany invaded Norway and Denmark, and when German forces launched another blitzkrieg in May against the Netherlands, Belgium, and Luxembourg, British and French troops went to their defense. But the intervention of the two countries barely slowed the German advance. Scarcely two weeks later, four hundred thousand Allied troops were backed up against the North Sea at the French town of Dunkirk. They barely escaped annihilation as they retreated across the Straits of Dover to England. Before the end of June, France would fall.

The first Englishwomen went to the front within a week of the outbreak of war. Among the last Allied troops to leave Paris when it fell were a platoon of women, bilingual telephone operators who stayed at their posts to keep the switchboards open as long as possible. Thirteen hundred British nursing sisters were in France and shared the hazards of evacuation at Dunkirk with the other members of the British Expeditionary Force. A wounded soldier described their heroism as the English waited and hoped for rescue:

> Out on that dreadful beach, with the sun pouring down on them, with German planes continually overhead and shells bursting all the time, they have worked without stopping for days past. If they have slept, they have done so on their feet, attacked by German planes and even by tanks, with machine-gun bullets whistling all round. I have seen them crawling into the open and dragging wounded men to shelter beneath sand dunes.
>
> I saw one part of them dressing wounded who were lying out in the open. A plane began bombing. They just laid down by their patients and continued bandaging. They have fetched food and water to assist the men. Angels is the only word you can use to describe them. I have seen some of them killed as they have gone about their work. We have asked them to go back in the rescue ships, but they have refused. Each one has said, "We shall go when we have finished this job—there's plenty of time, so don't worry about us."[4]

Actually, the nurses expected to be left behind with the wounded and taken prisoner. They heard the crackling voice on the BBC radio say, "England expects to be invaded by sea and air at any moment. You will allow no wounded man in a boat. England needs able-bodied soldiers." But the radio had also sent out a call to anyone in England who had a vessel that would float to take it to Dunkirk and rescue a soldier. The Royal Navy could do relatively little to help because its ships made such good targets. Then the little boats began to arrive. Civilian craft, including some Dutch and French boats, outnumbered naval vessels involved in the evacuation effort by more than three to one.[5] "People came to France in vessels that shouldn't have floated in a bathtub," one nurse recalled, "but they made it across the channel the ones that weren't blown out of the water by the Stutgars overhead."

More and more soldiers and nurses were rescued. Finally, only two nurses remained. They moved the wounded to the back of the beach and tried to hide them in foxholes, dispensing what medicine they had. Then the radio said, "All nurses not wounded will be in any available boat." The last nurse to leave went among the wounded one more time. "And I went from man to man," she remembered, "and not one man said, 'Don't leave me, sister.' I only remember the ones who said, 'Go home, sister, and fight.'"[6]

As the English soldiers and nurses waited for evacuation, other women caught in the path of the invasions were running for their lives. The most dramatic slaughter occurred in bombing attacks on cities—beginning with German bombs over England during the Battle of Britain in 1940 and ending with American atomic bombs on the Japanese cities of Hiroshima and Nagasaki in 1945, with a great many raids, some even more destructive, in between. But of the nearly fifty million soldiers and civilians estimated to have been killed in the war, only 3 percent were victims of air raids. As continuous fronts moved through entire countries, tens of millions of civilians died in the rubble of their homes or as they fled in terror.[7] Sometimes they were deliberately targeted.

Twelve English nurses who had been setting up a field hospital in Belgium were caught up among the refugees as they tried to make their way to Dunkirk. One of the four nurses who survived the retreat recalled,

Overhead we had to contend with the pride of the German Air Force. At that time, the Germans had a divebomber called a Stutgar and it was a deadly machine that day. The Stutgars were equipped with sirens on the wings of the plane, and pilot would come in and make a bombing run. He would release his bombs among the people along the road, and then he would make altitude and peel off and come in with his machine guns chattering. And as he peeled off to make a striking run against these defenseless people below, the wind would swing through the sirens on the wings, and it would create panic—which is what it was meant to do of course.

And it was my first experience with panic, and I remember how hard it was to fight down the urge to run. And I remember how sad it was too, because when we heard the planes in the sky, if there was a child near you, you grabbed a child and rolled into the ditch with it and hoped that the bullets would miss you this time. But for the unfortunate children who didn't have an adult to lie on top of them, the siren on the wings of the Stutgar did its work.

And these children would get up and run. And the pilots never let one live. Those children were literally cut in two with machine gun bullets. I learned then how hard it was to persuade the mother to go on and leave her seven-year-old child's corpse beside the road.[8]

But by no means did all civilians die running away. Everywhere, doing the best they could, men, women and children fought back. This guerrilla activity—or partisan warfare, as it was called at this time—played an essential part in the war. To conventional military historians, the civilian partisan activity is a mere footnote; they are more concerned with the large armies of uniformed soldiers and the new tactical elements of motorized weapons and air power. The partisans, however, are of particular interest since they offered the most visible combatant roles for women.[9]

PARTISAN WARFARE

CIVILIAN WOMEN FORCED TO fight in defense of their own lives and homes did not go to war for glory. In describing their decision to take up arms, they generally speak as though they had no choice. John Laffin described such a woman he knew personally:

One of the soldiers was a girl who served from 1941 to 1945 with a Yugoslav partisan band and who was reputed to have killed fourteen of the enemy, two of them with a knife. When I met her she impressed me with her sense of humor and her quiet common sense. She was a peasant girl and a lady and no man's mistress. Not that she was anti-man, she simply knew that a liaison within a group of men would create a dangerous situation. She was a soldier because she had to be; without a home, money or friends in 1941 there was no other way of life possible.[10]

A woman who fought with the Italian resistance said:

At that time it was clear that each Nazi I killed, each bomb I helped to explode, shortened the length of the war and saved the lives of all women and children. . . . I never asked myself if the soldier or SS man I killed had a wife or children. I never thought about it. In those situations you just don't think about anything but surviving and covering for your friends to help them survive.[11]

Nevertheless, there could be substantial satisfaction for women participating in partisan activity. Among comrades risking their lives together, individuals were respected for what they did rather than for what they were. Diamondo Grizona remembered that when she and her girl friends wanted to join the Greek resistance, "[Our parents warned that] our reputations would be ruined, no one would want to marry us, we would shame our fathers' names." But the resistance promised a new kind of self-respect. As Eleni Fourtouni says, "For the first time in the history of Greece, in the ranks of the Resistance movement, women and young people were treated as the equal of adult men." [12] The ELAS (National People's Liberation Army) not only trained women to use weapons but even put some of them in command of combat units. For girls who had been socialized to be meek and passive, the discovery that they could act despite their fears and carry out aggressive action was exhilarating.

In fascist Italy, the main duty of women was to produce babies. "What war is to men, so maternity is to women," was one of Mussolini's sayings. [13] But Italian women, like women everywhere, had a history of combining the two. They fought as guerrillas in the struggle for Italian independence in the nineteenth century, and during World War I they fought again along the northern borders of the country. Mussolini did not want women soldiers, but 10 percent of the Italian partisans who fought against fascism were women. [14] Carla Capponi and Marisa Musu, whose stories Shelly Saywell recorded in *Women in War,* were among the Gappisti, as they called themselves after their acronym, GAP (Groups of Partisan Action). "GAP was the armed section of the whole conspiracy," Capponi told the interviewer. "There were other sections—those who took care of disbanded soldiers and helped Allied prisoners to hide and escape, a political section involved in keeping the various groups co-ordinated, and then the armed section." Both Capponi and Musu volunteered for that service. "I wanted to be armed," Musu said. "I wanted to participate. I thought that armed resistance was the best and simplest solution." [15]

GAP found women especially useful for planting bombs, precisely because the Germans thought it impossible that women could do that. But male partisans were not always willing to give women other weapons. When Capponi joined, she brought her own weapon, the gun her father had used during World War I. One of the men took it from her, but she soon got another: "I was riding on the bus one day and happened to be standing close to a German soldier and I stole his gun, a Beretta sub-machine-gun. So that is how I regained a gun."[16]

Women resisters in France also had to overcome male reluctance to have them fight, but fight they did. Marie-Madeleine Foucade headed the Alliance network and directed more than three thousand agents.[17] In the battle to liberate Paris, both men and women fought in the streets. The Germans sent ten thousand Frenchwomen to the concentration camp at Ravensbruck, north of Berlin, almost all of them because of participation in resistance activities; only five hundred of those in Ravensbruck survived the war.[18]

Nancy Wake and Pearl Witherton, agents of Britain's Special Operations Executive, dropped behind the enemy lines into France and led partisan units into battle. One American woman, Virginia Hall, also operated behind enemy lines in Europe and was the only American civilian woman to receive the Distinguished Service Cross for heroism, a decoration awarded only for combat service. Hall was known as the "Limping Lady" because she had an artificial leg, the result of a prewar hunting accident. Working with the Office of Strategic Services, she organized an agent network, distributed radios, arranged parachute drops of weapons and supplies, and helped downed airmen reach escape routes. She also engaged in blowing up bridges and railway lines, cutting telephone wires, and derailing freight trains.[19]

Covert operations and partisan activity became particularly important in Yugoslavia where the regular army lasted less than two weeks after Germany attacked the Balkans in April 1941. In this region, as we have seen, traditions of fighting women stretched back into ancient times. Soldier girls were a theme of popular Balkan folktales.[20] Women of Serbia and Montenegro had been conspicuous in the struggle for independence from the Ottoman Turks. The Serbian tradition of "sworn virgins" had a counterpart in Montenegro, although it applied not to virgins but to widows. The *kult majke,* or cult of motherhood, encouraged widows to wear male clothing and go to war. While other women fought in Montenegrin armies, most women soldiers were widows. In 1858, an all-woman battalion was active in a battle between Turks and Montenegrins, and between 1916 and 1918 women fought against Austrian occupation.[21]

With Germany's defeat of the Yugoslav army and the division of parts of the country among the Axis powers, the National Liberation Army of partisans took up the fight to resist the Nazis in mountain strongholds. Women were among the first to volunteer. In the spring of 1941, thirty young women from the Bosnian village of Dvar enlisted, and the first woman honored as "national hero" came from that town. In Macedonia, two women were among the first to join partisan detachments, and three women were among the earliest members of the partisan unit formed in Slovenia. Fifty women were in the first Serbian detachments. Eventually about one hundred thousand women were recruited into the partisan army, making up about 12.5 percent of the total force. Two million women were "civilian" partisans. About 25 percent of the women in the army died during the war; the casualty rate among "civilian" women partisans was much higher.[22]

Guerrilla warfare draws on primal emotions. The cool professionalism of career soldiers does not motivate civilians drawn into war to protect their families. Atrocities were committed on all sides in the war in the Balkans, and some descriptions of Yugoslav women in action are reminiscent of the scenes in which Roman legions confronted Huns and Goths. Vladimir Dedijer, who served with the partisans, wrote,

> *Those women were a horror—Attila incarnate! I watched them simply shoot down Nazi prisoners. Once, two of them did a tap dance, in jack boots, on the stomach and genitals of a spread-eagled German officer. Another soldier had the fingers of each hand shot off, was castrated, and made to choke on his own testicles. One of our women, Mira, was a crack shot and had thirty-four Germans to her credit in combat, . . . not just prisoner killing, but in real fighting. . . . She was totally dedicated to killing Germans. She could use a machine pistol with the best of us."[23]*

A German war correspondent, Kurt Neher, described an episode in 1942 in which Axis forces broke through the partisan resistance and surrounded tens of thousands of civilians hiding in the forest of Mount Kozara:

> *And then came the most horrifying part of all that made everyone's blood run cold—a woman started screaming hard and long and hundreds took up her call. Men, women and children threw themselves with beastly intensity upon our lines. It seemed to us as if we were present at the instant of the forming of the primal human horde, with men rushing us in human waves, intent on self-destruction and mindless of all fear.[24]*

Thirteen thousand of these unarmed people were killed. Sixty-eight thousand who survived, including 23,000 children under fourteen, were sent to concentration camps, where most of them died.

THE SOVIET UNION

IN JUNE 1941, THE Germans invaded the Soviet Union, opening hostilities on a front two thousand miles long. The invading force was estimated at 3.6 million, while the Soviet army numbered only 2.9 million in the western region.[25] But the Soviets had an enormous reserve of men from which to draw—and also a large reserve of women. By the end of the war eight hundred thousand women were serving in the Soviet army and many thousands more joined the partisans. At their peak strength, at the end of 1943, close to a million women were in military service, about 8 percent of the total force.[26] The raw numbers reflect an unprecedented historical phenomenon. Although larger percentages of women may have fought with Mongols and Huns or in the armies of the ancient Amazons, never before in any army had so many women served as regular soldiers.

Some women were already on active duty in the Soviet army when Germany invaded. As we have seen, women combatants had served in the Russian army during World War I and in the Red Army during the civil war that followed. At the start of World War II, most of the Soviet women in uniform were nurses or doctors. But in the emergency the Soviets decreed that all women without children who were not otherwise engaged in war work could be called up for military service. Most did not wait to be drafted; volunteers were plentiful and included women with children and some girls who were little more than children themselves. Grief for loved ones killed and the stories of Nazi atrocities, especially those against women and children, motivated many women to enlist. Especially in the early days of the war, patriotism, a sense of duty, and the opportunity for adventure in which women might prove themselves in ways not possible in traditional women's roles also played a part.

Women served in every military specialty, including infantry, antiaircraft defense, armor, artillery, transportation, communications, and air combat, and they participated in every major engagement of the war. They wore standard uniforms and greatcoats, often cut their hair short or shaved their heads, and were frequently mistaken for boys. Komsomol (Young Communist League) units trained about 250,000 women to use weapons, and 150 women graduated from the Central Sniper Training Center for Women every two months.[27] By the end of the war these snipers had killed 11,280 enemy soldiers. One woman sniper, Nona Solovei, is said to have killed an entire German company in twenty-five days.[28] Antiaircraft defense became a women's specialty, with women officers and hundreds of thousands of women firing the guns. A German pilot, who had flown in the African campaign, said, "I would rather fly ten times over the skies of Tobruk than to pass once through the fire of Russian flak sent up by female gunners."[29]

There was still room in this war for individual initiative, even in the Soviet Union. Many women were assigned to tanks, but Mariya Oktyabrskaya bought her own tank after her tanker husband was killed. She named it Front-Line Female Comrade and took it into combat; she was killed near Vitebsk in 1944.[30]

The Soviet women who flew combat missions during World War II are currently the subjects of a flurry of interest.[31] Their history is both important and fascinating, but it has tended to eclipse the stories of the far more numerous women who were engaged in ground or naval warfare. Although these combat veterans have not yet been the subject of a full, scholarly study, oral histories and translated memoirs give a sense of the richness of evidence available.[32]

Shelly Saywell interviewed thirty Soviet women veterans and was surprised to find that "the tough, hardened individuals who had fought in trenches alongside men, simply did not appear." She continued "Instead I met women whose passions and sensitivities reflected a real horror of war, who cried through much of our time together and who remembered death, not glory."[33] They also recalled some extraordinary experiences.

Katyusha Mikhaylova served as a marine, a soldier attached to a naval vessel, in what Saywell describes as "the most traditional and chauvinistic service and the most resistant to allowing women into combat." When she answered a radio call for volunteers for a unit about to form and approached the commander, he laughed at her and said, "If Peter the First [the founder of the Russian navy] heard that you wanted to enlist in the navy, he would turn over in his grave." Mikhaylova retorted, "Well, whatever Peter the First thought is history. I'm a Soviet girl, and we are equal in this country." But she had to go over his head to get in: "I decided to write to Naval High Command in Moscow. I told them I had enlisted when I was only fifteen, that I had taken part in battles near Moscow and been wounded, that I had served almost a year as a nurse on a sanitary ship. Now my native city Leningrad was under blockade, people were dying of hunger in the streets and I wanted to defend my country." The commander got orders to take

Mikhaylova aboard. She was not warmly welcomed: "One of the sailors walked up to me and handed me a baby's pacifier. He said, 'This is for you. When we go into battle we won't have time to baby you, so take this.' I said, 'We'll see who is going to take care of whom.'"[34]

Mikhaylova was the only woman in the battalion, and because of her nursing experience, she went into combat carrying a medical bag along with grenades and a machine gun. A Soviet journalist described her first amphibious operation:

> It was the capture of Temryuk. They made a landing in the flood plain while mortar shell explosions caused pillars of water to rise in quiet backwaters, bullets made water boil and the reeds, cut down as if by an invisible scythe, fell on top of the marines' heads. She was there, in the midst of all this mess, stood in salty water up to her chest, fired and dragged the wounded into boats. It was only a tiny town, but it was paid for with a very high price; more than half the battalion fell there, in the flood plain and on the coast."[35]

After that, the marines who had ridiculed her came one by one and apologized.

A second collection of oral histories by the journalist S. Alexiyevich was published in Moscow in an English translation in 1988 but quickly went out of print.[36] Because the writer was Russian and of an age to identify as a granddaughter of the veterans she interviewed, her book contains even more intense material. While Saywell's subjects cried during interviews, Alexiyevich pushed hers even harder:

> They begin telling their stories quietly and then, towards the end, they are almost shouting. Then they sit depressed and confused and you feel guilty, because you know that when you leave they'll be swallowing pills, taking sedatives. Their sons and daughters look at you pleadingly, making signs: "Isn't it enough? She shouldn't be upset." And you've got only one justification: their living voices will be preserved by the tape and the sheet of paper, and although these are not everlasting, they are still more durable than the best human memory. Even so, it has been very hard to sit and listen to the women's stories, to say nothing of the way the women themselves felt.[37]

In their honesty, Alexiyevich's subjects described experiences and commented on events that have always been present when women went to war but have not before entered the historical record so clearly.

Sgt. Albina Alexandrovna Gantimurova had just finished seventh grade when she enlisted. When she got her first rifle, she wondered when she would be as big as her weapon. Before the war ended, she had been decorated many times for valor, but the first award is the one she most cherishes:

> *The soldiers were lying low. "Forward! For Motherland!" came an order but no one rose. The order was sounded once again to no effect. I took my hat off for them to see that I was a girl and rose to my feet. . . . The rest of the company rose and we all went into battle.*
>
> *I was awarded that medal and that same day we went on a mission. It was then that I had my first period, you know . . . I saw blood and shrieked:*
> *"I've been wounded. . . . "*
> *Among the scouts on that mission was an elderly man—a doctor's assistant. "Where's the wound?" he rushed to me.*
> *"I don't know . . . But here's blood. . . . "*
> *And he told me everything, as if he were my father.*[38]

Other women recalled how their menstrual periods stopped entirely during the war; many never recovered their fertility. "The war not only took our youth away," said one, "it robbed many of motherhood as well. It deprived girls of a woman's greatest joy."[39]

Some women already had babies when they went to war. Those serving with the partisans, like women with the ancient nomadic tribes, had no choice but to combine fighting and maternity. There was no safe place to leave an infant. "I had my daughter in 1943," said Maria Timofeyevna Saritskaya-Radyukovich, "giving birth to her in a haystack on a marsh. I dried the swaddling clothes on myself, putting them under my bosom and warming them up in this way, and would use them again to swaddle the baby." When the baby was three months old, the mother went out on missions to smuggle medical supplies to the partisans. "I brought medicines, bandages and serum from the town, putting them between the baby's arms and legs in swaddles. Wounded soldiers were dying in the forest and I had to go. Nobody else managed to pass the German and police sentries. I alone could do it." She deterred searches by rubbing the infant with salt and putting garlic in the swaddling, to make it turn red and cry, telling the sentries it had typhus. "I find it hard even to speak about it now. . . . My poor little baby."[40] Another partisan fighter gave birth to a son three days before the war began and told this story:

Beginning with the early days of the German invasion we sought to pick up every cartridge in the forest and to amass weapons. Mother would not let me go: "Where are you off to with the baby in your arms? You have no fear of God!" "And what about them? Do they fear God?" I replied. . . . I distributed leaflets and collected information, all the while carrying my baby in my arms. I was risking two lives at a go and shed rivers of tears.

My little son died. I was not with him, but it was through my fault: I was with the partisans at the time. He was burnt together with my mother. When I reached our house . . . the earth was still warm. . . . All that I managed to find was a few grammes of bone ashes.[41]

Raisa Grigoryevna Khasenevich had two children, a daughter of two and a son not quite four. Since the boy was easier to take care of, she left him with her mother-in-law when she went to join the partisans. She carried her daughter with her. On one mission, she was taking a typewriter with a German keyboard through a swamp to another band of partisans. She said, "The men took nothing more than a rifle with them, but I carried a rifle, a typewriter and Elochka."[42]

In the regular army, women did not carry babies, but they often accomplished feats that in retrospect left them astonished by their own strength. Alexiyevich received this letter from Maria Petrovna Smirnova (Kukharskaya), who was awarded the highest decoration of the International Committee of the Red Cross, the Florence Nightingale Gold Medal:

On December 25, 1942, our 333rd Division of the 56th Army seized a height on the approaches to Stalingrad. The Nazis were determined to recapture it at any cost, and the fighting began. German tanks started the attack but were stopped by our artillery. The Nazis rolled back and there he was, a wounded lieutenant, gunner Kostya Khudov, lying in no-man's land. The medical orderlies who tried to haul him back to our lines, were killed. So were two of the sheep-dogs of the medical corps (it was the first time I had seen them). I felt it was my turn. I removed my cap with ear-flaps, stood upright and started singing, first softly, then louder and louder, our favoirte prewar song "I Saw You off for You to Perform a Feat of Valour." Both sides, ours and the German, stopped firing. I reached Kostya, bent over him, put him on the tow-sledge and pulled it towards our lines. As I did so I had one thought in mind: I hope they won't shoot me in the back. Better in the head. But not a single shot

was fired before I reached our lines. . . . Our uniforms were always covered
with blood so that there were never enough clean ones for us. . . . In all, I res-
cued 481 wounded from under fire. One reporter calculated that I had rescued
a whole rifle battalion![43]

And this from A. M. Strelkova:

When we found ourselves at the front line, we proved to be capable of
greater endurance than those who were older. I don't know how to explain
this. We carried men who were twice or three times our own weight. On top of
that, we carried their weapons, and the men themselves were wearing great-
coats and boots. We would hoist a man weighing 80 kilograms onto our backs
and carry him. Then we would throw the man off and go to get another one—
also weighing 70 or 80 kilograms. And we did this five or six times during an
attack. Our own weight was often some 48 kilograms, the weight of a ballet
dancer. I can't imagine how we managed.[44]

The experiences and memories that remained with these Russian women
after the war changed them. They had taken part in a kind of activity men
did not want to associate with their wives or the mothers of their children:
"The fighting was heavy. I saw hand-to-hand fighting. . . . That was awful. A
person becomes something . . . it isn't for human beings. . . . Men strike,
thrust their bayonets into stomachs, eyes, strangle one another. Howling,
shouts, groans . . . . It's something terrible even for war, it's more terrible
than anything else." Women combatants had not merely witnessed such gris-
ly episodes, they had been active participants: "In the morning the entire
battalion was drawn up and these cowards were brought out in front of the
men. The sentence was read out: death by firing squad. Seven soldiers were
needed to carry out the sentence. . . . Three men stepped forward, the others
held back. I took a sub-machine gun and stepped forward. Everyone else followed when I did that. . . . There could be no forgiveness. Because of them
such brave boys had been killed."[45]

Some women veterans married men they had served with during the war,
but many soldiers would not consider marrying a woman who had been in
combat. One woman reported,

A man returned and there he was, a hero. An eligible young man! But if it
was a girl, then immediately people looked askance: "We know what you did
there!" . . . And the whole of the suitor's family would think: should he marry

her? To tell the truth, we concealed the fact that we had been at the front, we did not want to tell people about it. . . .A strange fate indeed! First to have the strength needed to become extraordinary. Heroines! And then to find the strength to become ordinary girls. Marriageable girls.[46]

GERMANY

IF SOVIET WOMEN SOLDIERS sometimes appeared monstrous even to their own countrymen, they seemed even more ghastly to their German enemies. Any lingering reluctance to have women assume an equal military role in the Soviet Union was dwarfed by Nazi attitudes. The Germans counted tens of thousands of Soviet women among their prisoners of war. They contemptuously called them *flintenweiben*, or rifle women.

Hitler, like Mussolini, believed the duty of women was to obey fathers and husbands and to make babies. Of course, he made a few exceptions. Women auxiliaries were recruited for the Schutzstaffe (SS) elite guard to work in concentration camps to which women prisoners of war (POWs) were sent. They also worked in those camps that held the victims of the Nazi campaign to "purify" the race. Female concentration guards proved themselves as sadistically cruel as the male officers.[47] And then there was Hanna Reitsch.

Hanna Reitsch was a pioneer woman glider pilot who tested military aircraft for the Luftwaffe. In 1937, Hitler gave her the honorary rank of *Flugkapitän*, or flight captain. She flew all aircraft in Germany's growing inventory. Reitsch was the first woman to pilot a helicopter, and Hitler gave her the Iron Cross for testing a device designed to cut the cables of British barrage balloons over London. She also tested the Me-163, an experimental rocket plane that could climb to 30,000 feet in 90 seconds and reach a speed of 600 miles an hour. On its fifth flight, the plane crashed, and Reitsch spent more than five months in the hospital.

As the war turned against Germany, Reitsch offered to form a squadron of women pilots "to fight for the Fatherland on the same terms as the men of the Luftwaffe and without any privileges or restrictions." The Nazis turned her down. Reitsch then set to work planning a suicide squadron that could hit production centers in England or target Allied warships in the Atlantic. The craft used was the V-1 rocket provided with a seat for the pilot but no landing gear: this was a one-way mission. After Reich tested a prototype with special landing skids, Hitler gave his approval. The Allies landed in Normandy in June 1944 and forced an end to the war before the suicide device could be used.[49]

In the closing days of World War I, Germany had developed the Rear-Area Women's Auxiliary program. Several hundred working-class women were recruited in 1917 as civilian laborers in supply and ammunition depots, veterinary hospitals, and similar places where they took over tasks formerly done by soldiers. As the war ended, other civilian women were being trained for a women's signal auxiliary, but they never deployed. None of these women wore uniforms, held military rank, or received any arms training. Even the nurses were civilians.[50]

At the beginning of World War II about one hundred forty thousand civilian women were working for the German military; about one-third were in clerical positions, and the rest were unskilled laborers. Civilians were forbidden to work for deployed forces, but after the fall of France large numbers of German women—wives, girlfriends, and female relatives—went to the field army units hoping to find jobs and be with loved ones. The rule against employing civilians was reaffirmed, but the need for people to perform clerical work that could not safely be trusted to Frenchwomen revived the idea of a women's auxiliary.

The Signal Auxiliary was the first to be restored. This time its members wore the Red Cross women's uniform with military insignia. Soon after, the Staff Auxiliary, also uniformed, was organized for the army. The German navy and air force auxiliaries followed. In the air force, large numbers of women became Antiaircraft Auxiliaries, and later in the war some were trained as aircraft mechanics. But all these "civilian" women were told firmly that they must not think of themselves as soldiers like the Russian *flintenweiben*. They must never actually fire a weapon, not even to protect themselves from capture or death.[51] In 1945, all of the women's auxiliaries were combined in the Armed Services Women's Auxiliary Corps.[52]

In the last desperate weeks of the war, Hitler approved a plan to create a women's combat battalion on a trial basis. The women's infantry battalion, like the Russian Battalion of Death in World War I, was intended, in part, as a means of shaming male soldiers who by now were deserting in droves. But the war ended before the plan could be implemented.[53]

Soviet troops invaded from the east as Allied forces came in from the west. Thousands of these "civilian" women auxiliaries were captured. Those captured by Allied forces were treated as POWs, and all except the SS women were quickly released. On the eastern front, however, they were treated ruthlessly by the Soviets, who had suffered greatly and had no sympathy for Nazis, even for unarmed civilians working for the military while under orders not to protect themselves.

THE UNITED STATES

THE WAR THAT RAGED over most of the globe ended without raining death and destruction on the people living in the United States. A few American civilians died in the Japanese attack at Pearl Harbor on December 7, 1941, and American citizens living in the Philippines were captured by the Japanese. In the continental United States, apprehension arose about possible submarine attacks on the East Coast and Japanese balloon bombs on the West Coast. Americans pulled down their window shades, crouched under dining room tables, and sat for long periods in darkened rooms for air raid drills. But there were few successful attacks on the continental United States and only one that claimed lives: a Japanese balloon bomb exploded in Oregon on May 5, 1945, killing Elsie Mitchell and five neighborhood children while they were on a picnic.[54] Compared with the other belligerents, Americans suffered a trifling number of civilian casualties. American military, both men and women, also suffered lower casualty rates than those of other nations.

In June 1940, after English forces had escaped from Dunkirk, Great Britain stood alone against a seemingly unstoppable German force. The war came across the English Channel as German planes bombed the length of the home island as far north as Scotland.

Although bound by several neutrality acts, passed because of revisionist thinking about the country's role in World War I and the influence of strong pacifist ideals, the United States relaxed a provision of the legislation to permit the supply of war materials to Great Britain and concluded a defense agreement with that nation in September 1940. That same month, Italy and Japan contracted an alliance with Germany, pledging joint action if any member went to war with the United States. Despite enormous sympathy for the English, America remained out of the war until the Japanese attacked Pearl Harbor. Congress's declaration of war on Japan was followed by a declaration of war on the United States by Hitler and Mussolini, bringing America into the conflict more than two years after its outbreak.

At this time, the only women in the American military were nurses.

Until 1920, members of the Army and Navy Nurse Corps technically remained civilians. Both the War Department and the army surgeon general argued against giving women military rank because "that might give them hierarchical superiority to male officers" and because "military rank should be reserved for those in combat."[55] Somewhat greater recognition came in 1920 when army nurses were given a status called relative rank. That meant they would have insignia and military titles, from second lieutenant to major (or the Navy equivalents), but they would not have either authority and privileges or pay equal to male commissioned officers. On duty, they were still addressed as "Miss."

During World War II, almost all the American women in the combat zones were nurses, who continued to be perceived as somehow different from ordinary women. In addition to members of the Army and Navy Nurse Corps, Red Cross nurses and other civilian medical personnel were sent into war zones closed to most American military women. American nurses were in the thick of the action in both Europe and the Pacific from the start, and 201 army nurses lost their lives, 16 as a result of enemy action. Both army and navy nurses were on duty at Pearl Harbor during the Japanese attack. Others served on Bataan and Corregidor when the Japanese invaded the Philippines. The Japanese captured five Navy nurses on Guam, and sixty-seven army nurses and eleven navy nurses were taken prisoner in the Philippines.[56]

In Europe, one army nurse was taken prisoner by the Germans after a plane crash over Aachen. Four army nurses received the Silver Star for gallantry in action at the Anzio beachhead, where approximately two hundred nurses landed with the first assault group.[57] Army and Red Cross nurses followed the troops ashore at Normandy on D-Day plus 4.[58] In 1945, twelve flight nurses flew into Iwo Jima while the battle was raging and landed on the beach under a barrage of fire. Kathryn Van Wagner, who was among them, recalls, "The fighting was going on very close to the plane. On one of my missions when I was standing next to the plane, a marine handed me a trench mortar and said, 'Do you want to shoot the Japanese' and I said 'Sure.' So I just dropped the mortar round in the slot and it shot right over a hill."[59]

Despite the clear fact that American nurses were in the hottest combat zones, the belief that women were not sent into harm's way, so essential to the myth of war as an exclusively male activity, persisted among Americans.

Edward E. Rosenbaum, a doctor with a medical unit, remembers, "Many times an injured soldier would come out of shock or wake from anesthesia, and he would see one of the women and thank God, mistakenly believing he was out of the combat zone. No such luck."[60] The selective memory supporting the myth is reflected in the work of many historians. We now have a substantial number of books dealing with American women who served in the armed forces during World War II,[61] and some general studies of women's other roles in the war years,[62] but we still lack a comprehensive study of military nursing.[63]

Once in the war, the American military's need for women in nonmedical roles was evident immediately. But the same objection to giving women equal status that were raised for nurses blocked the creation of a regular women's corps. Early in 1941, when the army learned that Rep. Edith Nourse Rogers intended to introduce such legislation, the War Department's assistant chief of staff for personnel commissioned a study "to permit the organization of a women's force along the lines which meet with War Department approval, so that when it is forced upon us, as it undoubtedly will be, we shall be able to run it our way."[64] The result was legislation establishing the Women's Army Auxiliary Corps (WAAC) in May 1942, an organization of civilian women who would have a rank equivalent to nurses and a "director," not a "commander," at its head. Col. Oveta Culp Hobby became the director, and women began to sign up.

Despite vigorous efforts to keep women away from the actual killing that was the business of war, some WAACs came much closer to weapons than any of its founders envisioned. Gen. George C. Marshall, army chief of staff, was aware of the success the British had had with women working with antiaircraft artillery. Mixed-gender regiments had been operating in England since November 1941 and had brought down enemy planes, but there was always one male assigned to fire the weapon. Englishwomen were killed in action, but they did not kill.[65]

Marshall ordered an experiment in training the WAAC for antiaircraft duties to see how much work they could do with the batteries short of firing the guns or handling ammunition. Even with these restrictions, such assignments would be highly controversial, so Marshall ordered this one kept secret.[66] The women were employed in two mixed batteries in the Washington, D.C., area from December 1942 until the following August. An inspection was scheduled for January 15, 1943. At the last minute, General

Marshall had to back out because his presence was required at the Casablanca Conference. Another general attended in his place. An incident during the inspection makes a telling contrast to the total immersion in combat that Soviet women soldiers were experiencing at this time. It is difficult to remember that this was the same war. Major Elma Hilliard Grahn, who headed the secret experiment, reported,

> As Colonel Hobby, General Edwards, General Lewis, Colonel Timberlake and others went through the barracks on the 15th, there was one enlisted woman in bed. When Colonel Hobby asked her why, she said that on sick call the doctor had said she should stay in bed in quarters that day. Colonel Hobby solicitously asked, "Well, what is the matter?"
>
> "My back hurts; I have a backache."
>
> "How did you get that?"
>
> "Oh," she said, "on the machine gun." At that Colonel Hobby's mouth became a thin, tense line. She turned on General Lewis and Colonel Timberlake and said, "It was understood that the women would not be on the guns."
>
> Upon checking I learned that the enlisted woman had been too embarrassed in the presence of male officers to say that it was her menstrual period causing her pain. But I also learned that when the women were off duty at the Arboretum, where there wasn't much in the way of recreation, the enlisted men had shown the Waacs how to field-strip a machine gun and put it back together.[67]

It should be added that the experiment was a success, although it was discontinued because by this time the need for antiaircraft protection had diminished.

At the same time that the civilian WAACs were being evaluated for possible close combat support, problems with the whole idea of a military auxiliary were surfacing. Although the women did the same jobs as the soldiers, they operated under an entirely separate set of regulations. They had no binding contract and could resign any time they wished, which could be decidedly inconvenient during a military operation. If they were sent overseas, they would not have the legal protection of military members as prisoners of war or the right to veterans' hospitalization if they were wounded. They could not be flexibly assigned, and it was unclear which army procedures applied to WAACs.

Under pressure to expand the corps and after extensive debate, Congress passed a bill establishing the Women's Army Corps (WAC), whose members would have full military status but be assigned to a separate branch of the army. Between July and September 1943, WAACs were sworn in anew as WACs. Earlier, in July 1942, a bill was signed into law establishing the Navy Women's Reserve and the Marine Corps Women's Reserve. These were not separate organizations but were part of the regular structure of their respective services. Immediately, the Navy established a women officers training school, soon to be followed by schools for enlisted women. In November, the Marine Corps began planning for women, and the first inductees signed up in February 1943.

Navy women soon came to be known by the acronym WAVES (Women Accepted for Volunteer Emergency Service), and Marine Corps women were known as Women Marines. The Coast Guard women, who entered into service after authorizing legislation was passed in the late fall of 1942, were called SPARs (from the Coast Guard motto, "Semper Paratus—Always Ready"). Special names gave the impression that the women were somehow separate from the "real" services.

THE SLANDER CAMPAIGN

During World War II, none of the other combatant nations made so great an effort simultaneously to bring women into war work and to maintain a perception of gender segregation. Because the real horrors of the war, the realities of partisan combat and the devastation of cities, never came to the United States, matters not of concern to top military leadership in other nations loomed large in America. An example was a full-scale investigation of a phenomenon known as "the slander campaign."[68] When the first negative publicity about military women appeared, it was believed to be the work of enemy agents, an orchestrated effort designed to hinder recruitment of women or to encourage women to desert.

Sniggering directed at women who worked for armies was centuries old. From the references to "whore sergeants" in early modern times to the rumors of wanton behavior by British women serving in France during the First World War, women concerned about their reputations among civilians, whatever their actual conduct, were well advised to avoid the company of military men. That was why military families, in which the wife was herself the child of a soldier, were essential in maintaining military establishments.

Even nursing sisters did not escape speculation about their eroticism. Hirschfeld's salacious scholarly study, *The Sexual History of the World War,* informed readers that "a considerable portion of the female nurses were impelled to nursing by quite other than patriotic and humanitarian motives" and that "social scientists [regard] . . . nursing activities as one way of sublimating the libido and achieving sexual pleasure."[69] In particular, Hirschfeld said, nurses enjoyed carrying bedpans because it brought them close to male genitalia. He quoted a regimental physician who confessed he believed such nursing duties damaged women: "The shock which the female nervous system derives eventually makes nurses entirely unfit for marriage. It is a problem, but one would be insane to worry about problems during the war."[70] The same sentiments expressed by the learned gentleman were shared by others who had grosser ways of articulating them, most of them certainly never put on paper. Women probably overheard some of this talk, but essentially this was "manly" conversation not fit for mixed company.

In the United States, with its long history of isolation from European wars and traditional suspicion of standing armies, even male military officers had to struggle for respect. In Europe aristocrats and royalty wore military uniforms. In America the profession of arms attracted few members of the elite and the peacetime army none at all. So when large numbers of uniformed women became visible in American cities in 1943, many people were ready to believe the worst about them. And to men who had no female relatives in uniform, stories about wild, lecherous, "Waccies" seemed like harmless fun. A congressman from Alabama said WAC stories were "like traveling salesman jokes" and were "the way this country keeps its sense of humor."[71]

Colonel Hobby, however, was not amused. Rumors grew more vicious following congressional hearings in March 1943 in which army leaders emphasized that military women made it possible to send more men to the battlefields. Those already on duty, they claimed, had released for combat a number of men as large as that which had defeated German forces in North Africa. Hobby was convinced that having learned of the value of her women, the Nazis were out to sabotage the WAAC.

In May, Hobby asked for an investigation, and her request went through channels: from the Army Service Forces to the G-2 Division (military intelligence), the general staff, and on to the Federal Bureau of Investigation (FBI), which was outside the army's jurisdiction. Then, in mid-June, the G-2

Division changed its mind and made investigating the slander an army priority. A letter to the FBI stated, "Consequent to the formation of such a women's auxiliary to any of the military services, a certain amount of indecent humor was to be expected. However, the inevitable so-called humor first has been supplemented and subsequently replaced by a circulation of plainly vicious rumors. . . . [W]hat appears to be a concerted campaign has assumed such proportions as seriously to affect morale and recruiting."[72] One example of these rumors was a story spread almost simultaneously in, among other cities, New York, Washington, D.C., Kansas City, and Minneapolis that large numbers of pregnant WAACs were being shipped home from overseas. Actually only one woman serving in North Africa had become pregnant, and she was married to an army officer who spent leave with her. But folklore needs no facts. At Hampton Roads, Virginia, it was "common knowledge" that 90 percent of the WAACs were prostitutes and 40 percent were pregnant. In the Sixth Service Command, word spread that when army physicians examined WAAC applicants, they rejected all virgins. A War Department circular with obscene "specifications" for WAACs was reproduced and passed from hand to hand, eventually reaching even the foxholes of New Guinea.

The last straw came on June 8 when a nationally syndicated column called *Capitol Stuff* made the following revelation: "Contraceptives and prophylactic equipment will be furnished to members of the WAAC, according to a supersecret agreement reached by high-ranking officers of the War Department and the WAAC Chieftain, Mrs. William Pettus Hobby. . . . It was a victory for the New Deal Ladies. . . . Mrs. Roosevelt wants all the young ladies to have the same overseas rights as their brothers and fathers."[73] There was not a scrap of evidence for this story. The War Department could have forced the columnist to retract the statement, but some people thought that dignifying the piece with a reply would just spread the story more widely and make matters worse. The effect on the WAACs and their families was devastating.

A male army officer described the impact of the *Capitol Stuff* story in his command:

It raised hell with that company. Long distance calls from parents began to come in, telling the girls to come home. The younger girls all came in crying, asking if this disgrace was what they had been asked to join the Army for. The older ones were just bitter that such lies could be printed. It took all the pride and enthusiasm for the Army right out of them.[74]

An enlisted woman described it from another perspective:

I went home on leave to tell my family it wasn't true. When I went through the streets, I held up my head because I imagined everybody was talking about me, but when I was at last safe inside our front door, I couldn't say a word to them. I was so humiliated I just burst out crying, and my people ran and put their arms around me and cried with me. I couldn't understand how my eagerness to serve our country could have brought such shame on all of us.[75]

Even Director Hobby could not keep her voice steady when she told her staff about the story.

A flood of denials, of the *Capitol Stuff* story as well as other derogatory rumors, followed. President Franklin Delano Roosevelt and Mrs. Roosevelt, the secretary of war, members of Congress, and military officers denounced the newspaper columnist as buying into a Nazi agenda. Eleanor Roosevelt said, "Americans fall for Axis-inspired propaganda like children." Gen. Brehon B. Somervell of the Armed Services Forces told a congressional committee that an Axis sympathizer had spread the rumors, and Rep. Edith Nourse Rogers stated, "Nothing would please Hitler more" than to discredit WAACs. Rep. Mary Norton agreed, saying, "Loose talk concerning our women in the Armed Services cannot be less than Nazi-inspired." Under this pressure, the columnist retracted his story, but stubbornly insisted that his informant, an "intelligent and trustworthy" official, swore that he had seen the supersecret agreement with his own eyes. Despite the retraction, other periodicals continued to reprint the column.[76]

In June 1943, military leaders around the world had full agendas. The German army was gearing up for another summer offensive against the Russians; American, British, and Canadian forces were preparing a mass amphibious invasion in Sicily; and Australian and American troops and sea and air groups were poised for a concerted offensive in the South Pacific. Against this background, the U.S. Army's Military Intelligence Service, supported by the FBI, launched a full-scale investigation of possible Axis influence in spreading dirty stories about American service women. The investigation was exhaustive, involving hundreds of interviews. Specific stories were traced to their origins as elaborate files of notes and records were collected and analyzed.[77] The conclusion: the Axis had virtually nothing to do with originating or spreading slander against American military women.

Only one rumor showed any trace of Axis involvement. The tales of thousands of pregnant WAACs being shipped home at a time when only a few hundred were stationed overseas came down to an incident in North Africa when three WAACs, the pregnant wife and two women who were ill, were sent home. The Axis radio station DEBUNK announced that twenty WAACs were evacuated because of pregnancy. But this Nazi contribution to the scandal was negligible compared to that of a Coast Guard lieutenant who told friends that he had been part of an armed guard on a ship returning with 150 pregnant WAACs. The guard was necessary "to keep some of them from jumping overboard." A navy commander repeated the story, raising the number to 300. By the time a navy enlisted man told the story, the number of pregnant WAACs had ballooned to 250,000.[78]

No other case revealed even the smallest trace of Axis influence, nor did a search of German intelligence files after the war. The investigators concluded that the rumors originated with "Army personnel, Navy personnel, Coast Guard personnel, business men, women, factory workers and others, most of whom [had] completely American backgrounds."[79]

Slander of women soldiers continued throughout the war. The worst came from overseas where most male soldiers had not even seen a WAAC (or a WAC). Letters home that mentioned the servicewomen were overwhelmingly hostile; soldiers threatened to divorce wives or repudiate girlfriends who were so shameless as to enlist. Eventually WAC leaders learned to grit their teeth and endure the situation. As one commented, "Men have for centuries used slander against morals as a weapon to keep women out of public life." And even Colonel Hobby concluded after the war, "I believe now that it was inevitable; in the history of civilization, no new agency requiring social change has escaped a similar baptism. I feel now that nothing we might have done could have avoided it."[80]

Actually, the military kept its women under extremely strict discipline. A reporter looking for the wild WAACs in North Africa found that they began their workday at 6:00 A.M., riding together to their jobs in a military bus, worked a long hard day, and then "retired to the convent" for an 8:00 P.M. curfew. Some of them returned to work in the evening, and they were allowed a once-a-week pass to stay out socially until 11:00 P.M.[81]

Similar strict discipline was applied to the civilian women recruited for wartime service as pilots. The Women Airforce Service Pilots, or WASP, was born in August 1943 when two separate women pilots' programs, both civilian, merged. One was a training program founded by Jacqueline Cochran; the other was a ferrying program founded by Nancy Love. Cochran was director of the new organization and enforced strict military-style discipline on the trainees in addition to a supplemental code of conduct that required that they behave as "ladies" under all circumstances. The WASPs jokingly referred to their organization as "Cochran's Convent. " But the women aviators were well aware that they were doing challenging and dangerous work. They flew every kind of plane in the American arsenal and thirty-eight of them died in service.[82] The WASP and the women who flew for the British Air Transport Auxiliary shared much of the prestige and glamour associated with male pilots in the war, whom they freed to fly combat missions.[83]

Combining "respectability" with military service was particularly difficult for American women of color, who faced not only gender discrimination but race discrimination as well. The Women's Army Corps followed army policy and practiced racial segregation (except among officers) and also set a 10.6 percent quota for "Negro" units, which was never filled. The WAVES accepted no black women until the last months of the war, after the navy ended segregation for men. Two black trainees in the last WAVES officer class were commissioned, and only seventy-two black women became enlisted WAVES.[84]

The widespread assumption that the function of female auxiliaries, whatever the official pretense might be, were actually recruited to service the men as "clean" prostitutes intensified when the women were black. The first request for black WAACs from the European theater put the matter so bluntly that the secretary of war's civilian aide protested that "the assignment of units of the WAAC to afford companionship for soldiers would discredit that organization" and was "contrary to its whole plan and purpose."[85]

The casual assumption that black women had only one function in the military existed in the stateside installations as well. The first units of black women sent to Fort Huachuca in Arizona had a particularly difficult time in this respect during the early weeks following their arrival. Colonel Hobby continued to receive very explicitly worded requests. The inspector general at Sioux Falls, South Dakota, wanted black WACs trucked up from Des Moines "to make up for the recreational deficiencies of Negro men" at the air base. Hobby coolly replied that War Department policy forbade the removal of any WACs from their jobs to be "social companions."[86]

When American commanders in Europe found that Hobby would not permit black WACs to be placed in uncontrolled small field units near black male soldiers, they decided they did not want them at all. Only pressure from the National Association for the Advancement of Colored People and others forced the War Department to order the European theater to accept them for overseas duty. Grudgingly, the command requisitioned eight hundred black WACs to set up half of a central postal directory. The result was deployment of the 6888th Central Postal Battalion, which arrived in Europe under the command of Maj. (later Lt. Col.) Charity Adams in February 1945.[87]

The strict supervision of American military women and nurses kept them off-limits to servicemen looking for a good time. The alternative for commanders who did not believe that enforcing celibacy on males was realistic was to fall back on traditional ways of protecting their men from venereal disease: regulating civilian prostitutes. Unfortunately, this military approach ran into civilian opposition from those who believed prostitution itself was responsible for venereal disease. "Blitz the Brothels" was the cry in 1940 as the armed forces, the U.S. Public Health Service, the Federal Security Agency, and the American Social Health Association joined forces to pass legislation "For the Control of Venereal Diseases in Areas Where Armed Forces or National Defense Employees Are Concentrated." They succeeded with the passage of the so-called May Act in July 1941 which prohibited prostitution near military bases. What followed was a great deal of amateur prostitution.[88] *Time* magazine described the situation in the navy's principal East Coast port:

> *Whereas before Pearl Harbor, the majority of Norfolk's prostitutes were professionals, today probably 85% to 90% are amateurs. Many are young girls lured to Norfolk by the promises of big paying jobs. Hundreds of these girls arrive every week. They hang around bus terminals while phoning for a room somewhere. . . . Farm girls and clerks from small towns find it easy to have all the men they want. . . . [M]any do not charge for their services.*[89]

In San Antonio, Texas, the professional prostitutes complained that "the young chippies who work[ed] for a beer and a sandwich" not only cut into their business but were chiefly responsible for the spread of venereal disease.[90] A physician writing in the *American Medical Journal* agreed: "The oldtime prostitute in a house or formal prostitute on the street is sinking into second place. The new type is the young girl in her late teens and early twenties . . . who is determined to have one fling or better. . . . The carrier and disseminator of venereal disease today is just one of us, so to speak."[91]

In the war zones, where food was scarce, the equivalent of "a beer and a sandwich" would be a feast for a family. An American medical officer in Italy wrote, "Women of all classes turned to prostitution as a means of support for themselves and their families. Small boys, little girls and old men solicited on every street for their sisters, mother, and daughters and escorted prospective customers to their homes."[92] Gen. George Patton charged ahead with what he saw as the only sensible response to reality. He put U.S. Army medical teams into the six largest houses of prostitution in Palermo and announced that they were open for business,[93] but most field commanders were more subtle. They simply instituted an off-limits policy that directed officers and men to supervised establishments while both their headquarters and the War Department could deny that such a policy existed.[94]

The Germans left the traditional European brothel system intact, both as a proven method of controlling disease and as an adjunct to their intelligence operations. A famous Berlin establishment known as the Salon Kitty was remodeled by the German Security Service to conceal bugging devices used to spy on pro-German foreign diplomats as well as its own officers.[95] The partisan resistance also made use of the "closed houses," which had their own intelligence network. Escaping Allied pilots downed over France or other occupied countries could be smuggled out on routes that included stops at brothels. Roxanne Pitt, who ran an escape route, recalled a problem she had with a very nice young man she brought to such an establishment:

One day I escorted to a brothel in Montmartre a shy young English pilot who looked such an innocent Mummy's Darling that it seemed immoral to leave him there. As I heard later, he was so bashful that when la sous maîtresse showed him into the salon he caused some innocent merriment among the visitors. One of them must have described his behavior as a good story, for it came to the ears of the Gestapo, a member of which visited the brothel a few days later posing as a Frenchman. The manageress saw through him at once but concealed the fact. It seemed likely that a Gestapo raid was imminent. In such cases the usual procedure was to pair off the refugee with one of the girls, but this young man had been brought up so strictly that he seemed incapable of playing his part; and so he was dressed up as a prostitute instead.[96]

JAPAN

ALONE AMONG THE BELLIGERENTS in World War II, the Japanese military aggressively conscripted women to provide sex for its soldiers. The "comfort women," as the Japanese called them, were confined in filthy shanties and forced to have sex with soldiers, who were rotated through the "facilities for sexual comfort" day and night at fifteen-minute intervals. A few of these sex slaves came from Japan; many more came from China, Taiwan, the Philippines, and Indonesia, where Dutch women were taken along with the native women. But the greatest number of comfort women came from Korea. In all, the total number of women who were sex slaves in brothels operating from China and Indochina to Burma, Southeast Asia, and the South Pacific may have been as high as two hundred thousand. Thousands of the women died, many of venereal disease, and others were killed outright by their "clients."

For almost fifty years, the history of the comfort women was unknown. Those who survived the ordeal were shunned by their families, particularly in Korea, where virginity was demanded of brides, making it impossible for former comfort women ever to marry. Then in December 1991, as world attention focused on the fiftieth anniversary of Pearl Harbor, some of the victims overcame their shame and began to tell their stories. Their painful accounts described Japanese soldiers sweeping into villages and forcing girls in their teens or even younger into waiting trucks at gunpoint.

Three of the now-elderly Korean victims went to Tokyo to file suit against the Japanese government, demanding $160,000 each for their coercion into prostitution. At that time, the Japanese government insisted that all prostitution was handled by civilian entrepreneurs and the Japanese army was not involved. But Yoshimi Yoshiaki, a history professor at Chuo University, knew that to be false. He collected a number of documents signed with the personal stamps of leaders of the high command which bore such titles as "Regarding the Recruitment of Women for Military Brothels" and handed them over to a newspaper reporter. Finally, in August 1993, the Japanese government admitted the facts.[97]

Comfort women and nurses were the only women employed by the Japanese military in large numbers. The Confucian philosophy of Japan was in many ways compatible with the fascism of Germany and Italy. E. O. Reischauer described it as "the product of a patriarchal and strongly male-dominated society in China [which] saw women as important for bearing children and perpetuating the family more than as helpmates or objects of love."[98] Yet there was also a military tradition for women in Japan.

In A.D. 200, Jing ö-kögö, wife of the fourteenth emperor of Japan, took over his planned campaign to conquer Korea after his death. The pregnant empress carried out the invasion and brought three kingdoms under Japanese rule before returning to Japan in time to give birth to the future emperor.[99] In 660, the empress Kögyku-tennö died on her way to battle in Korea at the age of sixty-eight.[100] During its feudal period Japan had many noted women warriors, the most famous of whom was Tomoe Gozen. This eleventh-century swordswoman is described in the medieval epic *Heike Monogatori* as a "match for god or devil." In one battle, "when all the others had been slain, among the last seven rode Tomoe."[101] According to an early-eighteenth-century source, fighting women were common enough among the samurai to make facial hair an important part of a warrior's costume:

> *The warriors of old cultivated mustaches, for as proof that a man had been slain in battle, his ears and nose would be cut off and brought to the enemy's camp. So that there would be no mistake as to whether the person was a man or a woman, the mustache was cut off with the nose. At such a time the head was thrown away if it had no mustache, for it might be mistaken for that of a woman. Therefore, growing a mustache was one of the disciplines of a samurai so that his head would not be thrown away upon his death.*[102]

Because there is so little English-language literature on Japanese women during World War II, it is difficult to critique official statements that no Japanese women had combat roles in the war. A recent writer stated flatly, "At no time before 1967 have Japanese women been trained to replace men in any military function."[103] There are, however, a few bits of evidence to the contrary, suggesting that investigation of nonofficial Japenese sources, particularly collections of oral histories, might prove to be fruitful.

The Japanese had one very high profile covert operative, Kawashima Yoshiko, described by some newspapers as the "Joan of Arc of Manchuria." She began working as a secret agent before the war and often wore male clothing. One man described her as "strikingly attractive, with a dominating personality, almost a film-dram figure, half tom-boy and half heroine, and with this passion for dressing up as a male. Possibly she did this to impress the men, or so that she could more easily fit into the tightly-knit guerrilla groups without attracting too much attention."[104] According to the American *Literary Digest,* "whenever a section of the Japanese Army found itself in difficulties, rumor was that Yoshiko was on her way to join them. When her name was mentioned, it invoked victory and inspired the troops."[105]

Photographs from the war years show Japanese women in home guard units preparing to fight as a final line of resistance should the home islands be invaded. Wealthy matrons trained in rifle units as others of lower rank dug bomb shelters and set up barbed-wire, pillboxes, and booby traps along the shoreline. In the summer of 1945, Japanese soldiers began training civilian women to use bamboo staves to repel the coming invasion with the "Spirit of Three Million Spears." Some of the women, at least, realized this was a fatuous effort. "The enemy will attack with bombs and guns," one wrote. "It is absurd to meet them with such weapons."[106]

Most women's units never saw combat. A notable exception was the so-called Lily Brigade (Himeyuri Butai). The unit was organized on March 23, 1945, in response to the impending American invasion of Okinawa. It consisted of 223 field hospital nurses, most of them high school girls and their teachers. Many died in the battle and many more committed suicide rather than surrender, bringing the total casualties suffered by the brigade to 167. There is a monument to them in the city of Itoman on Okinawa, and they were the subject of both a best-selling novel and a movie in Japan.[107]

During the battle of Okinawa, U.S. Marines found the bodies of two Japanese women with those of seven male soldiers, all of whom were killed while trying to infiltrate marine lines. The women had hand grenades but were not carrying rifles. Marine officers at the time said this was one of only a few instances when women had been found with Japanese soldiers.[108] During the same battle, there was evidence of women flying kamikaze missions. Pvt. Howard E. Kern told reporters he had seen the body of a woman about eighteen or twenty years old in the cockpit of a plane that crashed into a ship at anchor.[109]

Perhaps the most intriguing scrap of evidence comes from much earlier in the war, long before those final desperate days when even Hitler was contemplating putting women in combat. The Associated Press reported on November 30, 1942 that Japanese women fought in the Guadalcanal campaign. The story quoted a marine corporal, Richard Fraley, who was home on furlough after fifty-six days fighting in the Solomon Islands. "Several times our gunners have picked off Jap snipers in the trees in the jungles, only to find that they were women in uniform," he said. "Once a bomber crashed near us and when the boys ran to the scene of the wreck they found a Jap girl lying near by dead and with her uniform partially blown off. They thought she might have been the bombadier or wireless operator."[110]

WORLD WAR II AND HISTORICAL MEMORY

AS WE WOULD EXPECT, the history of World War II continues to document most fully those women's roles that complement the old mythic tale of men as heroes and women as helpmates or victims.[111] Rosie the Riveter[112] and the women who were victims of the Holocaust[113] are subjects of a substantial number of volumes.

Recently, women in the American military services have begun to be recognized for having done their part to "free a man to fight," but few of them served in combat areas. Those who were most frequently in combat zones, the nurses, are less likely to be mentioned than other women in uniform. Women who fought as covert operatives or guerrillas outside a recognized military organization gain some attention, as do women war correspondents, but the civilian WASPs, who never deployed in a combat zone, and the Soviet women flyers who were in the thick of air action are the most popular nontraditional heroines. Most books about women who flew have been written by journalists or independent scholars, often flyers themselves, outside the academic mainstream.[114]

While we still lack scholarly monographs on uniformed women of any nation in ground combat, scholarly work on military prostitution has been published.[115] Although there are memoirs and oral histories from women combatants, they have so far not attracted the interest of academic historians in either military history or women's studies. So, as we enter the final chapters of women's military history, the half century following World War II, the myth persists, particularly in the United States, that deploying women warriors is an unprecedented experiment.

CHAPTER TEN

THE COLD WAR

ALTHOUGH WORLD WAR II proved to be the last global war, it took several decades for people to realize how much things had changed. After 1945 there was great fear of another war, a World War III, in which the two superpowers, the United States and the Soviet Union, would again square off, mobilizing mighty armies, sending tanks rumbling down networks of superhighways, and perhaps using tactical nuclear weapons. From the first use of the atomic bomb in Japan, it was obvious that these weapons were so much more powerful than older explosives that their use in substantial numbers would for all practical purposes mean the end of the world for humanity. This was a fact of such magnitude, appearing so suddenly, that its meaning is still being digested.

After World War II ended, the developed nations continued to expect the history of war to continue as it had in the past, with security and victory going to the side with the best weapons and training. An arms race began. In 1949, the Soviet Union developed its own atomic bomb, and in 1952, Great Britain achieved this capability, followed by France in 1960 and communist China in 1964. At the same time, the leading nations vied for the support of less developed nations through diplomacy and economic and military aid. In 1949, the former enemies of fascism developed a policy of containment against Soviet expansion by forming the North Atlantic Treaty Organization (NATO). On their side, the communists formed the Warsaw Pact.

The cold war, which endured more than forty years, consumed huge sums of money on weapons development and construction. Despite mutual efforts toward strategic arms limitation in the 1970s, weapons sales became the world's most profitable industry, rivaled only by drug sales. Eventually the cost of the arms race cracked the Soviet economic system, and "the evil empire" so feared by the West crumbled into dust. World War III never happened.

Instead, during the second half of the twentieth century, insurgent, guerrilla, and terrorist activities, which formerly had been minor elements in wars between great nations, became the main action. Mighty armies with the latest high-tech weapons discovered they could not defeat, or even locate, guerrillas living among civilians. Petty warriors, described as warlords, thugs, or terrorists, resisted capture and were indifferent to the huge nuclear arsenals of the great powers.

Ever since the Western nations had begun to claim colonies across the globe, they had consumed a disproportionate share of the world's wealth. After World War II, modern forms of communication, including movies and television, allowed people in underdeveloped nations, now popularly known as the Third World, to see how people in the developed nations live. While millions in the Third World died of starvation and disease, people in Europe and the United States found garbage disposal to be a growing problem. Grotesquely, at the height of the cold war, Americans ranking their fears in public opinion polls regularly put the fear of growing fat at the top of the list, above cancer and nuclear holocaust.

People living in the underprivileged nations resented and resisted the old colonial systems that took their labor and raw materials and left them living at a subsistence level and worse as their populations increased. As newly invigorated rebellions sprang up to resist the colonial powers now weakened by two world wars, the Western nations struggled to understand what was happening. They considered most independence movements part of an international communist conspiracy, a planned expansion of the Soviet Union. Third World rhetoric and Soviet foreign policy encouraged this perception. Anticolonial revolutionaries used Marxist terminology, though most learned Marxism from books or in Western universities rather than through indoctrination by master manipulators in the Kremlin. The Soviet leaders, fearing encirclement by capitalist enemies and another world war, strove to stay strong and encouraged any movement that would nibble away at Western power.

The anticolonial wars that followed World War II took the techniques of small-scale civilian resistance into the European colonial empires. As the British discovered during the American Revolution, locally based military units cannot defeat regular troops in open battle, but neither can they be defeated as they melt into the general population. They can make it very expensive for a colonial power to maintain its authority. Immediately following World War I, the Irish Free State won its independence from England using such tactics, and simultaneously Turkish nationalists successfully resisted partition in what the Soviets called a "national liberation war," a term that would reappear after World War II.

There are no battlefields in guerrilla war, and some would say that the kind of violence involved should not be described as combat.[1] Killing with booby traps or land mines or with snipers is not the same as participating in massed formation in a bayonet charge. Still, women, both as combatants and as military leaders, have always been prominent in guerrilla movements, although scholarship in the field largely ignores them.[2] In the military theaters of the cold war thousands of women fought in wars of revolution in Africa, Asia, and Latin America. Some of the wars were Marxist, some were liberal, and some were simply nationalist. A striking similarity is the speed with which the contributions of women to these wars either were deliberately suppressed or were easily forgotten in the postrevolutionary period. Rarely did the military service of women bring any improvement in their peacetime status.[3]

In 1945 the United States was the world's most powerful military force, but Americans were glad that the war was over, and the nation rapidly demobilized. Because the Soviet Union still controlled East Germany as well as all the Eastern European countries, America's remaining military forces were either stationed in Europe or poised to intervene if the Soviet Union attempted to invade Western Europe. And because the United States was the sole nuclear power at that time, American military and political leaders felt a nuclear strike would be the obvious way to halt such an invasion. But nothing happened in Europe. Instead, a civil war in China ended with a victory for Mao Tse-tung, and the communist People's Republic of China was established in 1949, drawing attention to communist expansion in Asia.

A few months later, a communist North Korean People's Army crossed the 38th parallel in an attempt to reunite the peninsula, which had been divided by American and Soviet occupying forces as a temporary expedient after the defeat of Japan. Thus it was in Korea, where partisans of the two halves of the peninsula were already battling before the North Korean invasion, that Americans went to war again in 1950.

THE KOREAN POLICE ACTION

WHAT HAPPENED IN KOREA was a peculiar sort of military activity. No war was declared, and no peace was concluded. There was no drive for total victory, partly because of fear that a war would be started with China, and neither side used nuclear weapons. Later it would be said that the action in Korea was "the wrong war, in the wrong place, at the wrong time." Whatever the nature of the United Nations (UN)military action in Korea, women from a number of nations were on active duty from the start. There were not many, only 22,000 U.S. women, and one-third of these were health professionals. By law, the WACs, the WAVES, the Women Marines, and the new Women in the Air Force (WAFs) could enlist numbers only up to 2 percent of total military strength in each service, but they had fewer than half that many when the war began.[4]

U.S. Army nurses were in Korea four days after the first troops landed. Two days after that, twelve nurses went to the war zone at Taejon with a mobile army surgical hospital (M*A*S*H). (Not many years later, the description of M*A*S*H nurses in the popular television series would make certain no one forgot that women had served under fire in Korea.) Within a year, the size of the Army Nurse Corps increased by one-half, to 5,400; most of its members were veterans of World War II who had joined the reserves. Far fewer women in the other services were in reserve units. The military refused to send any women except nurses into the combat zone anyway, although WACs and WAFs served in Japan, Okinawa, Iwo Jima, and the Philippines. Other women in all the services replaced military men in the States so that men could go overseas.

A year after the war began, there were still far fewer women in the line components than there were requests for them coming in from the field. Although women had never made up more than 2 percent of the force during World War II, all the services had planned at the beginning of the war for a great many more. The army and air force said that at least 10 percent of their strength could be female, while the navy estimate was for 15 percent of its officers and 12 percent of its enlisted force. Even the Marine Corps projected a need for 7 percent.

But it proved impossible to meet even the more modest 2 percent goal, and by mid-1951 the women's forces made up only 1 percent of the total armed force strength. Anna Rosenberg, the assistant secretary of defense for manpower, then suggested to Secretary of Defense George C. Marshall that he form a committee of fifty prominent women to help the recruiting effort. The result was the Defense Advisory Committee on Women in the Services (DACOWITS), an organization still in existence today. The members used their personal influence as well as their committee service to carry out their mission: to inform the public about military recruiting needs, to reassure parents about care and supervision of the young women who joined the military, to let young women know about career opportunities, and to raise the prestige of military women in the public mind. Their goal was to recruit 72,000 women within a year, most of them in line rather than health care specialties. A rumor circulated in Washington, D.C., that if the services did not meet their goals, Congress would consider drafting women.

The well-publicized recruiting campaign was a dismal failure. The WAC, which hoped to grow from 13,000 to 32,000 had fewer than 10,000 women a year later—a net loss. The navy and Marine Corps made modest gains. The overall total for the three women's services was still less than 1 percent of the total armed forces. The secretary of the army was so concerned by this shortfall that he told the Department of Defense he was preparing legislation to make Selective Service legislation applicable to women as well as men. Before any action could be taken on his proposal, the war ended. For the next ten years, the women's services remained small because only men continued to be subject to the draft. In 1959, another rumor circulated that Congress was considering eliminating women from the peacetime forces entirely.[5]

THE VIETNAM CONFLICT

THE KOREAN WAR BORE only a superficial resemblance to the wars the United States had participated in earlier in the century. The next deployment of American troops had an even more surreal quality. The United States drifted into military involvement in Vietnam in the 1950s. What was officially known as the Vietnam Conflict—since, again, Congress did not declare war—bore even less resemblance to the military operations of earlier times.

Young people raised on John Wayne movies discovered that Vietnam was nothing at all like World War II. The conflict lasted from 1958, when the first official American military advisers arrived, to 1973, when American troops pulled out—longer than any previous American war. It seemed impossible to win. Somehow, technologically unsophisticated peasants were able to frustrate the best efforts of the superbly trained and equipped Americans. The longer combat in Vietnam lasted, the less sense it made to the young men drafted to serve there. For women who had volunteered for military service, the experience often was even more stressful.

Most military women sent to Vietnam served in the traditional woman's role, as nurses. In that capacity they saw more death and pain close up than combat soldiers did, and they agonized over their inability to save the young men in their care. Improvements in medical technology and speedy evacuation saved grotesquely injured soldiers who earlier would have died on the field. These wounded now came under the care of young women fresh out of nursing school. Decades later, many nurse veterans still have nightmares about wounded men and corpses. Nurses suffered physically as well as emotionally; nine army nurses died in Vietnam.[6]

For the few military women in the line, the situation was also disorienting. As part of the effort to make military service more attractive to women volunteers, the services deliberately downplayed the connection of enlistment with the possibility of exposure to fighting. Nonnursing personnel did not have the training, clothing, or equipment necessary to function effectively in the field. Even weapons familiarization was eliminated from WAC training because, according to the WAC director, Col. Elizabeth P. Housington, it was "a waste of time" that "failed to contribute to the image we want to project."[7]

American civilian women, however, could go where regulations prohibited sending women in uniform. Dr. Eleanor Ardel Vietti went to Vietnam to work for the Christian Missionary Alliance at a station about eight miles from Ban Me Thuot. In 1962, she and two men were taken prisoner; today her name remains on the POW/MIA list among those "presumed dead." Women journalists and Central Intelligence Agency personnel as well as American Red Cross nurses and other humanitarian volunteers went to the war zone. Sixty-two civilian women died there.[8]

American servicewomen, however, were kept out of harm's way. A WAC lieutenant complained, "What kind of delicate creatures do the brass think we are? There's a war going on in Vietnam but you have to be a civilian to get assigned there. Women are fighting in the jungles with the Viet Cong. Yet we aren't allowed to dirty our dainty hands."[9] By war's end, approximately 7,500 American military women had served in Vietnam, but fewer than 1,200 were WACs, WAFs, or Women Marines.

For Vietnamese women, the war was much simpler. Whether they allied themselves with the American-backed South Vietnamese forces, took the side of the insurgents, or just tried to protect themselves and their families, they knew exactly why they were there. Vietnam was their home.

As we have seen, every nation has had a history of women in war. The Vietnamese tradition extended back to A.D. 43, when Trung Trac organized a peasant revolt against the Chinese governor of the area. Her sister, Trung Nhi, fought with her and was even more famous in battle. In the year A.D. 40, the sisters led an army of eighty thousand against the governor, who fled to China. Their victory marked the first time in one thousand years that Vietnam had been free of Chinese domination. The Trungs held sixty-five fortified towns and trained thirty-six other women generals, including their mother. One of these, Phyung Thi Chinh, reportedly gave birth on the battlefield and returned to the fray with the infant strapped on her back. Eventually, the Chinese brought in reinforcements and defeated the sisters, who escaped capture by performing ceremonial suicide.[10] In the third century, Trieu Thi Thinh raised one thousand troops in another revolt against the Chinese. She wore golden armor and rode into battle mounted on an elephant. Her revolt lasted only six months, and she, too, committed suicide. But she was remembered for her defiant cry, "I want to rail against the wind and the tide, kill the whale in the sea, sweep the whole country to save the people from slavery, and I refuse to be abused."[11]

Fighting foreign invaders made up a good part of Vietnamese history. In 1887, the French unified Vietnam and ruled the region as a French colony. After World War II, one million Vietnamese women fought in an independence movement to expel the French. A defeat by the Vietminh in the north of the country broke the French command and brought about the division of Vietnam through an international agreement in 1954. Then the United States decided to pick up where the French left off and lend support to South Vietnam, fearing that the revolt by the communist north was part of a larger Soviet strategy. Many women who were veterans of the earlier conflict became leaders in the war against the Americans. Military activity in Vietnam included both conventional armies and guerrillas.[12]

In 1965, the U.S. Army sent a WAC major and one woman noncommissioned officer to help the South Vietnamese organize and train their Women's Armed Forces Corps.[13] In 1966, about three thousand women were in this service, but their experience had been quite different from that of American WACs. Although many performed administrative and clerical tasks, some were combat troops who had gone into action long before their American advisers arrived.[14] Like American WACs, the first Vietnamese women recruits were well-educated city girls, and few of them had ever done any manual labor. Their proficiency as combat troops, displayed in an action at Hoc Mon early in 1962, demonstrated what training could accomplish. At Hoc Mon a patrol of fifteen women soldiers ambushed and killed twenty-five Viet Cong guerrillas.[15] Still, it turned out that keeping these educated women for clerical and staff assignments was a better use of womanpower, and rural women soon replaced them in combat assignments.

Particularly useful for combat roles were enlisted women recruited in the mountainous region of Min Top. Early in the twentieth century, a Swedish mining company worked in Min Top. When the company crew abandoned the location, they left behind large numbers of children with fair skin and light hair. Over the years, Swedish genes spread widely in the region, producing what were known as the "big people of Min Top." Swedish women tend to be large even by American standards; compared with typical Vietnamese people, among whom both men and women are small, they were enormous. The Min Top women could easily lift heavy machine guns and set up tree traps and rope and bamboo snares. They also had remarkable endurance. One of them, Dho Minde, was said to have run forty-five miles through thick jungle when pursued by insurgent forces.

The leaders of the Min Top women and other peasant women soldiers were Hui Po Yung, who had been a physical education instructor in Saigon, and Ding Le Tunn, the daughter of a French officer. Western observers in the 1960s said that the only other women soldiers of the postwar period as good as these Vietnamese were the Kikuyu women who fought in the Mau Mau insurgency in Kenya in the 1950s.[16]

An example of the women's army in action occurred in 1962, a day's march from the village of Kong Loc. The leaders divided the force of fifty women into two halves, and when the Viet Cong attempted to ambush one, the other took them from the rear. In this engagement they killed twenty-two Viet Cong; only one of their own was killed, and seven were wounded.

The South Vietnamese military included a few prominent women in the regular army. Most notable was Madame Ho Thi Que, known as the "Tiger Lady of the Mekong Delta." The mother of seven children, Madame Ho rose to the rank of master sergeant in the elite Vietnamese 44th Rangers. She led men into action and was three times decorated for valor. As so many other women soldiers have done, the Tiger Lady also worked as a field medic and a nurse.[17]

The enemy faced by the American-backed Army of the Republic of South Vietnam (ARVN) included both the North Vietnamese Army and an insurgent force known as the Viet Cong. Both forces had women members. A May 1970 intelligence report described an army outpost in the jungle near Champassak, observing, "The camp is notable also for the reported presence of several dozen North Vietnamese WACs."[18] Women were even more prominent among the insurgents, where they worked as intelligence agents, nurses, and soldiers, usually combining the functions so that a captured Viet Cong "nurse" received no mercy. When American and South Vietnamese troops captured the major Viet Cong headquarters at Nui Coto in 1969, they discovered photographs showing women fighters in checkered scarves, brandishing AK-47s. Two years later, forty or fifty women were serving on the front line in the Viet Cong 101st Independent Regiment, and a number died in combat. Women made up between one-third and one-half of Viet Cong troops and about 40 percent of regimental commanders.[19] Among the best known woman field commanders was Hong, who led a Viet Cong battalion in a major engagement near Da Nang that ended with an ARVN retreat. United Press International reported in 1974 that she was "both feared and respected by the men under her command." Nguyen Thi Dinh was deputy commander of the entire Viet Cong insurgent operation in the south. A political and a military leader, Dinh was honored by Vietnamese officials at the time of her death in 1992; they described her as "the outstanding woman in Vietnam's modern history."[20]

A few all-woman platoons specialized in reconnaissance, communications, commando operations, and nursing. Tran Thi Gung commanded the all-woman C3 company that trained with the North Vietnamese Special Forces for small unit infantry fighting. Training included using side arms and rifles, throwing hand grenades, wiring and detonating mines, and assassination. Such women were among the special forces that penetrated the American base at Cu Chi in February 1969, where they destroyed all the

Ch-47 Chinook helicopters and killed thirty-eight Americans. But the most famous of the all-woman squads was one that took part in the Tet offensive a year earlier. The unit consisted of eleven girls; the oldest was nineteen. They were said to have killed one hundred twenty American soldiers.[21] A recent documentary, *As the Mirror Burns,* shows women who raised their children underground in the Viet Cong tunnel systems as they conducted insurgent operations.[22]

In North Vietnam, civilian women trained in hand-to-hand combat and were the core of the village self-defense teams, making up as much as 80 percent of the home guard forces. They fortified the villages with trenches, traps, and spikes and brought down hundreds of American planes with anti-aircraft weapons. Those living in fishing hamlets shelled American warships from the shore. Women also worked on repair crews to restore roads after bombing attacks. Young women without children carried supplies down the Ho Chi Minh Trail for the units in the south. These women, said to have "feet of brass and shoulders of iron," each carried a forty-pound pack for the three-month march down the trail, which was a regular target for American bombing.

Although many Vietnamese women had combat roles, many also were forced into the ancient role of rape victim. Thanks to Susan Brownmiller's interviews for her pioneering study, *Against Our Will,* we have evidence of rape in Vietnam that goes beyond the bare catalogs of atrocity stories compiled by investigators of earlier wars. Journalists covering the Vietnam conflict did not file stories on rape, but in interviews with Brownmiller they spoke at length on a matter that, at the time, had not seemed fit to print.

The Associated Press correspondent Peter Arnett, who covered Vietnam for eight years, knew about rapes committed by the South Vietnamese army. Indeed, reporters accompanying the army were often so close to the scene of gang rapes that they could hear the woman screaming. In contrast he told Brownmiller "that it was common knowledge among the Saigon press corps that the Vietcong and North Vietnamese Army rarely committed rape." If one of their soldiers did commit rape, the punishment was severe. Arnett had seen documents taken from dead Viet Cong referring to soldiers guilty of the crime. "The VC would publicize an execution for rape," Arnett said. "Rape was a serious crime for them. It was considered a serious political blunder to rape and loot. It just wasn't done. At the same time they made women who were raped by the other side into heroines, examples of enemy atrocity."²³ The CBS correspondent Dan Rather, who spent a year in Vietnam, told Brownmiller,

Rape was not something that was foremost in my mind when I talked to people. My average story was shooting, shelling and bombing. The pattern was to jump on a helicopter, shoot a story very quickly and ship the film back to Saigon. I never did a rape story, and if you had been doing my job I don't think you would have, either. Everywhere you looked there was a horror and a brutality. Rape may have been mentioned to me several times while I was in Vietnam. When you see women crying, and you see that universal look of bitterness and anger, you find out about rape. My own limited experience led me to conclude that everybody who passed through a village did it—steal a chicken and grab a quick piece of ass, that sort of thing. Based on my own experience I would have to say that the Americans and the Korean troops were probably the worst—they had the least to lose—but I wouldn't build any case for the other side's superior morality. Vietnam was a loosely organized gang war, and the women caught it from all sides.²⁴

One atrocity did eventually make the news: the My Lai massacre of March 16, 1968. Seymour M. Hersh, of the *New York Times*, broke the story and later published a book giving an unflinching and detailed account of the destruction of My Lai and its people by American soldiers. The members of Charlie Company in the Americal Division had been abusing women near their base camp in Qung Ngai Province for a month before the My Lai incident. Everyone knew about it, but no one had been reprimanded. One participant in a gang rape even recorded it for posterity, clicking away with his Instamatic camera while the peasant woman who had been working in a field with her baby beside her suffered and died.

Most American soldiers were not rapists, but they had the normal male interest in sex. The presence of American troops created a flourishing business for sex workers in all the ports the men visited—from Bangkok and the Philippines to the war zone itself. Before the United States intervened in the war, the French armies fighting the rebels went to Indochina with mobile field brothels staffed by women from Algeria, another French colony. The American military had two types of organized prostitution, one favored by the Marine Corps and the other by the army. According to Peter Arnett, the marine base at Danang at first organized trips to town for the battalions once a month, but "the men would hit town like animals, they couldn't cope, it was pure chaos." So the marine command decided to confine the men to base and tolerate the inevitable appearance of a shantytown known as "Dogpatch," a community of brothels, massage parlors, and dope dealers ringing the base. "The marines would bust through the wire at night," Arnett explained. "The marine command could live with that."[25]

The army solution was to establish official military brothels within the perimeter of the base camps. Known as "Disneylands," "Sin Cities," and "boom-boom parlors," they operated in the tradition of European regulated prostitution. Arnett described the Lai Khe "recreation area," a one-acre compound surrounded by barbed-wire with MPs guarding it. Inside, soldiers could buy hot dogs, hamburgers, souvenirs, and sex. Two concrete barracks one hundred feet long were equipped with two bars, a bandstand, and sixty curtained cubicles, each furnished with a table covered by a thin mattress. The prostitute working this station could earn more than her soldier clients by turning only eight or ten tricks a day, so she did her best to please. Prostitutes wore elaborate bouffant hairdos, heavy makeup, and often had their breasts enlarged with silicone in deference to Western preferences. Civilians recruited the prostitutes for the army, but army medics checked them for venereal disease and in at least one command gave them daily shots of penicillin.[26]

THE ALL-VOLUNTEER MILITARY

AS THE ASIAN WAR dragged on, increasing numbers of Americans came to believe that U.S. involvement was a bad idea. Although casualties were light compared to other wars of modern times, the deaths were real and harder to bear because they seemed meaningless, especially to young people. Many young men took measures to avoid the draft, some fleeing the country. At that time, eighteen-year-olds did not have the right to vote, but males of that age were subject to compulsory military service. In the United States, no government policy could stand indefinitely against the force of public opinion, and the war was brought to a halt in 1973. Even before that, eighteen-year-olds were enfranchised. At the end of the war the draft was abolished, and in 1977 amnesty was declared for war resisters. Meanwhile fighting continued between the two sides in Vietnam, and the country was finally reunified in 1975 under a communist regime that became embroiled in fighting with Cambodia.

The elimination of the draft fundamentally changed the nature of military service in the United States. Actually, Americans had tolerated a draft for only a few decades; they had prided themselves on the absence of a standing army and the tradition of civilian soldiers who would turn out to defend their lives and liberties, as did the patriots of Massachusetts at Lexington and Concord. But creating a large, peacetime, all-volunteer force meant that military career offerings had to compete with civilian career opportunities to attract young people. The kind of recruit the services wanted would not tolerate the humiliating and abusive forms of training accepted by draftees. Simultaneously, the introduction of increasingly sophisticated weapons systems made technological skill more important in recruits than their muscle mass.

Had the United States faced a concrete threat, such as Soviet tanks rumbling down the New Jersey turnpike toward Washington, D.C., realism might have forced immediate radical changes in the military. But there was no such threat then, nor has there been in all the years since. Consequently, often to the bewilderment of other nations, the United States began in the early 1970s to engage in agonized debates on issues only a nation with a history that included so little experience of invasion and war could afford to take seriously. Two of these issues focus on gender.

Everyone has opinions on "women in combat" and "gays in the military," both of which are talk show staples, so there is no need to go into the arguments here. Since neither side in these discussions is interested in listening to the other, the debate is repetitious and impossible to resolve.[27] The two subjects converge, however, in the rarely mentioned issue of "lesbians in the military," a subject about which something new remains to be said. Although seldom recognized as a topic, military lesbians have a distinct history of their own.

Lesbians became visible enough by the end of World War II to cause amendment of the centuries-old "slander campaign" against women in the military. Where once it was said, "All military women are whores," the amended version is "All military women are either whores or dykes."

Simple name-calling is nothing new. Women intellectuals as far back as the Renaissance were accused of having "a male mind in a female body" and sometimes worried about this themselves, although most were intelligent enough to observe other women and realize that the capacity for logical thought was reasonably widespread among both sexes. In the nineteenth century, as some Western women entered the professions and could support themselves without marriage, those who moved into male territory could expect to be called "unnatural." A writer outraged by the Grimké sisters, who lectured against slavery in the 1830s, wrote, "These Amazonians are their own executioners. They have unsexed themselves in public estimation." He reassured himself by stating his certainty that they would remain "spinsters" and be unable to "perpetuate their race" because they could never attract husbands.[28] But Angelina Grimké married Theodore Weld and had three children, and Sarah made her home with them. The sisters continued their political activity.

In the nineteenth century, however, many women deliberately chose not to marry. Louisa May Alcott wrote an article entitled "Happy Women" about "old maids." In it she listed "all the busy, useful, independent spinsters [she knew]," for, she said, "liberty is a better husband than love to many of us."[29] In the decades following the Civil War, which had killed off many eligible young men and also left many widows, large numbers of respectable women lived without a man. Of course there were critics. As early as 1867, the Reverend John Todd was fulminating against the new trend:

The root of the great error of our day is, that woman is to be made independent and self-supporting, precisely what she never can be, because God never designed she should be. Her support, her dignity, her beauty, her honor, and happiness lie in her dependence as wife, mother, and daughter. Any other theory is rebellion against God's law of the sexes, against marriage, which it assails in its fundamental principles, and against the family organization, the holiest thing that is left from Eden.[30]

In the decades before World War I, the number of never-married women in America was at an all-time high, and the proportion of voluntary spinsters was greatest among the most highly educated women. The public admired them, and the bold, independent "new woman" who drove motor cars, piloted planes, and had adventures was the epitome of the "American girl." During World War I, recruiting posters featured girls with boyish figures and bobbed hair in male military uniforms saying to the male thinking of enlisting, "I wish I were a man. I'd join the Navy," or "If you want to fight, join the Marines."

Some of these "new women" merely delayed marriage, but others stayed single permanently. Few could afford to live alone even if they wanted to.

Living with family meant always being on call for baby-sitting or caring for the sick. Living with a male friend was out of the question for a decent woman. So they lived with women friends. Did they love each other? Of course. Did they have sexual relations with each other? The new openness about sex in the twentieth century meant that someone was bound to ask that question.

Katharine Bement Davis studied a sample of clubwomen and college graduates born about 1880 and found that 50 percent of the single women and 30 percent of the married women had intense emotional relationships with other women and that half of these were "accompanied by mutual masturbation, contact of genital organs or other physical expressions recognized as sexual in character."[31] Dr. Robert L. Dickinson, who did not think to ask such intimate questions when he first went into medical practice, started to keep records after World War I. Eventually he had three hundred fifty patients willing to discuss their sexual practices and found that twenty-eight had genital relationships with other women. He saw nothing wrong with it. In 1934 Dickinson wrote, "Homosexuality had been stressed far beyond its numerical significance or its importance as a harmful interference with normal response. Physiology is teaching us that we are all in some degree bisexual and that we possess some sex traits other than those characteristic of our overt type, with two series of stages between extreme masculinity and complete femininity." Because female homosexual behavior was so common, he said that "to stamp such activity a 'perversion' . . . is to lack a sense of proportion, if not sound judgement." What was deviant, however, and he was very firm on this point, was for a woman to refuse to marry.[32]

Lillian Faderman, a pioneer in lesbian history, describes the inconsistency of social attitudes toward independent women. "Perceptions of emotional or social desires, formations of sexual categories, and attitudes concerning 'mental health' are constantly shifting," she writes, "not through the discovery of objectively conceived truths, as we generally assume, but rather through social forces that have little to do with the *essentiality* of emotions or sex or mental health. Affectional preferences, ambitions, and even sexual experiences that are within the realm of the socially acceptable during one era may be considered sick or dangerous or antisocial during another—and in a brief space of time attitudes may shift once again, and yet again."[33]

During World War I, the dashing young women who went to the front won praise and admiration. During the depression years of the thirties, a single woman working to support herself would more likely be denounced for selfishly stealing a job from a man who was head of a family. And the popularization of Freud and the writing of other "sexologists" made the newly discovered category "lesbian" a household word. Then some women, recognizing themselves in the doctors' descriptions, self-identified as lesbians. In big cities, these women discovered each other and, interacting as members of a distinct community, created the first lesbian subculture. With World War II, the demand for women's labor rose dramatically, and girls were urged to put on pants to work in the war industries or to join the military themselves. Fleischmann's yeast ran an advertisement showing a young woman in uniform on a motorcycle, proclaiming, "This is No Time to be Frail! . . . The dainty days are done for the duration."[34]

Young women who took up the challenge tasted independence and met many other women at work. With so many men away at war, women did not view their new female acquaintances as sexual rivals in the hunt for a husband. Instead, they discovered women could be serious, self-sufficient human beings. In 1942, there was a word for this kind of female friendship if a woman chose to accept it. A woman who volunteered to harvest crops with the civilian Women's Land Army during the war recalls that she noticed two women acting affectionately toward each other. A third woman told her, "It's called lesbianism. There's really nothing wrong with it."[35]

During World War II, the military disqualified homosexuals from service for the first time. But WAC officers were specifically ordered not to seek out or punish lesbian activity. They were to take note of lesbian relationships, even those that took the form of sexual expression, "only in so far as the manifestations undermine the efficiency of the individual concerned and the stability of the group." Discharges were only for cases that were universally demoralizing. The order further stated, "Any officer bringing an unjust or unprovable charge against a woman in this regard will be severely reprimanded."[36] Faderman concludes that "few women who loved other women had serious difficulty during the war, since the military needed all the women it could get who would do their jobs and not disrupt the functioning of the service. Lesbians understood that if they practiced a modicum of discretion they would be quite safe."[37]

After the war, social attitudes abruptly reversed again. Experts told women that "feminists" of any kind needed psychoanalysis because "healthy" women wanted only to marry and have babies. The number of never-married women plummeted as pressure grew to marry, and marry young. By 1950, the mean age of marriage for women in the United States was at a historic low, 20.2 years. No wonder there was a baby boom, and no wonder the military found it impossible to meet its Korean War recruiting goals. Aside from the more attractive jobs in the civilian sector, the military competed with a nesting trend. The distinction between "deviant" unmarried women and those with a marriage certificate widened. The "real" woman was a wife. All others were pitiable failures, prostitutes, or lesbians.[38]

Women who chose to remain single and had only platonic relationships with their women friends would not self-identify as lesbians whatever the psychologists might say. Then Betty Friedan wrote of "the problem that has no name," in her book, *The Feminine Mystique,* published in 1963.[39] She asserted that it was perfectly normal for educated women to want to do more with their lives than nurture husbands and raise children. Soon there was yet another category a woman might select for self-identification: "lesbian feminist," a term describing women who for political reasons chose to bond with other women rather than with a man. By 1970, there were several types of lesbians. For some women, lesbianism was a genetic orientation they were born with. For others, it was a political choice. For still others, it might be a sudden revelation or personal insight that could come relatively late in life after many years of marriage.

During the same decade in which the United States developed its all-volunteer military, lesbian feminists spoke of building a "lesbian nation."[40] This utopian concept aimed to construct an alternative to patriarchy. The adherents of this movement were the first to use the phrase "politically correct" to describe the high standard of personal behavior necessary in their self-conscious promotion of a radical political agenda that included abstinence from drugs and alcohol, vegetarianism, sensitivity to all forms of bigotry, and opposition to "militarism." A "politically correct" lesbian would not join the military and would condemn any woman who did as supporting the "male war machine." But many lesbians were not feminists, and many feminists were not lesbians. And many women who considered themselves neither lesbians nor feminists in those years were entering the nontraditional occupations that paid better and had greater status than those dominated by women.

Ten years after the draft ended, the new all-volunteer military included large numbers of women moving into senior positions and pushing for the removal of limitations on the kinds of assignments they could fill. Some of these were self-identified but carefully closeted lesbians.[41] They did not welcome publicity about their lifestyle, which was no longer tolerated as it had been during World War II. Publicity came anyway. In 1976, two years after enlisting in the U.S. Army, a drill sergeant, Miriam Ben-Shalom, told her commander and other soldiers that she was a lesbian. Many years of litigation followed as Ben-Shalom took her case all the way to the Supreme Court in her battle to remain in the service. Although the final ruling went against her, Ben-Shalom had some victories along the way. The army was forced to allow her back on duty in 1987, and from then until 1990 she was the only acknowledged "homosexual" in any branch of service. Since Ben-Shalom's case involved a person who claimed to be homosexual without engaging in homosexual conduct, the military scrambled to revise its rules to cover those who might be celibate but still "desired" to engage in homosexual activity.[42]

After the new rule was promulgated, any woman who preferred flat shoes to pumps and pants to skirts was a suspected lesbian. And the better a woman performed her job, the more likely she was to be considered a lesbian. In the witch-hunts of the 1980s and 1990s women were many times more likely than men to be discharged for suspected homosexual tendencies. As witch-hunting peaked in 1990, a memo from the admiral heading the navy's Atlantic command helpfully described the "stereotypical lesbian" as "hardworking, career-oriented, willing to put in long hours on the job and among the command's top professionals." He ordered the nearly two hundred ships and forty shore installations in his command to deal "firmly" with them.[43]

During the 1980s, any woman who was particularly good at her job and refused a male sexual advance became vulnerable to charges that could end her military career. Ironically, if the Supreme Court ultimately rules against the ban on military service by homosexuals, the largest number of beneficiaries will be the thousands of hard-driving professional military women who happen to be straight (as most of them are) but are presently vulnerable to charges that they are not.

Meanwhile, after American withdrawal from Vietnam, the new all-volunteer military planned and conducted training exercises focused on repelling a Soviet invasion of Europe. But there was no real fighting. Years passed, and soon a younger generation of military leaders that had no first-hand experience of any kind of combat was accustomed to the presence of women in the ranks. In 1978, the WAC became part of the regular army. The first women graduated from the service academies in 1980, and women made up a substantial proportion of the force in all the uniformed services. Then a brief U.S. military action in Grenada in 1983 brought army and air force women under fire, although that fact was not widely publicized.[44] A second brief action in Panama brought women of the all-volunteer force under fire again, this time with a hail of publicity. In particular, the media descended on Capt. Linda Bray, who ordered an assault on a Panamanian dog kennel. Journalists declared that no woman in history had performed so gallant a deed. The pressure of this publicity, which made her the unwilling symbol of the "women in combat" controversy, quickly ended her military career.[45]

A third action, the Gulf War, put women in a glare of publicity from the start. This high-tech conflict to force the withdrawal of Iraqi forces from Kuwait resulted in few deaths on the UN side. But several U.S. women were killed, and two became prisoners of war while the whole world watched on cable television. The Gulf War ended with the Iraqi leader, Saddam Hussein, cast as a new Hitler, still in power. The limits of conventional military operations were now blazingly clear. At precisely this moment, however, Americans became obsessed with women as potential combatants. Heated debate took place in what approached a historical vacuum. A respected reference work for young people published in 1994 solemnly informed students, "During the Gulf War, women for the first time served alongside men in combat regions."[46]

THE ISRAELI EXPERIENCE

FOR MOST OF THE years since World War II, Americans have taken a myopic view of women's military activity. When the subject of women in combat is raised, appeals are usually made to the history of U.S.women in military service since World War I or, occasionally, to the experiences of Russian women in World War II. Most frequently, however, those opposed to the extension of opportunities for women in the American military point to the presumed history of Israeli women, which we will turn to now.

Of the many limited wars fought around the globe since World War II, those between the state of Israel and neighboring Arab nations have been of particular interest in the United States. Common knowledge about the role of women in the Israeli military—the sort repeated by newspaper columnists and talk show hosts who cite no specific evidence—goes this way: At one time Israel "experimented" with the use of women in combat. The experiment was a failure. The Israeli military discovered that Arab males fought to the death rather than accept the shame of surrendering to women, so using women in combat made engagements more costly in casualties. Also, women soldiers captured by Arabs suffered unspeakable abuses, which Israeli civilians could not tolerate. Thus the image of heroic Israeli women combat soldiers following in the gory footsteps of Deborah and Judith is a myth.

The Israeli military itself has worked to destroy the impression that women ever fought for the nation. Israel's conscription law applies to both men and women, but any woman may be exempt by claiming that service would conflict with traditional religious practices. Women recruits go into a separate women's army corps, Chail Nashim in Hebrew, known by the acronym CHEN, meaning "charm." A typical statement is the following from the *Israel Defense Forces Spokesman,* an official publication of the Israel Defense Forces (IDF):

> *Sorry to disappoint you if you have been influenced by the Hollywood image of Israeli girl soldiers being Amazon-type warriors accoutred in ill-fitting male combat fatigues and toting sub-machine guns. Today's female soldiers are trim girls, clothed in uniforms which bring out their femininity. They play a wide variety of noncombat, though thoroughly essential roles, within the IDF framework and within certain sectors of the civilian community.*[47]

What this description conceals is the history of women who fought for Israel in organizations other than CHEN and predating the organization of the IDF.

Ancient Palestine was ruled for only a few hundred years by the Israelites, who won it over a period of time from the Canaanites and fought to hold it against the Philistines. Their kingdom split, and the northern half, Israel, was conquered by the Assyrians, and, later, the southern half, Judah, was conquered by the Babylonians and Persians before becoming part of the Roman Empire at the start of the Christian era. The Romans did not believe in coddling their colonists; they destroyed much of the city of Jerusalem in A.D. 70 when the Jews revolted. After another revolt in 132, the Romans punished insurrectionists by executing more than half a million men in more than a thousand villages. Left without a homeland, the Jews dispersed to other parts of the world.

At the end of the nineteenth century, Jews known as Zionists began to return to Palestine with the goal of creating a nation that would belong to them. Since they were not welcomed peacefully by the Arabs, who had considered the land their home for centuries, the Jewish immigrants organized for self-defense. The first organization was a secret society, the Bar Glora, founded in 1907. This group had at least two women members: Manya Shochat and Esther Becker. Two years later, Bar Glora became Hashomer, whose members were dedicated to guarding the settlements. The role of women in the organization was debated; some women and men supported equal participation for women, other women and men opposed it. The outcome of the debate was the establishment of two distinct roles for women. Some were recognized in the organization because they were wives of members. Others, like Manya Shochat and Rachel Yanait, were full members, in meetings and trusted with policy matters.[48]

At the end of World War I, the victorious powers agreed to put Palestine, which had been part of the Ottoman Empire, under the control of Great Britain. The Arabs stepped up their attacks on Jewish settlers and the Hashomer was inadequate to meet defense needs. Following attacks on Jerusalem and Jaffa in 1921, a new underground organization called the Haganah (Defense) was formed, which was to include all able-bodied Jews, men and women alike. A secret organization, it did not keep records, and its history comes from diaries and oral histories. Mina Ben Zvi, a Haganah officer, stated to an interviewer:

> Haganah women were a direct link from the Hashomer woman. I was not given to hero worship, but they were my role models. They nurtured us, my generation, and gave us the assurance that if they could do it, so could we. In 1933, when I finished my studies, I joined the Haganah. We fought against separation and wanted mixed platoons of men and women. There were those who disagreed, and they were sent to prepare sandwiches and do first aid. We wanted to take part in combat and fought for the same training. This training took place in cellars, in the Technion (the Israel Institute of Technology). I was then sent to Juara for officer training, where there were about four women to forty men. Women in the Haganah were devoted, disciplined, and conscientious. It was natural for them to do what they did, not because they were feminists, but because they felt strongly for what was being fought for.[49]

In 1936, as Arab attacks continued, Yitzhak Sadeh formed a small unofficial elite unit called the Nodedet (Patrol), composed of young volunteers from Haganah. Their mission was attack rather than defense, and they went after Arab guerrillas in their own villages. Sopshana Spector, who later would be a member of the general staff of the Palmach, remembered being the "one girl among Yitzhak Sadeh's boys."[50]

In May 1939, just when persecution of Jews by Nazis increased the numbers wanting to leave Europe for Palestine, Great Britain issued a White Paper putting a cap on immigration. When the war against Hitler began, David Ben-Gurion described the position of the Jews in Palestine: "We will fight the war as if there is no White Paper and we will fight the White Paper as if there is no war."[51] During World War II, Jewish women in Palestine served in two distinct organizations: the Auxiliary Territorial Services (ATS), run by the British, and the Palmach (Assault Companies), an arm of the Haganah. The Palmach specialized in the most difficult and dangerous assignments.[52]

When the Palmach was first formed, the Haganah chief of staff forbade recruitment of women. But Israel Livartovsky, the commander of the Jerusalem company, disobeyed, and in the winter of 1941–42 the first women were recruited. By 1944, need outweighed ideological reluctance. Socialist youth movement groups known as the Hachsharot reached an agreement with the Palmach not to discriminate against their girls. One-half of each core group of recruits would be female.[53]

Meanwhile, as the war turned in favor of the Allies, a separate Jewish military group called the Irgun began to target Great Britain. The Irgun was a small organization; during the period of its greatest activity, only about two thousand members participated, some four hundred of them female. These women undertook a great deal of dangerous work, but only a few of them were in combat. Yet, according to E. Lankin, a member of the Irgun High Command, "It was because of the reluctance of the men that the girls were not included more often in the actions. They were a wonderful group of girls, who without hesitation performed their duties under the most difficult conditions. They often showed greater zeal, greater responsibility than the men. . . . [T]his I saw. . . . [A]nd there were some girls who were better in the action than some of the men."[54]

After World War II was won, the United Nations voted to partition Palestine into separate Jewish and Arab states. Britain refused to help implement the UN decision and withdrew its forces on expiration of its mandate in May 1948. The Jews proclaimed the state of Israel and fought the Arabs in a war that ended on January 7, 1949. During this war, women participated through the Palmach at all levels. This is where the "amazon-type" woman soldier so repellent to the more recent CHEN flourished, and women veterans of this war are still alive to tell their stories. There were five women commanding combat units. Col. Meir Pa'il recalls, "Women were excellent—there was not a single incident of a female soldier not behaving correctly."[55] The women who were taken out of combat were those in the Haganah.

In the spring of 1948, two women officers who had served with the ATS during World War II were asked to form a women's battalion in Jerusalem which would put women into more restricted roles of the type they held in the British women's auxiliary. Esther Herlitz, one of those officers, says, "One of the things we had to do was to take the Haganah girls out of the frontline. It was a decision about which there is controversy till this day. . . .The Haganah girls didn't like it, especially the radar girls. It kept them from getting good jobs in the army, in lower ranks, and out of decision making posts. They resented it."[56]

With independence, the state of Israel created a new defense establishment. Now that the war was over, the orthodox religious minority insisted that it was contradictory to the "spirit of Israel" for women to bear arms. In deference to these beliefs, the Defense Service Law of 1949 set the policy that limited participation of women in the Israeli military until 1995, when the Israeli Supreme Court ruled against the ban on combat training.[57] At the time of its passage, Ben-Gurion, the first prime minister, said, "We are told that women are not drafted into any other army in the world. We, too, have no intention of putting women into combat units, though no one can be sure that, should we be attacked and have to fight for our lives, we should not call on services of every man and woman. But the law in question deals with a peacetime situation, and we want to give women only the most basic training."[58]

Thus it was not the inability of Jewish women to perform well in combat that transformed the heroic Palmach women into the charming ladies of the Israeli Defense Forces; it was a policy decision, and one that could only be made in the luxury of peacetime. As for the fear that women prisoners would be mistreated, that, too, was based on prejudice rather than fact. According to Meir Pa'il,

To the best of my knowledge those few Jewish girls, soldiers and civilians, who happened to fall alive into Arab armies' hands were treated in

a respectable manner. The most important case concerning the question occurred some time before the Six Day War, when a bus carrying about 30 women soldiers happened to cross the Lebanese borders by mistake, was captured by Lebanese armed forces and brought back after a few days to Rosh Hasnikre. According to the girls' report, the Lebanese treated them honorably.[59]

Finally, as to the alleged propensity of Arab males to fight to the death rather than be taken alive by women, the sole recorded contemporary first-hand observation on the subject reveals just the opposite. Lionel Tiger, author of *Men in Groups,* records, "A Canadian soldier connected with the U.N. Truce Commission has noted that Israeli women are sent out on guerrilla raids in certain areas. Rather than engaging in battle with them, apparently many of their opponents surrender or retreat when it is clear females are involved. The theory is that this happens for essentially religious reasons: a man killed by a woman cannot have a desirable after-life."[60]

URBAN GUERRILLA WARFARE

HAVING WON INDEPENDENCE, THE state of Israel developed a modern military on the Western model, with expensive high-tech weapons, including a nuclear capability. Meanwhile, more than one million Arabs who had lived in Palestine either became refugees or were forced into refugee camps.[61] They wanted their homes back, but Israel's legitimacy was confirmed by the United Nations and the Palestinians could not challenge the Israelis through conventional military means. As the women bore children and the population grew, refugee camps became ever more crowded and frustration and resentment mounted. The Palestinians therefore found a new form of guerrilla warfare, commonly called urban guerrilla warfare or terrorism, particularly attractive.

Terrorism does not fit the models of conventional warfare, but it is a disciplined use of lethal force for socially sanctioned purposes. When used by recognized nations, it is called state-sponsored terrorism. The Palestinians lacked a state, but in 1958 they formed a secret society named al-Fatah dedicated to destroying Israel. In 1964, al-Fatah joined with other groups of Palestinians to create the Palestine Liberation Organization (PLO). Except for having no territory, the PLO operated as a government, and subsidiary groups around the world launched attacks against Israel.

Technically, terrorists are noncombatants because international law does not recognize the legitimacy of urban guerrilla warfare. Yet its practitioners consider themselves soldiers who apply alternative tactics to achieve political and military objectives. Terrorists, like advocates of saturation bombing, believe that large numbers of civilian casualties will result in the overthrow of repressive regimes. Urban guerrilla warfare has attracted large numbers of women. A terrorist needs no great strength and is not required to endure the harsh conditions of living in the field; all that is necessary are courage and steady nerves. Modern explosives, which eventually may include nuclear devices, are the terrorist's weapon of choice. For more than a century, women have been prominent among those assembling and planting bombs.

Eileen MacDonald interviewed an assortment of women terrorists for her book, *Shoot the Women First.*[62] Her subjects did not use the word *terrorist* to describe themselves; they prefer the designation "freedom fighters." Some were nationalists, such as the Palestinians and the members of the Irish Republican Army. Others were political revolutionaries, such as German Red Army Faction (successor to the Baader-Meinhof group) and the Italian Red Brigades. A list of "most wanted fugitives" published by *The European* in August 1993 listed three women among its "ten most wanted men." One of these, Andrea Klump, was believed to have participated in the bombing of a discotheque frequented by members of the American military in the Spanish town of Rota in 1988.

Then there are state-sponsored terrorists who take orders from an established government. Kim Hyun Hee carried out such a mission for North Korea in 1987, placing a bomb on Korean Air Flight 858, which exploded in the air, leaving no survivors.[63] Islamic fundamentalists, whose allegiance is transnational, accept similar missions. Christian Lochte directs a German antiterrorist operation and told MacDonald, "For anyone who loves his life, it is a very clever idea to shoot the women first. From my experience women terrorists have much stronger characters, more power, more energy. There are some examples where men waited a moment before they fired, and women shot at once. This is a general phenomenon with terrorists."[64]

In addition to nationalism and political or economic motivations, religious motives began to fuel terrorist activity in the last decades of the twentieth century, just as they supported wars in earlier eras. And as in all earlier wars, women have had a part to play. To outsiders, Islamic fundamentalism may appear misogynistic. Women are excluded from political decision making. They may not go out in public without a male escort or drive an automobile. Polygyny is accepted, and adulterous women are publicly stoned to death. To those who do not wear it, the chador, the voluminous, heavily veiled, black robe that is required garb for Islamic women, seems a symbol of oppression. But many Islamic women see it as a symbol of their religious dedication, and they fight in the jihad, or holy war, against the secular evil represented by the West and more liberal Arabs. An eyewitness described events in Tehran on September 8, 1978 as women played their part in the revolution that overthrew the shah of Iran:

> There are thousands of people in the streets. You can see the women; in one hand they are holding up banners and flags, in the other they carry children. . . . The masses in the streets are faced with American-trained soldiers and American weapons. . . . It is Black Friday. The regime's troops attack the demonstrators at Jaleh Square. Women in Islamic clothing are in the front lines shouting slogans, protecting their husbands, marching behind them. They think because they are women the soldiers will not shoot. A few moments later the massacre starts. Perpetual machine gun firing shakes the streets. Hundreds of blood-soaked bodies cover the ground, among them innumerable women wrapped up in their black Islamic garment. A badly wounded woman is lying on the ground bleeding. She doesn't scream for help, she doesn't complain. She only says Allah-Akbar [God is great] until she dies. This is the woman that Islam builds.[65]

During the six-year war between Iran and Iraq that broke out in 1980 following the fundamentalist victory over the shah of Iran, whole regiments of women trained for combat. Reuters news service described a camp training women commandos in the use of automatic weapons, the American M-16 and the Soviet AK-47, as well as machine guns, mortars, and bazookas. "This Islamic Republic shows that women are valued," said a woman recruit holding up a Kalashnikov rifle through a gap in her black chador. "We are worth as much as a man and probably more. I don't know how to use this yet, but I am ready to fight."[66] Women sometimes train in all-female camps, but they are also seen in news clips training along with men. News photographers captured images from a camp training Islamic women terrorists, showing women in chadors marching and drilling in separate units but carrying out the same exercises as the men. The secret training camp was in the Sudan, not far from Cemetery 117 where the woman known as Burial 44 died 8,500 years ago at Jebl Sababa.

CHAPTER ELEVEN

THIRD WORLD WARS

IN FEBRUARY 1992, THE presidents of the United States and Russia jointly announced a formal end to the cold war following the breakup of the Soviet Union. As the threat of Armageddon faded away, numerous smallscale conflicts erupted in eastern European states that had been controlled by the Soviet Union, and minor wars that had raged for years in Asia, Africa, and Latin America became more visible. In the wake of the cold war, large numbers of humans around the globe were killing their fellows or being killed by them. They did not need tanks, jet aircraft, or submarines; the weapons of choice in the 1990s were lightweight inexpensive assault rifles and cheap antipersonnel land mines. In 1996, there were at least fifty unresolved low-intensity conflicts that could be described as wars. Ninety percent of these were internal, and the overwhelming majority of the casualties were civilian women and children.

The armies waging these wars are often scarcely recognizable as military organizations. Atrocities are the norm. Arms manufacturers keep the soldiers of these militias, or death squads, or warlord gangs well supplied with weapons, and international drug dealers supply many of them with chemicals to keep their will to kill high. These armies often feel no obligation to defend noncombatants but compete with them for food and humanitarian aid.

✦ ✦ ✦

WOMEN COMBATANTS AROUND THE WORLD

WOMEN AND CHILDREN HAVE been highly visible as victims in wars of the Third World, but those who look closely find them in combat roles as well. Until recently, the weight of weapons made it impractical to use children in any but combat support roles. Today girls and boys with assault rifles are the equals of adults. The AK-47 can be stripped and reassembled by a child of ten, and the American-made M-16s are so easy to use that they have been called "the transistor radio of modern warfare."[1]

Because so many low-intensity wars have been raging simultaneously in recent years, it is impossible to do more than highlight a few examples in this brief history. For those living through the events, each of these wars has elements of horror and heroism to fill a thick volume. Many women veterans of recent wars have told their stories, and a growing number are available in English translations. The stories of other women warriors are known only through the writings of journalists and outside observers. Their activities run the gamut from primitive to highly sophisticated. Their motives extend from the simple need to protect their homes to a wish to spread a universal messianic ideal. Below is a sample of women who have fought in wars at the turn of the millennium.[2]

In 1987, an army commanded by Alice Lakwena, called Messiah by her followers, challenged the National Resistance Army (NRA) of Uganda. They tied down thousands of Ugandan troops and threatened the Owen Falls bridge, which was landlocked Uganda's main link to the outside world. Lakwena's troops went to war accompanied by wives, children, and cattle. Their primary weapons were charms of shea nut oil that they smeared over their bodies as protection against bullets. Lakwena also provided charms of snake bone and beeswax, which her followers said turned into hordes of snakes or swarms of bees that could be hurled at enemies like hand grenades. The NRA had modern small arms and some artillery.

Two years later, Lakwena's Holy Spirit movement was still intact, although she retreated into Kenya after two-thirds of her army of seven thousand was killed. Most of her followers had only magic weapons, but they fearlessly advanced on NRA lines, clapping and singing hymns. And some of them had grenades and machine guns. Observers said it was the most violent cult seen in Africa since the Maji Maji rebellion against the Germans in 1905 in what is now Tanzania.[3]

In 1989, after the Soviet Union failed to suppress guerrilla activity in Afghanistan, the government there recruited a special guard to defend against mujahedin rebels. A *Washington Times* reporter interviewed one woman in a mostly-male contingent guarding Kabul. Nafizy Kareem wore a uniform consisting of "red lipstick and earrings, chipped nail polish, low-heeled dress shoes, maroon kneesocks, and camouflage skirt and blouse." She held the rank of third lieutenant. "I have never fought in a war," the seventeen-year-old told the reporter, "but if the guerrillas come, I am ready. The difficult condition our country is in causes us to fight side-by-side with our brothers." She fired off thirty blasts from her Kalashnikov assault rifle to emphasize the point. "I feel like a brave man when I shoot it," she said.[4]

Mujahedin opposed to Islamic fundamentalism created the well-equipped, uniformed National Liberation Army (NLA) operating against Iran from bases in Iraq. A woman, Maryam Rajavi, is their commander, and 70 percent of her top officers are women. About a third of the total force is female. Women serving in the infantry are armed with Kalashnikov assault rifles and rocket-propelled grenade launchers. They also pilot helicopters. When watching a military review of tanks, a Western observer could identify the women by their bright red head scarves. The men who serve with them have no problem taking orders from women. Mahboub Sabahti, deputy to a woman tank repair workshop commander said, "It was under Maryam Rajavi that we evolved from an infantry army to an armored force, so it's a great source of pride to be commanded by women. It's something we welcome, not merely accept, and there will be an explosion of women's energies when the mullahs are overthrown."[5] Since its establishment in Iraq in 1986, the NLA has met Iranian forces on the battlefield twice. In 1988, the army advanced more than one hundred miles into Iran, and in 1991 they fought the Revolutionary Guard when it invaded Iraq in the aftermath of the Persian Gulf War.

The Shining Path guerrilla movement in Peru, which has operated for almost forty years, has always had a woman as second in command. In 1992, 40 percent of its members and almost half of the ruling central committee were women. Women led armed bands in the field and were popularly believed to be more ruthless than the men.[6] And among the Nicaraguan contras, women served as platoon commanders and in the ranks. Photographs from the last major battle of the contra war show women commandos supporting nursing babies in their arms, carrying combat packs on their backs, and balancing AK-47s on their shoulders while advancing to the front under fire from Sandinista BM-21 rocket launchers.[7]

On the island of Sri Lanka off the coast of India, civil war has raged since 1983. Women are engaged as combatants on both sides. The rebels, the Liberation Tigers of Tamil Eelam, are an independence movement of ethnic Tamil against the Sinhalese majority. There is a strong feminist theme in the Tigers' rhetoric, which may explain why an estimated two-thirds of its combat force is female. The Tiger women are a separate cadre, trained since 1987 in an all-woman camp and operating since 1989 within an all-woman leadership structure. Sri Lankan government forces also recruit women. Of the 107 cadets graduating in 1997 from the Kotelawala Defense Academy at Ratmalann, 17 were women. Authorities invited journalists to interview one of these who was quoted as saying, "I have a dream. One day, when I get married, have children and retire, I could tell them battlefield stories about how we saved our nation."[8]

Eritrea fought one of the longest wars of modern times in a struggle for independence from Ethiopia that ended in May 1991. Backed at different times by the United States, the Soviet Union, and Israel, its army was among the best equipped in Africa. Women made up about one-third of the combat troops. In 1988, a Western observer wrote of them, "There is an almost neuter quality to female Eritrean guerrillas. After years of living in the field exactly like the men, they have come to resemble them physically. Their hair is short, their hands and feet callused, their legs sinewy. Though men and women sleep side-by-side in the cramped front-line quarters, sex is said to be rare and pregnancies are unusual."[9]

Similar circumstances prevailed in other integrated armies during protracted conflicts. Thus a woman who fought with Zimbabwe's liberation army in the 1970s wrote, "In Zambia I was trained with men and I ended up feeling like a man. . . . I went on guard and didn't even attend to my monthly periods. I lived like a man."[10] But war does not necessarily affect female biological functions. During the Eritrean war, wounded veterans manufactured feminine hygiene products for women in the field, and Joyce "Teurai Ropa" (Spill-Blood) Nhongo, a Zimbabwe commander, fought off a Rhodesian attack just two days before giving birth.[10]

Third World women warriors emphasize that their military role is not a matter of choice. They are not engaged in a feminist crusade and have no interest in establishing a "right to die in combat." Women who fight see combat as a grim necessity, not as an empowering adventure, and their military contribution rarely brings any permanent improvement in their status. Hewit Moges, who was the subject of a *Wall Street Journal* article on February 13, 1990, had been at the front for thirteen years during the Eritrean war. As a married woman with a child, she had one month's leave a year. Unmarried soldiers got no leave. A man who fought under her command said of her, "When it's a hard climb, she runs up the mountain. When it's a battle, she's in front of the troops, and when someone is wounded, she's the one who carries him from the field." Her comment on her life as a soldier was, "Everywhere in Eritrea there is death, whether you are at the front line or not. If it were possible to have a settled, peaceful life we wouldn't have to be here at all." After this war, the traditions of arranged marriage, male-dominated families, and denial of property rights to women resurfaced. A woman veteran interviewed in 1993 said, "To change this society of ours, we have to work hard—even more than we struggled at the front."[12]

In former Yugoslavia, women soldiers participated in the ethnic warfare that broke out after the collapse of the Soviet Union—*kindze* in the Serbian forces and *gardistas* in the Croatian. An Agence France-Presse photograph dated November 10, 1994, showed a unit of Bosnian women undergoing combat training. With the region's long tradition of combatant women, women soldiers became mass media heroines in their homelands. Newspapers quote them boasting, "The twelve of us against three hundred armed Croatians," or "I beheaded several children; I killed ten Serbian soldiers with my rifle." In December 1991 the first women's battalion of the war mobilized in Gina, a Croatian city populated mainly by Serbs. The women took an oath "to fight against all the enemies of the Serbs, under the protection of God." In Pofalici, a northern Sarajevo neighborhood, different motives brought together the women who formed a sixty-member infantry unit about six months later. Its members were Muslims, Serbs, and Croats who fought in defense of their homes rather than for an ideal of ethnic purity. One of them told a reporter, "Some of us made the decision out of revenge. Most of us saw the need to help. The men were wounded; we had to replace them. There was no choice."[13] Another added, "What I do now is because I miss the life I used to have. I'm fighting for the life they took away from me. I think I have the right to live like other girls in the rest of Europe."[14]

+ + +

THE LAST SUPERPOWER

AFTER THE DISINTEGRATION OF the Soviet Union, the United States was the sole power capable of waging the sort of high-tech war that American military planners had envisioned as the only significant threat following World War II.

After the Gulf War, American women going into harm's way were no longer a novelty. More combat jobs, including the most glamorous jobs in combat aviation, opened to women, and women were soon flying combat missions over Iraq and Bosnia.[15] Popular debate about whether women should be in combat continued unabated without reference to what women were doing. Instead the American public focused on sex in the military. To the amazement and amusement of other nations, Americans in the last decade of the twentieth century appeared to have discovered for the first time that soldiers and sailors were not always chaste and chivalrous.[16] The American people ignored issues of planetary significance to focus instead on instances of sexual misbehavior by military members ranging from rape and violent assault to adultery and too-close friendships within a chain of command.[17]

Meanwhile, some Americans were more concerned about erosions of morality and ethical standards in the federal government and what appeared to them to be dangerous abuses of power by government law enforcement agencies. To protect themselves against the armed police forces of a government they viewed as having ceased to serve the people, they organized citizens' militias, citing the Sixth Amendment of the Constitution as the source of their legitimacy. As usual in guerrilla armies, women moved into prominent roles. A journalist who interviewed both men and women in 1996 for an article on American militia women concluded, "Regardless of age, education or financial status, all of the women have one thing in common. They all believe the future and stability of their country are in danger. They all regard the grasp of power by government as unconstitutional and the abuse of power by some law enforcement groups as a threat to the future of their families and their way of life."[18]

Although the conservative ideology of the American militias might suggest intolerance of women as soldiers, focus on mission overcomes ideology. Col. James A. McKinzey, co-founder and commander of the Missouri 51st Militia, said, "When I ask one of our militia women to do a job, I don't have to check to see if it's getting done. If I need information or intelligence, a militia woman will get it for me. Some say that they do not want a woman next to them in a foxhole. I say: if she can hit her target and keep her cool, I don't care." Col. Stephanie Birmingham, commander of the Chattanooga Militia in Tennessee and mother of three, told the journalist, "I joined the militia to join forces with like-minded individuals who are God-fearing, peace-loving, freedom-loving Constitutionalists willing to go the extra mile to return the hearts and minds of Americans to the Constitution on which this country was founded." Although the militia women interviewed all emphasized that they considered taking up arms to be a last resort, all were proficient in handling weapons.[19]

THE NEW WORLD DISORDER

IN THE YEARS BETWEEN the end of World War II and the fall of the Berlin wall in 1989, as we waited for a possible nuclear war and prepared for it, the planet experienced a human invasion of unprecedented dimensions. It began immediately after the end of World War II and continued at an accelerating pace, creating psychological stresses and growing pressure on planetary ecology. It threatened to destroy civilization and all life on Earth as we have known it. Still, no one fears these invaders as European tribes once feared Romans or Mongols. The invaders arrive quietly, unarmed and innocent. They are only babies. Billions of babies.

In all of history prior to 1945, women's fecundity was encouraged by the makers of military policy. A nation with a growing population might be a threat to its neighbors, but from its own perspective, more babies now meant more soldiers in the future. Indeed, a common explanation for the presumed absence of women in dangerous military roles was the need to preserve the ability to replace the dead. But after World War II, unprecedented population growth began to strain national resources and create poverty rather than military power. Developed nations no longer needed massive armies; technology and skilled soldiers would balance any disadvantage in numbers. For undeveloped nations, higher rates of population growth led to crises and conflicts.

By the early sixties, human population was growing at a rate of 2 percent and the number of people on the planet was doubling every thirty-five years. Soon more people were living on the planet than the total of all who had lived on it in the millennia before 1950. For a while there was reason to fear that there would be no end to this "baby boom" and that the planet might be populated beyond its ability to support life. Then, on February 14, 1978, UN officials announced that, for the first time in three million years of human experience, world population growth had started leveling off. It now appears that it will stabilize sometime in the twenty-first century.[20]

The pressure of growing population is still a major concern, however, and it underlies all post-World War II conflicts. Humans living in over-crowded conditions become hostile. If food and water become scarce because of competition for these basic resources, frightened humans are likely to fight over them before seeking constructive negotiated solutions.[21]

The population explosion caused other problems as well. As all of us who have caught a cold after a long airline flight or after attending a movie in a packed theater know, people in crowded conditions are vulnerable to disease. Ever since the rise of the first cities, urban dwellers have experienced more illness than those in the country. Now population density is increasing so rapidly that even people in a privileged nation such as the United States are aware of it. Our distress is reflected, for instance, in concern over the problem of illegal aliens.

In 1990, American population density was 70.3 persons per square mile; by 1995, it had risen to 70.4. Compare this to the situation in Rwanda where despite war, famine, and disease, UN census data recorded that the population density of 715 persons per square mile in 1990 had grown to 806 two years later, an increase of 11.3 percent. Some experts say population density in some parts of the world could eventually go as high as 3,000 people per square mile.[22]

The increase in the number of humans on Earth has resulted in changes in the world of microorganisms that prey on us. Frequent air travel has thoroughly mixed once-isolated gene pools of humans and microbes, and sexual promiscuity among those with access to a range of prospective partners gave another boost to microbe activity. In 1989, just as our fears of the cold war ended, scientists came to the chilling conclusion that in competition for the top of the food chain on the planet, the microbes were decisively winning. Microbes have been evolving far more rapidly than we have, "adapting to changes in their environments by mutating, undergoing high-speed natural selection, or drawing plasmids and transposons from the vast mobile genetic lending library in their environments."[23] The AIDS epidemic is only one among many deadly threats.

Statistical analysis of demographic data reveals that under certain circumstances women lower their fecundity naturally without any coercion. When women are educated, when they have self-respect, and when they have sufficient resources to allow them to hope their own efforts can create a better future, birthrates drop. This can be observed even among teenage girls in the United States. Women who are aware of a world of opportunity beyond motherhood contrast sharply with the traditional ideal of conservative societies where women were expected to remain "barefoot and pregnant in the kitchen." In parts of the world where girl children are still sold into sexual slavery and where women are helplessly trapped in abusive marriages, the notion of granting full human rights to females is revolutionary.

Some nations, notably China, which has been notorious for human rights abuses, have taken coercive measures to force the limitations of families, including forced abortions and deliberate neglect of orphans. In other nations, moral objections to abortion or to any birth control other than abstinence seem to be working in the opposite direction. In Croatia, nationalists fearing population decline for their own ethnic group at the end of a smoldering civil war have tried to encourage larger families and to ban mention of the global population explosion from schoolbooks.[24]

When women in the Third World are raised to higher status, they do more than limit the size of their families; they also are the group most likely to take action to increase the food supply and control disease. Grassroots humanitarian organizations believe that investment in women's enterprises is the best intervention they can make in developing nations where women do most of the farming. And UNICEF discovered during the 1970s that women were the key to implementing public health measures. Educated women support vaccination programs, understand the need for clean water supplies, and persuade family members to seek professional medical aid before an entire village becomes infected.

It has been tempting for feminists to believe that emancipated women would also put an end to war. Unfortunately, forgiving one's human enemies is not as easy as accepting the logic of adopting public health measures. While there are many women who do become peace activists, as many men have, others put their nation, race, or class above gender or appeals to a common humanity. In South Africa, Winnie Mandela's conversion from nonviolence to terrorism illustrates well how a talented and educated woman can burn for revenge when confronted with murder and injustice.

+ + +

HUMANITARIANS

THROUGHOUT HISTORY A FEW people saw their mission in wartime as healing rather than killing. These humanitarians have not necessarily been peacemakers or even antiwar but saw their task as moderating the violence and horror. In the Middle Ages, churches provided safe haven and religious orders provided food and medical care for war's victims, both soldiers and civilians.

The nineteenth century saw the birth of a number of quasi-military humanitarian organizations. The clearest example is the Salvation Army, which adopted uniforms and a military rank structure as it carried out its nonviolent humanitarian campaigns. In 1994, Lt. Lisa Brodin, a young American Salvation Army officer, was part of an eight-member team sent to work with refugees and unaccompanied minors in Rwanda. The first task was to meet the immediate need for food and to distribute seed for the fall planting. Then the team split up, with one officer in charge of building reconstruction and water system rehabilitation and two officers in charge of rehabilitating the health and nutrition centers in a neighboring community and working to set up schools. Lieutenant Brodin was put in charge of the program for unaccompanied children. Since the team's logistics officer was ill, she arranged all the logistics for the program and trained her own staff members, "20 very bright women from Kayenzi." In her diary, she described the first day of the program's operation:

> We interviewed and enrolled 60 families, weighing and measuring the children and giving them two-week supplementary rations of food, including protein biscuits. We've worked with local leaders to identify those families with foster or malnourished children.
>
> Most of the children we measured were under the 80th percentile on the weight-for-height scale, but we noticed two who were extremely malnourished. One father came with his infant so emaciated that his skin hung on his tiny frame. His mother died during the war and the father couldn't find any milk for the child. We gave him some milk and Mrs. Major Sewell, a nurse, carefully explained what needed to be done for the baby. This work is rewarding but heartbreaking at times like these.[25]

Other humanitarian organizations active in war relief work are the International Committee of the Red Cross and, more recently, Doctors without Borders. The leadership of these organizations is predominantly male, but women are also recruited, and their roles have expanded during recent decades just as they have in military institutions.

Humanitarian workers go unarmed into war zones and do not take sides in conflicts. As we have seen, the women nurses among them have been exposed to greater danger and suffered greater casualties than women serving in regular armies. Because killing was not part of their mission, however, their activities have been identified with traditional female support roles and are usually accepted as suitable for women even by those who otherwise disapprove of women becoming active in war zones. Opponents of women in combat rarely say that Red Cross nurses should be excluded from wartime service.

With the end of the cold war and the dramatic downsizing of the American military, the United States revised the stated mission of its armed forces. Public opinion in the 1990s was reluctant to approve wars but appeared willing to support humanitarian missions for the armed forces, so the military began conducting "peace maneuvers."

In 1993, the army's basic operations manual, 100-5, introduced a separate chapter on "operations other than war," and began production of a special manual on peace operations.[26] In March 1995, the National Military Strategy, the Pentagon's basic policy statement, added sustaining peace to the roles of American troops. "U.S. Military strategy must be intrinsically constructive, proactive and preventive, helping to reduce the sources of conflict," the document states.[27]

The first major humanitarian mission undertaken by the American military was Operation Provide Comfort, which took place in the wake of Operation Desert Storm in the Gulf War and brought aid to the Kurds in northern Iraq. Missions to Somalia and Bosnia followed. Unlike civilian relief workers, military humanitarians, both those with national armies and those serving with the United Nations forces, go armed, and there are combat roles associated with their missions. But just as the media paid scant attention when the first American women flew combat missions over Iraq and Bosnia, Kurdish, Somali, and Bosnian women combatants were ignored as reporters focused on rape victims. Thus women in war who play roles that do not match gender expectations continued to be invisible.[28]

Those experts with experience in relief and rehabilitation operations in the Third World are divided as to whether involvement of military organizations in humanitarian work is desirable. The notion of warriors working as nonviolent peacemakers is certainly novel, and skepticism about their ability to remain focused on humanitarian ends is understandable. Military personnel are divided as well. Particularly in the United States, where no war has been fought in the homeland for more than a century, the soldier as a symbol of rugged masculinity has considerable appeal. This raises the question, as Cynthia Enloe frames it, "Are UN Peacekeepers Real Men?"[29] One cannot imagine Rambo working as a water purification specialist.

WARRIORS FOR A NEW MILLENNIUM

MILITARY PROFESSIONALS, AS THEY have always done, look to the past when they plan for the future. But avoiding the mistakes of the last war has never been enough to deal with the realities of new forms of conflict, and it is likely to be even less useful when applied to real-life situations in the future. The threats to world security already upon us in the closing years of the twentieth century are not susceptible of military solutions. Weapons will not halt epidemics or prevent global warming. The violent fantasies of modern filmmakers notwithstanding, humans will need a different kind of hero if we are to save the planet. A few people in the Pentagon have already been thinking this way.

In the 1970s, Jim Channon, a U.S. Army lieutenant colonel, created what at the time seemed a highly eccentric model of a multinational army of the future. In a multimedia presentation created for the army's Task Force Delta, then headquartered at Carlisle Barracks in Pennsylvania, he described the personnel and mission of what he called the "First Earth Battalion."[30] The first loyalty of the "warrior-monks" of the First Earth Battalion is the planet. These men and women go into combat zones to implement nondestructive methods of conflict resolution. Instead of weapons, they bring music native to the region. Instead of training to "kill people and break things," they study psychology, languages, and conflict resolution negotiation techniques based on the premise that everyone can win when all parties are heard and respected.[31]

In the early 1980s, certain senior officers in the army's Special Operations division began to investigate the possibility of enhancing the skills of individual soldiers by employing a holistic approach based on the practices of warriors who had made martial arts a spiritual path. Native American warriors, the samurai of ancient Japan, and various sects of monks and nuns had used combat training to further their personal growth as well as to serve a higher cause. One of the officers supporting the project gave it the code name the *Trojan Warrior Project,* reasoning "that soldiers initiated this way, perhaps like the Greek warriors hidden in the belly of a wooden horse, would be an elite cadre converted to the leading edge of inner technologies in the belly of the U.S. Army." The logo for the operation was a flying horse above two crossed light sabers with the inscription *Vi Cit Tecum,* which means "May the Force Be with You."[32]

Twenty-five soldiers went through the Trojan Horse program. None of them were women, because at the time no women could serve in the special forces, but the instructors faced the question of whether a woman could be a warrior and agreed that gender was no barrier.[33] Experts in the martial arts appear to be agreed on this point. For example, the air force major Forrest E. Morgan, author of *Living the Martial Way,* notes in his introduction, "To avoid awkward 'he and she' sentence structures, I tend to refer to warriors in the masculine gender. I don't mean this to imply women can't be warriors. Some of the greatest warriors in history were women, and there are great ones with us today."[34] Another martial arts instructor recently collected a book of stories of women warriors throughout history with the explicit purpose of encouraging women to claim their "martial self" which he found the only element lacking in his female martial arts students.[35]

Still, recruiting for a humanitarian organization such as the Salvation Army does not appeal to the same motives that bring young people to enlist in the military services. It remains to be seen whether established military organizations have the will to alter their traditional cultures rapidly enough to take up the role of peaceful warrior. Many, if not most, military professionals have contempt for practitioners of nonviolence and would not take kindly to training that emphasized meditation over weight-lifting and valued gentleness over aggressive force.[36] In the past, warriors who viewed their calling as a spiritual path have insisted on distinguishing themselves from mercenaries and professional soldiers who kill for pay. Although the call to "be all that you can be" may attract young people to both military and humanitarian organizations, the humanitarians do not offer a stable career, money for college, or even the assurance of a regular paycheck.

Nevertheless, there is clearly a need for armies of dedicated people willing to give up the comfort of civilian life in order to take the necessary actions to avert catastrophe in the decades ahead. Going to the aid of cholera victims or dismantling toxic waste sites, attempting therapeutic intervention between people possessed by murderous rage or restoring the integrity of the rain forests will be hard, dirty, dangerous work calling for all the martial virtues of courage, discipline, loyalty, and a willingness to sacrifice.

That women will answer the call to such service is inevitable; they have always done so, and around the world they are already working locally on such projects. Indeed, if the visions of the First Earth Battalion and the Trojan Warrior Project came to dominate military organizations, we would certainly find women more conspicuous in the ranks and in leadership roles than ever before in history. The new warrior role model offers an androgynous ideal, equally appropriate for men and women, a role that combines the protector and the nurturer, joining the best of the soldier's military virtues with the best of the motherly roles of teacher, nurse, and comforter. Should armies of the future be composed of such warriors, history might finally overcome the cultural amnesia of centuries, be able to acknowledge the presence of women in the struggle to save our planet in these perilous times, and remember women's valorous acts.

NOTES

Preface

1. An important exception is the work of Barton C. Hacker who almost twenty years ago wrote, "Women, sometimes in great numbers have always played military roles. . . . Without women, armies would rarely have functioned as well, might even have failed to function at all." Barton C. Hacker, "Where Have All the Women Gone? The Pre-Twentieth-Century Sexual Division of Labor in Armies," *MINERVA: Quarterly Report on Women and the Military 3*, no. 1 (Spring 1985): 107. See also Barton C. Hacker, "Women and Military Institutions in Early Modern Europe: A Reconnaissance," *Signs: Journal of Women in Culture and Society 6*, no. 4 (1981): 643–71.

2. John Keegan, *A History of Warfare* (New York: Alfred A. Knopf, 1993), 76.

3. Collective biographies of women warriors have been popular for centuries. A recent example is Jessica Amanda Salmonson, *The Encyclopedia of Amazons: Women Warriors from Antiquity to the Modern Era* (New York: Paragon House, 1991). Salmonson made no attempt to assure factual accuracy in her entries, and the collection includes fictional and mythological figures from Aphrodite to Wonder Woman and an assortment of violent women who had no connection with warfare, including performers like Annie Oakley and gangsters like Gallus Mag. The first scholarly encyclopedia of women combatants, *Military Women Worldwide: A Biographical Dictionary,* edited by Reina Pennington, will be published by Greenwood Press. Other recent books about women warriors, all of which focus exclusively on combatant roles and none of

which attempt to place the stories in the context of broader military history, are Julie Wheelwright, *Amazons and Military Maids: Women Who Dressed as Men in Pursuit of Life, Liberty and Happiness* (London: Pandora Press, 1989); Tim Newark, *Women Warlords: An Illustrated History of Female Warriors* (London:Blandford, 1989); and David E. Jones, *Women Warriors: A History* (Washington, D.C.: Brassey's, 1997).

4. In addition to Keegan, *A History of Warfare*, other well-known histories of war are William H. McNeill, *The Pursuit of Power* (Chicago: University of Chicago Press, 1982), and Robert L. O'Connell, *Of Arms and Men: A History of War, Weapons and Aggression* (New York: Oxford University Press, 1989).

5. Mariah Burton Nelson, *The Stronger Women Get, the More Men Love Football* (New York: Harcourt, Brace, 1994), 198.

CHAPTER ONE: *Introduction: Definitions and Presuppositions*

1. Alice S. Rossi, ed., *The Feminist Papers from Adams to de Beauvoir* (New York: Columbia University Press, 1973), 428.

2. Personal communication, August 2, 1993.

3. Holly Devor, *Gender Blending: Confronting the Limits of Duality* (Bloomington: Indiana University Press, 1989), 10.

4. Wesley Thomas, quoted in Leslie Feinberg, *Transgender Warriors: Making History from Joan of Arc to Dennis Rodman* (Boston: Beacon Press, 1996), 27.

5. Nickie Roberts, *Whores in History: Prostitution in Western Society* (London: HarperCollins, 1992); *Women of the Light: The New Sacred Prostitute* (Secret Garden video, October 1994).

6. Ralph Dennison, "LBJ," in Al Santoli, *Everything We Had: An Oral History of the Vietnam War by Thirty-three American Soldiers Who Fought It* (New York: Ballantine Books, 1981), 251–252.

7. Feinberg, *Transgender Warriors*, 92.

8. Sally Miller Gearhart, "The Spiritual Dimension: Death and Resurrection of a Hallelujah Dyke," in Ginny Vida, ed., *Our Right to Love: A Lesbian Resource Book* (Englewood Cliffs, N.J.: Prentice-Hall, 1978), 187.

9. Arther Ferrill, *The Origins of War: From the Stone Age to Alexander the Great* (London: Thames and Hudson, 1985), 10–11.

10. Nancy Carlsson-Paige and Diane E. Levin, *Who's Calling the Shots?*

How to Respond Effectively to Children's Fascination with War Play and War Toys (Philadelphia: New Society Publishers, 1990), 31.

11. For example, the writing of Audré Lorde, who identifies herself as a "Black lesbian feminist warrior poet" and an enemy of militarism, is permeated with horrific war imagery. See Audré Lorde, *Our Dead Behind Us* (New York: W. W. Norton, 1986). Mary K. DeShazer, "'Sisters in Arms': The Warrior Construct in Writings by Contemporary U.S. Women of Color," *National Women's Studies Association Journal* 2, no. 3 (Summer 1990), 349–373.

12. Sue Mansfield, *The Gestalts of War: An Inquiry into Its Origins and Meanings as a Social Institution* (New York: Dial Press, 1982), 20–40.

13. Martin Van Creveld, "Why Men Fight," in Lawrence Freedman, ed., *War* (New York: Oxford University Press, 1994), 88–89.

14. Anne E. Hunter, ed., *On Peace, War, and Gender: A Challenge to Genetic Explanations* (New York: Feminist Press, 1991), 115; Olivia Vlahos, *New World Beginnings: Indian Cultures in the Americas* (New York: Viking Press, 1970), 268.

15. Jessica Mayer, "Women and the Pacification of Men in New Guinea" in *Women and the Images of Women in Peace and War: Cross-Cultural and Historical Perspectives* (Madison: University of Wisconsin Press, 1988), 148–65.

16. In the 1980s academic feminists describing themselves as "relational feminists," "difference feminists," "social feminists," or "neofeminists" emphasized the peaceful, nurturing qualities that they argued were uniquely female. Joan C. Williams "Deconstructing Gender," *Michigan Law Review* 87 (February 1989): 797. Popular writers followed the trend, for instance, Sara Ruddick, *Maternal Thinking: Toward a Politics of Peace* (Boston: Beacon Press, 1989); and Laura Shapiro, "Guns and Dolls: Scientists Explore the Differences Between Girls and Boys," *Newsweek*, May 28, 1990, 56.

17. Hunter, *On Peace, War, and Gender*, 168–71.

18. Susan Brownmiller, *Against Our Will: Men, Women and Rape* (New York: Simon & Schuster, 1975); Ruth Siefert, "Rape in Wars: Analytical Approaches," *MINERVA: Quarterly Report on Women and the Military* no. 2 (Summer 1993): 17–22; Yuki Tanaka, *Hidden Horrors: Japanese War Crimes in World War II* (Boulder, Colo.: Westview Press, 1996), 107.

19. Antonia Fraser, *The Warrior Queens: The Legends and the Lives of the Women Who Have Led Their Nations in War* (New York: Vintage Books, 1990).

20. Among biographies of the queen are William Thomas Walsh, *Isabella of Spain: The Last Crusader* (New York: McBride, 1930), and Malveena

McKendrick, *Ferdinand and Isabella* (New York: American Heritage, 1968). The most recent is Peggy K. Liss, *Isabel* (Oxford: Oxford University Press, 1992).

21. A recent book in which soldiers are seen as both victimizers and victims in war is Tanaka, *Hidden Horrors*.

CHAPTER TWO: *Prehistory*

1. Ferrill, *The Origins of War*, 23–24; Fred Wendorf, ed., *The Prehistory of Nubia* (Dallas: Southern Methodist University Press, 1968), 2: 954–95.

2. The scientific literature on this subject is enormous and impossible to summarize in a note. An inspiring as well as accessible study, which has thorough documentation, is Riane Eisler, *The Chalice and the Blade: Our History, Our Future* (San Francisco: Harper & Row, 1987). See also Richard A. Gabriel, *The Culture of War: Invention and Early Development* (New York: Greenwood Press, 1990), 19-21; Geraldine J. Casey, "Eleanor Leacock, Marvin Harris, and the Struggle over Warfare in Anthropology," in Hunter, *On Peace, War, and Gender,* 18.

3. Eisler, *The Chalice and the Blade,* 13, 42, 71.

4. Richard B. Lee, "What Hunters Do for a Living, or, How to Make Out on Scarce Resources," in Richard B. Lee and Irven DeVore, eds., *Man the Hunter* (Chicago: Aldine Publishing Co., 1968), 36–43.

5. Rosalind Miles, *The Women's History of the World* (New York: Harper & Row, 1988), 5, 14.

6. Quoted in Hunter, *On Peace, War, and Gender,* 18.

7. Gwynne Dyer, *War* (Homewood, Ill: Dorsey Press, 1985), 6.

8. Richard Strozzi Heckler, *In Search of the Warrior Spirit* (Berkeley, Calif.: North Atlantic Books, 1990), 105–11.

9. C. Lumholtz, *Among Cannibals: An Account of Four Years' Travels in Australia and of Camp Life with the Aborigines of Queensland* (New York: C. Scribner's & Son, 1889), 123–27.

10. Inenäus Eibl-Eibesfeldt, *The Biology of Peace and War: Men, Animals, and Aggression* (New York: Viking Press, 1979), 173–74.

11. Ibid.

12. Lawrence H. Keeley, *War Before Civilization: The Myth of the Peaceful Savage* (New York: Oxford University Press, 1996), 64–65.

13. Lewis Mumford, *The City in History: Its Origins, Its Transformations, and Its Prospects* (New York: Harcourt, Brace & World, 1961), 44.

14. Dyer, *War*, 11.

15. Keegan, *A History of Warfare*, 160–61 .

16. Eisler, *The Chalice and the Blade*, 43–45.

17. John Pfeiffer, *The Origins of Society and Prehistory: A Pre-History of the Establishment* (New York: McGraw Hill, 1977), 21–22.

18. Gabriel, *The Culture of War*, 12.

19. Ibid., 37.

20. Ibid., 20–35.

21. Ibid., 80.

22. Cyrus Gordon, *Common Background of Greek and Hebrew Civilizations* (New York: W. W. Norton, 1965); Saul Levin, *The Indo-European and Semitic Languages* (Albany: State University of New York Press, 1971). See also Merlin Stone, *When God Was a Woman* (New York: Harcourt Brace Jovanovich, 1976).

23. June Nash, a student of the Aztec culture of ancient Mexico, points to "the interrelationships between male specialization in warfare, predatory conquest, state bureaucracy . . . and the differential access to its benefits between men and women." June Nash, "The Aztecs and the Ideology of Male Dominance," *Signs: Journal of Women in Culture and Society* 4 (1978): 350.

24. Eisler, *The Chalice and the Blade*, 57–58; Yigael Yadin, *The Art of Warfare in Biblical Lands in the Light of Archaeological Study* (New York: McGraw Hill, 1963) 2: 253–87; Chaim Herzog and Mordechai Gichon, *Battles of the Bible* (New York:Random House, 1978).

25. All references are to the Revised Standard Version of *The Holy Bible* (New York: Thomas Nelson, 1952).

26. Num. 31: 8–18, 32.

27. Gabriel, *The Culture of War*, 63.

28. See, e.g., Deut. 31:16.

29. Josh. 2:10.

30. Ibid., 2:14.

31. Ibid., 2:15–16.

32. Ibid., 6:21–25, 27.

33. Michael Grant, *The History of Ancient Israel* (New York: Charles Scribner's Sons, 1984), 56–57.

34. Judges 5:25–27.

35. Ibid., 5:24.

36. Apocrypha, Book of Judith.

37. Georges Contenau, *Everyday Life in Babylon and Assyria* (New York: St. Martin's Press, 1954), 65–66.

38. Ibid., 68.

39. Herodotus, *The Histories*, trans. Aubrey de Selincourt (New York: Penguin Books, 1988), 115.

40. See, e.g., Joan Oates, *Babylon* (London: Thames and Hudson, 1989), lii; A. T. Olmstead, *History of the Persian Empire* (Chicago: University of Chicago Press, 1948), 118, 163, 321–22, 380.

41. Herodotus 4.118.

42. Ibid., 4.15.

43. M. A. Groushko, *Cossack: Warrior Riders of the Steppes* (New York: Sterling, 1992), 11.

44. W. B. Emery, *Archaic Egypt* (Harmondsworth: Penguin Books, 1987), 32, 65–69, 94, 126.

45. John Ray, "Hatshepsut, the Female Pharaoh," *History Today* 44, no. 5 (May 1994): 23–29; J. E. Manchip White, *Ancient Egypt: Its Culture and History* (New York: Dover Publications, 1970), 165–67.

46. N. G. L. Hammond and H.H. Scullard, *The Oxford Classical Dictionary*, 2d ed. (Oxford: Clarendon Press, 1970), 50; Abby Wettan Kleinbaum, *The War Against the Amazons* (New York: New Press, 1983), 1-3.

47. Kleinbaum, *The War Against the Amazons*, 21, quoting Strabo, *Geography* 2.5.3–4.

48. Ibid.

49. Sarah B. Pomeroy, *Goddesses, Whores, Wives, and Slaves: Women in Classical Antiquity* (New York: Schocken Books, 1975), 23–24.

50. Notable among recent works on African women in the ancient world are Heinrich Loth, *Woman in African Art* (Westport, Conn.: Lawrence Hill, 1978); and Ivan van Sertima, *Black Women in Antiquity* (New Brunswick, N.J.: Transaction Books, 1984; rev. 1988).

51. Florence Mary Bennett, *Religious Cults Associated with the Amazons* (New York: AMS Press, 1967).

52. Barbara G. Walker, *The Woman's Encyclopedia of Myths and Secrets* (San Francisco: Harper & Row, 1983), 58–60.

53. Keegan, *A History of Warfare*, 179–82.

54. Herodotus 4.117.

55. T. Sulimirski, *The Sarmatians* (New York: Praeger,1970), 66.

56. Ibid, 55–58.

57. Groushko, *Cossack,* 46.

58. Sulimirski, *The Sarmatians,* 48.

59. Keegan, *A History of Warfare,* 34.

60. Gabriel, *The Culture of War,* 84; N. K. Sandars, *The Sea Peoples: Warriors of the Ancient Mediterranean, 1250-1150 B.C.* (London: Thames and Hudson, 1978).

61. Eisler, *The Chalice and the Blade,* 114; Albert Bates Lord, *The Singer of Tales* (Cambridge, Mass.: Harvard University Press, 1960), 141–57; Albert Bates Lord, *Epic Singers and Oral Tradition* (Ithaca: Cornell University Press, 1991), 38–48. See also Adam Parry, ed., *The Making of Homeric Verse: The Collected Papers of Milman Parry* (Oxford: Clarendon Press, 1971).

62. Sue Mansfield, "In the Shadow of Andromache's Loom," *MINERVA: Quarterly Report on Women and the Military,* 2, no. 4 (Winter 1984): 60–83.

63. Homer, *The Iliad,* trans. A. Lang, W. Leaf, and E. Meyers, ed. G. Highet (New York: Modern Library, 1950), 6.254–61.

64. Ibid., lines 43–45.

65. Ibid., 24.581–89.

66. Ibid., 3.189, 6.186.

67. Thomas Day Seymour, *Life in the Homeric Age* (New York: Macmillan, 1907), 628.

68. Salmonson, *The Encyclopedia of Amazons,* 189–90; Donald Sobol, *The Amazons of Greek Mythology* (Cranbury, N.J.: Barnes and Noble, 1973).

69. Kleinbaum, *The War Against the Amazons,* 22–25.

70. Ibid., 14; Dietrich von Bothmer, *Amazons in Greek Art* (Oxford: Clarendon Press, 1957), 1–5.

71. Hippocrates wrote (3.321), "There is a Scythian race . . . which differs from other races. Their name is Sauromatae. Their women ride, shoot, and throw javelins while mounted. . . . They have no right breast because when they are babies, their mothers apply a red-hot bronze instrument to the right breast and cauterise it, so its growth is arrested and all its strength and bulk are diverted to the right shoulder and arm."

72. For example, Herodotus, *Histories* 4.110.

73. Kleinbaum, *The War Against the Amazons,* 8–9.

74. Ibid., 9.

75. A project that has recently excavated graves of women warriors in Russia is directed by Jeannine Davis-Kimball of the Center for the Study of Eurasian Nomads. See Jeannine Davis-Kimball, "Warrior Women of the Eurasian Steppes, *Archaeology* 50, no. 1 (January/February 1997): 44–48 Jeannine Davis-Kimball, Leon Yablonsky, L. T. Iablonskii, V. Demkin, *Kurgans on the Left Bank of the Ilek: Excavations at Pokrovka, 1990-1992* (Berkeley, Calif.: Zinat Press, 1995).

CHAPTER THREE: *Classical Warfare*

1. There are many fine translations of the major classical texts. The Loeb Classical Library series provides the original language on the left-hand page and an English translation facing it plus a full index for each author. For on-line research, the best place to start is at the Internet Classics Archive, http://webatomics.com/Classics/Search/index.html.

2. Xenophon, *Cyropaedia* 4.2.29.

3. T. Sulimirski, *The Sarmatians,* 55–61.

4. Specialists criticize the ancient writers, including Herodotus, for exaggerating their figures and use formulas of their own to give what they believe are more accurate statistics. Estimating the size of crowds is an uncertain business even today. Rather than enter into these controversies, I will simply report what the sources say, acknowledging that they may be imprecise.

5. Herodotus, *Histories,* 1.270.

6. Ibid.

7. Plutarch, *Moralia, trans.* Frank Cole Babbit (Cambridge, Mass.: Harvard University Press, 1983), 473–582. In this same section, entitled "Bravery of Women," Plutarch describes how the women of Chios defended their city against attack by Philip of Macedon.

8. Plutarch, *Pyrrhus* 34.1–3.

9. Herodotus, *Histories* bk. 4.

10. Polyaenus, *Strategies of War.*

11. Victor Davis Hanson, ed., *Hoplites: The Classical Greek Battle Experience* (London: Routledge, 1991), 135.

12. Thucydides 2.45.2.

13. Homer, *Odyssey* 13.412; Strabo, *Geography* 10.13.

14. Humfrey Michell, *Sparta* (Cambridge: Cambridge University Press, 1952), 47, 53.

15. Ibid., 46.

16. Elizabeth Fisher, *Woman's Creation: Sexual Evolution and the Shaping of Society* (New York: McGraw Hill, 1979), 333.

17. Quoted in Michell, *Sparta*, 47.

18. Hanson, *Hoplites*, 29–30; Yvon Garlan, *War in the Ancient World: A Social History*, trans. Janet Lloyd (London: Chatto and Windus, 1975), 172; Xenophon, *Anabasis*. 5–6.1.1–13.

19. Plutarch, *Moralia* 3.459, 463.

20. Garlan, *War in the Ancient World*, 90; Hanson, *Hoplites*, 113; Donald W. Engels, *Alexander the Great and the Logistics of the Macedonian Army* (Berkeley: University of California Press, 1978), 11–13.

21. Garlan, *War in the Ancient World*, 136.

22. Ferrill, *The Origins of War*, 184.

23. Gabriel, *The Culture of War*, 98.

24. Robin Lane Fox, *The Search for Alexander* (Boston: Little, Brown, 1980), 123.

25. N. G. L. Hammond, *A History of Greece to 322 B.C.* (Oxford: Clarendon Press, 1986), 607, 621; Olmstead, *History of the Persian Empire*, 436, 483, 487, 499.

26. Quoted in Newark, *Women Warlords*, 20.

27. Kleinbaum, *The War Against the Amazons*, 20.

28. Ibid., 265, 368–69.

29. Ibid., 368–69.

30. Ibid., 381–82.

31. William L. Langer, ed., *Encyclopedia of World History*, 5th ed. (Boston: Houghton Mifflin, 1968), 99; H. A. Omerod, *Piracy in the Ancient World* (New York: Doreste, 1987), 169–75.

32. Dyer, *War*, 42.

33. Trevor N. Dupuy, *Understanding War: History and Theory of Combat* (New York: Paragon House, 1987), 82–84.

34. Michael Grant, *Gladiators* (New York: Delacorte Press, 1967), 33–34; John K. Evans, *War, Women and Children in Ancient Rome* (London: Routledge, 1991), 130–31; Jane F. Gardner, *Women in Roman Law and Society* (London: Croom Helm, 1986), 247–48; Salmonson, *The Encyclopedia of Amazons*, 100–2.

35. Roland Auguet, *Cruelty and Civilization: The Roman Games* (London: Ruskin House, 1972), 166–67, 169. A photograph of the plaque is facing p. 176.

36. Quotation from an extended attack on freeborn women practicing various forms of martial arts: Juvenal 6.246–67.

37. Plutarch, *Caius Marius* para. 25.

38. Mary Ritter Beard, *Woman as Force in History: A Study in Traditions and Realities* (New York: Macmillan, 1946), 288.

39. Plutarch, *Caius Marius* para. 40.

40. Tacitus, *Germania,* quoted in Beard, *Woman as Force in History,* 289.

41. Dio Cassius, *Roman History* 3.23, quoted in Nora Chadwick, *The Celts* (Harmondsworth: Penguin Books, 1970), 50.

42. Dio Cassius, *Roman History,* quoted in Newark, *Women Warlords,* 86.

43. Fraser, *Warrior Queens,* 74.

44. Ibid., 66–67.

45. Peter Marsden, *Roman London* (London: Thames and Hudson, 1980), 31.

46. Tacitus, *Annals* 3.1; Dio 3.23.

47. A modern scholar who gives an estimate of 15,000 to 20,000 is Graham Webster, *The Roman Imperial Army of the First and Second Centuries A.D.* (Totowa, N.J.: Barnes and Noble, 1985), 229.

48. Peter Salway, *Roman Britain,* (New York: Oxford University Press, 1981), 77.

49. Webster, *Roman Imperial Army,* 122–32.

50. Tacitus, *Annals* 14.45.

51. Christoph Bulst, "The Revolt of Queen Boudicca in A.D. 60: Roman Politics and the Iceni," *Historia* 10 (1961): 506.

52. Michael Grant, *Cleopatra: A Biography* (New York: Barnes and Noble, 1972); Emil Ludwig, *Cleopatra* (New York: Viking Press, 1937).

53. Nabia Ab-bott, "Pre-Islamic Arab Queens," *American Journal of Semitic Languages and Literature,* 58 (1941): 1–22.

54. Trebellius Pollio's description of Zenobia is in *Scriptores Historia Augusta,* with an English translation by David Magie (London:Heinemann, 1932), 3:135–43.

55. A classic account of Zenobia's history is that of Zosimus, a fifth-century Greek who wrote a history of the Roman Empire up to 410: *The History of Count Zosimus, Sometimes Advocate and Chancellor of the Roman Empire* (London: Primted for J. Davis by W. Green and T. Chaplin, 1814), 21 ff. A recent biography is Agnes Carr Vaughan, *Zenobia of Palmyra* (New York: Doubleday, 1967).

56. Newark, *Women Warlords,* 64.

57. Ibid., 72.

58. Ibid.

59. *The History of Count Zosimus,* 27.

60. Quoted in Newark, *Women Warlords,* 73.

61. Fraser, *The Warrior Queens,* 125; *Scriptures Historia Augusta,* 3:141, 259.

62. Quoted in Newark, *Women Warlords,* 73.

63. Garlan, *War in the Ancient World,* 90, quoting Onasander 1.12.

64. G. R. Watson, *The Roman Soldier* (Ithaca: Cornell University Press, 1969), 134. For legislation regarding soldier marriages, see also Michael Grant, *The Army of the Caesars* (New York: Charles Scribners' Sons, 1974), 78 ff.; 92 ff., 242, 258.

65. Lucian's last hetaerae conversations, quoted in Wilhelm Haberling, "Army Prostitution and Its Control: An Historical Study," in Victor Robinson, ed., *Morals in Wartime* (New York: Publishers Foundations, 1943), 11.

66. Titus Livius, *History of Rome,* cited in Haberling, "Army Prostitution, 12.

67. Watson, *The Roman Soldier,* 135.

68. Haberling, "Army Prostitution," 13.

69. Watson, *The Roman Soldier,* 141.

70. Grant, *The Army of the Caesars,* 284.

CHAPTER FOUR: *European Warfare*

1. Geoffrey Parker, "Taking Up the Gun," in Robert Cowley, ed., *Experience of War* (New York: W. W. Norton, 1992), 127–39.

2. The Chinese tradition of military women is described in chapter 7. Japanese women warriors are discussed in chapter 9, and the Vietnamese tradition is discussed in chapter 10.

3. William of Malmesbury, *Chronicle of English Kings,* trans. J. A. Giles, (London, 1847), 109.

4. F. T. Wainwright, "Aethelflaed, Lady of the Mercians," in Clemoes, ed., *The Anglo-Saxons* (London: Bowes & Bowes, 1959); G. N. Garmonsway, trans., *The Anglo-Saxon Chronicles* (London: Dent, 1953); Megan McL-aughlin, "The Woman Warrior: Gender, Warfare, and Society in Medieval Europe," *Women's Studies* 17 (1990): 193–209.

5. William of Malmesbury, *Chronicle of English Kings,* quoted in Tim Newark, *Women Warlords,* 94.

6. Saxo Grammaticus, *The History of the Danes,* quoted in Jones, *Women Warriors,* 157.

7. Saxo Grammaticus, *The History of the Danes,* quoted in Salmonson, *The Encyclopedia of Amazons,* 269.

8. Saxo Grammaticus, *The History of the Danes,* quoted in Salmonson, *The Encyclopedia of Amazons,* 105.

9. The most recent full-length biography in English is Mary Huddy, *Matilda Countess of Tuscany* (London: John Long, 1906). Another is Nora Duff, *Matilda of Tuscany* (London: Methuen, 1902). Briefer treatments are Valerie Eads, "The Campaigns of Matilda of Tuscany," *MINERVA: Quarterly Report on Women and the Military* 4, no. 1 (Spring 1986): 167–81, Fraser, *The Warrior Queens,* ch. 9; and Ferdinand Schevil, *History of Florence* (New York: Harcourt, Brace, 1936), chap. 5. A definitive biography of Matilda as a military leader, currently in preparation, is Valerie Eads, *Mighty in War: The Military Career of the Countess Matilda.*

10. Duff, *Matilda of Tuscany,* 91.

11. Quoted in Newark, *Women Warlords,* 106.

12. See Charity Cannon Willard, *Christine De Pizan: Her Life and Works* (New York: Persea Books, 1984).

13. A translation by W. Caxton (London, 1490) was reprinted in London, 1932.

14. The most recent such work is Salmonson, *The Encyclopedia of Amazons,* which unfortunately contains numerous factual errors. A more scholarly work in this genre is Guida M. Jackson, *Women Who Ruled* (Santa Barbara, Calif.: ABC-CLIO, 1990).

15. Haberling, "Army Prostitution," 16, citing Albertus Aquensis, Ekkehard of Jerusalem, and the chronicle of the monk Berthold.

16. I Cor. 7.36–37.

17. Barbara G. Walker, *The Woman's Encyclopedia of Myths and Secrets* (San Francisco: Harper & Row, 1983), 585–86.

18. Ibid., 16–17.

19. Palgrave, quoted in Fraser, *The Warrior Queens,* 111; Ellen C. Clayton, *Female Warriors: Memorials of Female Valour and Heroism, from the Mythological Ages to the Present Era* (London: Tinsley Brothers, 1879), 1:88.

20. Quoted in Miles, *The Women's History of the World,* 66.

21. Ibid., 66–67.

22. Quotations from Haberling, "Army Prostitution," 18. A recent edition of the source is Hamilton Alexander Rosskeen Gibb, ed., *The Life of Saladin: From the Works of Imad ad-Din and Baha ad-Din* (Oxford: Clarendon Press, 1973).

23. Amy Kelly, *Eleanor of Aquitaine and the Four Kings* (Cambridge, Mass.: Harvard University Press, 1950), 34–38.

24. Haberling, "Army Prostitution," 18.

25. Ibid., 20.

26. Ibid., 19.

27. Ibid., 21, quoting "the monk du Vigeois transmitted to us by Velly."

28. Keegan, *A History of Warfare*, 188.

29. Robert Briffault, *The Mothers,* abr. Gordon Rattray Taylor (New York: Atheneum, 1977), 100; David Nicolle, *The Mongol Warlords: Genghis Khan, Kublai Khan, Hugelu, Tamerland* (Poole, Dorsett: Firebird Books, 1990), 6, 11, 78, 173–74.

30. René Grousset, *The Empire of the Steppes: A History of Central Asia,* trans. Naomi Walford (New Brunswick, N.J.: Rutgers University Press, 1970), 268.

31. Quoted in Dyer, *War,* 45.

32. Froissart, *Chronicles of England, France, and Spain,* trans. T. Johnes, (New York: E.P. Dutton, 1961), 34–36.

33. Quoted in Newark, *Women Warlords,* 127.

34. Ibid., 128.

35. Haberling, "Army Prostitution," 22.

36. Ibid., 22–23.

37. Ibid., 27, quoting J. de Lavardian.

38. Ibid., 27–28, quoting Barante.

39. Ibid., 38.

40. Ibid., 38–39.

41. Ibid., 37.

42. Quoted in Haberling, "Army Prostitution," 27.

43. Ibid., 40.

44. Claude Quétel, *History of Syphilis,* trans. Judith Braddock and Brian Pike, (Baltimore: Johns Hopkins University Press, 1992), 4–5.

45. Haberling, "Army Prostitution," 41–42.

46. Ibid.

47. Larry H. Addington, *The Patterns of War through the Eighteenth Century* (Bloomington: Indiana University Press, 1990), 87.

48. Haberling, "Army Prostitution," 44, referencing Schiller, *History of the Thirty Years War.*

49. Quoted in Haberling, "Army Prostitution," 42.

50. Ibid., 43 quoting Wallhausen, *Defensio patriae* (1621).

51. Ibid., 35.

52. Hacker, "Where Have All the Women Gone?" 118–19.

53. Haberling, "Army Prostitution," 43.

54. Ibid., 33–34.

55. Noel T. St. John Williams, *Judy O'Grady and the Colonel's Lady: The Army Wife and Camp Follower Since 1660* (London: Brassey's, 1988), 14.

56. Haberling, "Army Prostitution," 34, quoting Gustav Freytag.

57. Fronsperger's *Kriegesbuch* of 1598 as quoted in Herman Heinrich Ploss, Max Bartels, and Paul Bartels, *Woman in the Sexual Relation: An Anthropological and Historical Survey,* rev. and enl. Ferd F. Von Reitzenstein, trans. Eric Dingwall (New York: Medical Press of America, 1964), 99.

58. H. J. C. Von Grimmelshausen, *Simplicius Simplicissimus,* ed. George Schulz-Berend (Indianapolis: Bobbs Merrill, 1965), 221.

59. Ibid.

60. For women sailors in the age of sail, see Linda Grant De Pauw, *Seafaring Women* (Boston: Houghton Mifflin, 1982); Suzanne J. Stark, *Female Tars: Women Aboard Ship in the Age of Sail* (Annapolis, Md.: Naval Institute Press, 1996; and Margaret S. Creighton and Lisa Norling, eds., *Iron Men, Wooden Women: Gender and Seafaring in the Atlantic World, 1700–1920* (Baltimore: Johns Hopkins University Press, 1996).

61. Rudolf M. Dekker and Lotte C. van de Pol, *The Tradition of Female Transvestism in Early Modern Europe* (New York: St. Martin's Press, 1989), xv, quoting Nicholas Witsen from J. F. Gebhart, *Het leven van mr. Nicholas Cornelisz, Witsen* (Utrecht, 1882) 2:408.

62. Diane Dugaw, *Warrior Women and Popular Balladry, 1650–1850* (Cambridge: Cambridge University Press, 1989), 5, 157, 156.

63. Brigitte Erikson, ed., "A Lesbian Execution in Germany, 1721: The Trial Records," *Journal of Homosexuality* 6 (1980–81): 33.

64. Dekker and van de Pol, *The Tradition of Female Transvestism,* 16.

65. Ibid.

66. Ibid., 14.

67. Ibid., 60–61.

68. Marjorie Garber, *Vested Interests: Cross-Dressing and Cultural Anxiety* (New York: Routledge, 1992), 131.

69. The autobiographical manuscript fragments are in the University of

Leeds Brotherton Collection. The most recent biography of d'Eon is Gary Kates, *Monsieur d'Eon Is a Woman: A Tale of Political Intrigue and Sexual Masquerade* (New York: Basic Books, 1995). See Also Edna Nixon, *Royal Spy: The Strange Case of the Chevalier d'Eon* (New York: Reynal, 1965); Gary Kates, "D'Eon Returns to France: Gender and Power in 1777," in Julia Epstein and Kristina Straub, eds., *Body Guards: The Cultural Politics of Gender Ambiguity* (New York: Routledge, 1991), 167–94.

CHAPTER FIVE: *The Age of Revolution*

1. Gwyn Jones, *The North Atlantic Saga: Being the Norse Voyages of Discovery and Settlement to Iceland, Greenland, America* (New York: Oxford University Press, 1986), 183.

2. Ibid.

3. Ian K. Steele, *Warpaths: Invasions of North America, 1513–1765* (New York: Oxford University Press, 1986).

4. Alvin M. Josephy, Jr., *The Patriot Chiefs: A Chronicle of American Indian Resistance* (New York: Viking Press, 1961).

5. Ibid.

6. Langer, *Encyclopedia of World History.* 551.

7. James Axtell, "The Vengeful Women of Marblehead: Robert Roules's Deposition of 1677," *William and Mary Quarterly* 31 (1974): 647–52. This was not an isolated incident. For other New England women praised as "fighting Jaels" in the colonial years, see Laurel Thatcher Ulrich, *Good Wives: Image and Reality in the Lives of Women in Northern New England 1650–1750* (New York: Oxford University Press, 1982), 167–83.

8. Cotton Mather, *Magnalia Christi Americana* (New York: Russell & Russell, 1967); "Diary of Samuel Sewall," Massachusetts Historical Society, *Collections,* 5th ser., 5 (1878): 452–53; "Journal of Rev. John Pike," Mass. Hist. Soc. *Proceedings* 14 (1875–76): 131.

9. Jean Bethke Elshtain, *Women and War* (New York: Basic Books, 1987), 175–76 has a photograph of one monument.

10. Caleb Butler, *History of the Town of Groton, Including Pepperel and Shirley from the First Grant of Groton Plantation in 1655* (Boston: Press of T. R. Marvin, 1848), 336–37; C. Shattuck, *Military Record of Pepperell, Mass.* (Nashua, N.H.: H. R. Wheeler, Steam Bok and Job Printer, 1877), 8; Mary L. Shattuck, *The Story of Jewett's Bridge* (n.p., 1912).

11. Nancy Van Alstyne, who gave birth to fifteen children, was popularly

known as "Patriot Mother of the Mowhawk Valley" because of her prowess as an Indian fighter. Linda Grant De Pauw, *Four Traditions: Women of New York During the American Revolution* (Albany: New York State Bicentennial Commission, 1974), 28.

12. Anne Newport Royall, *The Black Book: or, A Continuation of Travels in the United States* (Washington, D.C.: Printed for the author, 1828–29).

13. The first published study of American camp followers was Walter Hart Blumenthal, *Women Camp Followers of the American Revolution* (Philadelphia: George S. MacManus, 1952). The original printing was an edition of three hundred copies. The subject remained neglected for another forty years until it was taken up by Holly A. Mayer, "Belonging to the Army: Camp Followers and the Military Community During the American Revolution" (Ph.D. dissertation, College of William and Mary, 1990). Her book with the same title was published by University of South Carolina Press in 1996.

14. Marvin L. Brown, Jr., trans., *Baroness von Riedesel and the American Revolution: Journal and Correspondence of a Tour of Duty, 1776–1783* (Chapel Hill: University of North Carolina Press, 1965), 57–61. See also Louisa Hall Tharp, *The Baroness and the General* (Boston: Little, Born, 1962), 218–19.

15. Reginald Hargreaves, *The Bloodybacks: The British Serviceman in North America, 1655–1783* (London: Rupert Hart-Davis, 1968), 251.

16. Blumenthal, *Women Camp Followers*, 63.

17. Linda Grant De Pauw, *Four Traditions*, 23–24.

18. Ibid., 27.

19. Linda Grant De Pauw, *Founding Mothers: Women of America in the Revolutionary Era* (Boston: Houghton Mifflin, 1975), 172.

20. Mayer, "Belonging to the Army," 300.

21. De Pauw, *Founding Mothers*, 183.

22. Mayer, "Belonging to the Army," 137, 294.

23. Ibid., 137.

24. Edward Bangs, ed., *Journal of Lieutenant Isaac Bangs, April 1 to July 29, 1776* (Cambridge, Mass.: John Wilson & Son, 1890), 29.

25. Ibid.

26. Ibid., 136–38.

27. Williams, *Judy O'Grady and the Colonel's Lady*, 44.

28. Mayer, "Belonging to the Army," 54.

29. De Pauw, *Four Traditions*, 32.

30. Don N. Hagist, "The Women of the British Army During the American Revolution," *MINERVA: Quarterly Report on Women and the Military* 13, no. 2 (Summer 1995): 63.

31. Sir Leslie Stephen, ed., *Dictionary of National Biography* (London: Smith, Elder, 1889–1906), 614.

32. Ibid.

33. Patrick J. Leonard, "Ann Bailey: Mystery Woman Warrior of 1777," *MINERVA: Quarterly Report on Women and the Military* 11, nos. 3 and 4 (Fall/Winter 1993): 1–4.

34. Linda Grant De Pauw, "Women in Combat: The Revolutionary War Experience," *Armed Forces and Society* 7 (1981): 209–26.

35. John Keegan, *A History of Warfare,* 342–43.

36. The documentary records of Deborah's life show that Samson is the correct spelling. Her father, grandfather, and great-grandfather were Samsons, and her marriage was recorded with the spelling Samson. The corruption of the spelling of the family name did, however, occur in her lifetime and was not entirely the fault of Horace Mann. Her brother was a Samson at the time of his marriage but became Sampson in the Federal Census of 1790. See Emil F. Guba, *Deborah Samson alias Robert Shurtliff: Revolutionary War Soldier* (Plymouth, Mass.: Jones River Press, 1994), 22–23, 27, 29.

37. There are a number of books on Deborah intended for a juvenile audience. A recent biography directed to a popular audience is a collaboration between a journalist and a psychoanalyst who uncritically accept Horace Mann's fictionalizing as truth: Lucy Freeman and Alma Bond, America's *First Woman Warrior: The Courage of Deborah Sampson* (New York: Paragon House, 1992). Alfred Young is currently writing the first serious scholarly study under the title *Masquerade.*

38. Carol Klaver, "An Introduction to the Legend of Molly Pitcher," *MINERVA: Quarterly Report on Women and the Military* 7, no. 2 (Summer 1994) 35–61; D. W. Thompson, "Goodbye, Molly Pitcher," *Cumberland County History,* 5, no. 1 (Summer 1989): 3–26.

39. For a wildly elaborated account in what purports to be a serious work of history, see John Laffin, *Women in Battle* (London: Abelard-Schuman, 1967), 101.

40. De Pauw, "Women in Combat," 215.

41. Benjamin F. Lossing, *Pictorial Field Book of the American Revolution* (New York: Harper, 1851), 2:164n.; See also John Todd White, "The Truth About Molly Pitcher," in James Kirby Martin and Karen R. Stubaus, eds., *The*

American Revolution: Whose Revolution, (Huntington, N.Y.: Robert F. Krieger, 1977), 99–105.

42. Thompson, "Goodbye, Molly Pitcher."

43. Carlisle *(Pennsylvania) Herald,* May 18, 1876.

44. John B. Landis, "Molly Pitcher": *A Short History of Molly Pitcher, the Heroine of Monmouth* (Carlisle, Pa.: Corman, 1905); Jeremiah Zeamer, "Molly Pitcher Story Analysed," *Carlisle (Pennsylvania) Volunteer,* February 20, 1907.

45. (New York) *National Advocate,* March 7, 1822.

46. Ibid.

47. A photograph of this pitcher appears on 8 of Thompson, "Goodbye, Molly Pitcher."

48. Joseph Martin, *Private Yankee Doodle,* ed. George F. Scheer, (Boston: Little, Brown, 1962), 132–33; Waldo Journal, quoted in William S. Stryker, *The Battle of Monmouth* (Princeton University Press, 1927), 189–90. An anonymous oil painting done in the last half of the nineteenth century and now owned by the Monmouth County Historical Association, Freehold, New Jersey, shows a second combatant woman at the cannon.

49. Edward H. Hall, *Margaret Corbin, Heroine of the Battle of Fort Washington, 16 Nov. 1776* (New York: American Scenic and Historic Preservation Society, 1932); William Henry Egle, *Pennsylvania Women in the American Revolution* (Harrisburg, Pa.: Harrisburg Publishing Co., 1898), 52–54. By a strange quirk of history, Margaret Corbin is the only individual who can be positively identified as having filled an artillery position at that battle. See William Paul Deary, "Toward Disaster at Fort Washington, November 1776" (Ph.D. dissertation, George Washington University, 1996).

50. Lossing, *Pictorial Field Book,* 2:164.

51. Between 1787 and 1790, New York Deputy Commissary William Price wrote occasional letters to Secretary of War Henry Knox on behalf of women who were caring for "Capt. Molly." The letters never identify this charity case by her full name. James W. Wensyel, "Captain Molly," *Army* 31, no. 11 (November 1981): 52. Some of these letters were printed in Edward C. Boynton, *History of West Point and Its Military Importance During the American Revolution* (New York: D. Van Nostrand, 1871).

52. Landis, "Molly Pitcher."

53. Olwen H. Hufton, *Women and the Limits of Citizenship in the French Revolution* (Toronto: University of Toronto Press, 1992), 7.

54. Darlene Gay Levy and Harriet B. Applewhite, "Women and Militant

Citizenship in Revolutionary Paris," in Sara E. Meltzer and Leslie W. Rabine, eds., *Rebel Daughters: Women and the French Revolution* (New York: Oxford University Press, 1992), 83.

55. Elizabeth Roudinesco, *Théroigne de Méricourt: A Melancholic Woman during the French Revolution*, trans. Martin Thom (London: Verso, 1991), 23.

56. Lujo Bassermann, *The Oldest Profession: A History of Prostitution*, trans. James Clough (London: Barker 1967), 213.

57. Darlene Gay Levy et al., eds., *Women in Revolutionary Paris* (Urbana: University of Illinois Press, 1979), 72–74.

58. Jane Abray, "Feminism in the French Revolution," *American Historical Review* 80 (1975): 51.

59. Levy et al., *Women in Revolutionary Paris*, 225–7; Abray, "Feminism in the French Revolution," 49.

60. Elshtain, *Women and War*, 63, 67.

61. Quoted in Marilyn Yalom, *Blood Sisters: The French Revolution in Women's Memory* (New York: Basic Books, 1993), 203.

62. Ibid., 200–01.

63. Ibid., 199.

64. Ibid., 199–200.

65. *Dorothy Carrington, Napoleon and His Parents* (New York: E. P. Dutton, 1990), 222 n.56.

66. English-language biographies of Letizia Bonaparte include Clara Gilbert Martineau, *Madame Mère: Napoleon's Mother*, Trans. Frances Partridge (London: J. Murray, 1978); Robert McNair Willson, *Napoleon's Mother* (Philadelphia: J. B. Lippincott, 1933); and Monica Stirling, *A Pride of Lions* (London, Collins, 1961).

67. Haberling, "Army Prostitution," 57–58.

68. Ibid., 67.

69. Clayton, *Female Warriors*, 2:82.

70. Sir John Carr, *Descriptive Travels in the Southern and Eastern Parts of Spain and the Balearic Isles* (London: Sherwood, 1809), 32.

71. John R. Elting, *Swords Around a Throne: Napoleon's Grande Armée* (New York: Free Press, 1988), 612.

72. Oscar Paul Gilbert, *Women in Men's Guise* (London: John Lane, 1932), 88.

73. Thérèse Figueur, *Un ancien de 15e dragons* (Bordeaux: Editions Delmas, 1936).

74. Gilbert, *Women in Men's Guise*, 80; Francis Gribble, *Women in War* (New York: E. P. Dutton, 1917), 21–23.

75. Clayton, *Female Warriors*, 2:91.

76. Nadezhda Durova, *The Cavalry Maiden: Journals of a Russian Officer in the Napoleonic Wars*, trans. Mary Fleming Sirin (Bloomington: Indiana University Press, 1988), ix.

77. Ibid., 227.

78. Clayton, *Female Warriors*, 2:62–63.

79. Ibid., 230.

CHAPTER SIX: *Nineteenth-Century Warfare*

1. *Russkii Invalid* (St. Petersburg), January 4, 1855, quoting the *Neue Preussische Zeitung*. I am grateful to Mark Conrad for sharing these news clippings with me.

2. The best-known memoir of a camp follower of this period is Mary Seacole, *Wonderful Adventures of Mrs Seacole in Many Lands*, intro. by William L. Andrews (New York: Oxford University Press, 1990). Elizabeth Davis, a former domestic servant and hospital nurse, was the only paid nurse of the Crimean War to publish her memoirs. She was often sharply critical of Nightingale. Elizabeth Davis, *The Autobiography of Elizabeth Davis, a Balaklava Nurse*, ed. J. Williams (London: Hurst and Blackett, 1857).

3. Hacker, "Women and Military Institutions in Early Modern Europe," 666

4. Cecil Woodham-Smith, *Florence Nightingale, 1820–1910* (New York: McGraw Hill, 1951), 85.

5. The Nightingale bibliography is enormous. See W. J. Bishop and Goldie S. Bishop, *A Biobibliography of Florence Nightingale* (London: Dawsons of Pall Mall for the International Council of Nurses, 1962). Recent works are F. B. Smith, *Florence Nightingale: Reputation and Power* (New York: St. Martin's Press, 1982); M. E. Baly, *Florence Nightingale and the Nursing Legacy* (Dover, N.H.: Croom Helm, 1986); and E. Garnett, *Florence Nightingale's Nuns* (New York: Farrar, Straus & Cudahy, 1961).

6. Woodham-Smith, *Florence Nightengale*, 93.

7. The best biographies of Barry are Isobel Rae, *The Strange Story of Dr. James Barry* (London: Longmans, Green, 1958); and June Rose, *The Perfect Gentleman: The Remarkable Life of Dr. James Miranda Barry, the Woman Who Served as an Officer in the British Army from 1815 to 1859* (London: Hutchinson, 1977). The Barry Papers in the Muniment Room of the Royal Army

Medical Corps, London contain documents discovered by both of these biographers. The Public Record Office has Barry's "Statement of Home and Foreign Services" (WO:25/3899).

8. Rae, *The Strange Story of Dr. James Barry*, 96–97, 100; Rose, *The Perfect Gentleman*, 133–42.

9. Rose, *The Perfect Gentleman*, 30.

10. Ibid., 24.

11. Ibid., 13.

12. Among the scholarly works already in print are C. Kay Larson, "Bonny Yank and Ginny Reb," *MINERVA: Quarterly Report on Women and the Military* 8 no. 1 (Spring 1990): 33–49 and "Bonny Yank and Ginny Reb Revisited," ibid., 10 no. 2 (Summer 1992): 35–61; DeAnne Blanton, "Women Soldiers of the Civil War," *Prologue: Quarterly of the National Archives* 11 (Spring 1993): 27–33; Lauren Cook Burgess, ed., *An Uncommon Soldier: The Civil War Letters of Sarah Rosetta Wakeman, alias Private Lyons Wakeman, 153rd Regiment, New York State Volunteers* (Pasadena, Md.: The MINERVA Center, 1994).

13. Harry Besançon Papers, diary, May 26, 1864; and A. Jackson Crossly to Samuel Bradbury, Headquarters, Army of the Potomac, May 29, 1864. Both documents are in the Manuscript Department, William R. Perkins Library, Duke University.

14. Quoted in Thomas Lowry, *The Story the Soldiers Wouldn't Tell: Sex in the Civil War* (Mechanicsburg, Pa.: Stackpole Books, 1994), 35. The manuscript is at the Chicago Historical Society.

15. Paul Haas, ed., "A Volunteer Nurse in the Civil War: The Letters of Harriet Douglas Whetten," *Wisconsin Magazine of History* 48, no. 3 (Spring 1965): 217.

16. Lt. Col. Fremantle, *Three Months in the Southern States* (New York: John Bradburn, 1864), 172–73.

17. "Civil War Letters of Herman Weiss and Wife Adeline Weiss," in *An Immigrant Goes to War*, published in History, vol. 4, ed. Harlan B. Phillips (N. D.: Meredian Books, 1961). I am grateful to Lauren Cook Burgess for sharing her copy of this rare publication.

18. Ibid.

19. Ibid.

20. Alexander H. Sheridan, *Personal Memoirs* (New York: Charles L. Webster & Co., 1888), 252–55.

21. Richard Miller Devens, *The Pictorial Book of Anecdotes and Incidents of the War of the Rebellion* (Hartford: Hartford Publishing Col, 1867), 622–23.

22. James H. Guthrie Diary, October 19, 1862 quoted in Michael Fellman, "Women and Guerrilla Warfare," in Catherine Clinton and Nina Silber, eds., *Divided Houses: Gender and the Civil War* (New York: Oxford University Press, 1992), 157.

23. Fazar Kirkland, *Reminiscences of the Blue and Gray, 1861–1865* (Chicago: Preston, 1866), 173.

24. Mary A. Livermore, *My Story of the War* (Hartford, Conn.: A. D. Worthington, 1889), 119–20.

25. An edited collection of all the Lucy Brewer books has recently been published: David A. Cohen, ed., *"The Female Marine" and Related Works,* (Amherst: University of Massachusetts Press, 1997).

26. David S. Reynolds, *Beneath the American Renaissance* (New York: Alfred A. Knopf, 1988), 347.

27. Quoted in Sylvia Dannett, *She Rode with the Generals: The True and Incredible Story of Sarah Emma Seelye, Alias Franklin Thompson* (New York: Thomas Nelson & Sons, 1960), 24.

28. S. Emma E. Edmonds, *Nurse and Spy in the Union Army* (Hartford, Conn.: W. S. Williams, 1986).

29. Loreta J. Velazquez, *The Woman in Battle: A Narrative of the Adventures and Travels of Madame Loreta Janeta Velazquez, Otherwise Known as Lt. Harry T. Buford, CSA* (Richmond, Va.: Dustin, Gilman, 1876), 42.

30. Papers of Gen. James Longstreet, Letter to Miss E. W. Pech, June 15, 1888, Special Collections Library, Duke University; Richard Hall, *Patriots in Disguise: Women Warriors of the Civil War* (New York: Paragon House, 1993), 207–8. Hall has discovered considerable "circumstantial support" for Velazquez's narrative and is continuing this research. The request of a soldier named H. T. Buford for a commission, dated July 27, 1863, is in the Records of the Confederate Secretary of War, Registers of Application for Appointments, in Record Group 109 at the National Archives.

31. Velazquez, *The Women in Battle*, 47, 49.

32. Ibid., 44.

33. Mary Elizabeth Massey, *Bonnet Brigades* (New York: Alfred A. Knopf, 1966), 74. See also Lowry, *The Story the Soldiers Wouldn't Tell*, 154–55.

34. Massey, *Bonnet Brigades*, 71.

35. Quoted in Burgess, *An Uncommon Soldier*, 11.

36. Edmonds, *Nurse and Spy*, quoted in Jane E. Schultz, "Women at the Front: Gender and Genre in Literature of the American Civil War" (Ph.D. dissertation, University of Michigan, 1988), 305. Emphasis in original.

37. Schultz, "Women at the Front," 278.

38. Hall, *Patriots in Disguise*, 23–25; Gerhard Glausius, "The Little Soldier of the 95th: Albert D. J. Cashier," *Journal of the Illinois State Historical Society* 51, no. 4 (Winter 1958): 380–87.

39.After a long period of neglect, a gratifying number of scholars have taken up the study of Civil War nurses. In addition to those cited, see Nina Bennett Smith, "The Women Who Went to the War: The Union Army Nurse in the Civil War" (Ph.D. dissertation, Northwestern University, 1981); Nina B. Smith, "Men and Authority: The Union Army Nurse and the Problem of Power," *MINERVA: Quarterly Report on Women and the Military* 6, no. 4 (Winter 1988): 25–42; Ann Douglas Wood, "The War within a War: Women Nurses in the Union Army," *Civil War History* 18, no. 3 (September 1972): 197–212; Patricia Paquette, "A Bandage in One Hand and a Bible in the Other: The Story of Captain Sally L. Thompkins (CSA)," *MINERVA: Quarterly Report on Women and the Military* 8, no. 2 (Summer 1990): 47–54; Peggy Brase Siegel, "She Went to War: Indiana Women Nurses in the Civil War," *Indiana Magazine of History*, 86, no. 1 (March 1990), 1–27; Jane E. Schultz, "The Inhospitable Hospital: Gender and Professionalism in Civil War Medicine," *Signs: Journal of Women in Culture and Society* 17 (1992): 262–92.

40. Schultz, "Women at the Front," 36–38; Philip A. Kalisch and Beatrice J. Kalisch, "Untrained But Undaunted: The Women Nurses of the Blue and Gray," *Nursing Forum* 15, no. 1 (1976): 4–33.

41. Just as women veterans of World War II and Vietnam have done, army nurses of the Civil War worked to preserve their own history when they found histories of the war ignored their service. Thirty years after the war, Mary G. Holland collected sketches of wartime service from fellow nurses and published them together with a portrait of each woman. The book has recently been reissued: Mary G. Holland, *Our Army Nurses* (Roseville, Minn.: Edinborough Press, 1997).

42. Schultz, "Women at the Front," 147.

43. Ibid., 99, 123n.

44. Ibid., 100.

45. Ibid., 178n.

46. Ibid., 153.

47. Ibid., 103.

48. Steven Roca, "Permission to Come on Board: Women Nurses on the USS Red Rover, 1861–1865," paper delivered at "Lead, Blood and Tears," Conference on Women and the Civil War, Hood College, June 28, 1997.

49. Schultz, "Women at the Front," 69.

50. Livermore, *My Story of the War,* 246.

51. Schultz, "Women at the Front," 3–5.

52. The only book-length biography of Dr. Walker is Charles McCool Snyder, *Mary Walker: The Little Lady in Pants* (New York: Vantage Press, 1962).

53. Two recent biographies of this most famous of American women nurses are Elizabeth Brown Pryor, *Clara Barton: Professional Angel* (Philadelphia: University of Pennsylvania Press, 1987); and Stephen Oates, *A Woman of Valor: Clara Barton and the Civil War* (New York: Free Press, 1994).

54. The Uniform Code of Military Justice that replaced the Articles of War in 1950 also permitted court-martial of civilians. In 1960, the Supreme Court declared the practice in peacetime is unconstitutional. Maurer Maurer, "The Court-Martialing of Camp Followers, World War I," *American Journal of Legal History* 9 (1965): 203–15.

55. Agnes Salm-Salm, *Ten Years of My Life* (London: Richard Bentley, 1876), 1:37.

56. George Augustus Sala, *My Diary in America in the Midst of the War* (London: Tinsley Brothers, 1865), 1:359.

57. Schultz, "Women at the Front," 222.

58. Salm-Salm, *Ten Years of My Life,* 1:37.

59. Schultz, "Women at the Front," 106–7.

60. Ibid., 186–87; Livermore, *My Story of the War,* 114–16; Ernest Edward East, "Lincoln's Russian General," *Journal of the Illinois State Historical Society* 52 no. 1 (Spring 1959): 106–22. A. I. Startsev, "Ivan Turchaninov and the American Civil War," in Norman E. Saul et al., eds., *Russian-American Dialogue on Cultural Relations, 1776–1914* (Columbia: University of Missouri Press, 1997), 107–27. Extracts from Nadine Turchin's journal for the period May 1863 to April 1864, translated from the French, are in *Journal of the Illinois State Historical Society* 52 (February 1977): 27–89. Documents relating to her application for a pension are in *US Statutes at Large* 32:1330–31.

61. *Canton* (Ohio) *Repository,* December 30, 1895, 5.

62. For example, Frank Moore, *Women of the War: Their Heroism and Self-Sacrifice* (Hartford, Conn: S. S. Scranton, 1866); and Linus Pierpont Brockett and Mary Vaughan, *Women's Work in the Civil War* (Philadelphia: Ziegler,

McCurdy; Boston: R. H. Curran, 1867). An excellent recent work that includes biographies of Annie Ethridge and Mary Tepe and dozens of other women who had some part in the historic events at Gettysburg is Elaine F. Conklin, *Women at Gettysburg, 1863* (Gettysburg, Pa.: Thomas Publications, 1993).

63. John W. Halley, *The Rebel Yell and the Yankee Hurrah: The Civil War Journal of a Maine Volunteer, 17th Maine Regiment,* ed. Ruth L. Silliker (Camden, Maine: Down East Books, 1985), 64.

64. Schultz, "Women at the Front," 278.

65. Susie King Taylor, *A Black Woman's Civil War Memoirs,* ed. Patricia W. Romero (New York: Marcus Wiener, 1988), 61.

66. Ibid., chap. 5.

67. *Journal of the Afro-American Historical and Genealogical Society* (Spring/Summer 1991): 33.

68. Quoted in Peter Bardaglio, "Children of Jubilee: African American Childhood in Wartime," in Clinton and Silber, *Divided Houses,* 225.

69. Bardaglio, "Children of Jubilee" 225–26.

70. Gerald Schwartz, ed., *A Woman Doctor's Civil War: Esther Hill Hawks' Diary* (Columbia: University of South Carolina Press, 1984), 34.

71. Massey, *Bonnet Brigades,* 262; Lowry, *Stories the Soldiers Wouldn't Tell,* 157–58, 193.

72. Margaret Leech, *Reveille in Washington, 1860–1865* (New York: Harper & Row, 1941), 261 ff.; Lowry, *The Story the Soldiers Wouldn't Tell,* 62–63, 73–75.

73. Bell Irvin Wiley, *The Life of Billy Yank: The Common Soldier of the Union* (Baton Rouge: Louisiana State University Press, reissued 1978), 258, 260.

74. Ibid, 259.

75. Massey, *Bonnet Brigades,* 228–29.

76. Brockett and Vaughan, *Women's Work in the Civil War,* 781.

77. James Reston, Jr., *Sherman's March and Vietnam* (New York: Macmillan, 1984), 92–93.

78. H. E. Sterx, *Partners in Rebellion: Alabama Women in the Civil War* (Rutherford, N.J.: Fairleigh Dickinson University Press, 1970), 45.

79. Catherine Clinton, "Plantation Mistress," in Richard N. Current, ed., *Encyclopedia of the Confederacy* (New York: Simon and Schuster, 1993), 3:1218.

80. Schultz, "Women at the Front," 259.

81. Ibid.

82. Fellman, "Women and Guerrilla Warfare," 157.

83. Massey, *Bonnet Brigades,* 105.

84. Fellman, "Women and Guerrilla Warfare," 156.

85. Edmonds, *Nurse and Spy,* 92–97.

86. Phoebe Yates Pember, *A Southern Woman's Story: Life in Confederate Richmond,* ed. Bell I. Wiley, (Jackson, Tenn.: McCowat-Mercer Press, 1959), 150–51.

87. Velazquez, *The Woman in Battle,* 416.

88. Massey, *Bonnet Brigades,* 105.

89. Ibid., 300.

90. There are only two serious biographies of Tubman. The first was originally published in 1886 but exists in a modern edition: Sarah H. Bradford, *Harriet Tubman: The Moses of Her People* (New York: Corinth Books, 1961). The other is Earl Conrad, *Harriet Tubman* (Washington, D.C.: Associated Publishers, 1943).

91. Hall, *Patriots in Disguise,* 166.

CHAPTER SEVEN: *The Age of Imperialism*

1. Fray Gaspar de Carvajal, *The Discovery of the Amazon,* ed. José Toribio Medina, trans. Bertram J. Lee (New York: Dover Publications, 1988); Newark, *Women Warlords,* 31–40.

2. Briffault, *The Mothers,* 99.

3. Catalina De Erauso, *Lieutenant Nun: Memoir of a Basque Transvestite in the New World,* trans. Michele Stepto and Gabriel Stepto (Boston: Beacon Press, 1996).

4. For more about Indian women as warriors, see Valerie Sherer Mathes, "Native American Women in Medicine and the Military," *Journal of the West* 21, no. 2 (1982): 41–48; Josephy, *The Patriot Chiefs;* Carolyn Thomas Foreman, *Indian Women Chiefs* (Washington, D.C.: Zenger, [1954] 1976); Carolyn Niethammer, *Daughters of the Earth: The Lives and Legends of American Indian Women* (New York: Collier, 1977); Bernice Medicine, "Warrior Women/Sex Role Alternatives for Plains Indian Women," in Patricia Albers and Bernice Medicine, eds., *The Hidden Half: Studies of Plains Indian Women* (Lanham, Md.: University Press of America, 1983) 267–80; James Axtell, ed., *The Indian People of Eastern America: A Documentary History of the Sexes* (New York: Oxford University Press, 1981); Margot Liberty, "Hell Came with

the Horses: Plains Indian Women in the Equestrian Era, " *Montana* 32 (Summer 1982): 41–48.

5. Harold W. Felton, *Nancy Ward, Cherokee* (New York: Dodd, Mead, 1975); Norma Tucker, "Nancy Ward, Ghigua of the Cherokees," *Georgia Historical Quarterly* 53 (June 1969): 192–200; Ben Harris McClary, "Nancy Ward," *Tennessee Historical Quarterly* 21 (December 1962): 352–64.

6. Briffault, *The Mothers,* 99.

7. Frank B. Linderman, *Pretty-shield: Medicine Woman of the Crows* [original title *Red Mother,* published 1932] (New York: John Day, 1972), 227–31.

8. Don Rickey, Jr., *Forty Miles a Day on Beans and Hay: The Enlisted Soldier Fighting the Indian Wars* (Norman: University of Oklahoma Press, 1963), 131.

9. Few historians take note of laundresses. An important exception is Patricia Y. Stallard, *Glittering Misery: Dependents of the Indian Fighting Army* (Fort Collins, Colo.: Old Army Press, 1978), chap. 3. See also Miller J. Stewart, "Army Laundresses: Ladies of the 'Soap Suds Row,'" *Nebraska History* 61, no. 4 (1980): 421–24.

10. Stallard, *Glittering Misery,* 59.

11. Ibid., 59–60.

12. Elizabeth B. Custer, *Boots and Saddles or Life in Dakota with General Custer* (New York: Harper & Row, 1885), 94–96, 188–92; Rickey, *Forty Miles a Day,* 170–71; Katherine G. Fougera, *With Custer's Cavalry: From the Memoirs of the Late Katherine Gibson* (Caldwell, Idaho: Caxton, 1940), 222–23.

13. Anne M. Butler, "Military Myopia: Prostitution on the Frontier," *Prologue* 13, (Winter 1981), 233–50.

14. Stallard, *Glittering Misery,* 63–64.

15. Ibid., 64.

16. Adjutant General's Office, General Orders No. 37, *Index of General Orders, 1878* (Washington, D.C.: Government Printing Office, 1879), 8.

17. Helen Diner, *Mothers and Amazons: The First Feminist History of Culture* (New York: Anchor Books, 1973), 176–86; Jackson, *Women Who Ruled,* 1–3.

18. Fraser, *The Warrior Queens,* 241, 242. See also David Birmingham, *Trade and Conflict in Angola: The Mbundu and Their Neighbors under the Influence of the Portuguese* (Oxford: Oxford University Press, 1966), 6.

19. Filippo Pigafetta, *A Report of the Kingdom of Congo and of the Surrounding Countries,* quoted in Kleinbaum, *The War Against the Amazons,* 132.

20. Quoted in Melville J. Herskovits, *Dahomey: An Ancient West African Kingdom* (Evanston: Northwestern University Press, 1967), 85.

21. F. E. Forbes, *Dahomey and the Dahomans,* quoted in Herskovits, *Dahomey,* 85.

22. John Duncan, *Travels in Western Africa,* quoted in Newark, *Women Warlords,* 46–47.

23. Quoted in Herskovits, *Dahomey,* 88.

24. Quoted in Newark, *Women Warlords,* 47.

25. Richard Burton, *A Mission to Gelele, King of Dahome,* Quoted in Newark, *Woman Warlords,* 48

26. A. H. Atteridge, "The Forest Fighting in Dahomey: 1892," in A. Forbes, et al eds., *Battles of the 19th Century* (London: Cassell, 1896) 647–58.

27. In addition to references cited below, those interested in learning more on women in India will find valuable information in Kenneth Ballhatchet, *Race, Sex, and Class under the Raj: Imperial Attitudes and Policies and Thier Critics, 1793–1905* (London: Weidenfeld and Nicolson, 1980), and Douglas Peers, *Between Mars and Mammon: Colonial Armies and the Garrison State in India, 1819–1835* (New York: St. Martin's Press, 1995). These books also contain extensive bibliographies.

28. Quoted in F. C. G. Page, *Following the Drum: Women in Wellington's Wars* (London: Andre Deutsch, 1986), 3.

29. Rudyard Kipling, "The Married Man," in *The Definitive Edition of Rudyard Kipling's Verse* (London: Hodder and Stoughton, 1948), 474.

30. Byron Farwell, *Mr. Kipling's Army: All the Queen's Men* (New York: W. W. Norton, 1981), 225.

31. Ibid.,233.

32. Ibid., 231, 231–32.

33. Ibid., 237.

34. Ibid., 232.

35. Myrna Trustram, *Women of the Regiment: Marriage and the Victorian Army* (Cambridge: Cambridge University Press, 1984), 120.

36. Ibid., 120–21.

37. Ibid., 132.

38. Farwell, *Mr. Kipling's Army,* 226.

39. Ibid.

40. Haberling, "Army Prostitution," 8.

41. Williams, *Judy O'Grady and the Colonel's Lady*, 155.

42. Ibid., 157.

43. English-language biographies include D. V. Tahmankar, *The Ranee of Jhansi* (London: Macgibbon and Kee, 1958); Sir John Smyth, *The Rebellious Rani* (London: Muller, 1966); Shyam Narain Sinha, *Rani Laksmi Bai of Jhansi* (New Delhi: Chugh Publications, 1980); Joyce Lebra-Chapman, *The Rani of Jhansi: A Study in Female Heroism in India* (Honolulu: University of Hawaii Press, 1986).

44. Tahmankar, *The Ranee of Jhansi*, 19.

45. Ibid., 67.

46. Thomas Lowe, *Central India During the Rebellion of 1857 and 1858* (1860), 233.

47. Ibid., 263.

48. Quoted in Fraser, *The Warrior Queens*, 294.

49. Ibid., 295.

50. Quoted in Byron Farwell, *The Great Anglo-Boer War* (New York: Harper & Row, 1976), 4.

51. Quoted in Emanoel Lee, *To the Bitter End: A Photographic History of the Boer War, 1899–1902* (Harmondsworth: Penguin Books, 1985), 19.

52. Ibid., 42.

53. Quoted in Fraser, *The Warrior Queens*, 184.

54. Quoted in Farwell, *The Great Anglo-Boer War*, 367.

55. Ibid.

56. Farwell, *The Great Anglo-Boer War*, 397. For additional information on women in the concentration camps, see Peter Warwick, ed., *The South African War: The Anglo-Boer War, 1899–1902* (Harlow, Exxex: Longman, 1980).

57. Ibid., 410.

58. Viscountess Milner, *My Picture Gallery, 1886-1901* (London: John Murray, 1951), 180.

59. Quoted in Farwell, *The Great Anglo-Boer War*, 249.

60. Ibid.

61. Farwell, *The Great Anglo-Boer War*, 402–3.

62. Ibid., 403.

63. Lee, To the Bitter End, 186; *Farwell, The Great Anglo-Boer War*, 419;

Emily Hobhouse, *The Brunt of the War and Where It Fell* (London: Methuen, 1902).

64. Farwell, *The Great Anglo-Boer War,* 404.

65. Ibid., 410.

66. Ibid., 418.

67. Ibid., 369.

68. Ibid., 391.

69. Ibid., 406.

70. Ibid., 403.

71. Ibid., 244.

72. Ibid., 243.

73. Ibid., 243–44.

74. Laffin, *Women in War,* 53.

75. Briffault, *The Mothers,* 99.

76. Haberling, "Army Prostitution," 84.

77. Martha L. Crawley, "The Science of Right Living: The Navy Medical Department in the Progressive Era" (Ph.D. dissertation, George Washington University, 1989), 212.

78. Mary B. Dearing, "Anita Newcomb McGee," in Edward T. James, ed., *Notable American Women: A Biographical Dictionary* (Cambridge, Mass.: Belknap Press, 1971), 2:464–66. There is no book-length biography of Dr. McGee.

79. Personal communication, Xiaolin Li, May 25, 1995.

80. Kwok Kian-Chow, "The Tomb of Fu Hao" (M.A. thesis, University of British Columbia, 1984), and "Quadrilateral Patterning in the Tomb of Fu Hao," *Indo-Pacific Prebetary Association Bulletin* 11 (1991): 72–178.

81. For the study of Chinese women in war, English-language sources of any kind are sparse. The most valuable work to date is that of Xiaolin Li: Mady Wechsler Segal, Xiaolin Li, and David R. Segal, "Role of Women in the Chinese People's Liberation Army," *MINERVA: Quarterly Report on Women and the Military* 10, no. 1 (Spring 1992): 48–55, and her Ph.D. dissertation, "Women in the Chinese Military" (University of Maryland, 1995). She is currently writing a book entitled *Women in the Chinese Military: A History and Sociological Analysis* (Greenwood Press). Chapter 1 of Maxine Hong Kingston's autobiographical work, *The Woman Warrior: Memoirs of a Girlhood Among Ghosts*

(New York: Vintage Books, 1975), describes the Chinese woman warrior tradition. See also Louise Anne May's Ph.D. dissertation, "Worthy Warriors and Unruly Amazons: Sino-Western Historical Accounts and Imaginative Images of Women in Battle" (University of British Columbia, 1985); and Jia Lin Bao, ed., *Collected Works on the History of Chinese Women* (Tai Pei: Mu Tong, 1979).

82. Personal communication, Xiaolin Li, May 25, 1995.

83. Segal, Li, and Segal, "The Role of Women in the Chinese People's Liberation Army," 50.

Dr. Li, whose generosity in sharing her research was invaluable to me, began her graduate studies in the United States after an eighteen-year military career in the PLA. Her mother was also a verteran, and her family's tradition of military service inspired her research. As the history of China's military women becomes more widely known, we can hope that many more scholarly studies will be written and published in English.

CHAPTER EIGHT: *The Great War*

1. The "compulsive masculinity" term is used by Betty Roszak and Theodore Roszak, eds., *Masculine/Feminine* (New York: Harper & Row, 1969), esp. 90–92, 102. See also Michael C. C. Adams, *The Great Adventure: Male Desire and the Coming of World War I* (Bloomington: Indiana University Press, 1990).

2. Judith Wishnia, "Pacifism and Feminism in Historical Perspective," in Hunter, ed., *On Peace, War, and Gender,* 84–91; Sandi Cooper, "Women in War and Peace, 1914–1945," in Renate Bridenthal, Susan Stuard, and Merry Wiesner, eds., *Becoming Visible: Women in European History,* 3d ed. (Boston: Houghton Mifflin, 1998), 439–60, and "Women's Participation in European Peace Movements: The Effort to Prevent World War I," in Ruth Roach Pierson, ed. *Women and Peace* (London: Croom Helm, 1987), 51–75.

3. Theodore Roosevelt, *The Strenuous Life* (New York: The Review of Reviews, 1904).

4. Mark Gerzon, *A Choice of Heroes: The Changing Face of American Manhood* (Boston: Houghton Mifflin, 1982), 51. See also Joe L. Dubbert, *A Man's Place* (Englewood Cliffs, N.J.: Prentice-Hall, 1979).

5. Gerzon, *A Choice of Heroes,* 36; Roszak and Roszak, *Masculine/ Feminine,* 90–92, 102.

6. Gerzon, *A Choice of Heroes,* 52.

7. Ibid., 54.

8. Quoted in Caroline E. Playne, *Society at War, 1914-1916* (Boston: Houghton Mifflin, 1931), 134.

9. Lillian Faderman, *Odd Girls and Twilight Lovers: A History of Lesbian Life in Twentieth-Century America* (New York: Columbia University Press, 1991), 63; Radclyffe Hall, "Miss Ogilvy Finds Herself" and *The Well of Loneliness* (New York: Covici Friede, 1928).

10. Laffin, *Women in Battle,* 52, 62-3.

11. Ibid., 62.

12. Jonathan Katz, *Gay American History: Lesbians and Gay Men in the U.S.A.* (New York: Avon Books, 1976) 905.

13. Laffin, *Women in Battle,* 62–63.

14. Dekker and van de Pol, *The Tradition of Female Transvestism,* 42; Wheelwright, *Amazons and Military Maids,* 115-116; Edith Durham, *High Albania* (London: Virago Press, 1985), 80.

15. Laffin, *Women in Battle,* 57.

16. Wheelwright, *Amazons and Military Maids,* 108–9.

17. Flora Sandes published two autobiographies: *An English Woman-Sergeant in the Serbian Army* (London: Hodder and Stoughton, 1916) and *The Autobiography of a Woman Soldier: A Brief Record of Adventure with the Serbian Army, 1916-1919* (London: Witherby, 1927). See also Alan Burgess, *The Lovely Sergeant* (London: Heinemann, 1963).

18. Wheelwright, *Amazons and Military Maids,* 35.

19. Ibid., 148.

20. Sandes, *The Autobiography of a Woman Soldier,* 38.

21. Dorothy Lawrence, *Sapper Dorothy Lawrence: The Only English Woman Soldier, Late Royal Engineers, 51st Division, 179th Tunnelling Co., BEF* (London: John Lance, 1919).

22. "Soldier Hides Wife on Army Transport," *New York Times,* July 16, 1917; "Mrs. Hazel Carter of Douglas, Arizona, was determined to go to France," *New York Times,* July 17, 1917.

23. Dekker and van de Pol, *The Tradition of Female Transvestism,* 32.

24. Wheelwright, *Amazons and Military Maids,* 33.

25. Rosetta Forbes, *Women Called Wild* (London: Grayson and Grayson, 1935), 65.

26. Marina Yurlova, *Cossack Girl* (London: Cassell, 1934) 32–33, 36.

27. Maria Bochkareva, as told to Isaac Don Levine, *Yashika: My Life as a Peasant Officer and Exile* (New York: Frederick A. Stokes, 1929); Richard Stites, *The Women's Liberation Movement in Russia: Feminism, Nihilism and Bolshevism* (Princeton: Princeton University Press, 1978), 295–300; Wheelwright, *Amazons and Military Maids,* 125–26.

28. Bochkareva, *Yashika,* 209; Wheelwright, *Amazons and Military Maids,* 126; Anne Elliot Griesse and Richard Stites, "Russia: Revolution and War," in Nancy Loring Goldman, ed., *Female Soldiers—Combatants or Noncombatants? Historical and Contemporary Perspectives* (Westport, Conn.: Greenwood Press, 1982), 65.

29. Louise Bryant, *Six Red Months in Russia: An Observer's Account of Russia Before and During the Proletarian Dictatorship* (London: Heinemann, 1918), 212–18.

30. Wheelwright, *Amazons and Military Maids,* 129.

31. Bryant, *Six Red Months in Russia,* 212–18.

32. Griesse and Stites, "Russia: Revolution and War," 64–65.

33. Wheelwright, *Amazons and Military Maids,* 129.

34. Laffin, *Women in Battle,* 54–56.

35. Dorothy Schneider and Carl J. Schneider, *Into the Breach: American Women Overseas in World War I* (New York: Viking Press, 1991), 12.

36. Ettie A. Rout, *Two Years in Paris* (London, 1923), cited in Harry Benjamin, "Morals versus Morale in Wartime," in Robinson, *Morals in Wartime,* 189.

37. Magnus Hirshfeld, *The Sexual History of the World War* (New York: Panurge Press, 1934), 146.

38. Quoted in Hirshfeld, *The Sexual History of the World War,* 147–48.

39. James A. Sandos, "Prostitution and Drugs: The United States Army on the Mexican-American Border, 1916-1917," *Pacific Historical Review* (1980): 621–45.

40. Etienne Ribaud, "Maternal Impregnation in Wartime," in Robinson, *Morals in Wartime,* 93.

41. Williams, *Judy O'Grady and the Colonel's Lady,* 176.

42. According to Hirshfeld, "the exact figures on this subject are lacking, since at the end of the war all these records were purloined by the notorious Gômbôs, now one of the leaders of the Hungarian Fascists, but at that time a member of the general staff." *The Sexual History of the World War,* 179–81.

43. Ibid., 180.

44. Diana Condell and Jean Liddiard, *Images of Women in the First World War 1914-1918* (London: Routledge & Kegan Paul, 1987), 72, 160, 104, 83, 105. This splendid collection of illustrations says far more about the work of Englishwomen during the war than words can. Two other recent books on the subject are Arthur Marwick, *Women at War, 1914-1918* (London: Croom Helm, 1977), and Gail Braybon, *Women Workers in the First World War: The British Experience* (London: Croom Helm, 1981).

45. Condell and Liddiard, *Images of Women,* 105.

46. Ibid., 107.

47. Ibid., 113; Angela Woollacott, *On Her Their Lives Depend: Munitions Workers in the Great War* (Berkeley: University of California Press, 1994).

48. Candall and Liddiard, *Images of Women,* 136.

49. Valerie Moolman, *Women Aloft* (Alexandria, Va.: Time-Life Books, 1981), 30.

50. B. Robertson, ed., *Air Aces of the 1914–18 War* (Los Angeles: Aero Publications, 1964).

51. Moolman, *Women Aloft,* 31–33.

52. Joy Bright Hancock, *Lady in the Navy: A Personal Reminiscence* (Annapolis, Md.: Naval Institute Press, 1972), 22, 23, 113.

53. Jean Ebbert and Marie-Beth Hall, *Crossed Currents: Navy Women from WW I to Tailhook* (Washington, D.C.: Brassey's, 1993), 4–6, 12.

54. Eunice Desser, *The First Enlisted Women, 1917–1919* (Philadelphia: Dorrance, 1955), 62; Linda L. Hewitt, *Women Marines in World War I* (Washington, D.C.: U.S. Marine Corps, 1974), v, 4, 25, 41.

55. A. Lincoln Lavine, *Circuits of Victory* (Garden City, NY: Country Life Press, 1921), is a history of the Army Signal Corps in World War I; Karen L. Hillerich, "Black Jack's Girls," *Army* 32, no. 12 (December 1982): 44–48.

56. Hillerich, "Black Jack's Girls," 45.

57. Ibid., 46.

58. Ibid.

59. Merle Anderson, "My Battle with the Pentagon," unpublished manuscript, undated. Anderson was the most persistent advocate of recognition of Signal Corps women.

60. Quoted in Madeleine Zabriskie Doty, *Short Rations: Experiences of an American Woman in Germany* (New York: A. L. Burt, 1917), 90.

61. Ibid.

62. Robert V. Piedmont and Cindy Gurney, eds., *Highlights in the History of the Army Nurse Corps* (Washington, D.C.: U.S. Army Center of Military History, 1987), 9–12.

63. A recent survey of American women's service in World War I, which includes many photographs, is Lettie Gavin, *American Servicewomen in World War I* (Niwot: University of Colorado Press, 1997).

64. No comprehensive bibliography of women's published memoirs from World War I exists, although the number of memoirs printed is substantial. A useful list of American memoirs is in Schneider and Schneider, *Into the Breach*. Most of the books were produced in small editions by small presses and have long been out of print. Some oral histories were also collected from women who served in World War I, but the interest in women's military history came too late to capture as many stories as one could wish for. Unpublished letters and journals are additional sources that are still largely in private hands.

60. Vera Brittain, *Testament of Youth* (London: Victor Gollancz, 1933), 656. Other English-language works by women based on their war experiences are Mary Borden, *The Forbidden Zone* (London: Heinemann, 1929); Enid Bagnold, *A Diary without Dates* (London: Heinemann, 1918); and Irene Rathbone, *We that Were Young* (London: Chatto & Windus, 1932).

CHAPTER NINE: *The Second World War*

1. The publication of personal narratives and the collection of oral histories of American women alone has already outpaced the ability of bibliographers to keep up with them. In addition to material cited in these notes, the stories women have so far shared only with other women veterans can still become part of history. The reunions of World War II veterans in all nations witness the retelling of old stories, which will disappear with this generation if they are not recorded in permanent form.

2. Dyer, *War*, 90–91.

3. A monograph focused on women's roles in this war is Mary Nash, *Defying Male Civilization: Women in the Spanish Civil War* (Denver: Arden Press, 1995).

4. John Laffin, *Women in Battle*, 64–65.

5. Martin Gilbert, *The Second World War: A Complete History* (New York: Henry Holt, 1989), 72, 80, 83.

6. Eve Gordon, "War Stories," *MINERVA: Quarterly Report on Women and the Military* 7, nos. 3 and 4 (Fall/Winter 1989): 69–70.

7. Dyer, *War,* 90.

8. Gordon, "War Stories," 68–69.

8. Because the home guard role is more easily accepted for women than regular military service, there is much more written about women partisans of World War II than about women serving in regular military units. In terms of numbers, there were far more women in combatant roles in the Red Army alone than in partisan forces. Many scholars feel that popular works have romanticized and grossly exaggerated the importance of women partisans and dismiss them as of slight military significance in the war. For one who disagrees, see Kenneth D. Slepyan, "'The People's Avengers': Soviet Partisans, Stalinist Society and the Politics of Resistance, 1941–1944," (Ph.D. dissertation, University of Michigan, 1994).

10. Laffin, *Women in Battle,* 12.

11. Shelley Saywell, *Women in War: From World War II to El Salvador* (Ontario: Penguin Books, 1985), 85.

12. Eleni Fourtouni, *Greek Women in Resistance* (New Haven, Conn.: Thelphini Press, 1986).

13. Victoria de Grazia, *How Fascism Ruled Women: Italy, 1922–1945* (Berkeley: University of California Press, 1992), 74.

14. Saywell, *Women in War,* 74.

15. Ibid., 81.

16. Ibid., 82.

17. Marie Madeleine Fourcade, *Noah's Ark* (New York: E. Dutton, 1974).

18. Ibid., 38. The most recent survey of women in the French resistance is Margaret Collins Weitz, *Sisters in the Resistance: How Women Fought to Free France, 1940–1945* (New York: John Wiley, 1995).

19. Margaret Rossiter, *Women in the Resistance* (New York: Praeger, 1986).

20. Jan Öjvind Swahn, *The Tale of Cupid and Psyche* (Lund: C. W. K. Gleerup, 1955), 222, 247, 270–73, 436–38.

21. Barbara Jancar, "Yugoslavia: War of Resistance," in Goldman,*Female Soldiers,* 87.

22. Ibid., 91.

23. Vladimir Dedijer, *With Tito Through the War: Partisan Diary, 1941–1944* (London: Alexander Hamilton, 1951).

24. Quoted in "Waldheim Admits Link to 'Pacification,'" *Washington Post,* October 30, 1986, A50.

25. I. C. B. Dear and M. R. D. Foot, eds., *The Oxford Companion to World War II* (Oxford: Oxford University Press, 1995), 109.

26. K. Jean Cottam, "Soviet Women in Combat in World War II: The Ground Forces and the Navy," *International Journal of Women's Studies* 3 (1980): 345–47.

27. K. Jean Cottam, ed. and trans., *The Golden-tressed Soldier* (Manhattan, Kans.: MA/AH, 1983), introd.

28. Griesse and Stites, "Russia: Revolution and War," 69.

29. Ibid.

30. Ibid., 69–70.

31. The first English-language book on this subject was Bruce Myles, *The Night Witches: The Untold Story of Soviet Women in Combat* (Novato, Calif.: Presidio, 1981), which suffered from the author's need to conduct interviews through Soviet interpreters. A Canadian researcher, K. Jean Cottam, did valuable service by translating a series of Soviet sources, including *Soviet Airwomen in Combat in World War II* (Manhattan, Kans.: MA/AH, 1983). A recent popular piece, based on new interviews with women veterans, is Reina Pennington, "Wings, Women, and War," *Air & Space* 8, no. 5 (December 1993/January 1994): 74–85. Pennington's master's thesis with the same title (University of South Carolina, 1993) will soon be published by the University of Kansas Press.

32. In addition to the materials cited above, see K. Jean Cottam, *The Girl from Kashin: Soviet Women in Resistance in World War II* (Manhattan, Kans.: MA/AH, 1984); and Anne Noggle, *A Dance with Death: Soviet Airwomen in World War II* (College Station: Texas A&M University Press, 1994).

33. Saywell, *Women in War,* 132.

34. Ibid., 147.

35. Ibid., 148.

36. S. Alexiyevich, *War's Unwomanly Face* (Moscow: Progress Publishers, 1988).

37. Ibid., 54.

38. Ibid., 34–36.

39. Ibid., 154, 158.

40. Ibid., 39–40.

41. Ibid., 40.

42. Ibid., 216–18.

43. Ibid., 55.

44. Ibid., 56.

45. Ibid., 107, 109.

46. Ibid., 189–90.

47. For the oral history of a woman SS guard, see Allison Owings, *Frauen: German Women Recall the Third Reich* (New Brunswick, N.J.: Rutgers University Press, 1995).

48. A recent biography of this unusual woman is Dennis Piszkiewicz, *From Nazi Test Pilot to Hitler's Bunker: The Fantastic Flights of Hannah Reitsch* (Westport, Conn.: Praeger, 1997).

49. Moolman, *Women Aloft,* 154–57. Reitsch and Melitta Schilla-Stauffenberg, another woman test pilot, were the only women to be awarded the Iron Cross (first class). D'Ann Campbell, "Women in Combat: The World War II Experience in the United States, Great Britain, Germany, and the Soviet Union," *Journal of Military History* 57 (April 1993): 317n.

50. Jeff M. Tuten, "Germany and the World Wars," in Goldman, *Female Soldiers,* 49. See also Jill Stephenson, *Women in Nazi Society* (New York: Harper & Row, 1975); and Leila Rupp, *Mobilizing Women for War: German and American Propaganda, 1939-1945* (Princeton: Princeton University Press, 1978).

51. Tuten, "Germany and the World Wars," 55. There may have been occasional exceptions to the weapons rule in areas close to the Russian front. Campbell, "Women in Combat," 317.

52. Louise Willmot, "Women in the Third Reich: The Auxiliary Military Service Law of 1944," *German History* 2 (1985): 10–20.

53. Campbell, "Women in Combat," 317–18.

54. Associated Press, Washington, D.C., May 31, 1945; Associated Press, Lakeview, Ore., June 1, 1945.

55. Piedmont and Gurney, *Highlights in the History of the Army Nurse Corps,* 18.

56. A recently published memoir by a POW nurse is Dorothy Still Danner, *What a Way to Spend a War: Navy Nurse POWs in the Philippines* (Annapolis, Md.: Naval Institute Press, 1995).

57. C. Kay Larson, *'Til I Come Marching Home: A Brief History of American Women in World War II* (Pasadena, Md.: The MINERVA Center, 1995), 73–74.

58. The first American woman to go ashore was probably the war correspondent Martha Gellhorn, who stowed away on a water ambulance on D-Day plus one. Martha Gellhorn, *The Face of War* (New York: Atlantic Monthly Press, 1988), 109–20.

59. Kathryn Van Wagner, "Flight Nurse at Iwo," *Navy Medicine* 86 (March/April 1995): 9.

60. Edward E. Rosenbaum, "The Doctor Is In," *New Choices* (July 1989): 25.

61. Mattie E. Treadwell, *United States Army in World War II, Special Studies, the Women's Army Corps* (Washington, D.C.: U.S. Department of the Army, 1954); Hancock, *Lady in the Navy;* Ebbert and Hall, *Crossed Currents;* Peter A. Soderbergh, *Women Marines: The World War II Era* (West-port, Conn.: Praeger, 1992); Judy Barrett Litoff and David C. Smith, *We're in this War, Too: World War II Letters from American Women in Uniform* (New York: Oxford University Press, 1994).

62. D'Ann Campbell, *Women at War with America: Private Lives in a Patriotic Era* (Cambridge, Mass.: Harvard University Press, 1984); Susan M. Hartmann, *The Home Front and Beyond: American Women in the 1940's* (Boston: Twayne, 1982).

63. General histories of nursing that pay some attention to military medicine are Philip A. Kalisch and Beatrice J. Kalisch, *The Advance of American Nursing* (Boston: Little, Brown, 1978); and Mary M. Roberts, *American Nursing: History and Interpretation* (New York: Macmillan, 1954); Judith Bellafaire, *The Army Nurse Corps in World War II* (Washington, D.C.: U.S. Army Center of Military History, 1993); George Korson, *At His Side: The Story of the American Red Cross Overseas in World War II* (New York: Coward-McCann, 1945). Important contributions have recently been made by Barbara Tomblin: "Beyond Paradise: The U.S. Navy Nurse Corps in the Pacific in World War II," pt. 1, *MINERVA: Quarterly Report on Women and the Military* 11, no. 2 (Summer 1993): 33–53, and pt. 2, Ibid., 11, nos. 3–4 (Fall/Winter, 1993): 37–56; and *G.I. Nightingales: The Army Nurse Corps in World War II* (Lexington: University Press of Kentucky, 1996) See also Doris M. Sterner, *In and Out of Harm's Way: A History of the Navy Nurse Corps* (Seattle: Peanut Butter Press, 1997).

64. Jeanne Holm, *Women in the Military: An Unfinished Revolution,* rev. ed. (Novato, Calif.: Presidio, 1992), 22.

65. Campbell, "Women in Combat," 306–13.

66. Treadwell, *The Women's Army Corps,* 301–2; Campbell, "Women in Combat," 303–6.

67. Elna Hilliard Grahn, *In the Company of WACS* (Manhattan, Kans.: Sunflower University Press, 1993), 35, 39.

68. Treadwell, *The Women's Army Corps,* 191–218.

69. Hirscheld, *The Sexual History of the World War,* 53, 54.

70. Ibid., 56, 57.

71. Treadwell, *The Women's Army Corps,* 218.

72. Ibid., 201.

73. Ibid., 203.

74. Ibid., 204.

75. Ibid.

76. Ibid., 205.

77. Ibid., 206 n 59. The complete investigation file is in G-2 files, MID 322.12 WAAC in the National Archives of the United States.

78. Treadwell, *The Women's Army Corps,* 218.

79. Ibid., 216.

80. Ibid., 218.

81. Ernie Pyle, "Roving Reporter," July 9, 1943 (syndicated column).

82. Deborah G. Douglas, *United States Women in Aviation, 1940-1985* (Washington, D.C.: Smithsonian Institution Press, 1991), 52.

83. As was the case for Soviet women during World War II, the American women flyers, a small elite group, have received much more extensive study than other women veterans. Book-length studies include Sally Van Wegener Keil, *Those Wonderful Women in Their Flying Machines: The Unknown Heroines of World War II* (New York: Rawson, Wade, 1979); and Marianne Verges, *On Silver Wings: The Women Airforce Service Pilots of World War II* (New York: Ballantine Books, 1991). Several of these dynamic, articulate women have written their own histories: Jean Hascall Cole, *Women Pilots of World War II* (Salt Lake City: University of Utah Press, 1992); and Byrd Howell Granger, *On Final Approach: The Women Airforce Service Pilots of World War II* (Scottsdale, Ariz.: Falconer, 1991). A substantial number have published personal memoirs, and they are well represented in collections of oral histories. A recent academic study is Molly Merryman, *Clipped Wings: The Rise and Fall of the Women Airforce Service Pilots of World War II* (New York: New York University Press, 1997).

84. Ebbert and Hall, *Crossed Currents,* 86–87.

85. Treadwell, *The Women's Army Corps,* 597.

86. Ibid., 597–98.

87. Ibid., 599. See also Martha S. Putney, *When the Nation Was in Need: Blacks in the Women's Army Corps During World War II* (Metuchen, N.J.: Scarecrow Press, 1992); Charity Adams Early, *One Woman's Army: A Black Officer Remembers the WAC* (College Station: Texas A&M University Press, 1989); Brenda L. Moore, *To Serve My Country, to Serve My Race: The Story of the Only African-American WACs Stationed Overseas During World War II* (New York: New York University Press, 1996).

88. John Costello, *Virtue Under Fire: How World War II Changed Our Social and Sexual Attitudes* (Boston: Little, Brown, 1985), 213.

89. Ibid., 214.

90. Ibid.

91. Ibid., 213.

92. Ibid., 225.

93. Ibid., 224.

94. Ibid., 222.

95. Richard Symanski, *The Immoral Landscape: Female Prostitution in Western Societies* (Toronto: Butterworths, 1981), 101.

96. Ibid., 219.

97. *Minerva's Bulletin Board* 5, no. 2 (Spring 1992): 8–9. Many newspapers, including the *Washington Post* and the *New York Times,* published articles on the comfort women on August 5, 1993. The first book-length study in English is George Hicks, *The Comfort Women: Japan's Brutal Regime of Enforced Prostitution in the Second World War* (New York: W. W. Norton, 1994), which contains a select annotated bibliography but no footnotes.

98. E. O. Reischauer, *The Japanese* (Tokyo: Charles E. Tuttle, 1978), 205.

99. W. G. Aston, trans., *Nihongi: Chronicles of Japan from the Earliest Times to A.D. 669* (Rutland, Vt.: Charles E. Tuttle, 1972), 224–53.

100. Ibid., 296, 527–28.

101. Chieko Irie Mulhern, ed., *Heroic with Grace: Legendary Women of Japan* (Armonk, N.Y.: M. E. Sharpe, 1991).

102. Yamamoto Tsunetomo, *Hagakure: The Book of the Samurai,* trans. William Scott Wilson, (Tokyo: Kodansha International, 1979 [originally published 1716]), 165.

103. Karl L. Wiegand, "Japan: Cautious Utilization," in Goldman, *Female Soldiers,* 179.

104. Richard Deacon, *Kempei Tai: A History of the Japanese Secret Service* (New York: Berkley Books, 1985), 150.

105. Ibid., 151.

106. Thomas R. H. Havens, *Valley of Darkness: The Japanese People and World War Two* (New York: W. W. Norton, 1978), 188–9.

107. Ibid., 189; *Tomiko Higa, The Girl with the White Flag,* trans. Dorothy Britton (Tokyo: Kodansha International, 1991); Jo Nobuko Martin, *A Princess Lily of the Ryokyus* (Tokyo: Shin Nippon Kyoiku Tosho, 1984). A memoir by one of the women is Miyagi Kikuko, "Student Nurses of the 'Lily Corps,'" in Haruko Taya Cook and Theodore F. Cook, eds. *Japan at War: An Oral History* (New York: New Press, 1982), 354–63.

101. Associated Press, "With the Tenth Army on Okinawa," June 7, 1945.

109. Associated Press, Temple, Texas, June 13, 1945.

110. Associated Press, Akron, Ohio, November 30, 1942.

111. A useful bibliographic essay on American women, broader than the title of the book suggests, appears in Litoft and Smith, *We're in this War, Too,* 261–64.

112. Sherna Berger Gluck, *Rosie the Riveter Revisited: Women, the War and Social Change* (Boston: Twayne, 1987); Karen Anderson, *Wartime Women: Sex Roles, Family Relations and the Status of Women During World War II* (Westport, Conn.: Greenwood Press, 1981); Maureen Honey, *Creating Rosie the Riveter: Class, Gender and Propaganda During World War II* (Amherst: University of Massachusetts Press, 1984); Amy Kesselman, *Fleeting Opportunities: Women Shipyard Workers in Portland and Vancouver During World War II and Reconversion* (Albany: State University of New York Press, 1990); Ruth Milkman, *Gender at Work: The Dynamics of Job Segregation by Sex During World War II* (Urbana: University of Illinois Press, 1987); Leila Rupp, *Mobilizing Women for War;* Mary Martha Thomas, *Riveting and Rationing in Dixie: Alabama Women in the Second World War* (Tuscaloosa: University of Alabama Press, 1987).

113. An overview of the bibliography is Joan Ringelheim, "Women and the Holocaust: A Reconsideration of Research," in Judith Reesa Baskin, ed., *Jewish Women in Historical Perspective* (Detroit: Wayne State University Press, 1991), 243–64. A sampling of recent books by academics is Robin Ruth Linden, *Making Stories, Making Selves: Feminist Reflections on the Holocaust* (Columbus: Ohio State University Press, 1993); Lore Shelley, *Criminal Experiments on Human Beings in Auschwitz and War Research Laboratories: Twenty Women Prisoners' Accounts* (San Francisco: Mellen Research University Press, 1991); Ruth Schwertfeger, *The Women of Theresien-stadt: Voices from a*

Concentration Camp (New York: St. Martin's Press, 1989); Andreas Lixl, *Women of Exile: German-Jewish Autobiographies Since 1933* (New York: Greenwood Press, 1988); Marlene E. Heinemann, *Gender and Destiny: Women Writers and the Holocaust* (Westport, Conn.: Greenwood Press, 1986). Not all Nazi victims were passive. For women who fought back, see Vera Laska, *Nazism, Resistance and Holocaust in World War II: A Bibliography* (Metuchen, NJ: Scarecrow Press, 1985) and Hermann Langbein, *Against All Hope: Resistance in the Nazi Concentration Camps,* trans. Harry Zohn (New York: Continuum, 1996).

114. See note 72, above.

115. An example of scholarship on prostitution is Beth Bailey and David Farber, *The First Strange Place: Race and Sex in World War II Hawaii* (Baltimore: Johns Hopkins University Press, 1992). There is also untranslated literature on the Japanese "comfort women" as well as an unfootnoted popular work in English, Hicks, *The Comfort Women.*

CHAPTER TEN: *The Cold War*

1. John Keegan, *The Face of Battle* (New York: Vintage Books, 1977), 16.

2. See, for example, Robert B. Asprey, *War in Shadows: The Guerrilla in History* (Garden City, N.Y.: Doubleday, 1957), and Walter Laqueur, *Guerrilla: A Historical and Critical Study* (Boston: Little, Brown, 1976).

3. A valuable collection of articles on more than a dozen wars is Mary Ann Tetréault, ed., *Women and Revolution in Africa, Asia, and the New World* (Columbia: University of South Carolina Press, 1994).

4. Surveys of American women in military service since World War II include Holm, *Women in the Military*; Bettie J. Morden, *The Women's Army Corps, 1945-1978* (Washington, D.C.: U.S. Army Center of Military History, 1990); Ebbert and Hall, *Crossed Currents.* A useful brief summary is M. C. Devilbiss, *Women and Military Service: A History, Analysis, and Overview of Key Issues* (Maxwell Air Force Base, Ala.: Air University Press, 1990).

5. Holm, *Women in the Military,* 162.

6. The first book by a Vietnam era nurse was a novel published in 1982: Patricia L. Walsh, *Forever Sad the Hearts* (New York: Avon, 1982). This was followed a year later by a brutally honest biography: Lynda Van Devanter, with Christopher Morgan, *Home Before Morning: The True Story of an Army Nurse in Vietnam* (New York: Warner Books, 1983). The first anthology of military and civilian women's stories about Vietnam was Keith Walker, *A Piece of My Heart* (New York: Ballantine Books, 1985). Since then, published memoirs have

proliferated. A recent contribution is Winnie Smith, *American Daughter Gone to War: On the Front Lines with an Army Nurse in Vietnam* (New York: William Morrow, 1992). A scholarly historical study of Vietnam nursing, however, is yet to be written.

7. Holm, *Women in the Military*, 211.

8. Mary Haas, *Women's Perspectives on the Vietnam War* (Pittsburgh: Center for Social Studies Education, 1991), 16–17.

9. Ibid., 4.

10. Jackson, *Women Who Ruled*, 154–55. See also, Arlene Eisen-Bergman, *Women of Viet Nam* (San Francisco: People's Press, 1975).

11. Jackson, *Women Who Ruled*, 154.

12. William J. Duiker, "Vietnam: War of Insurgency," in Goldman, *Female Soldiers*, 107–22.

13. Holm, *Women in the Military*, 210.

14. Except where otherwise noted, the sources for the following paragraphs are Arlene Eisen, *Women and Revolution in Viet Nam* (Atlantic Highlands, N.J.: Humanities Press International, 1984), and Haas, *Women's Perspectives on the Vietnam War*.

15. Laffin, *Women in Battle*, 77–78.

16. Ibid., 78–79.

17. Ibid., 77; John Clarey, "Twilight Zone East," *Vietnam* 5, no. 4 (1992): 41–43.

18. Clarey, "Twilight Zone East," 42.

19. A 1968 U.S. intelligence report estimated that half of some guerrilla units were women. In the same year, the government of North Vietnam reported 250,000 women combatants killed, 40,000 wounded, and 36,000 captured as prisoners of war. Shelly Saywell, *Women in War*, 321n. The Women's Museum in Ho Chi Minh City estimates that by the time of American withdrawal, more than 70 percent of the guerrilla forces were women.

20. "Senior Vietcong Woman Dies," *Minerva's Bulletin Board* 5, no. 3 (Fall 1992): 3–4. See also Dinh's autobiography: *Nguyen Thi Dinh, No Other Road to Take* (Ithaca: Cornell University SEA Data Paper no. 102, June 1976).

21. "Eleven Girls of Hue Defeated One American Battalion," in *Scenes of the General Offensive and Uprising* (Hanoi: FLPH, 1968), 21–26.

22. Cristina Pozzan, *As the Mirror Burns* (Video Australia, 1990). See also Tom Mangold and John Penycate, *The Tunnels of Cu Chi* (London: Hodder and Stoughton, 1985), passim.

23. Susan Brownmiller, *Against Our Will*, 90–91.

24. Ibid., 91–92.

25. Quoted in ibid., 94.

26. Ibid., 95; Symanski, *The Immoral Landscape*, 102.

27. A handy summary of both sides of the debate is M. C. Devilbiss, "Women in Combat: A Quick Summary of the Arguments on Both Sides," *MINERVA: Quarterly Report on Women and the Military* 8, no. 1 (Spring 1990): 29–32.

28. Lee Virginia Chambers-Schiller, *Liberty a Better Husband, Single Women in America: The Generations of 1780-1840* (New Haven: Yale University Press, 1984), 1.

29. Ibid., 1.

30. Ibid., 190–91. Emphasis in original.

31. Katharine Bement Davis, *Factors in the Sex Life of Twenty-Two Hundred Women* (New York: Harper & Row, 1929), 247.

32. Ibid., 201.

33. Faderman, *Odd Girls and Twilight Lovers*, 119.

34. Ibid.

35. Ibid., 121.

36. Ibid., 123.

37. Ibid., 125.

38. Ibid., 130–38.

39. Betty Friedan, *The Feminine Mystique* (New York: W. W. Norton, 1963).

40. Jill Johnston, *Lesbian Nation: The Feminist Solution* (New York: Simon & Schuster 1973).

41. A collection of oral histories is Winni S. Webber, *Lesbians in the Military Speak Out* (Northboro, Mass.: Madwoman Press, 1993). Public tolerance of lesbians has increased dramatically since 1990, and lesbians are becoming more willing to share their histories openly. See, for example, Margarethe Cammermeyer, with Chris Fisher, *Serving in Silence* (New York: Viking Press, 1994); and the only slightly fictionalized account of a military career, Beth F. Coye, Commander, U.S. Navy (Ret.), *My Navy Too: A Political Novel Based on Real Life Experiences* (Ashland, Ore.: Cedar Hollow Press, 1997). Miriam Ben-Shalom's autobiography, *Out, On Point,* is in preparation.

42. Humphrey, *My Country, My Right to Serve*, 187–93.

43. Vice Admiral Joseph Donnell's memo dated July 24, 1990 was leaked to the press and generated a flurry of protests from gay and women's groups and their supporters. See, for instance, Jane Gross, "Navy Is Urged to Root Out Lesbians Despite Ability," *New York Times*, September 2, 1995.

44. The first description of army women's activity in Grenada was written by the senior woman officer on the scene and published a year after the events it describes: Ann Wright, "The Roles of Army Women in Grenada," *MINERVA: Quarterly Report on Women and the Military* 2, no. 2 (Summer 1984): 103-13.

45. "Combat Controversy Destroyed Her Career Says Linda Bray," *Minerva's Bulletin Board* 4, no. 2 (Summer 1991): 4-5.

46. John A. Garraty, ed., *The Young Reader's Companion to American History* (Boston: Houghton Mifflin, 1994), 52.

47. Quoted in Anne R. Bloom, "Israel: The Longest War," in Nancy Loring Goldman, *Female Soldiers*, 156.

48. Ibid., 140.

49. Ibid., 143.

50. Ibid.

51. David Ben-Gurion, *Israel: A Personal History* (Tel Aviv: American Israel Publishing Co., 1972), 54.

52. Bloom, "Israel: The Longest War," 144-46.

53. Ibid., 147-48.

54. Ibid., 148.

55. Ibid., 149.

56. Ibid., 151.

57. *Minerva's Bulletin Board* 9, no. 1 (Spring 1996): 7.

58. Ben-Gurion, *Israel*, 376.

59. Quoted in Bloom, "Israel: The Longest War," 156.

60. Lionel Tiger, *Men in Groups* (New York: Vintage Books, 1970), 104-5.

61. Two recent English-language books on Palestinian women are Elise G. Young, *Keepers of the History: Women and the Israeli-Palestinian Conflict* (New York: Teachers College Press, 1992); and Najjar Orayb Aref and Kitty Warnock, *Portraits of Palestinian Women* (Salt Lake City: University of Utah Press, 1992).

62. Eileen MacDonald, *Shoot the Women First* (New York: Random House, 1991).

63. Ibid., 33-62; See also Kim Hyun Hee, *The Tears of My Soul* (New York: William Morrow, 1993).

64. MacDonald, *Shoot the Women First,* xiv.

65. Freda Hussain and Kamelia Radwan, "The Islamic Revolution and Women: Quest for the Kuranic Model," in Freda Hussain, ed. *Freda Hussain Muslim Women* (London: Croom Helm, 1984), 44.

66. Reuters, September 19, 1985, quoted in Minou Reeves, *Female Warriors of Allah: Women and the Islamic Revolution* (New York: E. P. Dutton, 1989), 7–8.

CHAPTER ELEVEN: *Third World Wars*

1. Guy S. Goodwin-Gill and Ilene Cohn, *Child Soldiers: A Study on Behalf of the Henry Dunant Institute* (Oxford: Oxford University Press, 1994); Rachel Brett and Margaret McCallin, *Children: The Invisible Soldiers* (Geneva: Swedish Save the Children, 1996).

2. These examples are drawn primarily from issues of *Minerva's Bulletin Board,* an international news magazine on women and the military published quarterly by The MINERVA Center in Pasadena, Maryland. Zed Books, a London publisher specializing in books about Third World women, is a good source for English language materials. Among Zed Books publications are Helen Collinson, ed., *Women and Revolution in Nicaragua* (1990), and Tessa Cleaver and Marion Wallace, *Nambia Women in War* (1990).

3. *Minerva's Bulletin Board* 2, no. 1 (Spring 1989): 14.

4. Ibid.

5. *Minerva's Bulletin Board* 1, no. 3 (Fall 1988): 3; Reuters, Ashraf Camp, Iraq, November 6, 1995; "Mullahs, Look! Women, Armed and Dangerous," *New York Times International,* December 30, 1996.

6. *Minerva's Bulletin Board* 5, no. 3 (Fall 1992).

7. Timothy C. Brown, "Women Unfit for Combat? Au Contraire!" *Wall Street Journal,* September 30, 1997.

8. *Minerva's Bulletin Board* 10, no. 2 (Summer 1997): 1

9. Ibid., 1, no. 3 (Fall 1988): 3, no. 2 (Summer 1990): 5, no. 3 (Fall 1992).

10. Fraser, *The Warrior Queens,* 183, n80. On the war in Zimbabwe, see also Irene Staunton, ed., *Mothers of the Revolution: The War Experiences of Thirty Zimbabwean Women* (Bloomington: Indiana University Press, 1991).

11. "Women Make Up One-Third of Eritrean Guerrillas," *Minerva's Bulletin Board* 1, no. 3 (Fall 1988): 3–4; Miles, *The Women's History of the World,* 230.

12. "Eritrean Women Who Fought in the Trenches Now Battle Tradition," *The Washington Post,* June 25, 1993, A-30.

13. Stanislava Stasa Zajovic, "Ex-Yugoslavia," *Connexions,* no. 42 (1993): 19, 27.

14. "Sarajevo's Female Forces Fight 'to Live Like Girls,'" *Washington Times,* October 31, 1992, A1, A12.

15. "Navy Women are First to Fly Combat Missions," *Minerva's Bulletin Board* 7, nos. 3 and 4 (Fall/Winter 1994): 1; "Air Force Reservist Is First Woman to Fly Combat Over Bosnia," *Minerva's Bulletin Board* 8, no. 3 (Fall 1995): 1.

16. For discussion of sexual and nonsexual abuse of women beginning long before the Tailhook scandal focused attention on the issue see Donna M. Dean, *Warriors Without Weapons: The Victimization of Military Women* (Pasadena, Md: The Minerva Center, 1997).

17. Stories about military sex scandals filled the American popular media as well as the service publications such as *Navy Times* and *Army Times* from 1992 on. The first major scandal involved military aviators at the Tailhook Association's 1991 convention. For a survey, see Jean Zimmerman, *Tailspin: Women at War in the Wake of Tailhook* (New York: Doubleday, 1995); and Linda Bird Francke, *Ground Zero: The Gender Wars in the Military* (New York: Simon & Schuster, 1997). Major scandals hit the army in the fall of 1996 with the revelation of abuse of army women by drill sergeants at Aberdeen Proving Ground, Maryland, followed by charges of sexual assault against the army's senior enlisted member, Sgt. Maj. Gene McKinney.

18. Carolyn Hart, "Women Have Real Roles in Militias," *Media Bypass Magazine* 4, no. 10 (October 1996): 12.

19. Hart, "Women Have Real Roles in Militias, 12–13.

20. George Leonard, *The Silent Pulse* (New York: E. P. Dutton, 1978), 162.

21. A useful overview is Michael Renner, *Fighting for Survival: Environmental Decline, Social Conflict, and the New Age of Insecurity,* 2d ed. (New York: W. W. Norton, 1996).

22. Laurie Garrett, *The Coming Plague: Newly Emerging Diseases in a World Out of Balance* (New York: Farrar, Straus and Giroux, 1994), 572–73.

23. Ibid., 618. See also Kevin M. Cahill, MD, *Preventive Diplomacy: Stopping Wars Before They Start* (New York: Basic Books, 1996), especially the essay by Dr. Erin O'Brien.

24. Cynthia Enloe, *The Morning After: Sexual Politics at the End of the Cold War* (Berkeley: University of California Press, 1993), 241–43.

25. Lt. Lisa Brodin, "Rwanda Diary," *War Cry,* February 18, 1994, 14.

26. "New Twist for U.S. Troops: Peace Maneuvers," *Washington Post,* August 15, 1994, A1.

27. "Responsibilities of U.S. Military Expanded," *Washington Post,* March 9, 1995, A36.

28. *Minerva's Bulletin Board* 7, 3–4 (Fall–Winter 1994): 1; 8, no. 3 (Fall 1995): 1.

29. Enloe, *The Morning After,* chap. 1.

28. Marilyn Ferguson, *The Aquarian Conspiracy: Personal and Social Transformation in the 1980's* (Los Angeles: J. Tarcher, 1980), 347. See also Jim Channon, *Evolutionary Tactics: The First Earth Battalion Operations Manual,* (n. p.: privately published, 1982).

31. There is a growing literature on conflict resolution, and the emphasis on the "peace process" in various third world wars raging today reflects an understanding that negotiated agreements in which everyone wins are possible and infinitely preferable to warfare. A brief, easily understandable introduction to this subject is Arnold Gerstein and James Reagan, *Win-Win: Approaches to Conflict Resolution at Home, in Business, Between Groups, and Across Cultures* (Salt Lake City: Peregrine Smith Books, 1986). See also Robert J. Burrowes, *The Strategy of Nonviolent Defense: A Gandhian Approach* (Albany: State University of New York Press, 1996); I. William Zartman, ed., *Elusive Peace: Negotiating an End to Civil Wars* (Washington, D.C.: Brookings Institute, 1995).

32. Heckler, *In Search of the Warrior Spirit,* 2.

33. Ibid., 13.

34. Forrest E. Morgan, *Living the Martial Way: A Manual for the Way a Modern Warrior Should Think* (Fort Lee, N.J.: Barricade Books, 1992), 13–14.

35. Jones, *Women Warriors,* ix–xiii.

36. For examples of disciplines recommended for peaceful warriors, see Dan Millman, *Way of the Peaceful Warrior* (Tiburon, Calif.: H. J. Kramer, 1980), and Danaan Parry, *Warriors of the Heart* (Cooperstown, N.Y.: Sunstone Publications, 1989).

WORKS CITED

Abbott, Nabia. "Pre-Islamic Arab Queens." *American Journal of Semitic Languages and Literature,* 58 (1941): 1–22.

Abray, Jane. "Feminism in the French Revolution." *American Historical Review,* 80 (1975): 43–62.

Adams, Michael C. C. *The Great Adventure: Male Desire and the Coming of World War I.* Bloomington: Indiana University Press, 1990.

Addington, Larry H. *The Patterns of War through the Eighteenth Century.* Bloomington: Indiana University Press, 1990.

Alexiyevich, S. *War's Unwomanly Face.* Moscow: Progress Publishers, 1988.

Anderson, Karen. *Wartime Women: Sex Roles, Family Relations and the Status of Women During World War II.* Westport, Conn.: Greenwood Press, 1981.

Anderson, Merle. "My Battle With the Pentagon." Unpublished manuscript.

Aref, Najjar Orayb, and Kitty Warnock. *Portraits of Palestinian Women.* Salt Lake City: University of Utah Press, 1992.

Asprey, Robert B. *War in Shadows: The Guerrilla in History.* Garden City, N.Y.: Doubleday, 1957.

Aston, W. G., trans. *Nihongi: Chronicles of Japan from the Earliest Times to* A.D. *669.* Rutland, Vt.: Charles E. Tuttle, 1972.

Atteridge, A. H. "The Forest Fighting in Dahomey: 1892." In *Battles of the 19th Century,* edited by A. Forbes et al., 647–658. London: Cassell, 1896.

Auguet, Roland. *Cruelty and Civilization: The Roman Games.* London: Ruskin House, 1972.

Axtell, James. "The Vengeful Women of Marblehead: Robert Roules's Deposition of 1677." *William and Mary Quarterly* 31 (1974).

——ed. *The Indian Peoples of Eastern America: A Documentary History of the Sexes.* New York: Oxford University Press, 1981.

Bagnold, Enid. *A Diary without Dates.* London: Heinemann, 1918.

Bailey, Beth, and David Farber. *The First Strange Place: Race and Sex in World War II Hawaii.* Baltimore: Johns Hopkins University Press, 1992.

Ballhatchet, Kenneth. *Race, Sex, and Class under the Raj: Imperial Attitudes and Policies and Their Critics, 1793–1905.* London: Weidenfeld and Nicolson, 1980.

Baly, M. E. *Florence Nightingale and the Nursing Legacy.* Dover, N.H.: Croom Helm, 1986.

Bangs, Edward, ed., *Journal of Lieutenant Isaac Bangs, April 1 to July 29, 1776.* Cambridge, Mass.: John Wilson & Son, 1890.

Bao, Jia Lin, ed. *Collected Works on the History of Chinese Women.* Tai Pei: Mu Tong, 1979.

Bardaglio, Peter. "Children of Jubilee: African American Childhood in Wartime." In *Divided Houses: Gender and the Civil War,* edited by Catherine Clinton and Nina Silber, 213–29. New York: Oxford University Press, 1992.

Bassermann, Lujo. *The Oldest Profession: A History of Prostitution.* Translated by James Clough. London: Barker, 1967.

Beard, Mary Ritter. *Woman as Force in History: A Study in Traditions and Realities.* New York: Macmillan, 1946.

Bellafaire, Judith. *The Army Nurse Corps in World War II.* Washington, D.C.: U.S. Army Center of Military History, 1993.

Ben-Gurion, David. *Israel, a Personal History.* Tel Aviv: American Israel Publishing Co., 1972.

Benjamin, Harry. "Morals versus Morale in Wartime." *In Morals in Wartime,* edited by Victor Robinson, 177–203. New York: Publishers Foundation, 1943.

Bennett, Florence Mary. *Religious Cults Associated with the Amazons.* New York: AMS Press, 1967.

Birmingham, David. *Trade and Conflict in Angola: The Mbundu and Their Neighbors under the Influence of the Portuguese.* Oxford: Oxford University Press, 1966.

Bishop, W. J., and Goldie S. Bishop. *A Biobibliography of Florence Nightingale.* London: Dawsons of Pall Mall for the International Council of Nurses, 1962.

Blanton, DeAnne. "Women Soldiers of the Civil War." *Prologue: Quarterly of the National Archives* 11 (Spring 1993): 27–33.

Bloom, Anne R. "Israel: The Longest War." *In Female Soldiers—Cambatants or*

Noncombatants? Historical and Contemporary Perspectives, edited by Nancy Loring Goldman, 137–62. Westpoint, Conn.: Greenwood Press, 1986.

Blumenthal, Walter Hart. *Women Camp Followers of the American Revolution.* Philadelphia: George S. MacManus, 1952.

Bochkareva, Maria, as told to Isaac Don Levine. *Yashika: My Life as a Peasant Officer and Exile.* New York: Frederick A. Stokes, 1929.

Borden, Mary. *The Forbidden Zone.* London: Heinemann, 1929.

Boynton, Edward C. *History of West Point and Its Military Importance During the American Revolution.* New York: D. Van Nostrand, 1871.

Bradford, Sarah H. *Harriet Tubman: The Moses of Her People.* New York: Corinth Books, 1961.

Braybon, Gail. *Women Workers in the First World War: The British Experience.* London: Croom Helm, 1981.

Brett, Rachel, and Margaret McCallin. *Children: The Invisible Soldiers.* Geneva: Swedish Save the Children, 1996.

Briffault, Robert. *The Mothers.* Abridged by Gordon Rattray Taylor. New York: Atheneum, 1977.

Brittain, Vera. *Testament of Youth.* London: Victor Gollancz, 1933.

Brockett, Linus Pierpont, and Mary C. Vaughan. *Women's Work in the Civil War.* Philadelphia: Ziegler, McCurdy; Boston: R. H. Curran, 1867.

Brodin, Lisa. "Rwanda Diary." *War Cry,* February 18, 1994, 14.

Brown, Marvin L., Jr. trans. *Baroness von Riedesel and the American Revolution: Journal and Correspondence of a Tour of Duty, 1776–1783.* Chapel Hill: University of North Carolina Press, 1965.

Brownmiller, Susan. *Against Our Will: Men, Women and Rape.* New York: Simon & Schuster, 1975.

Bryant, Louise. *Six Red Months in Russia: An Observer's Account of Russia Before and During the Proletarian Dictatorship.* London: Heinemann, 1918.

Bulst, Christoph. "The Revolt of Queen Boudicca in A.D. 60: Roman Politics and the Iceni." *Historia* 10 (1961): 496–509.

Burgess, Alan. *The Lovely Sergeant.* London: Heinemann, 1963.

Burgess, Lauren Cook, ed. *An Uncommon Soldier: The Civil War Letters of Sarah Rosetta Wakeman, alias Private Lyons Wakeman, 153rd Regiment, New York State Volunteers.* Pasadena, Md.: The MINERVA Center, 1994.

Burrowes, Robert J. *The Strategy of Nonviolent Defense: A Gandhian Approach.* Albany: State University of New York Press, 1996.

Butler, Anne M. "Military Myopia: Prostitution on the Frontier." *Prologue* 13 (Winter 1981): 233–250.

Butler, Caleb. *History of the Town of Groton, Including Pepperel and Shirley from the First Grant of Groton Plantation in 1655.* Boston: Press of T. R. Marvin, 1848.

Cahill, Kevin M., M.D. *Preventive Diplomacy: Stopping Wars Before They Start.* New York: Basic Books, 1996.

Cammermeyer, Margarethe, with Chris Fisher. *Serving in Silence.* New York: Viking Press, 1994.

Campbell, D'Ann. *Women at War with America: Private Lives in a Patriotic Era.* Cambridge, Mass.: Harvard University Press, 1984.

———. "Women in Combat: The World War II Experience in the United States, Great Britain, Germany, and the Soviet Union." *Journal of Military History* 57 (April 1993): 301–23.

Carlsson-Paige, Nancy, and Diane E. Levin. *Who's Calling the Shots? How to Respond Effectively to Children's Fascination with War Play and War Toys.* Philadelphia: New Society Publishers, 1990.

Carr, Sir John. *Descriptive Travels in the Southern and Eastern Parts of Spain and the Balearic Isles.* London: Sherwood, 1809.

Carrington, Dorothy. *Napoleon and His Parents.* New York: E. P. Dutton, 1990.

Casey, Geraldine J. "Eleanor Leacock, Marvin Harris, and the Struggle over Warfare in Anthropology." *In On Peace, War, and Gender: A Challenge to Genetic Explanations,* edited by Anne E. Hunter, 1–33. New York: Feminist Press, 1991.

Chadwick, Nora. *The Celts.* Harmondsworth: Penguin Books, 1970.

Chambers-Schiller, Lee Virginia. *Liberty a Better Husband, Single Women in America: The Generations of 1780–1840.* New Haven: Yale University Press, 1984.

Channon, Jim. *Evolutionary Tactics: The First Earth Battalion Operations Manual.* N. p.: privately published, 1982.

"Civil War Letters of Herman Weiss and Wife Adeline Weiss." In *An Immigrant Goes to War,* History, vol. 4, edited by Harlan B. Phillips. N.p.: Meridian Books, 1961.

Clarey, John. "Twilight Zone East," *Vietnam* 5, no. 4 (1992): 41–43.

Clayton, Ellen C. *Female Warriors: Memorials of Female Valour and Heroism, from the Mythological Ages to the Present Era.* 2 vols. London: Tinsley Brothers, 1879.

Cleaver, Tessa, and Marion Wallace. *Nambia Women in War.* London: Zed Books, 1990.

Clinton, Catherine. "Plantation Mistress." In *Encyclopedia of the Confederacy,* edited by Richard N. Current, 3:1218–19. New York: Simon & Schuster, 1993.

Cohen, David A., ed. *"The Female Marine" and Related Works.* Amherst: University of Massachusetts Press, 1997.

Cole, Jean Hascall. *Women Pilots of World War II.* Salt Lake City: University of Utah Press, 1992.

Collinson, Helen, ed. *Women and Revolution in Nicaragua.* London: Zed Books, 1990.

Condell, Diana, and Jean Liddiard. *Images of Women in the First World War, 1914–1918.* London: Routledge & Kegan Paul, 1987.

Conklin, Elaine F. *Women at Gettysburg, 1863.* Gettysburg, Pa.: Thomas Publications, 1993.

Conrad, Earl. *Harriet Tubman.* Washington, D.C.: Associated Publishers, 1943.

Contenau, Georges. *Everyday Life in Babylon and Assyria.* New York: St. Martin's Press, 1954.

Cooper, Sandi. "Women's Participation in European Peace Movements: The Effort to Prevent World War I." In *Women and Peace,* Ruth Roach Pierson, 51–75, London: Croom Helm, 1987.

———. "Women in War and Peace, 1914–1945." In *Becoming Visible: Women in European History,* 3d ed., edited by Renate Bridenthal, Susan Stuard, and Merry Wiesner, 439–60. Boston: Houghton Mifflin, 1998.

Costello, John. *Virtue Under Fire: How World War II Changed Our Social and Sexual Attitudes.* Boston: Little, Brown, 1985.

Cottam, K. Jean. *The Girl from Kashin: Soviet Women in Resistance in World War II.* Manhattan, Kans.: MA/AH, 1984.

———. "Soviet Women in Combat in World War II: The Ground Forces and the Navy," *International Journal of Women's Studies* 3 (1980): 345–47.

———. ed. and trans., *The Golden-tressed Soldier.* Manhattan, Kans.: MA/AH, 1983.

———. trans. *Soviet Airwomen in Combat in World War II.* Manhattan, Kans.: MA/AH, 1983.

Coye, Beth F. *My Navy Too: A Political Novel Based on Real Life Experiences.* Ashland, Ore.: Cedar Hollow Press, 1997.

Crawley, Martha L. "The Science of Right Living: The Navy Medical Department in the Progressive Era." Ph.D. dissertation, George Washington University, 1989.

Creighton, Margaret S., and Lisa Norling, eds. *Iron Men, Wooden Women: Gender and Seafaring in the Atlantic World, 1700–1920.* Baltimore: Johns Hopkins University Press, 1996.

Custer, Elizabeth B. *Boots and Saddles or Life in Dakota with General Custer.* New York: Harper & Row, 1885.

Custis, G. W. P. *Recollections and Private Memories of Washington.* N.p., 1859.

Danner, Dorothy Still. *What a Way to Spend a War: Navy Nurse POWs in the Philippines.* Annapolis, Md.: Naval Institute Press, 1995.

Dannett, Sylvia. *She Rode with the Generals: The True and Incredible Story of Sarah Emma Seelye, Alias Franklin Thompson.* New York: Thomas Nelson & Sons, 1960.

Davis, Katharine Bement. *Factors in the Sex Life of Twenty-Two Hundred Women.* New York: Harper & Row, 1929.

Davis, Elizabeth. *The Autobiography of Elizabeth Davis, a Balaklava Nurse.* Edited by J. Williams. London: Hurst and Blackett, 1857.

Davis-Kimball, Jeannine. "Warrior Women of the Eurasian Steppes." *Archaeology* 50, no. 1 (January/February 1997): 44–48.

Davis-Kimball, Jeannine, Leon Yablonsky, L. T. Iablonskii, and V. Demkin. *Kurgans on the Left Bank of the Ilek: Excavations at Pokrovka, 1990–1992.* Berkeley, Calif.: Zinat Press, 1995.

Deacon, Richard. *Kempei Tai: A History of the Japanese Secret Service.* New York: Berkley Books, 1985.

Dean, Donna M. *Warriors Without Weapons: The Victimization of Military Women.* Pasadena, Md.: The MINERVA Center, 1997.

Dear, I. C. B., and M. R. D. Foot, eds. *The Oxford Companion to World War II.* Oxford: Oxford University Press, 1995.

Dearing, Mary B. "Anita Newcomb McGee." In *Notable American Women: A Biographical Dictionary,* edited by Edward T. James, 2:464–66. Cambridge, Mass.: Belknap Press, 1971.

Deary, William Paul. "Toward Disaster at Fort Washington, November 1776." Ph.D. dissertation, George Washington University, 1996.

de Carvajal, Fray Gaspar. *The Discovery of the Amazon.* Edited by José Toribio Medina, translated by Bertram T. Lee. New York: Dover Publications, 1988.

Dedijer, Vladimir. *With Tito Through the War: Partisan Diary, 1941–1944.* London: Alexander Hamilton, 1951.

de Erauso, Catalina. *Lieutenant Nun: Memoir of a Basque Transvestite in the New World.* Translated by Michele Stepto and Gabriel Stepto. Boston: Beacon Press, 1996.

de Grazia, Victoria. *How Facism Ruled Women: Italy, 1922–1945.* Berkeley: University of California Press, 1992.

Dekker, Rudolf M., and Lotte C. van de Pol. *The Tradition of Female Transvestism in Early Modern Europe.* New York: St. Martin's Press, 1989.

Dennison, Ralph. "LBJ." In Al Santoli, *Everything We Had: An Oral History of the Vietnam War by Thirty-three American Soldiers Who Fought It,* 251–52. New York: Ballantine Books, 1981.

De Pauw, Linda Grant. *Founding Mothers: Women of America in the Revolutionary Era.* Boston: Houghton Mifflin, 1975.

———. *Four Traditions: Women of New York During the American Revolution.* Albany: New York State Bicentennial Commission, 1974.

———. *Seafaring Women.* Boston: Houghton Mifflin, 1982.

———. "Women in Combat: The Revolutionary War Experience." *Armed Forces and Society* 7 (1981): 209–26.

DeShazer, Mary K. "'Sisters in Arms': The Warrior Construct in Writings by Contemporary U.S. Women of Color." *National Women's Studies Association Journal* 2, no. 3 (Summer 1990): 349–73.

Desser, Eunice. *The First Enlisted Women, 1917–1919.* Philadelphia: Dorrance, 1955.

Devens, Richard Miller. *The Pictorial Book of Anecdotes and Incidents of the War of the Rebellion.* Hartford, Conn.: Hartford Publishing Co., 1867.

Devilbiss, M. C. *Women and Military Service: A History, Analysis, and Overview of Key Issues.* (Maxwell Air Force Base, Ala.: Air University Press, 1990.

———. "Women in Combat: A Quick Summary of the Arguments on Both Sides." *MINERVA: Quarterly Report on Women and the Military* 8, no. 1 (Spring 1990): 29–32.

Devor, Holly. *Gender Blending: Confronting the Limits of Duality.* Bloomington: Indiana University Press, 1989.

"Diary of Samuel Sewall." Massachusetts Historical Society Collection, 5th ser., 5 (1878): 452–53.

Diner, Helen. *Mothers and Amazons: The First Feminist History of Culture.* New York: Anchor Books, 1973.

Dinh, Nguyen Thi. *No Other Road to Take.* Ithaca: Cornell University SEA Data Paper no. 102, June 1976.

Doty, Madeleine Zabriskie. *Short Rations: Experiences of an American Woman in Germany.* New York: A. L. Burt, 1917.

Douglas, Deborah G. *United States Women in Aviation, 1940–1985.* Washington, D.C.: Smithsonian Institution Press, 1991.

Dubbert, Joe L. *A Man's Place.* Englewood Cliffs, N.J.: Prentice-Hall, 1979.

Duff, Nora. *Matilda of Tuscany.* London: Methuen, 1902.

Dugaw, Dianne. *Warrior Women and Popular Balladry, 1650–1850.* Cambridge: Cambridge University Press, 1989.

Duiker, William J. "Vietnam: War of Insurgency." In *Female Soldiers—Combatants or Noncombatants: Historical and Contemporary Perspectives,* edited by Nancy Loring Goldman, 107–22. Westport, Conn.: Greenwood Press, 1982.

Dupuy, Trevor N. *Understanding War: History and Theory of Combat.* New York: Paragon House, 1987.

Durham, Edith. *High Albania.* London: Virago Press, 1985.

Durova, Nadezhda. *The Cavalry Maiden: Journals of a Russian Officer in the Napoleonic Wars.* Translated by Mary Fleming Zirin. Bloomington: Indiana University Press, 1988.

Dyer, Gwynne. *War.* Homewood, Ill.: Dorsey Press, 1985.

Eads, Valerie. "The Campaigns of Matilda of Tuscany," *MINERVA: Quarterly Report on Women and the Military* 4, no. 1 (Spring 1986): 167–81.

Early, Charity Adams. *One Woman's Army: A Black Officer Remembers the WAC.* College Station: Texas A&M University Press, 1989.

East, Ernest Edward. "Lincoln's Russian General." *Journal of the Illinois State Historical Society* 52, no. 1 (Spring 1959): 106–22.

Ebbert, Jean, and Marie-Beth Hall, *Crossed Currents: Navy Women from WW I to Tailhook.* Washington, D.C.: Brassey's, 1993.

Edmonds, S. Emma E. *Nurse and Spy in the Union Army.* Hartford, Conn.: W. S. Williams, 1865.

Egle, William Henry. *Pennsylvania Women in the American Revolution.* Harrisburg, Pa.: Harrisburg Publishing Co., 1898.

Eibl-Eibesfeldt, Irenäus. *The Biology of Peace and War: Men, Animals, and Aggression.* New York: Viking Press, 1979.

Eisen, Arlene. *Women and Revolution in Viet Nam.* Atlantic Highlands, N.J.: Humanities Press International, 1984.

Eisen-Bergman, Arlene. *Women of Viet Nam.* San Francisco: People's Press, 1975.

Eisler, Riane. *The Chalice and the Blade: Our History, Our Future.* San Francisco: Harper & Row, 1987.

Elshtain, Jean Bethke. *Women and War.* New York: Basic Books, 1987.

Elting, John R. *Swords Around a Throne: Napoleon's Grande Armée.* New Free Press, 1988.

Emery, W. B. *Archaic Egypt.* Harmondsworth: Penguin Books, 1987.

Engels, Donald W. *Alexander the Great and the Logistics of the Macedonian Army.* Berkeley: Univ. of California Press, 1978.

Enloe, Cynthia. *The Morning After: Sexual Politics at the End of the Cold War.* Berkeley: University of California Press, 1993.

Erikson, Brigitte, ed. "A Lesbian Execution in Germany, 1721: The Trial Records." *Journal of Homosexuality* 6 (1980–81): 2–40.

Evans, John K. *War, Women and Children in Ancient Rome.* London: Routledge, 1991.

Faderman, Lillian. *Odd Girls and Twilight Lovers: A History of Lesbian Life in Twentieth-Century America.* New York: Columbia University Press, 1991.

Farwell, Byron. *The Great Anglo-Boer War.* New York: Harper & Row, 1976.

———. *Mr. Kipling's Army: All the Queen's Men.* New York: W. W. Norton, 1981.

Feinberg, Leslie. *Transgender Warriors: Making History from Joan of Arc to Dennis Rodman.* Boston: Beacon Press, 1996.

Fellman, Michael. "Women and Guerrilla Warfare." In *Divided Houses: Gender and the Civil War,* edited by Catherine Clinton and Nina Silber, 147–65. New York: Oxford University Press, 1992.

Felton, Harold W. *Nancy Ward, Cherokee.* New York: Dodd, Mead, 1975.

Ferguson, Marilyn. *The Aquarian Conspiracy: Personal and Social Transformation in the 1980's*. Los Angeles: J. P. Tarcher, 1980.

Ferrill, Arther. *The Origins of War: From the Stone Age to Alexander the Great*. London: Thames and Hudson, 1985.

Figueur, Thèrése. *Un ancien de 15e dragons*. Bordeaux: Editions Delmas, 1936.

Fisher, Elizabeth. *Woman's Creation: Sexual Evolution and the Shaping of Society*. New York: McGraw Hill, 1979.

Forbes, Rosetta. *Women Called Wild*. London: Grayson and Grayson, 1935.

Foreman, Carolyn Thomas. *Indian Women Chiefs*. Washington, D.C.: Zenger, [1954] 1976.

Fougera, Katherine G. *With Custer's Cavalry: From the Memoirs of the Late Katherine Gibson*. Caldwell, Idaho: Caxton, 1940.

Fourcade, Marie Madeleine. *Noah's Ark*. New York: E. P. Dutton, 1974.

Fourtouni, Eleni. *Greek Women in Resistance*. New Haven, Conn.: Thelphini Press, 1986.

Francke, Linda Bird. *Ground Zero: The Gender Wars in the Military*. New York: Simon & Schuster, 1997.

Fraser, Antonia. *The Warrior Queens: The Legends and the Lives of the Women Who Have Led Their Nations in War*. New York: Vintage Books, 1990.

Freeman, Lucy, and Alma Bond. *America's First Woman Warrior: The Courage of Deborah Sampson*. New York: Paragon House, 1992.

Freemantle, Lt. Col. *Three Months in the Southern States*. New York: John Bradburn, 1864.

Friedan, Betty. *The Feminine Mystique*. New York: W. W. Norton, 1963.

Froissart. *Chronicles of England, France, and Spain*. Translated by T. Johnes. New York: E. P. Dutton, 1961.

Gabriel, Richard A. *The Culture of War: Invention and Early Development*. New York: Greenwood Press, 1990.

Garber, Marjorie. *Vested Interests: Cross-Dressing and Cultural Anxiety*. New York: Routledge, 1992.

Gardner, Jane F. *Women in Roman Law and Society*. London: Croom Helm, 1986.

Garlan, Yvon. *War in the Ancient World: A Social History*. Translated by Janet Lloyd. London: Chatto and Windus, 1975.

Garmonsway, G. N., trans. *The Anglo-Saxon Chronicles*. London: Dent, 1953.

Garnett, E. *Florence Nightingale's Nuns*. New York: Farrar, Straus & Cudahy, 1961.

Garraty, John A., ed. *The Young Reader's Companion to American History*. Boston: Houghton Mifflin, 1994.

Garrett, Laurie. *The Coming Plague: Newly Emerging Diseases in a World Out of Balance*. New York: Farrar, Straus and Giroux, 1994.

Gavin, Lettie. *American Servicewomen in World War I*. Niwot: University of Colorado Press, 1997.

Gearhart, Sally Miller. "The Spiritual Dimension: Death and Resurrection of a Hallelujah Dyke." In *Our Right to Love: A Lesbian Resource Book*, edited by Ginny Vida, 187–93. Englewood Cliffs, N.J.: Prentice-Hall, 1978.

Gebhart, J. F. *Het leven var mr. Nicholas Cornelisz, Witson*. 2 vols. Utrecht, 1882.

Gellhorn, Martha. *The Face of War*. New York: Atlantic Monthly Press, 1988.

Gerstein, Arnold, and James Reagan. *Win-Win: Approaches to Conflict Resolution at Home, in Business, Between Groups, and Across Cultures*. Salt Lake City: Peregrine Smith Books, 1986.

Gerzon, Mark. *A Choice of Heroes: The Changing Face of American Manhood*. Boston: Houghton Mifflin, 1982.

Gibb, Hamilton Alexander Rosskeen, ed. *The Life of Saladin: From the Works of Imad ad-Din and Baha ad-Din*. Oxford: Clarendon Press, 1973.

Gilbert, Martin. *The Second World War: A Complete History*. New York: Henry Holt, 1989.

Gilbert, Oscar Paul. *Women in Men's Guise*. London: John Lane, 1932.

Glausius, Gerhard P. "The Little Soldier of the 95th: Albert D. J. Cashier." *Journal of the Illinois State Historical Society* 51, no. 4 (Winter 1958): 380–87.

Gluck, Sherna Berger. *Rosie the Riveter Revisited: Women, the War and Social Change*. Boston: Twayne, 1987.

Goodwin-Gill, Guy S., and Ilene Cohn. *Child Soldiers: A Study on Behalf of the Henry Dunant Institute*. Oxford: Oxford University Press, 1994.

Gordon, Cyrus. *Common Background of Greek and Hebrew Civilizations*. New York: W. W. Norton, 1965.

Gordon, Eve. "War Stories." *MINERVA: Quarterly Report on Women and the Military* 7, nos. 3–4, (Fall/Winter 1989): 67–89.

Grahn, Elna Hilliard. *In the Company of WACS*. Manhattan, Kans.: Sunflower University Press, 1993.

Grammaticus, Saxo. *The History of the Danes*. Translated by Peter Fisher, edited by Hilda Ellis Davidson. Cambridge: D. S. Brewer, 1979.

Granger, Byrd Howell. *On Final Approach: The Women Airforce Service Pilots of World War II*. Scottsdale, Ariz.: Falconer, 1991.

Grant, Michael. *The Army of the Caesars*. New York, 1974.

———. *Cleopatra: A Biography*. New York: Barnes and Noble, 1972.

———. *Gladiators*. New York: Delacorte Press, 1967.

———. *The History of Ancient Israel.* New York: Charles Scribner's Sons, 1984.

Gribble, Francis. *Women in War.* New York: E. P. Dutton, 1917.

Griesse, Anne Elliot, and Richard Stites. "Russia: Revolution and War." In *Female Soldiers Combatants or Noncombatants?: Historical and Contemporary Perspectives,* edited by Nancy Loring Goldman, 61–84. Westport, Conn.: Greenwood Press, 1982.

Groushko, M. A. *Cossack: Warrior Riders of the Steppes.* New York: Sterling, 1992.

Grousset, René. *The Empire of the Steppes: A History of Central Asia.* Translated by Naomi Walford. New Brunswick, N.J.: Rutgers University Press, 1970.

Guba, Emil F. *Deborah Samson alias Robert Shurtliff: Revolutionary War Soldier.* Plymouth, Mass.: Jones River Press, 1994.

Haas, Mary. *Women's Perspectives on the Vietnam War.* Pittsburgh: Center for Social Studies Education, 1991.

Haas, Paul, ed. "A Volunteer Nurse in the Civil War: The Letters of Harriet Douglas Whetten." *Wisconsin Magazine of History* 48, no. 3 (Spring 1965): 205–21.

Haberling, Wilhelm. "Army Prostitution and Its Control: An Historical Study." In *Morals in Wartime,* edited by Victor Robinson, 3–90. New York: Publishers Foundation, 1943.

Hacker, Barton C. "Where Have All the Women Gone? The Pre-Twentieth Century Sexual Division of Labor in Armies." *MINERVA: Quarterly Report on Women and the Military* 3, no. 1 (Spring 1985): 107–48.

———. "Women and Military Institutions in Early Modern Europe: A Reconnaissance." *Signs: Journal of Women in Culture and Society* 6, no. 4 (1981): 643–71.

Hagist, Don N. "The Women of the British Army During the American Revolution," *MINERVA: Quarterly Report on Women and the Military* 13, no. 2 (Summer 1995): 29–85.

Hall, Edward H. *Margaret Corbin, Heroine of the Battle of Fort Washington, 16 Nov. 1776.* New York: American Scenic and Historic Preservation Society, 1932.

Hall, Radclyffe. "Miss Ogilvie finds Herself" and *The Well of Loneliness.* New York: Covici Friede, 1928.

Hall, Richard. *Patriots in Disguise: Women Warriors of the Civil War.* New York: Paragon House, 1993.

Halley, John W. *The Rebel Yell and the Yankee Hurrah: The Civil War Journal of a Maine Volunteer, 17th Maine Regiment.* Edited by Ruth L. Silliker. Camden, Maine: Down East Books, 1985.

Hammond, N. G. L. *A History of Greece to 322 B.C.* Oxford: Clarendon Press, 1986.

Hammond, N. G. L., and H. H. Scullard, *The Oxford Classical Dictionary,* 2d ed. Oxford: Clarendon Press, 1970.

Hancock, Joy Bright. *Lady in the Navy: A Personal Reminiscence.* Annapolis, Md.: Naval Institute Press, 1972.

Hanson, Victor Davis, ed. *Hopolites: The Classical Greek Battle Experience.* London: Routledge, 1991.

Hargreaves, Reginald. *The Bloodybacks: The British Serviceman in North America, 1655–1783.* London: Rupert Hart-Davis, 1968.

Hart, Carolyn. "Women Have Real Roles in Militias," *Media Bypass Magazine* 4, no. 10 (October 1996): 12–13, 49.

Hartmann, Susan M. *The Home Front and Beyond: American Women in the 1940's.* Boston: Twayne 1982.

Havens, Thomas R. H. *Valley of Darkness: The Japanese People and World War Two.* New York: W. W. Norton, 1978.

Heckler, Richard Strozzi. *In Search of the Warrior Spirit.* Berkeley, Calif.: North Atlantic Books, 1990.

Hee, Kim Hyun. *The Tears of My Soul.* New York: William Morrow, Inc., 1993.

Heinemann, Marlene E. *Gender and Destiny: Women Writers and the Holocaust.* Westport, Conn.: Greenwood Press, 1986.

Herodotus. *The Histories.* Translated by Aubrey de Selincourt. New York: Penguin Books, 1988.

Herskovits, Melville J. *Dahomey: An Ancient West African Kingdom.* Evanston, Ill.: Northwestern University Press, 1967.

Herzog, Chaim, and Mordechai Gichon. *Battles of the Bible.* New York: Random House, 1978.

Hewitt, Linda L. *Women Marines in World War I.* Washington, D.C.: U.S. Marine Corps, 1974.

Hicks, George. *The Comfort Women: Japan's Brutal Regime of Enforced Prostitution in the Second World War.* New York: W. W. Norton, 1994.

Higa, Tomiko. *The Girl with the White Flag.* Translated by Dorothy Britton. Tokyo: Kodansha International, 1991.

Hillerich, Karen L. "Black Jack's Girls." *Army* 32, no. 12 (December 1982): 44–48.

Hirshfeld, Magnus. *The Sexual History of the World War.* New York: Panurge Press, 1934.

Hobhouse, Emily. *The Brunt of the War and Where It Fell.* London: Methuen, 1902.

Holland, Mary G. *Our Army Nurses.* Roseville, Minn.: Edinborough Press, 1997.

Holm, Jeanne. *Women in the Military: An Unfinished Revolution,* rev. ed. Novato, Calif.: Presidio, 1992.

Homer. *The Iliad.* Translated by A. Lang, W. Leaf, and E. Meyers, edited by G. Highet. New York: Modern Library, 1950.

Honey, Maureen. *Creating Rosie the Riveter: Class, Gender and Propaganda During World War II*. Amherst: University of Massachusetts Press, 1984.

Huddy, Mary. *Matilda Countess of Tuscany*. London: John Long, 1906.

Hufton, Olwen H. *Women and the Limits of Citizenship in the French Revolution*. Toronto: University of Toronto Press, 1992.

Hunter, Anne E., ed. *On Peace, War, and Gender: A Challenge to Genetic Explanations*. New York: Feminist Press, 1991.

Hussain, Freda, and Kamelia Radwan. "The Islamic Revolution and Women: Quest for the Kuranic Model." In *Muslim Women*, edited by Freda Hussain, 44–67. London: Croom Helm, 1984.

Jackson, Guida M. *Women Who Ruled*. Santa Barbara, Calif.: ABC-CLIO, 1990.

James, Edward T., ed. *Notable American Women: A Biographical Dictionary*. Cambridge, Mass.: Belknap Press, 1971.

Jancar, Barbara. "Yugoslavia: War of Resistance." In *Female Soldiers—Combatants or Noncombatants?: Historical and Contemporary Perspectives*, edited by Nancy Loring Goldman, 85–105. Westport, Conn.: Greenwood Press, 1982.

Johnston, Jill. *Lesbian Nation: The Feminist Solution*. New York: Simon & Schuster, 1973.

Jones, David E. *Women Warriors: A History*. Washington, D.C.: Brassey's, 1997.

Jones, Gwyn. *The North Atlantic Saga: Being the Norse Voyages of Discovery and Settlement to Iceland, Greenland, America*. New York: Oxford University Press, 1986.

Josephy, Alvin M., Jr. *The Patriot Chiefs: A Chronicle of American Indian Resistance*. New York: Viking Press, 1961.

"Journal of Rev. John Pike." *Massachusetts Historical Society Proceedings* 14 (1875–76): 131.

Kalisch, Philip A., and Beatrice J. Kalisch. *The Advance of American Nursing*. Boston: Little, Brown, 1978.

———. "Untrained But Undaunted: The Women Nurses of the Blue and Gray." *Nursing Forum* 15, no. 1 (1976): 4–33.

Kates, Gary. "D'Eon Returns to France: Gender and Power in 1777." In *Body Guards: The Cultural Politics of Gender Ambiguity*, edited by Julia Epstein and Kristina Straub, 167–94. New York, Routledge: 1991.

———. *Monsieur d'Eon Is a Woman: A Tale of Political Intrigue and Sexual Masquerade*. New York: Basic Books, 1995.

Katz, Jonathan. *Gay American History: Lesbians and Gay Men in the U.S.A.* New York: Avon Books, 1976.

Keegan, John. *The Face of Battle*. New York: Vintage Books, 1977.

———. *A History of Warfare*. New York: Alfred A. Knopf, 1993.

Keeley, Lawrence H. *War Before Civilization: The Myth of the Peaceful Savage*. New York: Oxford University Press, 1996.

Keil, Sally Van Wegener. *Those Wonderful Women in Their Flying Machines: The Unknown Heroines of World War II*. New York: Rawson, Wade, 1979.

Kelly, Amy. *Eleanor of Aquitaine and the Four Kings*. Cambridge, Mass.: Harvard University Press, 1950.

Kesselman, Amy. *Fleeting Opportunities: Women Shipyard Workers in Portland and Vancouver During World War II and Reconversion*. Albany: State University of New York Press, 1990.

Kian-Chow, Kwok. "Quadrilateral Patterning in the Tomb of Fu Hao." *Indo-Pacific Prehistory Association Bulletin* 11 (1991): 72–78.

Kikuko, Miyagi. "Student Nurses of the Lily Corps.'" In *Japan at War: An Oral History*, edited by Haruko Taya Cook and Theodore F. Cook, 354–63. New York: New Press, 1982.

Kingston, Maxine Hong. *The Woman Warrior: Memoirs of a Girlhood Among Ghosts*. New York: Vintage Books, 1975.

Kipling, Rudyard. "The Married Man." *The Definitive Edition of Rudyard Kipling's Verse*. London: Hodder and Stoughton, 1948.

Kirkland, Fazar. *Reminiscences of the Blue and Gray, 1861–1865*. Chicago: Preston, 1866.

Klaver, Carol. "An Introduction to the Legend of Molly Pitcher." *MINERVA: Quarterly Report on Women and the Military* 7, no. 2 (Summer 1994): 35–61.

Kleinbaum, Abby Wettan. *The War Against the Amazons*. New York: New Press, 1983.

Korson, George. *At His Side: The Story of the American Red Cross Overseas in World War II*. New York: Coward-McCann, 1945.

Laffin, John. *Women in Battle*. London: Abelard-Schuman, 1967.

Landis, John B. "Molly Pitcher": *A Short History of Molly Pitcher, the Heroine of Monmouth*. Carlisle, Pa.: Corman, 1905.

Lane Fox, Robin. *The Search for Alexander*. Boston: Little Brown, 1980.

Langbein, Hermann. *Against All Hope: Resistance in the Nazi Concentration Camps*. Translated by Harry Zohn. New York: Continuum, 1996.

Langer, William L., ed. *Encyclopedia of World History*, 5th ed. Boston: Houghton Mifflin, 1968.

Laqueur, Walter. *Guerrilla: A Historical and Critical Study*. Boston: Little, Brown, 1976.

Larson, C. Kay. "Bonny Yank and Ginny Reb." *MINERVA: Quarterly Report on Women and the Military* 8, no. 1 (Spring 1990): 33–49

———. "Bonny Yank and Ginny Reb Revisited." *MINERVA: Quarterly Report on Women and the Military* 10, no. 2 (Summer 1992): 35–61.

————. *'Til I Come Marching Home: A Brief History of American Women in World War II*. Pasadena, Md.: The MINERVA Center, 1995.

Laska, Vera. *Nazism, Resistance and Holocaust in World War II: A Bibliography*. Metuchen, N.J.: Scarecrow Press, 1985.

Lavine, A. Lincoln. *Circuits of Victory*. Garden City, N.Y.: Country Life Press, 1921.

Lawrence, Dorothy. *Sapper Dorothy Lawrence: The Only English Woman Soldier, Late Royal Engineers, 51st Division, 179th Tunnelling Co., BEF.* London: John Lance, 1919.

Lebra-Chapman, Joyce. *The Rani of Jhansi: A Study in Female Heroism in India*. Honolulu: University of Hawaii Press, 1986.

Lee, Emanoel. *To the Bitter End: A Photographic History of the Boer War, 1899–1902*. Harmondsworth: Penguin Books, 1985.

Lee, Richard B. "What Hunters Do for a Living, or, How to Make Out on Scarce Resources." In *Man the Hunter*, edited by Richard B. Lee and Irven DeVore, 36–43. Chicago: Aldine, 1968.

Leech, Margaret. *Reveille in Washington, 1860–1865*. New York: Harper & Row, 1941.

Leonard, George. *The Silent Pulse*. New York: E. P. Dutton, 1978.

Leonard, Patrick J. "Ann Bailey: Mystery Woman Warrior of 1777." *MINERVA: Quarterly Report on Women and the Military* 11, nos. 3 and 4 (Fall/Winter 1993): 1–4.

Levin, Saul. *The Indo-European and Semitic Languages*. Albany: State University of New York Press, 1971.

Levy, Darlene Gay, and Harriet B. Applewhite. "Women and Militant Citizenship in Revolutionary Paris." In *Rebel Daughters: Women and the French Revolution*, edited by Sara E. Meltzer and Leslie W. Rabine, 79–101. New York: Oxford University Press, 1992

Levy, Darlene Gay, et al., eds. *Women in Revolutionary Paris*. Urbana: University of Illinois Press, 1979.

Li, Xiaolin. "Women in the Chinese Military." Ph.D. dissertation, University of Maryland, 1995.

Liberty, Margot. "Hell Came with the Horses: Plains Indian Women in the Equestrian Era." *Montana* 32 (Summer 1982): 41–48.

Linden, Robin Ruth. *Making Stories, Making Selves: Feminist Reflections on the Holocaust*. Columbus: Ohio State University Press, 1993.

Linderman, Frank B. *Pretty-shield: Medicine Woman of the Crows*. New York: John Day Company, 1972. Original title *Red Mother*, published 1932.

Liss, Peggy K. *Isabel*. Oxford: Oxford University Press, 1992.

Litoff, Judy Barrett, and David C. Smith. *We're in this War, Too: World War II Letters from American Women in Uniform*. New York: Oxford University Press, 1994.

Livermore, Mary A. *My Story of the War.* Hartford, Conn.: A. D. Worthington, 1889.

Lixl, Andreas. *Women of Exile: German-Jewish Autobiographies Since 1933.* New York: Greenwood Press, 1988.

Lord, Albert Bates. *Epic Singers and Oral Tradition.* Ithaca: Cornell University Press, 1991.

———. *The Singer of Tales.* Cambridge, Mass.: Harvard University Press, 1960.

Lorde, Audré. *Our Dead Behind Us.* New York: W. W. Norton, 1986.

Lossing, Benjamin F. *Pictoral Field Book of the American Revolution.* 2 vols. New York: Harper, 1851.

Loth, Heinrich. *Woman in African Art.* Westport, Conn.: Lawrence Hill, 1978.

Lowe, Thomas. *Central India During the Rebellion of 1857 and 1858.* N.p., 1860.

Lowry, Thomas P. *The Story the Soldiers Wouldn't Tell: Sex in the Civil War.* Mechanicsburg, Pa.: Stackpole Books, 1994.

Ludwig, Emil. *Cleopatra.* New York: Viking Press, 1937.

Lumholtz, C. *Among Cannibals: An Account of Four Years' Travels in Australia and of Camp Life with the Aborigines of Queensland.* New York: C. Scribner's & Son, 1889.

McClary, Ben Harris. "Nancy Ward." *Tennessee Historical Quarterly* 21 (December 1962): 352–64.

MacDonald, Eileen. *Shoot the Women First.* New York: Random House, 1991.

McKendrick, Malveena. *Ferdinand and Isabella.* New York: American Heritage, 1968.

McLaughlin, Megan. "The Woman Warrior: Gender, Warfare, and Society in Medieval Europe." *Women's Studies* 17 (1990): 193–209.

McNeill, William H. *The Pursuit of Power.* Chicago: University of Chicago Press, 1982.

Malmesbury, William of. *Chronicle of English Kings.* Translated by J. A. Giles. London, 1847.

Mangold, Tom, and John Penycate. *The Tunnels of Cu Chi.* London: Hodder and Stoughton, 1985.

Mansfield, Sue. *The Gestalts of War: An Inquiry into Its Origins and Meanings as a Social Institution.* New York: Dial Press, 1982.

———. "In the Shadow of Andromache's Loom." *MINERVA: Quarterly Report on Women and the Military* 2, no. 4 (Winter 1984): 60–83.

Marsden, Peter. *Roman London.* London: Thames and Hudson, 1980.

Martin, Jo Nobuko. *A Princess Lily of the Ryokyus.* Tokyo: Shin Nippon Kyoiku Tosho, 1984.

Martin, Joseph P. *Private Yankee Doodle.* Edited by George F. Scheer. Boston: Little Brown, 1962.

Martineau, Gilbert. *Madame Mère: Napoleon's Mother*. Translated by Frances Partridge. London: J. Murray, 1978.

Marwick, Arthur. *Women at War, 1914–1918*. London: Croom Helm, 1977.

Massey, Mary Elizabeth. *Bonnet Brigades*. New York: Alfred A. Knopf, 1966.

Mather, Cotton. *Magnalia Christi Americana*. New York: Russell & Russell, 1967.

Mathes, Valerie Sherer. "Native American Women in Medicine and the Military," *Journal of the West* 21, no. 2 (1982): 41–48.

Maurer, Maurer. "The Court-Martialing of Camp Followers, World War I." *American Journal of Legal history* 9 (1965): 203–15.

May, Louise Anne. "Worthy Warriors and Unruly Amazons: Sino–Western Historical Accounts and Imaginative Images of Women in Battle." Ph.D. dissertation, University of British Columbia, 1985.

Mayer, Holly A. "Belonging to the Army: Camp Followers and the Military Community During the American Revolution." Ph.D. dissertation, College of William and Mary, 1990.

Mayer, Jessica. "Women and the Pacification of Men in New Guinea." In *Women and the Images of Women in Peace and War: Cross-Cultural and Historical Perspectives*, edited by Sharon McDonald, Pat Holden, and Shirley Ardener. 148–65. Madison: University of Wisconsin Press, 1988.

———. *Belonging to the Army: Camp Followers and the Military Community During the American Revolution*. Columbia: University of South Carolina Press, 1996.

Medicine, Bernice. "Warrior Women—Sex Role Alternatives for Plains Indian Women. In *The Hidden Half: Studies of Plains Indian Women*, edited by Patricia Albers and Bernice Medicine, 267–80. Lanham, Md.: University Press of America, 1983.

Merryman, Molly. *Clipped Wings: The Rise and Fall of the Women Airforce Service Pilots of World War II*. New York: New York University Press, 1997.

Michell, Humfrey. *Sparta*. Cambridge: Cambridge University Press, 1952.

Miles, Rosalind. *The Women's History of the World*. New York: Harper & Row, 1988.

Milkman, Ruth. *Gender at Work: The Dynamics of Job Segregation by Sex During World War II*. Urbana: University of Illinois Press, 1987.

Millman, Dan. *Way of the Peaceful Warrior*. Tiburon, Calif.: H. J. Kramer, 1980.

Milner, Vicountess. *My Picture Gallery, 1886–1901*. London: John Murray, 1951.

Moolman, Valerie. *Women Aloft*. Alexandria, Va.: Time-Life Books, 1981.

Moore, Brenda L. *To Serve My Country, to Serve My Race: The Story of the Only African-American WACs Stationed Overseas During World War II*. New York: New York University Press, 1996.

Moore, Frank. *Women of the War: Their Heroism and Self-Sacrifice*. Hartford, Conn: S. S. Scranton, 1866.

Morden, Bettie J. *The Women's Army Corps, 1945–1978.* Washington, D.C.: U.S. Army Center of Military History, 1990.

Morgan, Forrest E. *Living the Martial Way: A Manual for the Way a Modern Warrior Should Think.* Fort Lee, N.J.: Barricade Books, 1992.

Mumford, Lewis. *The City in History: Its origins, Its Transformations and Its Prospects.* New York: Harcourt, Brace & World, 1961.

Mulhern, Chieko Irie, ed. *Heroic with Grace: Legendary Women of Japan.* Armonk, N.Y.: M. E. Sharpe, 1991.

Myles, Bruce. *The Night Witches: The Untold Story of Soviet Women in Combat.* Novato, Calif.: Presidio, 1981.

Nash, June. "The Aztecs and the Ideology of Male Dominance," *Signs: Journal of Women in Culture and Society* 4 (1978): 349–62.

Nash, Mary. *Defying Male Civilization: Women in the Spanish Civil War.* Denver: Arden Press, 1995.

Nelson, Mariah Burton. *The Stronger Women Get, the More Men Love Football.* New York: Harcourt, Brace, 1994.

Newark, Tim. *Women Warlords: An Illustrated History of Female Warriors.* London: Blandford, 1989.

Nicolle, David. *The Mongol Warlords: Genghis Khan, Kublai Khan, Hugelu, Tamerland.* Poole, Dorsett: Firebird Books, 1990.

Niethammer, Carolyn. *Daughters of the Earth: The Lives and Legends of American Indian Women.* New York: Collier, 1977.

Nixon, Edna. *Royal Spy: The Strange Case of the Chevalier d'Eon.* New York: Reynal, 1965.

Noggle, Anne. *A Dance with Death: Soviet Airwomen in World War II.* College Station: Texas A&M University Press, 1994.

Oates, Joan. *Babylon.* London: Thames and Hudson, 1989.

Oates, Stephen. *A Woman of Valor: Clara Barton and the Civil War.* New York: Free Press, 1994.

O'Connell, Robert L. *Of Arms and Men: A History of War, Weapons and Aggression.* New York: Oxford University Press, 1989.

Olmstead, A. T. *History of the Persian Empire.* Chicago: University of Chicago Press, 1948.

Omerod, H. A. *Piracy in the Ancient World.* New York: Doreste, 1987.

Owings, Allison. *Frauen: German Women Recall the Third Reich.* New Brunswick, N.J.: Rutgers University Press, 1995.

Page, F. C. G. *Following the Drum: Women in Wellington's Wars.* London: Andre Deutsch, 1986.

Paquette, Patricia. "A Bandage in One Hand and a Bible in the Other: The Story of Captain Sally L. Thompkins (CSA)." *MINERVA: Quarterly Report on Women and the Military* 8, no. 2 (Summer 1990): 47–54.

Parker, Geoffrey. "Taking Up the Gun." In *Experience of War*, edited by Robert Cowley, 127–39. New York: W. W. Norton, 1992.

Parry, Adam, ed. *The Making of Homeric Verse: The Collected Papers of Milman Parry*. Oxford: Clarendon Press, 1971.

Parry, Danaan. *Warriors of the Heart*. Cooperstown, N.Y.: Sunstone Publications, 1989.

Peers, Douglas. *Between Mars and Mammon: Colonial Armies and the Garrison State in India, 1819–1835*. New York: St. Martin's Press, 1995.

Pember, Phoebe Yates. *A Southern Woman's Story: Life in Confederate Richmond*. Edited by Bell I. Wiley. Jackson, Tenn.: McCowat-Mercer Press, 1959.

Pennington, Reina. "Wings, Women, and War," *Air & Space* 8, no. 5 (December 1993/January 1994): 74–85.

Pfieffer, Jon. *The Origins of Society and Prehistory: A Pre-History of the Establishment*. New York: McGraw Hill, 1977.

Piedmont, Robert V., and Cindy Gurney, eds. *Highlights in the History of the Army Nurse Corps*. Washington, D.C.: U.S. Army Center of Military History, 1987.

Piszkiewicz, Dennis. *From Nazi Test Pilot to Hitler's Bunker: The Fantastic Flights of Hannah Reitsch*. Westport, Conn.: Praeger, 1997.

Playne, Caroline E. *Society at War, 1914–1916*. Boston: Houghton Mifflin, 1931.

Ploss, Herman Heinrich, Max Bartels, and Paul Bartels. *Woman in the Sexual Relation: An Anthropological and Historical Survey*. Revised and enlarged by Ferd F. Von Reitzenstein, translated by Eric Dingwall. New York: Medical Press of New York, 1964.

Plutarch. *Moralia*. Translated by Frank Cole Babbit. Cambridge, Mass.: Harvard University Press, 1983.

Pomeroy, Sarah B. *Goddesses, Whores, Wives, and Slaves: Women in Classical Antiquity*. New York, Schocken Books, 1975.

———. *Women in Hellenistic Egypt: From Alexander to Cleopatra*. New York: Schocken Books, 1984.

Pozzan, Cristina. *As the Mirror Burns*. Video Australia, 1990.

Pryor, Elizabeth Brown. *Clara Barton: Professional Angel*. Philadelphia: University of Pennsylvania Press, 1987.

Putney, Martha S. *When the Nation Was in Need: Blacks in the Women's Army Corps During World War II*. Metuchen, N.J.: Scarecrow Press, 1992.

Quétel, Claude. *History of Syphilis*. Translated by Judith Braddock and Brian Pike. Baltimore: Johns Hopkins University Press, 1992.

Rae, Isobel. *The Strange Story of Dr. James Barry*. London: Longmans, Green, 1958.

Rathbone, Irene. *We that Were Young*. London: Chatto & Windus, 1932.

Ray, John. "Hatshepsut, the Female Pharaoh." *History Today* 44, no. 5 (May 1994): 23–29.

Reeves, Minou. *Female Warriors of Allah: Women and the Islamic Revolution.* New York: E. P. Dutton, 1989.

Reischauer, E. O. *The Japanese.* Tokyo: Charles E. Tuttle, 1978.

Renner, Michael. *Fighting for Survival: Environmental Decline, Social Conflict, and the New Age of Insecurity.* 2d ed. New York: W. W. Norton, 1996.

Reston, James, Jr. *Sherman's March and Vietnam.* New York: Macmillan, 1984.

Reynolds, David S. *Beneath the American Renaissance.* New York: Alfred A. Knopf, 1988.

Ribaud, Etienne. "Maternal Impregnation in Wartime." In *Morals in Wartime,* edited by Victor Robinson, 93–105. New York: Publishers Foundation, 1943.

Rickey, Don, Jr. *Forty Miles a Day on Beans and Hay: The Enlisted Soldier Fighting the Indian Wars.* Norman: University of Oklahoma Press, 1963.

Ringelheim, Joan. "Women and the Holocaust: A Reconsideration of Research." In *Jewish Women in Historical Perspective,* edited by Judith Reesa Baskin, 243–64. Detroit: Wayne State University Press, 1991.

Roberts, Mary M. *American Nursing: History and Interpretation.* New York: Macmillan, 1954.

Roberts, Nickie. *Whores in History: Prostitution in Western Society.* London: HarperCollins, 1992.

Robertson, B., ed. *Air Aces of the 1914–18 War.* Los Angeles: Aero Publications, 1964.

Roca, Steven. "Permission to Come on Board: Women Nurses on the *USS Red Rover,* 1861–1865. Paper delivered at "Lead, Blood and Tears," Conference on Women and the Civil War, Hood College, June 28, 1997.

Roosevelt, Theodore. *The Strenuous Life.* New York: Review of Reviews, 1904.

Rose, June. *The Perfect Gentleman: The Remarkable Life of Dr. James Miranda Barry, the Woman Who Served as an Officer in the British Army from 1815 to 1859.* London: Hutchinson, 1977.

Rosenbaum, Edward E. "The Doctor Is In," *New Choices* (July 1989): 24–26.

Rossi, Alice S., ed. *The Feminist Papers from Adams to de Beauvoir.* New York: Columbia University Press, 1973.

Rossiter, Margaret. *Women in the Resistance.* New York: Praeger, 1986.

Roszak, Betty, and Theodore Roszak, eds. *Masculine/Feminine.* New York: Harper & Row, 1969.

Royall, Anne Newport. *The Black Book: or, A Continuation of Travels in the United States* .Washington, D.C.: Printed for the author, 1828–29.

Ruddick, Sara. *Maternal Thinking: Toward a Politics of Peace.* Boston: Beacon Press, 1989

Rupp, Leila. *Mobilizing Women for War: German and American Propaganda, 1939–1945*. Princeton: Princeton University Press, 1978.

Sala, George Augustus. *My Diary in America in the Midst of the War*. 2 vols. London: Tinsley Brothers, 1865.

Salmonson, Jessica Amanda. *The Encyclopedia of Amazons: Women Warriors from Antiquity to the Modern Era*. New York: Paragon House, 1991.

Salm-Salm, Agnes. *Ten Years of My Life*. 2 vols. London: Richard Bentley, 1876.

Salway, Peter. *Roman Britain*. New York: Oxford University Press, 1981.

Sandars, N. K. *The Sea Peoples: Warriors of the Ancient Mediterranean, 1250–1150 B.C.* London: Thames and Hudson 1978.

Sandes, Flora. *The Autobiography of a Woman Soldier: A Brief Record of Adventure with the Serbian Army, 1916–1919*. London: Witherby, 1927.

———. *An English Woman-Sergeant in the Serbian Army*. London: Hodder and Stoughton, 1916.

Sandos, James A. "Prostitution and Drugs: The United States Army on the Mexican-American Border, 1916–1917." *Pacific Historical Review* (1980): 621–45.

Saywell, Shelley. *Women in War: From World War II to El Salvador*. Ontario: Penguin Books, 1985.

Schevil, Ferdinand. *History of Florence*. New York: Harcourt, Brace, 1936.

Schneider, Dorothy, and Carl J. Schneider. *Into the Breach: American Women Overseas in World War I*. New York: Viking Press, 1991.

Schultz, Jane E. "The Inhospitable Hospital: Gender and Professionalism in Civil War Medicine." *Signs: Journal of Women in Culture and Society* 17 (1992): 262–92.

———. "Women at the Front: Gender and Genre in Literature of the American Civil War." Ph.D. dissertation, University of Michigan, 1988.

Schwartz, Gerald, ed. *A Woman Doctor's Civil War: Esther Hill Hawks' Diary*. Columbia: University of South Carolina Press, 1984.

Schwertfeger, Ruth. *The Women of Theresienstadt: Voices from a Concentration Camp*. New York: St. Martin's Press, 1989.

Scriptors Historia Augusta. Translated by David Magie. 3 vols. London: W. Heinemann, 1932.

Seacole, Mary. *Wonderful Adventures of Mrs Seacole in Many Lands*. Introduction by William L. Andrews. New York: Oxford University Press, 1990.

Segal, Mady Wechsler, Xiaolin Li, and David R. Segal. "The Role of Women in the Chinese People's Liberation Army." *MINERVA: Quarterly Report on Women and the Military* 10, no. 1 (Spring 1992): 48–55.

Sertima, Ivan van. *Black Women in Antiquity*. New Brunswick, N.J.: Transaction Books, 1984; rev. 1988.

Seymour, Thomas Day. *Life in the Homeric Age.* New York: Macmillan, 1907.

Shapiro, Laura. "Guns and Dolls: Scientists Explore the Differences Between Boys and Girls." *Newsweek,* May 28, 1990, 56.

Shattuck, C. P. *Military Record of Pepperell, Mass.* Nashua, N.H.: H. R. Wheeler, Steam Bok and Job Printer, 1877.

Shattuck, Mary L. P. *The Story of Jewett's Bridge.* N.p., 1912.

Shaw, Clement. *Letizia Bonaparte.* London, 1928.

Shelley, Lore. *Criminal Experiments on Human Beings in Auschwitz and War Research Laboratories: Twenty Women Prisoners' Accounts.* San Francisco: Mellen Research University Press, 1991.

Sheridan, Alexander P. H. *Personal Memoirs.* New York: Charles L. Webster, 1888.

Siefert, Ruth. "Rape in Wars: Analytical Approaches." *MINERVA: Quarterly Report on Women and the Military* 11, no. 2 (Summer 1993): 17–22.

Siegel, Peggy Brase. "She Went to War: Indiana Women Nurses in the Civil War." *Indiana Magazine of History* 86, no. 1 (March 1990): 1–27.

Sinha, Shyam Narain. *Rani Laksmi Bai of Jhansi.* New Delhi: Chugh Publications, 1980.

Slepyan, Kenneth D. "'The People's Avengers': Soviet Partisans, Stalinist Society and the Politics of Resistance, 1941–1944." Ph.D. dissertation, University of Michigan, 1994.

Smith, F. B. *Florence Nightingale: Reputation and Power.* New York: St. Martin's Press, 1982.

Smith, Nina B. "Men and Authority: The Union Army Nurse and the Problem of Power." *MINERVA: Quarterly Report on Women and the Military* 6, no. 4 (Winter 1988): 25–42.

———. "The Women Who Went to the War: The Union Army Nurse in the Civil War." Ph.D. dissertation, Northwestern University, 1981.

Smith, Winnie. *American Daughter Gone to War: On the Front Lines with an Army Nurse in Vietnam.* New York: William Morrow, 1992.

Smyth, Sir John. *The Rebellious Rani.* London: Muller, 1966.

Snyder, Charles McCool. *Mary Walker: The Little Lady in Pants.* New York: Vantage Press, 1962.

Sobol, Donald. *The Amazons of Greek Mythology.* Cranbury, N.J.: Barnes and Noble, 1973.

Soderbergh, Peter A. *Women Marines: The World War II Era.* Westport, Conn.: Praeger, 1992.

Stallard, Patricia Y. *Glittering Misery: Dependents of the Indian Fighting Army.* Fort Collins, Colo.: Old Army Press, 1978.

Stark, Suzanne J. *Female Tars: Women Aboard Ship in the Age of Sail.* Annapolis, Md.: Naval Institute Press, 1996.

Startsev, A. I. "Ivan Turchinanov and the American Civil War." in *Russian-American Dialogue on Cultural Relations, 1776–1914.* Edited by Norman E. Saul et. al., 107–27. Columbia: University of Missouri Press, 1977.

Staunton, Irene, ed. *Mothers of the Revolution: The War Experiences of Thirty Zimbabwean Women.* Bloomington: Indiana University Press, 1991.

Steele, Ian K. *Warpaths: Invasions of North America, 1513–1765.* New York: Oxford University Press, 1994.

Stephen, Sir Leslie, ed. *Dictionary of National Biography.* London: Smith, Elder, 1889–1906.

Stephenson, Jill. *Women in Nazi Society.* New York: Harper & Row, 1975.

Sterner, Doris M. *In and Out of Harm's Way: A History of the Navy Nurse Corps.* Seattle: Peanut Butter Press, 1997.

Sterx, H. E. *Partners in Rebellion: Alabama Women in the Civil War.* Rutherford, N.J.: Fairleigh Dickinson University Press, 1970.

Stewart, Miller J. "Army Laundresses: Ladies of the Soap Suds Row.'" *Nebraska History* 61, no. 4 (1980): 421–24.

Stirling, Monica. *A Pride of Lions.* London: Collins, 1961.

Stites, Richard. *The Women's Liberation Movement in Russia: Feminism, Nihilism and Bolshevism.* Princeton: Princeton University Press, 1978.

Stone, Merlin. *When God Was a Woman.* New York: Harcourt Brace Jovanovich, 1976.

Stryker, William S. *The Battle of Monmouth.* Princeton: Princeton University Press, 1927.

Sulimirski, T. *The Sarmatians.* New York: Praeger, 1970.

Swahn, Jan Öjvind. *The Tale of Cupid and Psyche.* Lund: C. W. K. Gleerup, 1955.

Symanski, Richard. *The Immoral Landscape: Female Prostitution in Western Societies.* Toronto: Butterworths, 1981.

Tahmankar, D. V. *The Ranee of Jhansi.* London: Macgibbon and Kee, 1958.

Tanaka, Yuki. *Hidden Horrors: Japanese War Crimes in World War II.* Boulder, Colo.: Westview Press, 1996.

Taylor, Susie King. *A Black Woman's Civil War Memoirs.* Edited by Patricia W. Romero. New York: Marcus Wiener, 1988.

Tetréault, Mary Ann, ed. *Women and Revolution in Africa, Asia, and the New World.* Columbia: University of South Carolina Press, 1994.

Tharp, Louisa Hall. *The Baroness and the General.* Boston: Little, Brown, 1962.

Thomas, Mary Martha. *Riveting and Rationing in Dixie: Alabama Women in the Second World War.* Tuscaloosa: University of Alabama Press, 1987.

Thompson, D. W. "Goodbye, Molly Pitcher." Edited by Merri Lou Schaumann. *Cumberland County History* 6, NO. 1 (Summer 1989): 3–26.

Tiger, Lionel. *Men in Groups.* New York: Vintage Books, 1970.

Tomblin, Barbara. "Beyond Paradise: The U.S. Navy Nurse Corps in the Pacific in World War II," pt. 1 *MINERVA: Quarterly Report on Women and the Military* 2, no. 2 (Summer 1993): 33–53 and pt. 2, Ibid., 2, nos. 3 and 4 (Fall/Winter 1993): 37–56.

———. *G.I. Nightingales: The Army Nurse Corps in World War II.* Lexington: University Press of Kentucky, 1996.

Treadwell, Mattie E. *United States Army in World War II, Special Studies, the Women's Army Corps.* Washington, D.C.: U.S.Department of the Army, 1954.

Trustram, Myrna. *Women of the Regiment: Marriage and the Victorian Army.* Cambridge: Cambridge University Press, 1984.

Tschudi, Clara. *Napoleon's Mother.* London, 1900.

Tsunetomo, Yamamoto. *Hagakure: The Book of the Samurai.* Translated by William Scott Wilson. Tokyo: Kodansha International, [1716] 1979.

Tucker, Norma. "Nancy Ward, Ghigua of the Cherokees." *Georgia Historical Quarterly* 53 (June 1969): 192–200.

Tuten, Jeff M. "Germany and the World Wars." In *Female Soldiers—Combatants or Noncombatants? Historical and Contemporary Perspectives,* edited by Nancy Loring Goldman, 47–60. Westpoint, Conn.: Greenwood Press, 1982.

Ulrich, Laurel Thatcher. *Good Wives: Image and Reality in the Lives of Women in Northern New England 1650–1750.* New York: Oxford University Press, 1982.

Van Creveld, Martin. "Why Men Fight." In *War,* edited by Lawrence Freedman, 85–89. New York: Oxford University Press, 1994.

Van Devanter, Lynda, with Christopher Morgan. *Home Before Morning: The True Story of an Army Nurse in Vietnam.* New York: Warner Books, 1983.

Van Wagner, Kathryn. "Flight Nurse at Iwo." *Navy Medicine* 86 (March/April 1995): 8–11.

Vaughan, Agnes Carr. *Zenobia of Palmyra.* New York: Doubleday, 1967.

Velazquez, Loreta J. *The Woman in Battle: A Narrative of the Adventures and Travels of Madame Loreta Janeta Velazquez, Otherwise Known as Lt. Harry T. Buford, CSA.* Richmond, Va.: Dustin, Gilman, 1876.

Verges, Marianne. *On Silver Wings: The Women Airforce Service Pilots of World War II.* New York: Ballantine Books, 1991.

Vlahos, Olivia. *New World Beginnings: Indian Cultures in the Americas.* New York: Viking Press, 1970.

von Bothmer, Dietrich. *Amazons in Greek Art.* Oxford: Clarendon Press, 1957.

Von Grimmelshausen, H. J. C., *Simplicius Simplicissimus*. Edited by George Schulz-Behrend. Indianapolis: Bobbs Merrill, 1965.

Wainwright, F. T. "Aethelflaed, Lady of the Mercians." In *The Anglo-Saxons,* edited by P. Clemoes, 53–69. London: Bowes & Bowes, 1959.

Walker, Barbara G. *The Woman's Encyclopedia of Myths and Secrets.* San Francisco: Harper & Row, 1983.

Walker, Keith. *A Piece of My Heart.* New York: Ballantine Books, 1985.

Walsh, Patricia L. *Forever Sad the Hearts.* New York: Avon, 1982.

Walsh, William Thomas. *Isabella of Spain: The Last Crusader.* New York: McBride, 1930.

Warwick, Peter, ed. *The South African War: The Anglo-Boer War, 1899–1902.* Harlow, Essex: Longman, 1980.

Watson, G. R. *The Roman Soldier.* Ithaca: Cornell University Press, 1969.

Webber, Winni S. *Lesbians in the Military Speak Out.* Northboro, Mass.: Madwoman Press, 1993.

Webster, Graham. *The Roman Imperial Army of the First and Second Centuries A.D.* Totowa, N.J.: Barnes and Noble, 1985.

Wendorf, Fred, ed. *The Prehistory of Nubia.* 2 vols. Dallas: Southern Methodist University Press, 1968.

Weitz, Margaret Collins. *Sisters in the Resistance: How Women Fought to Free France, 1940–1945.* New York: John Wiley, 1995.

Wensyel, James W. "Captain Molly." *Army* 31, no. 11 (November 1981): 48–53.

Wheelwright, Julie. *Amazons and Military Maids: Women Who Dressed as Men in Pursuit of Life, Liberty and Happiness.* London: Pandora Press, 1989.

White, J. E. Manchip. *Ancient Egypt: Its Culture and History.* New York: Dover Publications, 1970.

White, John Todd. "The Truth About Molly Pitcher." In *The American Revolution: Whose Revolution,* edited by James Kirby Martin and Karen R. Stubaus, 99–105. Huntington, N.Y.: Robert F. Krieger, 1977.

Wiegand, Karl L. "Japan: Curious Utilization." In *Female Soldiers—Combatants or Noncombatants? Historical and Contemporary Perspectives,* edited by Nancy Loring Goldman, 179–88. Westport, Conn.: Greewood Press, 1982.

Wiley, Bell Irvin. *The Life of Billy Yank: The Common Soldier of the Union.* Baton Rouge: Louisiana State University Press, reissued 1978.

Willard, Charity Cannon. *Christine De Pizan: Her Life and Works.* New York: Persea Books, 1984.

Williams, Joan C. "Deconstructing Gender." *Michigan Law Review* 87 (February 1989): 798–845.

Williams, Noel T. St. John. *Judy O'Grady and the Colonel's Lady: The Army Wife and Camp Follower Since 1660*. London: Brassey's, 1988.

Willmot, Louise. "Women in the Third Reich: The Auxiliary Military Service Law of 1944." *German History* 2 (1985): 10–20.

Willson, Robert McNair. *Napoleon's Mother*. Philadelphia: J. B. Lippincott, 1933.

Wishnia, Judith. "Pacifism and Feminism in Historical Perspective." In *On Peace, War, and Gender: A Challenge to Genetic Explanations*, edited by Anne E. Hunter, 84–91. New York: Feminist Press, 1991.

Women of the Light: The New Sacred Prostitute. Secret Garden Video, October 1994.

Wood, Ann Douglas. "The War within a War: Women Nurses in the Union Army." *Civil War History* 18, no. 3 (September 1972): 197–212.

Woodham-Smith, Cecil. *Florence Nightingale, 1820–1910*. New York: McGraw Hill, 1951.

Woollacott, Angela. *On Her Their Lives Depend: Munitions Workers in the Great War*. Berkeley: University of California Press, 1994.

Wright, Ann. "The Roles of Army Women in Grenada." *MINERVA: Quarterly Report on Women and the Military* 2, no. 2 (Summer 1984): 103–13.

Wright, W. *An Account of Palmyra and Zenobia*. London, 1895.

Yadin, Yigael. *The Art of Warfare in Biblical Lands in the Light of Archaeological Study*, 2 vols. New York: McGraw Hill, 1963.

Yalom, Marilyn. *Blood Sisters: The French Revolution in Women's Memory*. New York: Basic Books, 1993.

Young, Elise G. *Keepers of the History: Women and the Israeli-Palestinian Conflict*. New York: Teachers College Press, 1992.

Yurlova, Marina. *Cossack Girl*. London: Cassell and Co., 1934.

Zajovic, Stanislava Stasa. "Ex-Yugoslavia." *Connexions*, no. 42 (1993): 19–27.

Zartman, I. William, ed. *Elusive Peace: Negotiating an End to Civil Wars*. Washington, D.C.: Brookings Institute, 1995.

Zeamer, Jeremiah. "Molly Pitcher Story Analysed," Carlisle (Pennsylvania) *Volunteer*, February 20, 1907.

Zimmerman, Jean. *Tailspin: Women at War in the Wake of Tailhook*. New York: Doubleday, 1995.

Zosimus, Count. *The History of Count Zosimus, Sometimes Advocate and Chancellor of the Roman Empire*. London: Printed for J. Davis by W. Green and T. Chaplin, 1814.

INDEX